THE

DRAGON

AND THE

MAPLE LEAF

ERRATA

p. 104, left column, third paragraph, Henry Louie, change number
 to read "K.7788."

p. 109, right column, bottom of second paragraph. The school
 was closed in 1946 not 1945. Change sentence to read: "The
 school was closed 15 July 1946."

p. 223, CCOS - Combined Chiefs of Staff (US & British) - add "and
 British"

p. 226, ISLD - change MI 9 to MI 6

P. 226, JCOS - Joint Chiefs of Staff (US) - remove "and British
 combined"

p. 233, delete "Chew, Stanley"

p. 239, add "Lee, Henry E. K.7577"

p. 241, Louie, Pte. Henry (Vancouver) "K.7788" - change number

THE DRAGON AND THE MAPLE LEAF

CHINESE CANADIANS IN WORLD WAR II

Marjorie Wong

Pirie Publishing
1994

Editing: John Meyers, Toronto

Typesetting: Parker Typesetting, London

Printed and Bound by: The Bryant Press Limited, Toronto

Dragon crest drawn by Capt(N) J.M. Thornton, OMM, CD
                 modified by Capt(N) E.K. Lee, OMM, CD

Care has been taken to trace the ownership of copyright material used in the text (including the illustrations). The author and publisher welcome any information enabling them to rectify any reference or credit in subsequent editions.

Canadian Cataloguing in Publication Data

Wong, Marjorie
    The dragon and the maple leaf

Includes bibliographical references and index.
ISBN 0-9698086-0-7 (bound)
ISBN 0-9698086-1-5 (pbk.)

1. World War, 1939-1945 - Participation, Chinese Canadian.* 2. Chinese Canadians - History - 20th Century.* I Title.

D768.15.W65 1994   940.54'04   C94-930749-1

Pirie Publishing
P.O. Box 39073
London, Ontario N5Y 5L1

CONTENTS

Foreword by Major H.J. Legg vii

Acknowledgements ix

Introduction 1

  I. The Great War 3
  II. Numbers available for Military Service 8
  III. Hong Kong and China 11
  IV. The Allied Air Services 19
  V. The Allied Navies 60
  VI. The Canadian Army 70
  VII. S-20 Japanese Language School 109
  VIII. Special Operations Executive 112
  IX. Recruitment and Training
     – Canada and Australia 123
  X. Recruitment and Training
     – Canada and India .146
  XI. Malaya Operations 159
  XII. Sarawak Operations 185
  XIII. Conclusion 216

Abbreviations and Glossary 221

Appendix - Chinese Canadian Veterans 232

Bibliography 247

Sketch Maps: Malaya 160
      Sarawak and British North Borneo 186-7
      Sibu area 206

Index 257

Foreword

by Major H. J. Legg, MBE, MC

In 1942/43 the tentacles of the Japanese offensive had reached out to Singapore, Burma, Borneo, and the Indonesian Archipelago and the Allies were faced with the daunting task of regaining the initiative. Special Operations Executive, which was meeting with much success in infiltrating enemy-occupied territory in France, weighed up the chances of embarking on similar operations behind the Japanese lines in the Far East. There was however, one mountainous obstacle. France was a European country, close to Britain, with pre-war contacts whose cooperation was assured if they could be contacted by British agents who could pass muster in a country where they were look-alikes. But the Far East was a different proposition. The comparatively few Europeans resident there were nearly all in Japanese prison camps in an area where any infiltrating European would stand out like a sore thumb and quickly be added to the quota of prisoners. The indigenous inhabitants of the occupied territories were an unknown quantity and to establish contacts and build up a resistance organization would clearly be a difficult and laborious operation and certainly could not be done easily by Europeans.

There was a glimmer of light however. Throughout the entire area there was a widespread sprinkling of ethnic Chinese who were long-established residents. If some of these could be contacted it might be possible to make a start—but the infiltraters would have to be Chinese and where could they be found?

The salvation was the Chinese Canadians resident in British Columbia but even here it was a case of starting from scratch as Government policy did not favour the enlistment of Chinese Canadians in the armed forces. How pressure from the British Government led to a change of policy is a long story but eventually the policy was changed in 1944, Chinese Canadians were recruited into the Army and the way was clear for S.O.E. to seek volunteers to engage in clandestine operations in Japanese-held territory.

It was with much satisfaction that I found myself selected to train the original group of thirteen in wireless at a secret training camp in the foothills of the Okanagan valley as, two decades earlier, I had been resident in China and Japan and had acquired a deep respect for the basic qualities of the Chinese character. The question asked was "would the Chinese Canadians have retained these qualities which we so much admired despite the conflicting pressures of life in a European-type milieu?"

The answer was clear within the first month of life in the camp, and it was "Yes, only more so." But there was one imponderable which had still to be resolved. It may be all very well to have strength of character but can that be translated into practical application? The task ahead of the trainees was to be infiltrated into enemy-held territory where there would be nobody to turn to for advice, support or even the means ofsubsistence. They would need to be resourceful, self-reliant, with the capacity for organization and leadership of the indigenous population of the land in which they found themselves—a tall order for young men with experience only of life in sophisticated cities.

When camp was struck four months later there were no more imponderables. They had given full promise of living up to the high standards which would be required of them. The proof lies in the fact that, of the five infiltrated into Borneo, four were awarded the M.M.; nine from Force 136 in India were competent interpreter-instructors in Malaya and a tenth as wireless operator with the Escape and Evasion Group in Singapore.

The particular small group with which we started was not unique. As this book will show there were many more Chinese Canadians who went on active service, and from the reports received, their achievements were of equally high order. Their service in two World Wars is eminently worthy of the present recording and I am grateful for having been given this opportunity of paying tribute to comrades who merit the admiration of all who place value on the finer qualities of mankind.

Wimborne, Dorset, England
31st October 1991

Acknowledgements

Chinese Canadian veterans freely told their stories and assisted in every way to compile and interpret this history of their war years. Their names are not listed here but each one's contribution was important. This is a very special group of Canadian men and women and it has been a privilege to meet and talk personally to so many of them.

Personal photographs and other artifacts have been photographed by Regan Photography of London, Ont. A few pictures have been obtained from National Archives of Canada, Photographic Division; from Canadian Forces Base, Ottawa; and from Her Majesty's Stationery Office, in London, England. Photographs have not been tidied up in any way, but remain true to the originals. Three items have been reduced in size – Colin Mackenzie's letter and the two Japanese surrender documents – and Mountbatten's "Order of the Day" has been retyped from a tattered flimsy.

National Defence Headquarters, Directorate of History, and National Archives of Canada, have both provided material. Glenn Wright at NAC was especially helpful. Gervase Cowell, SOE Adviser at the Foreign and Commonwealth Office in London, has searched out and made available many summaries and reports. Australian Archives and the Australian War Memorial have provided valuable materials.

Members of the *Semut* parties, especially Bob Long, wireless operator for *Semut I,* and Keith Barrie with *Semut III,* provided material for and read and commented on the Sarawak chapter. Maj. M.G. Levy (Retd), formerly with Force 136 in Malaya, has provided material for the action of his team, which included Henry Fung; he also read the manuscript for this chapter. P/O K.V. Aro has read and commented on the Allied Air Services chapter; he also supplied service information on P/O Quan Jil Louie. P/O Douglas Sam, his wife Ruby, and son Trevor, have also been very helpful. LAC Herby Chan in Winnipeg searched out veterans (and photographs) in his area of the country. Cedric and Albert Mah have given a great deal of attention to the China National Aviation Corporation portion. Bill Lore in Hong Kong gave in-depth help with names; his work is reflected in the "Appendix." Bud Burnke in London provided much needed advice on photographs of interest to collectors and curators. The responsibility for any inaccuracies or misinterpretations remaining are mine.

The London Public Library, Interlibrary Loan staff, has searched out books across the country and in every respect has proved most helpful. The libraries at the University of Western Ontario also provided needed material.

To the Royal Canadian Legion and all its branches across Canada, to the Army, Navy, and Air Force Veterans in Canada, Pacific Unit 280, and to the Canadian-Chinese Veterans Association of Victoria, a heartfelt thanks for their help. Members of the Canadian Radar Detachment in Australia, particularly Danny Arntsen and J. Terry Hanes, provided helpful material on the three members of the first group who went on to Manila for Repatriation of Prisoner of War duties.

I am grateful also to the *Toronto Star,* the *Western Producer,* and newspapers in the Maritimes for publishing my request for information in locating Chinese Canadian veterans; my thanks to all their readers who wrote that they 'knew of' or were 'in a unit with' someone and wrote to tell me about the person concerned.

A sincere thanks to Dr. David Stafford, Canadian Institute of International Affairs, who not only helped during a personal interview but also provided the material covering the training period of the 13 Chinese Canadians at the special training camp in the Okanagan Valley. Special thanks also to Dr. Ian K. Steele, whose record of students is still extant after more than twenty-five years, and to Dr. A.M.J. Hyatt, who gave guidance on the NRMA, both of the University of Western Ontario.

Financial assistance in researching material for this book has been provided by the Department of the Secretary of State, Ministry of Multiculturalism and Citizenship.

INTRODUCTION

The number of Chinese Canadians who served in the Second World War was small in comparison with the total number of Canadians in the three services, but their contribution was unique in the Southeast Asia and Southwest Pacific theatres, and they served with distinction in Canadian Defence and in both Italy and Northwest Europe. Chinese Canadians also served with the British in Hong Kong and China and a few served with American forces.

There is no mention of this contribution in the official histories of the Royal Canadian Navy, the Canadian Army, or the Royal Canadian Air Force. Nor do these histories mention the reluctance with which Chinese Canadians were allowed to enlist voluntarily in the RCAF in 1942, and the RCN in 1943. These histories also do not mention that they were not called up in Pacific Command under the National Resources Mobilization Act until August/September 1944. This reluctance was based on a Canadian government decision of late 1940 not to call up Chinese and Japanese Canadians.

Some of these political decisions, such as lack of the franchise for those from British Columbia, are discussed in the text if they had a bearing upon military service. Occasionally, the post-war occupation of a serviceman is given as well as his war service to demonstrate the abilities of this particular group of citizens; the reader should contrast these occupations with the pre-war conditions where they were restricted almost entirely to casual labour, restaurant, laundry, and other ethnic businesses. These war years saw the first lessening of discrimination even though Ottawa was ambivalent; these years were crucial in bringing about the civil and legal changes that allowed Chinese Canadians to work and live on the same footing as other Canadians.

The necessary political change in Ottawa occurred as the result of the request of the British War Office which required a greater number of Chinese Canadians for employment with Special Operations Executive than had already voluntarily enlisted in the Canadian Army. To meet the request of the War Office, Chinese Canadians in Pacific Command were called up for military service. Compulsory military service was coupled with the franchise. As a result, this account falls naturally into two divisions; the first part is an account of those in the Canadian and paramilitary services, the second is of those on loan to SOE.

The interpretation of Chinese names has presented a problem in that many Chinese Canadians have an English name and a Chinese name. Some men enlisted under and used their Chinese names; others used their English names only. All those called up in British Columbia in 1944 enlisted under the name appearing on their birth certificates, which may have been a name they had never used in daily life.

In addition, there are various methods of transliteration and romanization. Today the Pinyin system of romanization is the accepted system but this was not so when Chinese immigrants first came to Canada. Immigration officials anglicized the name without regard to any system. Some have attempted to legally correct the English version of their name, and this sometimes adds to the difficulty of identification.

Some but not all Chinese write the surname first followed by their personal names; the army was inclined to accept the last written name as the surname so that 'Young Wing Hay,' whose surname was 'Young,' became 'Hay, Young Wing,' on enlistment. Frequently the surname is followed by a generation name as in 'Ng Hoan,' which became 'Hoan' to Caucasians when the surname actually is 'Ng.' To add to the confusion, occasionally the generation name is written before the surname but this is rare. My apologies to those veterans whose names are given army fashion in the text and "Appendix"; these were the names by which they were known during the period. It was not possible to contact each person to verify the correct form.

There are also many duplicate names: there are at least seven called George Lee, with six called Tommy Wong, Frank Lee, and Edward Lee. Whenever possible, the service numbers have been given where these are known; otherwise, the identifying factor has been the place the man was from.

The ranks and awards are those that were current during the Second World War; they have not all been verified, nor have all awards been noted. Some ranks have been retained with unification of the Canadian forces but many others are no longer used. The "Abbreviations and Glossary" will help readers who are not familiar with these terms.

Country and place names given in the text are those commonly in use during the war period; thus, 'Siam' rather than 'Thailand,' 'Malaya' rather than 'Malaysia,' and 'Ceylon' not 'Sri Lanka.' The place names in China also follow the old spelling: 'Kwangtung' not 'Guangdong' and 'Hong Kong' not 'Xianggang.'

During the dedication ceremony at the former camp site of the Special Training School located about ten miles north of Penticton and across from Summerland on Lake Okanagan where 13 Chinese Canadians were trained in the summer of 1944, it was startling to learn that no one in attendance knew what the men had been trained to do in this secluded area. Members of the municipal, provincial, and federal governments, the Royal Canadian Legion, and the Army, Navy, and Air Force Veterans in Canada, along with survivors of the original group, attended the ceremony. An account of their military story needed to be written.

To those of us who grew up in an environment outside the influences of racial discrimination, it is on first reading difficult to comprehend the bitterness on both sides in the British Columbia vendetta against not only the Chinese but against all non-Caucasians. The federal government followed the provincial lead. Although Canada was fighting Germany and Italy, as well as Japan, these two nationalities were Europeans and Canadians with these origins suffered little inconvenience in comparison with those from Asia, especially Japanese Canadians. This background to Chinese Canadian participation in the Canadian military should be kept in mind when reading the following account.

A very short chapter on Chinese Canadian veterans of the Great War is ncluded. My thanks to the sons and daughters who provided the names and photographs of the few listed here. A very brief statement of their enlistment in the Canadian Army is given. A short account of the Chinese Labour Battalions from China that served in Europe and the Near East is also included.

Chapter I

THE GREAT WAR

There were 27,774 Chinese in Canada in 1911, with nearly 20,000 of this number living in British Columbia. The rest were scattered across the country with 1,787 in Alberta and only six in Prince Edward Island. Both Ontario and Quebec had growing numbers. Some would have been Canadian born, more would have been naturalized, but most would still have been Chinese nationals. By 1914, when Great Britain declared war on Germany and Austria, the number of Chinese in Canada had increased by another 10,000.

In spite of the discriminatory Head Tax of $500, Canadian born and naturalized Chinese Canadians were eager to prove their loyalty to their new country by offering their services to the military. British Columbia refused all such recruits and it was necessary for them to travel outside their home province to enlist. Alberta and Ontario were two provinces that willingly accepted them into the army.

According to some historical sources, 300 Chinese Canadians enlisted in the Canadian Army between 1914 and 1918. When figures for the two World Wars are compared, it would seem that 300 must be an inflated figure. The same historical sources give only an estimated 500 for the whole of Canada for the Second World War.[1]

However, there was at least one platoon of about 60 men composed mainly of Chinese Canadians in the 52nd Battalion (The New Ontario Battalion) who fought at Ypres in 1917.[2] The 52nd was raised by The Lake Superior Regiment in Port Arthur, Kenora, Fort Frances, and Dryden, Ont, but few of the originals would have remained by 1917. It should be noted that 42 Japanese Canadians also served in the 52nd Battalion and at least one platoon in each of the 10th and 50th Battalions were composed entirely of Japanese Canadians.

The Military Service Act of July 1917 brought in conscription, but Orientals were not conscripted.

A few of those Chinese Canadian volunteers who served in the Canadian Army in the Great War are noted below.

Pte. James Delbert Harold Chew, L.32372, enlisted in the Great War but his battalion number is not known. His regimental number indicates that he enlisted in Military District No. 12 in Saskatchewan in the Second War, but Chinese Canadians moved across the country looking for work and did not always remain settled in any one area.

Pte. Chew served in the Veterans Guard of Canada in the Second World War. Originally called the Veterans Home Guard when it was raised in May 1940, it was renamed the Veterans Guard of Canada in November. These veterans guarded Prisoner of War internment camps, important factories, and other vulnerable areas within Canada. Companies were employed at Canadian Military Headquarters in London, England, and other companies were stationed at times in the Bahamas, British Guiana, and Newfoundland.

– courtesy Shirley Louie
Hanson Lee

Hanson Lee from Kamloops, and Yee Chong Leong from Vernon, also enlisted in the Canadian Army; nothing more is known about either of these soldiers.

Y.C. Lee also came from Kamloops. He enlisted late in the war and did not serve overseas; he died in the early 1920s. Y.C. Lee was the father of Rifleman Robert Lee who enlisted in The Queens Own Rifles of Canada in the Second War.

Two brothers from Shuswap, BC, Wee Hong Louie and Wee Tan Louie, succeeded in joining the Canadian Army as well.

Wee Hong Louie was born in Shuswap, 2 July 1894. He enlisted 19 April 1917 in a Forestry Draft in Kamloops and arrived in England 7 December 1917 on the SS *Megantic*. Beginning as gunner, Wee Hong served in France attached to the 102nd RMR Regiment. He was later transferred to com-

munications as wireless operator; he then became a driver for VIPs.

He embarked on the *Northland* at Liverpool 13 May 1919, and arrived in Halifax on 23 May and was honourably discharged in Winnipeg, Man, on the 26th. Wee Hong Louie received the British War Medal and the Victory Medal.

He then attended the University of Chicago. After he graduated as an electrical engineer, he decided to settle in Orillia, Ont, where he proposed to set up his own electrical shop. For this purpose he purchased the West End Radio Shop and applied for a business

– courtesy Shirley Louie
Wee Hong Louie

licence. The licence was refused because he was Chinese. When he protested to the Prime Minister's office, the refusal was confirmed. As a result, Wee Hong bundled up his army uniform and his medals and sent them to

Mackenzie King saying this was not what he had fought for. King promptly returned the articles with a letter of apology and the requested licence was granted. Wee Hong operated his shop until his retirement in 1976.

His brother, Pte. William Thomas (Wee Tan) Louie, 3206975, was born 15 January 1889, also in Shuswap. Wee Tan picked his English name from a mail box he passed on his way to enlist in Calgary, a journey that took him three months on the horse he had saved money to buy in order to make the trip. Using the name William Thomas Louie, on 20 February 1918 Wee Tan signed on with the 10th Canadian Infantry Battalion raised by the Calgary Regiment, and embarked on SS *Scandinavian* for Bramshot, England, where he landed 3 April. He took his basic training in England.

Because he was small and very quick on his feet, Wee Tan served as runner in France, Holland, and Belgium. He was wounded in action and handicapped by a hearing loss from the noise of the shelling.

Wee Tan returned to Canada on the *Carmania* in March 1919 and was honourably discharged in Calgary 23 April. William Thomas Louie received the British War Medal and the Victory Medal.

Pte. Frederick Lee, 687931, from Kamloops, served in the 47th Battalion; he was killed in action 1 August 1917. The 47th Battalion was one of the twelve battalions in the 4th Canadian Division, Canadian Expedi-

– courtesy Norman Lee
Frederick Lee

– courtesy Shirley Louie
Wee Tan Louie

tionary Force. The battalion was raised in New Westminster, Vancouver, and Victoria, but few originals would have remained by 1917. The Battalion was renamed the 47th (Western Ontario) Battalion in February 1918.

The Chinese government at Peking declared war on Germany and Austria 14 August 1917. Even before the declaration of war, at the request of the British and French governments, 200,000 men were recruited and trained in the Chinese Labour Corps. Over one thousand had already sailed by the time the corps was named 21 February 1917.

These men were employed in France, North Africa, and Mesopotamia (modern Iraq).[3] Although only 84,000 crossed Canada in bond,[4] a total of 117,000 served in France according to the British Empire War Office. The rest had travelled by way of the Indian Ocean and Suez Canal. In France, they repaired roads, laid railway tracks, and loaded cargo in companies of 500.

Nearly 50,000 Chinese nationals were returned to China in 1919 crossing Canada again in sealed railway cars. They were held at William Head, the old quarantine station

The last group left France 1 April 1920. They had cleaned up the battlefields, searched for the dead, and collected stores. During their contract period with the British, many hundreds died when ships were torpedoed, from bombing and strafing, and from artillery shelling when they served near the battlefields.

The men in the Chinese Labour Corps were issued the British War Medal (a bronze version); a few received the Meritorious Service Medal; and at least two Distinguished Service Medals were awarded to members of the Corps.[6]

Little notice has been taken of the Chinese labour battalions employed in Africa and Mesopotamia, possibly because they did not cross Canada and Canadians were not generally involved in the African and Middle East campaigns.

Neither Chinese nationals nor

– CFB Ottawa PNR 82 490

Chinese Labour Battalion at William Head quarantine station, Vancouver Island, BC

about eight miles south of Esquimalt on Vancouver Island. A few managed to escape the pens when they rioted after waiting several months for shipment home.[5]

Canadian Chinese were able to vote in their respective countries during the First War, although wealthy overseas Chinese contributors to the new Chinese government had been rewarded by appointment to coveted posts in the homeland. Sun Yat-Sen had led the country in revolt against the monarchy in 1911, and was elected President of the United Provinces of China. After the abdication of Emperor Pu Yi, one of the warlords was elected President of the Republic and he in turn tried to seize absolute power. From the Revolution until 1949, internal affairs in China were not conducive to democratic government; some elections, however, appear to have taken place.

Before 1875 the Chinese had been able to vote in British Columbia; they had voted in Lillooet and Victoria in 1874 in a by-election and municipal election respectively, but they had been physically barred from voting in Nanaimo in the municipal election of 1873. In 1875 the BC Legislature removed all Chinese names from the voters' lists in the "Qualifications and Registration of Voters Act." Dominion voters' lists were based on the provincial lists. This federal restriction remained on an unofficial basis until after the Great War when the new "Dominion Elections Act" was passed. Thus Chinese Canadians in British Columbia were unable to vote federally nor were they able to vote on the municipal or provincial level. This fact accounts in part for their apparent acceptance of their political position in British Columbia until the Second World War brought the matter to the fore again.

As early as 1919 over 500 Chinese Canadians in Victoria petitioned the federal government with respect to the franchise. Again in 1940 the Chinese Canadians in Victoria sent a petition to Ottawa concerning the franchise and military service; they were not altogether passive as to their position in Canada.

Two of these disenfranchised citizens, William Thomas and Wee Hong Louie, were the uncles of Thomas Kwok Hung Wong who served in the RCAF in the Second War. The RCAF was the first of the Canadian services to accept Chinese Canadians on an equal basis.

NOTES

Personal information has come from relatives and friends of the few veterans named above.

1. All sources appear to rely on the figure appearing in the article by Carol F. Lee, "The Road to Enfranchisement: Chinese and Japanese in British Columbia," *BC Studies* No. 30 (Summer, 1976), p. 50. In a letter to the author from Miss Lee of 17 April 1991, she states that this figure was obtained from "a CP wire service article, 'Indians, Orientals in Army, Get B.C. Votes After War,' which appeared in the *Vancouver Herald* on March 28, 1945. The figure is attributed to Mr. Foon Sien, president of the Chinese Benevolent Association in Vancouver." Harry Con, Ronald J. Con, Graham Johnson, Edgar Wickberg, and William F. Willmott, *From China to Canada: a History of the Chinese Communities in Canada,* ed. by Edgar Wickberg (Toronto, 1988), (hereafter cited as Wickberg), pp. 200, 208, repeat 300 for the First War and give 500 for the Second (400 from British Columbia). Jin Tan and Patricia Roy use 50 as the number of Great War veterans granted the franchise in 1945 in *The Chinese in Canada* (Ottawa, 1985), p. 15. Professor Roy advised 1 March 1989 that the figure came from Carol F. Lee's article.

2. James Morton, *In the Sea of Sterile Mountains* (Vancouver, 1974), p. 229, admits that evidence for their participation was not located in Ottawa but that the 52nd Battalion information came from Gen. G.R. Pearkes.

3. William L. Langer (comp. and ed.), *An Encyclopedia of World History,* rev.ed., (Cambridge, Mass., 1952), p. 1117, appears to be the only source to give North Africa and Mesopotamia.

4. Elizabeth A. Tancock "Secret Trains Across Canada 1917-1918," reprinted from the *Beaver* in *Military Collector's Club of Canada* (Summer 1992), p. 68, gives the count by ship arriving in Canada of 84,244.

5. Morton, p. 232.

6. Information provided by Jack Leong of Victoria from articles by Ronald J. Jack and published in *Military Collectors' Club of Canada* (Winter 1987), "Awards to the Chinese Labour Corps, B.E.F.," and (Spring 1988), "C.L.C. Headdress and Cap Badge with Notes for Collectors."

Chapter II

NUMBERS AVAILABLE FOR MILITARY SERVICE

National Defence Headquarters and other federal departments produced several estimates of the number of Chinese Canadians available for military service, ranging from as high as 8,000 in British Columbia in 1940,[1] to a revised figure of 2,300 for all of Canada in 1942,[2] and a low figure of 400 two years later again for British Columbia alone.[3] Other estimates were suggested as well.[4] Finally, when Chinese Canadians were called up in September 1944 and British Security Coordination began its recruiting programme on behalf of SOE, National Defence didn't think there would be 150 men available.

Between 1940 and 1944 the estimates of the number of Chinese Canadians appears to have been made on unreliable data. It is stated in the "Report and Recommendations of the Special Committee on Orientals in British Columbia December 1940" that the statistics should be "accepted with some reservations due to the length of time that has elapsed since the last census." The misleading figure was 8,000 said to be available in British Columbia between the ages of 18 and 45 with most being in the upper age limit.

The "1940 Report" was prepared after the series of meetings in British Columbia which began in October; the 8,000 estimate was based on the 1931 census with unofficial attempts to update it. This figure also does not distinguish between Canadian born, naturalized British subject, and Chinese national. In the 1944 call up of Chinese Canadian recruits in British Columbia under NRMA, only Canadian born and naturalized Canadians were accepted; Chinese nationals could usually enlist voluntarily.

Between 1931 and 1941 there was a decline in the total number of Chinese in Canada of 11,892; the census figures for 1931 showed a total of 46,519, which had dropped to 34,617 in 1941. For British Columbia alone there were 8,520 fewer Chinese.[5] War had accelerated in China from the first Japanese inroads into Manchuria in 1931, but open war between China and Japan did not occur until 1937. By late 1940 many of the 8,000 figure cited in the "1940 Report" had already left the country. Those who reached Hong Kong and China were caught up in the Sino-Japanese conflict.

The return to Hong Kong and China was also partly the result of the Great Depression that hit Canada severely from 1929 to 1939. Although the Depression affected all Canadians, for the Chinese it was a double tragedy. There was little or no employment even as casual labour or in other traditional fields. The usual Chinese self-help programmes had broken down,[6] and public assistance was limited.

In Alberta for example, they received smaller relief payments, less than half that received by white indigents;[7] as a result three unemployed Chinese in Calgary died from malnutrition. Many others became homeless when the medical officer for the city condemned the buildings in which they lived.

Conditions in Alberta were not usually considered as severe as those prevailing in British Columbia. In Vancouver alone, between 1931 and early 1935, well over 100 Chinese died from starvation; several hundred destitute Chinese and 65 mental patients were repatriated to China, their passage paid by the BC government.[8]

In addition, many Chinese in Canada supported their relatives, often their wives and children, in the homeland. The number of wives in China was estimated at 13,174 in 1947.[9] Those who were still financially sound had sent their sons to China for their education. Whatever the men in Canada could save from their earnings was sent to their families through Hong Kong.[10] After the Exclusion Act of 1923[11] became effective, they were unable to bring their families to Canada, even if they had wanted to do so. With the threat of access to their families being cut off by the Japanese control of the coastal areas, especially around Canton, from 1938 on it was vital that members of the family return to assist them. Those who were able to do so returned to China.

Thus, of the 8,000 mentioned in the "1940 Report," a more realistic figure would seem to be about 400 available for military service in British Columbia.[12] This estimate appears to be borne out in the same "1940 Report," where it is noted that there were 500 Canadian born Chinese in that province with 200 naturalized.

In September 1944, 1,061 had been called up in British Columbia under NRMA but only 273 reported of whom 128 were considered physically fit and 19 were still pending. Allowing for rejection on medical grounds, for exemptions,[13] for the number who had returned to China, the number who were now over the age limits, and adding the number who had already voluntarily enlisted, 400 would seem to be a more reliable estimate.

The *Vancouver Sun* of 15 August 1944 reported on the notices being sent to "Chinese who are Canadians by birth or naturalization" for the army medical. In the *Sun* of 13 September, it was reported that of the first 100 draftees, 33 were accepted, 42 rejected, and 25 not yet cleared through their examination. In Victoria, 100 Chinese Canadians had also received call up notices.

There is no way of arriving at an exact figure. Chinese Canadians in Vancouver, however, erected a bronze plaque in the 1980s commemorating their service in the Second World War. This plaque contains 388 names,

with an additional 50 names on a smaller plaque added in 1989. Unfortunately, the service numbers were not collected along with the names and there are many duplicates and other discrepancies. For example, one listing for Ira Chan and two listings for Toy Chan are just one person. Deducting the duplicates on the main plaque leaves a total of about 325. In addition, those named were not all from British Columbia but include some servicemen from as far east as Montreal. The plaques do, however, give some idea of the numbers since the majority listed are from British Columbia. The plaques are mounted on the wall leading off Pender Street to the Sun Yat-Sen Gardens. Also commemorated on the walls are the 1500 Chinese who died building the railway.

If 400 seems to be a reasonable figure for British Columbia, with 53.8 percent of the Chinese Canadian population in 1941, then an additional 400 for the rest of Canada, with a total of 800 for the entire country, would seem to be a generous estimate, but it is only an estimate. There is apparently no record in Ottawa even though by 1944, as far as the Canadian Army was concerned, Chinese Canadians throughout Canada were "Allied Aliens" and subject to "investigation and report."

Although Ottawa claims that attestation forms did not request the nationality of recruits, such information was collected. The attestation forms did, however, ask for language capabilities, and very few Caucasians were proficient in Cantonese. Full particulars concerning each "Alien," and there were various categories, was to be "submitted through District Intelligence to NDHQ (M.I.3) on Personal History Form (Alien) and accompanied by the Army Examiner's Report." Applicants were all to be fingerprinted on the RCMP form; the form was then to be forwarded to Ottawa.[14]

Many of those who returned to Hong Kong and China participated in the war effort against the Japanese, both in the colony and on the mainland.

NOTES

1. "Report and Recommendations of the Special Committee on Orientals in British Columbia December 1940" in NAC, RG 27, Vol.1500, File 2-K-184, p.7.

2. Maj.-Gen. M. [*sic*] C. Murchie for CGS to GOCinC, Pacific Command, 13 April 1942, in D.Hist. 322.009, (D814).

3. 2 Sept. 1944 "Report of Proceedings of Committee formed to Study the Disposal of men of Chinese Racial Origin called up for Service under N.R.M.A.." in D.Hist. 322.009, (D478), p. 2.

4. Letter from Lt.-Gen. J.C. Murchie, CGS, 23 Sept. 1944, in D.Hist. 322.009, (D478).

5. Tan and Roy, *The Chinese in Canada,* pp. 9, 17; and Peter S. Li, *The Chinese in Canada* (Toronto, 1986), p. 61.

6. Wickberg, *China to Canada,* pp. 181-2.

7. Howard Palmer, *Patterns of Prejudice* (Toronto, 1985), pp. 145-7.

8. Wickberg, pp. 182, 184. All immigrants who became a charge on the public were liable to deportation; the provision did not apply only to the Chinese.

9. Reginald H. Roy, *For Most Conspicuous Bravery: a biography of Major-General George R. Pearkes, V.C., through Two World Wars* (Vancouver, 1977), p. 254.

10. Wickberg, p. 189.

11. *Statutes of Canada,* 13-14 George V, Chap. 38, an Act respecting Chinese immigration, short title *The Chinese Immigration Act, 1923,* is generally referred to as 'The Exclusion Act.'

12. Lee, "Enfranchisement," p. 58.

13. Copy of Telegram 11 Sept. 1944, in NAC, RG 27, Vol. 998, File 2-114-6.

14. D.Hist. 162.066, (D1), A.Q. Circular Letter W.33/1944, dated 8 July 1944, p. 4, section 9 (d) (i) and (ii). In Canadian practice, "M.I." stands for "Military Intelligence."

Chapter III

HONG KONG AND CHINA

From 1937, when the Japanese captured the port cities along the south China coast, to the fall of Canton in 1938, the turmoil within China and the lack of access through Canton left many Canadian Chinese in a precarious position. Many had returned to China because of the Great Depression in Canada, and for family or educational reasons, but many also returned in order to fight the Japanese. Thousands of refugees from Hong Kong and returned overseas Chinese were gathered in western Kwangtung. No remittances could reach them. Once war broke out between Japan and the United States and Great Britain 7 December 1941, shipping was not available for their return to Canada. Only a very few of these Canadians have been located.

There were six British battalions in Hong Kong when the Japanese attacked, including the two Canadian battalions, and six volunteer companies and artillery units in the Hong Kong Volunteer Defence Corps. The HKVDC was made up of many nationalities working in the colony: Danes, Poles, Czechs, English, and Portuguese, as well as Chinese, and a good many Eurasians.

Bombardier George L. Chow, No. 4136, born in Moose Jaw, Sask, had gone to Hong Kong in the mid 1930s. He served in the 5th Anti-Aircraft Battery of the HKVDC. At the start of the battles, the 5th AA Battery was stationed within the fortifications built at the top of Sai Wan Hill, Lyemun, on the island, The battery was heavily shelled by the Japanese on 15 December; one gun was knocked out. Air raids alternated with more heavy shelling until finally, on 18 December, all guns were knocked out. The 5th AA Battery was forced to surrender when the Japanese stormed the hill and the men were quickly overcome. The Japanese had made

two attempts to receive surrender from Maj.-Gen. C.M. Maltby, under a flag of truce, but these offers were rejected. Just before capitulation finally came on Christmas Day 1941, many members of the HKVDC had been allowed to go home, there to change into civilian clothes and remain free.

George Chow was one of those imprisoned in the Sham Shui Po Prisoner of War Camp, but he managed to escape 28 January 1942. During an arranged diversion, he slipped under the barbed wire, dashed across the street, and disappeared between some buildings.[1] George and his fiancée escaped to Macao and from there made their way to the Canadian Embassy at Chungking. After the war, he and his wife returned to Canada and settled in Toronto.

Elsie Wong from New Westminster, BC, had gone to Hong Kong for her training since she was unable to gain acceptance to a nursing programme in her home province. She graduated as a nurse from Queen Mary Hospital just as war broke out in the Pacific, and worked in Hong Kong and India.

Elsie and her husband Alfred Hoe, a veteran of the Hong Kong battles whom she had nursed when he was wounded, escaped to Kweilin and they were flown to Calcutta by Captain MacDonald of China National Aviation Corporation. In Calcutta, Elsie too worked for the CNAC. She was awarded the Defence Medal 1939-1945 for her efforts in nursing the wounded in Hong Kong during the battles. Elsie and her husband returned to Canada after the war where Alfred (who had been born in Penang, Malaya) became a naturalized Canadian in 1954.

Elsie's brother, Charles, a civil engineer, although remaining a civilian, was given military rank by the Nationalist Government to provide him with the financial means and position to operate a munitions-type factory. He joined his brother, Henry, and their mother, at Canton after the Japanese capitulated. Another brother, Dr. David Wong, a surgeon, who had received his education in Chicago, was not allowed to leave Hong Kong by the Japanese who took over government hospitals but did not interfere with private ones. David and Henry did not return to Canada after the war. Peter, a fourth brother, was also in Hong Kong at this time.

There were many guerrilla[2] groups operating in the Hong Kong and Canton areas: the Communist guerrillas, independent guerrillas and bandits, several Nationalist commands, and those adhering to the Japanese puppet government at Nanking. All the guerrillas were referred to as 'Communist' by the Nationalist Government but the label was not a true reflection of the political beliefs of all these groups.[3]

The United States Army Air Force and the Office of Strategic Services operated in Nationalist-controlled areas; the British Army Aid Group, set up in 1942, operated in these areas as well. The China theatre was under the control of Chiang Kai-Shek's Chief of Staff, Gen. Joseph W. Stilwell until late 1944, and Gen. Albert Wedemeyer through to capitulation.

Another who escaped from the colony was Col. (Dr.) Lindsay T. Ride; he had commanded the Hong Kong Field Ambulance in the HKVDC. By February 1942, Colonel Ride had concluded arrangements with Brig. G.E. Grimsdale, Military Attaché at the British Embassy in Chungking, to place the British Army Aid Group, an organization he had formed in Kwangtung, on an appropriate military basis.

The scheme was approved by Commander-in-Chief, India, and permission from Chiang Kai-Shek was obtained by the British Ambassador to China. The Generalissimo had been informed that good relations with the Communist guerrillas in the area between free China and Hong Kong would have to be maintained, and that General Tai Li would be kept advised. Tai Li was head of the Chinese secret service and with Chiang controlled not only the Chinese divisions fighting in northern Burma under General Stilwell but also the Chinese recruits obtained for Force 136. Ride was authorized to employ any servicemen who escaped from POW camps, and also civilian Chinese, most of whom had escaped from Hong Kong or been expelled by the Japanese.

BAAG was a temporary military unit established in southern Kwangtung Province to assist in prisoner escapes from Hong Kong, and to rescue evaders, usually downed American airmen. It also supplied medicines to the prisoners at Sham Shui Po and other POW and Internee camps in Hong Kong, whose health had deteriorated rapidly as a result of the starvation diet to which they were reduced. Information about the New Territories area was passed to the prisoners for their escape plans, particularly information that there were people ready to assist them into free China once they succeeded in breaking out of the camp. BAAG was also authorized to collect and distribute intelligence.

BAAG was MI 9 under another name and eventually became part of E Group (Escape & Evasion) in India. BAAG personnel were carried on the strength of Director of Military Intelligence at General Headquarters, Delhi.[4] MI 9 like SOE was a very secret organization. Members of these two secret organizations were generally carried on Military Intelligence rolls or on the General List. Rank was not geared to normal military usage because BAAG, again like SOE, was not a true military organization, although BAAG apparently was set up with a War Establishment. In England, MI 9 was tied to both the War Office and the Secret Intelligence Service.

Only three SOE members who had been 'leave behind' parties in Hong Kong when the Japanese invaded were allowed to remain in China. One of these was D. Ronald Holmes who was an SOE officer from the early days when he had been recruited into 'Z' Force; he had been a civil service cadet learning Cantonese and Mandarin in Hong Kong when war broke out. SOE was not allowed to operate as a unit by Chiang Kai-Shek and his advisers but individual members were acceptable; these individuals were employed by BAAG.

The base headquarters was established at Kukong, about 120 miles north of Canton in the northern part of Kwangtung, with an advanced headquarters at Waichow in the south. Lieut. D.R. Holmes worked at the Waichow headquarters when it was first set up about mid-July. There were forward aid posts close to Hong Kong with medical teams of doctors and orderlies who gave free medical aid to the villagers and guerrillas. These forward posts also assisted escapers.

Ride moved his headquarters in August from Kukong to Kweilin to cover all routes in and out of Hong Kong and Canton. Kweilin was closer to Chungking so that communications with the British Embassy were eased. An additional advance headquarters was set up at Samfou, in western Kwangtung, southwest of Canton, to cover the Macao exit routes. Smaller posts were set up to the west of Canton to cover the sea route from Hong Kong. By 1943 the whole of the Kwangtung coastline was covered by BAAG and its agents.

One of these agents was William Gun Chong, born in Vancouver 15 July 1911. Bill had been a driver in the Auxiliary, but managed to escape from Hong Kong to work as Agent No. 50 for BAAG. Auxiliary drivers had been employed by the Field Ambulance and by the military using commandeered civilian vehicles.

When he first escaped from the colony, Bill and two or three others walked for several days after leaving the New Territories. At a camp for Hong Kong refugees, Bill met a Canadian priest who wanted an ambulance driver for Burma. Bill volunteered for this work but the British were being driven out of Burma. Bill then volunteered for service with BAAG. His translation and interpretation skills would be of value to this new organization.

Bill Chong was one of the few trusted to carry drugs between medical posts. Drugs were a highly profitable black market com-

modity. Bill also assisted Lieut. D.R. Holmes during a bout with malaria. This was when the groups had first made their independent escapes in January and February 1942 and they had taken up temporary accommodation on two 'flower' boats, one as headquarters and the other as living and mess.

Bill was sent to Macao, a neutral area but intimidated and watched very carefully by the Japanese, to contact the British Consul, J.F. Reeves. Dr. Ride informed the Consul of Bill's trustworthiness and that he would be setting up permanent communications, including codes as a security measure, between Kweilin and Macao. Loyalty to BAAG was of prime importance and Bill Chong was one of its most outstanding members.

After the war, Bill continued to work for British Intelligence in Hong Kong until the mid 1950s when he returned to Canada. He received the British Empire Medal in 1947 for his work with BAAG in China.[5]

Major Holmes spent some time in the New Territories from August 1942 with four other members of a forward operational group. They investigated escape means for the POWs in Hong Kong and undertook a general reconnaissance of the area. The guerrillas were not very cooperative and they discouraged the investigations carried out by the team. Relations deteriorated to the point where Holmes withdrew the group but they had spent over three weeks in the area and had learned a great deal about Japanese dispositions as well as guerrilla methods. In this particular case the guerrillas were Communists and BAAG was under suspicion of being Nationalist controlled, which accounted for their lack of cooperation.

Holmes also reported on conditions in southeast Kwangtung in 1943; the harvest had failed and the destitute from Hong Kong had gathered there after escaping or being expelled by the Japanese. Action was taken to distribute rice and to inoculate against cholera.

Early in 1943 a BAAG team had been captured by guerrillas at a post between Mirs and Bias Bays, northeast of Hong Kong. Holmes and Vincent Yeung[6] were sent to negotiate their release. Holmes found that the guerrilla leader was more bandit than Communist and by paying a ransom, secured the party's release 25 December. Holmes and Yeung had walked some 450 miles to rescue the men.

Two other Canadian Chinese worked for BAAG. Maj. (Dr.) Raymond Harry S. Lee, although born in China, had moved to Vancouver with his family as a child. He was a graduate of Hong Kong University. Dr. Lee was in charge of the field medical service at Waichow. In 1943 he travelled to western Kwangtung and took charge of the relief operations in this famine and cholera infested area. Several thousand patients were treated in the hospital and two medical aid posts set up in the area. His nurse, Nellie Lim, was also from Vancouver.[7]

In addition to assisting escapees from Hong Kong, BAAG had set up medical clinics to minister to the Chinese throughout the Kwangtung area. BAAG handled 30,000 patients during the famine of 1943, and daily fed some 6,000 people.[8] Medical services were extended to the Chinese Army, since it had none of its own.

When Ride visited the 14th USAAF in Hengyang, he was instrumental in preventing the bombing of the Sham Shui Po POW Camp. From then on, Maj.Gen. Claire Chennault's headquarters was regularly supplied with information concerning Hong Kong and other intelligence to prevent any future incidents. The 14th USAAF was established in the late spring of 1943 under Chennault after the China Air Task Force, which had operated as part of the 10th USAAF for eight months, had been disbanded in March.

One of the Canadian members of the 14th was Stanley Lowe from Victoria, BC, who joined the USAAF in San Francisco. Stanley remained with the 14th in China until it was shunted aside in July 1945 and the 10th from India supplanted it. Chennault was retired in early August of the same year. President Roosevelt had died in April and this left Chennault without effective support in Washington. Wedemeyer at Chungking supported the dismissal. Stanley returned to San Francisco after the war.

The USAAF had frequently transported BAAG messages from headquarters to New Delhi or Chungking. In return, intelligence and weather reports received from the Hong Kong and Canton areas were delivered twice daily to the USAAF by BAAG. Eventually, an American intelligence officer was posted to BAAG but he in turn set up his own intelligence gathering system after a few months. In the late spring of 1943, BAAG and other British units in China required more reliable transport facilities between India and China than the casual basis that the newly established 14th USAAF, the Air Transport Command, and the CNAC could or would provide.

The Canadian Ambassador in Chungking, Maj.-Gen. Victor W. Odlum, in June 1943 wrote to External Affairs in Ottawa in an effort to persuade the Canadian government to contribute a squadron for the purpose of transporting needed supplies into China for British and Canadian use. He gave credit to the CNAC for carrying material into China and for carrying the King's Messenger and other diplomatic passengers weekly to Calcutta. CNAC could not, however, carry explosives for the "British guerilla School in China."

Odlum outlined the following problems with transportation in the theatre. When a British plane became available early in 1943 before the 14th USAAF had become fully established, landing facilities in China were refused. Red Cross supplies in particular deteriorated as they sat in India waiting to be transported. The offer of the Canadian Red Cross to purchase a plane for this purpose had been turned down by the American Red Cross in Washington. Instead, Stilwell offered the use of one plane once a week.

Odlum's request was apparently considered by the Prime Minister and National Defence (army and air), but no action was taken.[9] It was not until the end of 1943 that the Royal Air Force was allowed to fly one plane a week into Kunming; the number of planes was later increased to six.

Stanley Lowe and Bill Lowe

Of the Chinese from Hong Kong that BAAG helped to escape, over 200 were raised and trained as the China Unit and employed on guard duties at BAAG headquarters. This group was broken up when 127 volunteered as the Hong Kong Volunteer Company to fight with Maj.-Gen. Orde Wingate's Chindits, the Long Range Penetration Groups operating behind Japanese lines in Burma. A small part of the China Unit remained with BAAG.

F.W. (Mike) Kendall, whose background and association with Chinese Canadians will be described in a later chapter, worked for BAAG in southern China for a short period at its inception until July 1942; D.R. (Ronnie) Holmes and Vincent Yeung worked for BAAG from the early days until December 1944. Kendall, Holmes, and Yeung were the nucleus around which Kendall proposed to build a team that included 13 Chinese

Canadians he recruited and trained in the Okanagan Valley in the summer of 1944.

BAAG arranged on 13 August 1945 for Embassy orders to be sent in to the Colonial Secretary of Hong Kong, F.C. Gimson, interned at Stanley Camp, to set up the Colonial Administration even before the British Naval Task Force was able to enter the port. Japan capitulated 15 August but there was much confusion until the armistice was signed 2 September. The British Naval Task Force appeared off Stanley Point 29 August and anchored at Victoria. Meanwhile, Gimson had assumed the government of Hong Kong on 19 August; he was greatly handicapped in his efforts to re-establish the government because of the chaotic conditions.[10]

Ride, with Holmes and other BAAG members, flew to Hong Kong 2 September. The Recovery of Allied Prisoners of War and Internees (RAPWI) had already begun. All remaining BAAG members reached Hong Kong by the end of the year and on 31 December 1945, the unit was disbanded.

BAAG had been instrumental in assisting in the escape of 139 prisoners of war, 314 service escapers who were not interned, 33 American evaders, and 1,806 Chinese with non-Chinese nationality.

Albert Quon from Montreal was another Canadian left stranded in Hong Kong. Albert was able to make his way into China and served behind Japanese lines for eight months from late 1944 as interpreter with the OSS, while six American officers trained Chinese guerrillas with American equipment. Albert returned to Canada late in 1946.

Albert's brother, Herbert, served in OSS intelligence in China and remained with the Central Intelligence Agency for four or five years after the war. Their father had been Catering Superintendent for Canadian Pacific Steamship Lines in Hong Kong. Another brother, Lyman, acted as assistant to his father and, although a member of the HKVDC, had been sent to Singapore conducting refugees on one of the company's ships just before the Japanese attacked. Lyman Quon did not return to Hong Kong.

The Luey Kheong family from Calgary returned in the 1930s when the mother took the children back to China. The father died while they were absent and his body was shipped to the homeland for burial, as was customary. Three of the four boys, Harry, Joe, and Jack Kheong. joined the Chinese Air Force/aircraft factory; Ken, the youngest, attended school. At the outbreak of war in the Pacific, Harry was liaison officer between the American and Chinese Air Forces; Joe joined the Air Transport Command in a ground support role; Jack enlisted as a sergeant in the US Army in Kunming; and Ken attended school in Hong Kong. Ken was later evacuated to Chungking where he joined the US Army Quartermaster Corps, Service of Supply, as interpreter in the latter part of the War. Harry returned to Canada in the 1950s and worked at Canadair in Montreal until his retirement. Ken served as radio officer on merchant ships of various national registry for ten years, before returning to Canada in 1960. He then joined Transport Canada as flight service specialist until his retirement in 1986.

Lannie Yee, younger brother of Louey King of the first Australian group, served as messenger for the Chinese Nationalist Army; he was too young for any formal military role, even in the Chinese Army. A member of the second Australian group, Jan Yuen, had spent the years 1930 to 1937 in China. Victor Louie, who was dropped into Malaya in the summer of 1945, also spent the years from 1931 to 1938 in China.

Two brothers of K.C. (Charlie) Lowe, Huene and Harvey Lowe, worked in the Reserves Section of the Shanghai Volunteers in the US International Settlement. One of them described the work as "very light duties." They both returned to Canada, Huene in 1949 on the *General Gordon*.

Arthur Lee of Montreal was also employed by Canada Steamship Lines in Hong Kong. Arthur was able to pick up a propaganda leaflet dropped by Japanese aircraft over the city. Ross Mark from Toronto, although very briefly a member of the HKVDC, escaped into China and made his

British Officers and men! What do you expect in your useless resistance after having been cornered in this small island of Hongkong? If you are waiting for the Chungking troops to stir up the Japanese rear, it will only end in a fool's dream. The Malay Peninsula and the Philippines are now under the sway of Japanese forces and their fate is completely sealed.

Your comrades brought to Kowloon, have already been sent to Samchun and they are calmly enjoying a peaceful X'mas. You fare at the cross-road now. It's all up to you whether you prefer death or save your life for the future.

We will give you the last chance for your reconsideration. If you surrender to us, the ultimatum ends at the midnight of Dec. 26th.

JAPANESE ARMY

- courtesy Arthur Lee

Leaflet dropped by Japanese in Hong Kong

吾粉共甘同

由於大東亞戰爭的勃發
，日華兩國的關係，比
前加倍密切，已成必要
。日本帝國空前絕後的
大戰果，對於中國，也
是無限的欣喜和幸福。
如兄弟姊妹的日華兩國民
，應進一步互相理解，
共向大東亞共榮圈邁進
。緊記着吧！十二月八
日這一天！

way to Chungking. Dr. David Lin from Montreal, after graduating from the University of Toronto in 1937, worked in the 19th Hospital in Hong Kong from the late 1930s. It was difficult for Chinese Canadian professionals to open a practice in this country. They all returned to Canada after the war.

For many of those who had remained in Canada, their first preference was to serve in the Royal Canadian Air Force.

NOTES

Unless otherwise noted, personal information is from participants or their relatives.

1. Letters from Secretary, the Hong Kong POW Association, 1992; and David Bosanquet, *Escape through China: Survival after the fall of Hong Kong* (London, 1983), pp. 27, 52-53.
2. *Guerrilla* is a Spanish word meaning "small war"; it is also the diminutive of *guerre* "war," and seems to have various spellings.
3. Bosanquet, p. 122.
4. Edwin Ride, *BAAG: Hong Kong Resistance 1942-1945* (Hong Kong, 1981), p. 83.
5. Interview with William Chong in Victoria 1991; and Ride, *BAAG*, p. 211.
6. Sgt. Vincent (Vinnie) Yeung, RA, was a member of BAAG's field operations and intelligence branch from 1942. The name is spelled 'Young' in SOE records. Vincent was born in the West Indies and taken to China by his father when he was very young. He spoke the Hakka dialect.
7. Interview with William Chong; and see Ride, pp. 193, 195.
8. M.R.D. Foot and J.M. Langley, *MI9: the British Secret Service that Fostered Escape and Evasion 1939-1945 and its American Counterpart* (London, 1979), p. 266.
9. Odlum letter dated 1 June 1943, in NAC, RG 25, Vol. 2717, File 72-US-40.
10. James Leasor, "The Man Who Kept Hong Kong British" in *Telegraph: Sunday Magazine,* 12 August 1984.

Chapter IV

THE ALLIED AIR SERVICES

On the outbreak of war in September 1939, Chinese Canadians, like many other Canadians, were eager to join the Royal Canadian Air Force; many had been members of flying clubs and several had paid for their own flying training and were qualified pilots.

Chinese Canadians, however, were not allowed to enlist for aircrew in the RCAF throughout Canada until October 1942; volunteers for this service had to be of "pure European descent." Enlistment for aircrew was opened to Canadian Chinese in the fall of 1942, although the change had been proposed as early as 23 April 1941. Order in Council PC 79/11160[1] was approved 9 December 1942, which officially amended paragraph 227 (1) of *The King's Regulations and Orders for the Royal Canadian Air Force, 1924.* The racial requirement was dropped.

Those few who enlisted before October 1942, and there were a few, were restricted to ground duties. In October 1941 a letter from Ottawa to the commanding officer at the RCAF No. 2 Recruiting Centre in Calgary stated that "Orientals and Negroes who are British subjects cannot be barred from enlistment in any category in Ground Duties for which they might be qualified," but all applications from "coloured applicants" had to be submitted to "Headquarters for enlistment sanction." Although they would be accepted for ground duties, the official view was "actually the Air Force does not want coloured personnel because of the difficulties of racial differences." By March of 1942 the view had altered and now they would be accepted for the Special Reserve if they had the "temperament, adaptability and education." The ultimate question of suitability was now left up to the Selection Boards of recruiting centres.

The question had still not been resolved in Vancouver, however, as clarification was requested from Ottawa as late as November 1943 for enlistment in ground duties with "respect to Canadian born Chinese who are not subject to the regulations of the 'National Resources Mobilization Act.'"[2] In the matter of enlistment, Chinese Canadians appeared to have had an unfair advantage in remaining free to enlist in the RCAF, if they so wished, because they had not been called up under NRMA.

The RCAF accepted Chinese Canadians for aircrew from 1 October 1942 and this service never became entangled in definitions as to whether they were British subjects or Chinese nationals, unlike the Canadian Army which finally lumped all categories together as "Allied Aliens." At an inter-departmental meeting in April 1943, however, the RCAF spokesman declared that air force policy was "to accept aliens after vetting but not enemy aliens. Special regulations, however, apply to Orientals . . . [but] the general policy is to discourage their enlistment."[3] This spokesman appeared to be out of touch with what was occurring; several Chinese Canadians were already members of the RCAF.

Some of this change in thinking may have been encouraged by the fact that the Royal Air Force had sent a few Chinese to Canada for training in the British Commonwealth Air Training Plan, two or three of whom were killed in training accidents.[4]

Since they were not called up under NRMA in Pacific Command, those who wished to join the air force waited until the enlistment qualifications allowed them to volunteer in the service of their choice. Many had been advised that the change was forthcoming. Thus, quite unwittingly, the government's NRMA policy in British Columbia worked to the advantage of Chinese Canadians even though Vancouver brought this advantage to the attention of Ottawa. Those in the eastern provinces, however, were called up under NRMA in the regular way.

Because of this racial restriction many men who had tried to volunteer for the RCAF in provinces other than British Columbia before 1942 were reluctant to transfer to active status when called up under NRMA. Some of these men were already trained pilots and many became instructors in the BCATP in order to play an active role in their professional capacity and, in the case of one pilot, in order to avoid internment.

The BCATP was set up in 1939 to train not only Canadian aircrew but also aircrew from Great Britain, Australia, and New Zealand. The plan was finally wound down in March 1945. Technical training was centralized at St. Thomas, Ont, and was given to RCAF recruits only.

The Clayton Knight Committee, a non-governmental body to recruit Americans, was formed early in the war not only to recruit men to be trained for Allied service but also to locate instructors and staff pilots for the Elementary Flying Training and Air Observer Schools for the BCATP. The AOS were later renamed Air Navigation Schools. American recruits for the RCAF were not required to swear allegiance to King George VI; instead, they took an oath of obedience to superior officers. Americans also could transfer to their own forces should the United States enter the war. The committee became inactive from about February 1942, but some American recruits were still being accepted in the summer. Before 1942 many Chinese Canadians became instructors for BCATP since civilian instructors were employed in this programme.

A complete run down of all the manning depots and schools that were a part of the BCATP would be tedious; they will be mentioned only where Chinese Canadians instructed or were trained. From the few mentioned, the reader will have some idea of the various types and the vastness of the programme. Before the plan ended in March 1945, 131,553 pupils had graduated; RCAF graduates numbered 72,835, well over half.

Two civilian instructors for the BCATP were the brothers Albert and Cedric Mah, born 1920 and 1922, in Prince Rupert, BC. They had paid for their own pre-war pilot training at the Aviation College (California Flyers) in Los Angeles.

With a senior commercial pilot's licence, Pilot Albert Mah flew out of Edmonton and later moved to Canadian Pacific Airlines. Pilot Cedric Mah returned to Canada to fly under Capt. Wilfred R. (Wop) May, OBE, DFC. Refused by the RCAF, they both became instructors for the BCATP. Albert became an instructor at No. 2 AOS, Edmonton, from 1940 (where Captain May was the civilian manager until the school closed in 1944); he then became an instructor at No. 8 AOS, Ancienne Laurette, Quebec City, until 1943. Cedric was an instructor at No. 5 AOS, Winnipeg, from 1942 and at No. 2 AOS, Edmonton, until 1944.

Southeast Asia

When released from BCATP, Capt. Albert Mah joined China National Aviation Corporation in the spring of 1943, flying a CNAC DC-3 from Florida to Brazil, Ascension Island, Accra in Africa, and on to Khartoum and India.

Capt. Cedric Mah flew to India in 1944 by Air Transport Command in a DC-4, the new four-engine aircraft, via New York to Newfoundland, then to the Azores, Casablanca, Tripoli, Cairo, Iraq, to Abadan in Iran, and on to Karachi, Delhi, and Agra, ending at Calcutta.

"CNAC flights over the Himalayas began in 1942 with Douglas Dakota DC-3s, and in Dakota C-46 Commando Transports early 1944 with one third more capacity, on a contract basis packing freight for the American Military Commission in China," as Cedric Mah briefly described the purpose of these trips. Pan American Airways jointly owned the CNAC (the China Division of Pan Am) and recruited and trained pilots for the Hump

– photo by Louis Jacques, Weekend Magazine
Captain Albert Mah

service was called the Warhawk; in British service it was called the Tomahawk or Kittyhawk. It was a low-level, ground-attack aircraft. The crews trained in Burma and assisted the British Army when the Japanese invaded.

Chinese newsmen named the group "The Flying Tigers," in honour of the men who had fought "so furiously and had given such a good account of themselves" during the British retreat from Burma. The tiger had been China's national symbol from the founding of the Republic in 1911. American newsmen picked up the title and used "The Flying Tigers" in their own news stories about the group.

Major General Chennault then headed the China Air Task Force, a wing of the 10th USAAF, with headquarters in New Delhi, although Chennault's group operated within China. The China Air Task Force was disbanded 10 March 1943, and the 14th USAAF

run supplying Chiang Kai-Shek's Nationalist Armies. President F.D. Roosevelt made a special radio appeal for aircrew that encouraged several to transfer to this organization upon release from their current duties. Aircraft, of course, were obtained from the United States.

Claire Chennault's American Volunteer Group, the AVG, was disbanded 4 July 1942 after less than a year of service. Chennault was not a member of the United States Army Air Force during this period. From 1938 he had been a civilian air adviser in the employ of Chiang Kai-Shek and had been given the rank of colonel in the Chinese Air Force by the Generalissimo. In 1941 the United States government agreed to the funding of both Chennault and the AVG. The volunteers were recruited from the US army and navy to fly the P-40 fighters with which the AVG was equipped. The P-40 in American

Captain Cedric Mah

was formed with headquarters in China. The new unit grew to over 20,000 men with a corresponding increase in the number of aircraft, from the small group with which Chennault began. Chennault, however, had made no provision for ground defence and the Japanese captured his airfields, Lingling, and Kweilin, in late 1943 and early 1944, with the Americans destroying millions of dollars worth of airlifted supplies and equipment as they retreated.

By the fall of 1944, China's importance to the war effort had waned. General Stilwell, senior American military adviser to Chiang Kai-Shek, was replaced by Maj.Gen. Albert C. Wedemeyer, formerly chief of staff to Lord Louis Mountbatten in Southeast Asia Command. Lt. Gen. Daniel Sultan replaced Stilwell in command of the American, British, and Chinese troops in northern Burma. Now the theatre was more firmly divided into two separate commands: India-Burma and China-Burma.

When the AVG was disbanded in 1942, five pilots joined the China Air Task Force; 17 switched to the CNAC. By the end of 1943, CNAC had 43 qualified pilots with nearly a dozen in training. The pilots came from China, the United States, Australia, Canada, Great Britain, and Denmark: from the AVG, the Eagle Squadron, North Atlantic Ferry Command, the RAF, and the RCAF. Although money and adventure may have been the motivating factors, Canadian Chinese would also have seen the move as an opportunity to provide help to relatives in China.

The operating base for CNAC was Dinjan, Assam Province, in northeast India, with the Chinese base located at Kunming in Yunnan, the old Burma Road terminal. Maintenance, overhaul, and supply facilities were located at Dum Dum airport, Calcutta. After two or three weeks on operations at Dinjan, personnel spent time in Calcutta for rest and recreation as well as on refresher courses.

Three members of the crew pose with CNAC aircraft

On one trip just after the war ended, because of ice build-up, the snapping of a support in the under-carriage, and the loss of one engine, Cedric Mah jettisoned $800 million in Chinese paper money over the mountains in order to hold his altitude. Over a valley, he circled a lake for about 40 minutes and the ice began to melt at this lower altitude. The second engine returned to life but with less fuel than needed, he was forced to land in Kunming instead of Chungking as planned. The Kunming runway was surfaced with gravel. The money had been destined for the Bank of China in Chungking. Twenty-two DC-3 flights had preceded this one to deliver some $200 million in gold bullion from Calcutta to Chungking, an American government loan to China. Cedric made three trips on this delivery programme.[5]

Between Japanese fighters in the air and equally fierce Chinese Communists on the ground, the crews of CNAC braved these dangers and freakish weather hazards, especially during the monsoon periods from May to October, to ferry essential supplies to the Nationalist Chinese government. On 14 January 1945, 35 planes out of 300 despatched on the Hump run were lost in a storm; three were CNAC aircraft. By the end of the month CNAC had lost two more, "from an operational fleet of twenty-two aircraft."

The route covered 550 miles and took about three hours and twenty minutes. "The Hump Route" from Dinjan direct to Kunming, "on a clear day, minus enemy interception . . . could be flown at fifteen thousand feet skirting the mountain peaks. But at night or when the weather was bad an additional two to four thousand feet was needed to compensate for navigation and other errors." To avoid enemy interception, a dogleg to the north had to be made. "It took additional fuel and hours and put the crew over the higher Himalayas and 25,000 foot peaks, spawning ground of the world's worst weather and high speed jet streams."

A low route, the "scenic southern route" could be flown in extremely bad weather or at night when there was no moon. This route

crossed the Naga Hills, home of the Naga head hunters, over the upper Chindwin River in Burma, across the Hukawng Valley to Myitkyina and the Irrawaddy River, then on across the Salween and the Mekong Rivers, and the lofty Santsung Range, a spur of the Himalayas between the two rivers called the "graveyard of the Hump." Here the alpine and tropic airs met and fronts collided, forming monsoon storms. Clear of the mountains, the Yunnan plateau stretched out below and soon signs of civilization and then Kunming appeared.

Albert Mah made 420 return trips over the Hump in the final 18 months of the war; Cedric completed 400 missions. Chinese troops were airlifted to India for training before being sent to fight in Burma. Each load carried 35 to 40 men. The transports carried ammunition, gun powder, silver, aviation gasoline, TNT, and "massive amounts of paper currency to fuel inflation" into China, and tin, wood oil, tungsten, tea, mercury, silk, and hog bristles out.

Silk was urgently needed for parachute cloth even though nylon had been developed and was in production for this purpose. Lack of silk forced the British Army in Assam to develop a jute parachute for dropping stores which worked satisfactorily. Silk was also used as the material on which maps and sometimes codes were printed for SOE and MI 9, frequently in the form of a handkerchief.

CNAC tonnage out-performed the Air Transport Command, the US Army's freight service, until the last months of the war. There were over 400 pilots and co-pilots in the India-China Wing of Air Transport Command; when pilot numbers were increased to 750, the tonnage flown dropped. About 66 planes were lost by CNAC out of a total of 400 for the entire freight service.

In addition to the Hump run, CNAC also carried personnel to the Ledo Road construction, ferried rice to the Chinese road builders, made trips to Tibet, and supplied the American naval meteorologists on the Silk Road at Suchow, gateway to the Gobi Desert. Cedric Mah was involved in one of the Tibet runs when he recruited a Tibetan chieftain as interpreter to purchase a supply of horses for the war.[6]

On leave in 1944, Albert Mah rescued his young teen-age sister, Bernice, from a small village near Canton behind Japanese lines. She had been taken to China in August 1935 when their mother returned with her three daughters after the father died. The family had been trapped in Canton when the Japanese captured the city and surrounding area. Albert had made the trip through Japanese lines by sampan, cycling, and walking to deliver money to his mother. He was able to extricate his sister successfully but it was some time before she finally arrived in British Columbia.[7]

The mother and the two sisters left behind did not arrive in Vancouver until the summer of 1949. The girls had been born in Canada and they had no problem entering the country, but the mother had not been naturalized and she had remained abroad beyond the two-year limit. An order in council was passed 17 December 1948 to allow her re-entry.[8]

When Albert and Cedric Mah returned to Canada, they continued their flying careers, Cedric as commercial pilot and Albert as a NATO instructor at a school near Montreal. Before Albert's work began at NATO, the plane he was flying crashed near Terrebonne, Que, in February 1946. Kim Yuen Lee was with him at the time. Other than a broken bone or two, which soon mended, neither man received lasting injury. For Cedric Mah who remained in the west, a mountain in the BC coastal range was named Mount Ced Mah in 1953 "for outstanding service transporting and supplying a government survey party under difficult flying conditions."[9]

Tommy Wong, now living in Montreal, followed a pattern similar to the Mah brothers. Tommy came to Canada when he was three years old with his family settling in Moose Jaw. In 1938 Tommy was already a pilot and when war began he tried to enlist in the RCAF in Toronto but was refused because he was not of pure European descent. He was then called up under NRMA but refused to go saying that if he wasn't good enough for the air force,

Tommy Wong wearing the uniform and badges of No. 10 AOS, Chatham, NB, 1942

then he wasn't good enough for the army. He had also paid the Head Tax of $500, which only Chinese immigrants had to pay to enter Canada. The National Selective Service, having confirmed his pilot status, was apparently completely unaware of the RCAF restriction and called the nearest RCAF recruiting office in Toronto for confirmation. There was some sympathy for his position but, nevertheless, Tommy Wong was threatened with internment. Instead, he joined BCATP as instructor at No. 10 AOS, Chatham, NB.

When released from BCATP, he was offered a commission in Ferry Command (also a part civilian organization) or as pilot with CNAC. In 1943, Capt. Tommy Wong decided to join CNAC and flew to India to operate from Dinjan with the others.[10]

Tommy Wong also advises that "very recently the USA Government has passed a ruling with respect to civilian participation in the war effort with companies under contract to the US Government, such as Pan Am's CNAC, the US Ferry Command, Transport Command, and others, so that they will receive veteran status. It might be good to see the same sort of recognition obtained for Canadians in Canada."

Capt. Harold Chinn, born in Vancouver, received his pilot training in British Columbia before going to China in 1933 at the age of 21. At that time there was no employment in Canada for Chinese pilots. In China, Harold enlisted in the Canton Air Force and served in this organization from 1933 to 1935. He was in Shanghai from 1935 to 1937, and then became a CNAC transport pilot flying between Chungking, Kweiyang, and Hong Kong until Hong Kong fell to the Japanese in December 1941. In 1942 Harold Chinn joined CNAC on the Hump route operating with the others between Dinjan and Kunming. He flew over 600 flights on the Hump run, more than any other pilot in this organization.

When the war ended in 1945 Harold Chinn remained with the Central Air Transport Company (the new name for CNAC) operating within China. Returning to China after home leave in 1947, he flew a remodeled DC-4 from San Francisco to Shanghai for delivery to Chiang Kai-Shek as his personal plane. Two years later, he was again on leave in Canada when he received word that the Communists had taken over the country and there was no point in returning. When his wife and two children arrived in Canada, he was unable to obtain employment as a pilot since commercial organizations were still reluctant to hire Chinese Canadians. They moved to the United States where his family became American citizens but Harold still retains his Canadian citizenship.

Capt. Kuo Lim Mah, from Kelowna, BC, completed his flying training in Edmonton in 1933 and went to China shortly after. He joined the No. 6 Fighter Squadron of the Canton Air Force and then enlisted in the Central Government Air Force (the Canton Government joined the Central Government in 1936). In these organizations, he had been a fighter pilot. Retrained as a transport pilot, in 1942 he joined CNAC flying the Hump.

Kuo Lim Mah was killed 1 August 1944 when his aircraft failed to clear the cliff when taking off from Kunming.[11] An attempt through US Government sources to discover where he is buried has not proved successful, although his grave may be in a private cemetery near Canton.

There were several Canadian Chinese airborne radio operators working for CNAC: Enoch and Luke Bunn, brothers from Vancouver, Jack K. Dong, also from Vancouver, and Stanley Fong, and C.T. (Fatty) Fung. Enoch Bunn was in Hong Kong when the Japanese captured the colony. He escaped to China and on reaching Chungking worked first for the press attaché office of the British

Captain Harold Chinn

Embassy, then moved to the International Broadcasting Station. In 1944 Enoch went to India to work as radio operator for CNAC. He was one of the three-man crew (pilot, navigator, radio operator) on the Hump flights.

The airlift over the Hump was no longer required when the war ended but the Central Air Transport Company continued the routes within China. Many Hump pilots continued with this new organization. Although most of the Chinese Canadian pilots had returned to Canada long before 1949, Cedric Mah and many of the others had transferred to the Central Air Transport Company for a short time.

When Chiang Kai-Shek fled to Formosa in 1949 after the Great Yellow River Battle near Hsuchow in January, the Central Air Transport Company was unable to function, since the Chinese Nationalist Government owned 51 percent. Pan American Airways divested itself of its interest in the company and sold it to the Kuomintang Government. Mao Tse-Tung proclaimed the People's Republic of China 1 October 1949.

Discrimination followed the Canadian and American Chinese. The CNAC paid the Chinese, regardless of their nationality, at a lower rate than it did Caucasians. A Caucasian captain earned $800 a month as base salary for 60 hours' flying but captains with Chinese ancestry were paid $485. Overtime pay to Caucasians was $6 an hour which averaged another 65 hours and anything over 70 hours was at $20 an hour, but for the Chinese overtime pay was about $3.25 for anything over 60 hours. One Chinese Canadian pilot felt that discrimination was following him from country to country although in Canada he had been paid on an equal basis. As with Ferry Command crews, all living expenses had to be paid by the individual, and there were no disability or pension benefits when the war was over. After the war many CNAC pilots left that company for Central Air Transport Company where all were treated equally.

In addition to these pilots in CNAC, there were other Chinese Canadian pilots posted to India: two in the RAF and one in an RCAF Transport Squadron employed in Burma.

The headquarters of RCAF Squadrons No. 435 (Chinthe) and No. 436 (Elephant) were formed at Gujrat, India, in the fall of 1944, in spite of the adverse report made by the Canadian Air Liaison Mission to India in June 1944. This report concluded that RAF standards in India were unsuitable for Canadians with respect to accommodadation, food, hygiene, hospitalization, and welfare. Lt.-Gen. Sir William Slim's land campaign to retake Burma could not be undertaken without adequate air supply and Canada agreed to provide two squadrons. Air and ground crew were collected from England and Canada.

One of the pilots in No. 436 Squadron was F/O Hong Yuen Tso, J.44216, born 1919 in Canton, who came to Canada at the age of two and grew up in Victoria. Hong's grand-

Hong Yuen Tso

father had come to Canada a decade or two before the turn of the century and his father had been born in Canada. Hong's grandson, Eric, makes the fifth Canadian generation for this family.

Hong had tried to join the air force shortly after Pearl Harbor but he was refused. "I received a letter from Ottawa that Orientals were not being taken into aircrew; then they sent me a notice that Orientals would be accepted."

Hong finally joined the air force late in 1942 or early 1943. He went first to the Manning Pool at Edmonton and then began his ground school training at No. 2 Initial Training School, Regina College, in July 1943; next came No. 19 EFTS, Virden, Man, in October. He was at No. 17 Service Flying Training School, at Souris (just outside Winnipeg) by April 1944 when he was commissioned pilot officer. Crews were formed at No. 6 Operational Training Unit at Comox, BC, the end of August. They trained together as a crew on the DC-3.

Hong was trained as a transport pilot and received the equivalent of a transport pilot's rating. In his aircraft, they were all officers except the wireless airgunner. At graduation the top ten percent of the class was picked to go overseas. They left Lachine, near Montreal, and arrived in England in November 1944 where squadrons were formed; they then flew to Karachi, India.

By the end of November, No. 435 consisted of 20 Douglas Dakota DC-3s and No. 436 had 15. The squadrons were established for 25 aircraft each, 20 operational and five in reserve, but the aircraft were not yet all available. Apparently they operated below establishment level throughout their tour in Burma.

One of their first operations on arrival in India was to drop Indian paratroopers in training north of Karachi. The British officers would often hit the knuckles of the Indians with their pistols to force them to release their hold in order to make the jump. The action seemed brutal but perhaps it was necessary.

They towed a few gliders, "but that country wasn't made for gliders. . . . In Burma and India there was one mountain range after another and gliders were just impractical." Gliders, however, had been used for the Chindits on their second Long Range Penetration behind enemy lines so they had to undergo training in this method.

Jumpmasters (wireless airgunners) and kickers (many of them ground crew) were trained in India and the loads varied from animals to guns, from motor transport to the gasoline to operate them, from rice and other food to ammunition for all types of weapons. In addition, at least 20 fully equipped troops and 12 to 16 casualties could be transported in each aircraft.

Their first operational flying occurred when they assisted the RAF move to Imphal in the second week of December. No. 435 moved to Tulihal in the Imphal Valley on the 19th with the second squadron assisting them. The first sorties were flown the following day supporting the XIVth Army's advance on Shwebo, in spite of lack of accommodation, proper food, and equipment. Living conditions were never the best in the India theatre.

Kangla, near Imphal (Manipur) in Assam was the location for 436 Squadron when it moved in January 1945. Again, living conditions were very poor, including lack of water. By 15 January the squadron began support operations at Shwebo. Both squadrons were part of the Combat Cargo Task Force.

The Dakota was limited to an operational range of 250 miles, and as the army advanced, one squadron had to be relocated. Akyab and Ramree Islands on the Arakan coast had been captured late 1944 and early 1945. No. 436 moved south to Mawnubyin, Akyab Island, in March 1945 and was operational by the 20th, flying supplies to Myitche, Meiktila and Mandalay. Since these towns were still under dispute, the aircraft often came under fire while landing or dropping supplies. No. 435 also dropped supplies to the Mandalay fighting troops but was soon out of range as the army moved into the Meiktila-Toungoo-Pegu area. This squadron continued to fly supplies to the northern area of Burma.

The Americans at the bases in Akyab and Ramree were well supplied with a great variety of food and other amenities. Ships frequently entered the harbour carrying an abundance of supplies. "We used to envy them. The Canadians had to make do with bully beef, K-rations. But we were lucky in the Canadian Transport Squadron; we went to Calcutta every week, one plane a week, and brought back fresh meat."

The "tarmac was made up of interlocking steel plates; it's like a giant mechano set. Because of the heavy rainfall, this was how runways were built. We flew in the monsoons wearing raincoats. It rained a lot; every day it rained. We lived in a very primitive area in the jungle; everybody lived together, all the aircrew together and all the ground crew together."

All the officers rotated their duties and censored all mail entering and leaving the base. The RCAF Intelligence Branch performed the briefings.

"As a part of our kit when flying, we carried this cloth." As the picture shows the cloth was printed in colour with the Union Jack and, in English and about fifteen other languages, a message requesting help for the downed airman. The cloth was pinned to the back of the shirt or jacket so that it was easily visible. They also carried a map of Burma, waterproofed and rubberized, issued to them as a part of evasion training. Crews always had to carry the map with them in case they were forced down. They flew both day and night sorties.

Their flights were usually round trip although sometimes they "landed to bring back POWs, wounded, and emergency cases." Their supply drops were made from about 150 to 300 feet and there was no air protection. "We made some supply drops to Force 136 people. As soon as they cap-

tured a Japanese fighter strip, the army would tell us to drop fuel and rockets and munitions. We carried aviation fuel for fighter pilots." These were 50-gallon drums and they would have to land to deliver them, often on the front strip just captured from the enemy. These runways were very short but they were able to take off with a very heavy load.

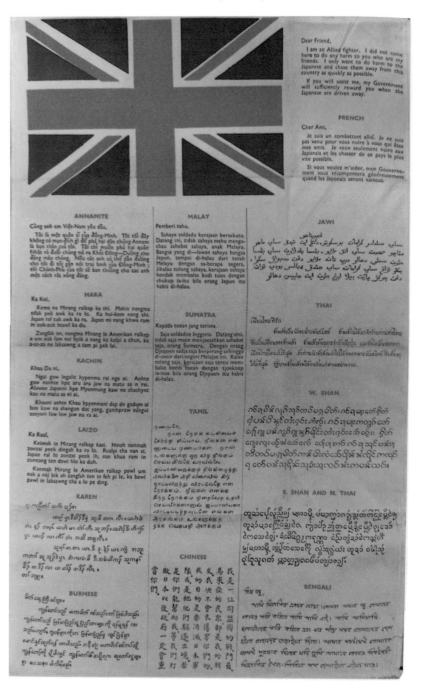

– *courtesy Hong Yuen Tso*
Silk panel fastened to flight jacket – part of Escape and Evasion kit

Jumpmasters, 20 wireless airgunners from each squadron, participated with the USAAF 317th and 319th Troop Carrier Squadrons in dropping paratroops to capture guns at Elephant Point outside Rangoon on 1 May 1945. Rangoon itself was entered two days later in Operation *Dracula* but the Japanese had already left.

Monsoon weather descended and lasted until September. On 12 May, No. 436 moved to Kyaukpyu, Ramree Island, just before the monsoon reached Akyab the end of the month. The USAAF squadrons were withdrawn 1 June; this left just seven squadrons to supply the same number of troops.

With the onset of the monsoon, the main difficulty was with the weather. No. 435, still at Imphal, supplied the northern area generally: Lashio, Bhamo, and Myitkyina, including civilians building the Ledo road. No. 436 remained based at Ramree supplying troops clearing pockets of Japanese resistance, evacuating casualties, and stocking rear airfield. Supply drops were also made to Force 136 guerrilla bands.

In August and September, both squadrons dropped supplies to Force 136 teams as they led their guerrillas against Japanese stragglers making for Siam. The weather and the difficulty of locating the dropping zones made these trips very hazardous. On 15 August, the day the Japanese capitulated, 436 Squadron delivered mail to all the stations; there were no other flights on this day. During the third week of August and until the end of the month, No. 436 Squadron evacuated casualties from Ramree and Akyab to Chittagong.

CNAC, now the Central Air Transport Company, tried to interest F/O Hong Yuen Tso in continuing to fly for that organization; he knew the routes and conditions and flew the same planes, although Central Air Transport Company was using the newer C-46. His bride, whom he had married just before going overseas, preferred to stay in Canada, so he did not take up the offer. He had been promoted to flying officer before he returned to England.

Surrender of the Japanese was taken in this area of Southeast Asia on 26 August although Tokyo had accepted unconditional surrender on the 15th. Shipping by sea to Rangoon and by land through Assam was able to supply most needs by the end of September. Many Canadians had become tour expired by August and on 9 September for No. 436, and 11 September for No. 435, the two Canadian squadrons left Burma. Before they left, however, one aircraft and crew were sent to Hong Kong 2 September in the belief that the two transport squadrons were the closest Canadians to the colony. When an engine failed in Bangkok, the trip was cancelled. The British Naval Task Force had entered Hong Kong 29/30 August and had accepted surrender.

The route back to England took the squadrons to Karachi, Palestine, Cairo, North Africa, and to Sardinia by 13 September 1945, and "north from there to Holmsley, England. Each pilot flew his own plane home. We flew the whole squadron back to England." The two squadrons now became a part of the 2nd Tactical Air Force.

Including those in the two Canadian Transport Squadrons, there were 3,110 Canadians in SEAC in January 1945; the others included those serving in RAF units, particularly the Liberator squadrons, and radar personnel. Although the process of withdrawal had begun by the end of May and was completed toward the end of September, many Canadians (there were still about 1700 after September) remained under RAF command in the theatre in the Liberator Squadrons. The BCATP provided many Canadian aircrew for this particular aircraft.

Malaria was a serious problem as were leeches and ticks. The number of casualties from disease in Burma and Malaya was greater than casualties inflicted by the Japanese. Worse than disease were the deadly snakes. Some of them managed to invade the aircraft and more than one pilot operated his plane very cautiously until the reptile could be safely jettisoned.[12]

Another Canadian posted to India-Burma was P/O Charlie Chow, J.35171, from Lethbridge, Alta. He joined the RCAF in the fall of 1942 and was posted to Edmonton Manning Depot. After SFTS at MacLeod (not far from Lethbridge) in September 1943, he completed his training at Charlottetown, PEI, in March 1944, and received his wings. Charlie Chow was then posted to the RAF OTU No. 31 at Debert, NS. One of the functions of this school was to ready aircrew for the delivery of aircraft in Ferry Command.

He flew a plane to India for Ferry Command and was then posted to RAF No. 117 (Transport) Squadron from August 1944. He completed his tour in June 1945 but remained in the theatre as training officer checking out new crews. Cedric Mah met him in May 1945 after Charlie had been posted to Akyab and Chittagong. He returned to England and was in Brussels by November 1945.

Charlie Chow was repatriated to Canada and released in Winnipeg 6 March 1946. The

**Charlie Chow
in Burma 1 August 1945**

– CFB Ottawa PL 60963

same year he went to China to fly for the Central Air Transport Company and returned to Canada in the spring of 1950. He re-enlisted in the RCAF in Winnipeg in the fall of 1951 for the Korean War but was killed at Carmen, Man, in February 1952 when his plane hit guy wires of the Canadian Broadcasting Corporation radio transmitter towers.

Sgt. Harry Gong from Clinton, BC, born 2 February 1920, also served in Southeast Asia Command. He enlisted in Montreal in the summer of 1943, took his basic training in Toronto and various other courses such as radio at Guelph, Ont, and Montreal, Que. He completed his training at St. Catharines and Trenton.

After completing his training, Harry Gong was posted for a short time to Calgary, and then to Halifax where he flew Hurricanes on Atlantic patrol. He was then posted in September 1944 to the RAF in India flying Spitfires. He returned to Canada in the spring of 1945 and was released at Sea Island, BC, August 1945.

In addition to SEAC, Chinese Canadians served in the RCAF and RAF in England; they were posted to Bomber Command, Coastal Command, Fighter Reconnaissance, and the 2nd Tactical Air Force. Many others served in Home Defence in Canada or were still in training when the war ended.

Bomber Command

The first Chinese Canadians joined Bomber Command in late 1943 or early 1944 after the Command had become well settled into its massive bombing campaign against strategic objectives in Germany. From 1943, area night raids of Bomber Command alternated with USAAF day attacks, frequently against the same target. In the spring of 1944, there was a shift to pre-invasion bombing; after D-Day, Bomber Command was often called upon to support the armies. It was released from the control of SHAEF in the fall of 1944 to continue its primary strategic function.

Ernie Thomas Lee, born in Windsor, Ont, enlisted in Kenora in 1942 at the same time as his brother, George. From Manning Depot in Brandon, Man, Ernie was posted to pre-training but washed out as pilot; he graduated as sergeant navigator from No. 5 AOS, Winnipeg. While on leave, Ernie was commissioned; he is possibly the first Chinese Canadian to receive a commission in the RCAF. He proceeded overseas late in 1943 or early 1944. After OTU he served in Bomber Command until 1945 and was then repatriated to Canada. Ernie Lee later died in a Canadian Military Hospital as a result of his war injuries. Ernie's mother was awarded the Silver Cross.

F/Lt. Harvey A. (Hal) Lee, navigator, from Hamilton, Ont, was considered overweight when he first tried to enlist. He slimmed down somewhat and was then accepted for training. Hal Lee had at first wanted to train as a pilot but after meeting other navigators, he decided he liked the men and the occupation, so was happy to remain in this group. When he reached England, he was posted to No. 405 (Vancouver) Pathfinder Squadron, which had been transferred to No. 8 Group in April 1943 based at Gransden Lodge.

The nickname or title following the squadron number indicates the civilian organization (such as service club or city council) that sponsored the particular squadron. These organizations supplied reading and writing material, cigarettes, chocolate bars, socks, sweaters, and so on, to members of their squadron. Some titles were official, that is, approved by Canadian Forces Headquarters; many titles were not.

After many postings from its formation in No. 4 Group in April 1941, including a stint in Coastal Command, No. 405 remained based at Gransden Lodge to the end of the war. No. 405 was the first Canadian squadron in Bomber Command and the only Canadian Pathfinder Squadron. It flew on more raids than any other Canadian squadron and casualties were heavy. The last mission was a night drop of supplies to Rotterdam 7 May 1945.

The Pathfinder squadrons were an elite group wearing their own distinctive badge of the RAF eagle worn below medal ribands. Consideration was given to increased rank and pay on operations, and for this purpose the Pathfinders received their own War Establishment. By the time Hal joined No. 405, 45 sorties constituted a tour although before this it had been 60. On completion of a tour a certificate was awarded. Hal Lee was repatriated and released in 1945.

From Winnipeg, F/O Navigator Jim Gen Lee, J.42216, served in RAF No. 101 Squadron, No. 1 Group, based at Ludford Magna. This squadron was the only one in Bomber Command equipped with *Airborne Cigar* (ABC). Each plane in the squadron was fitted with the jamming device and carried a crew member who spoke German. Many German speakers came from Kitchener, Ont, which has a large German-speaking commu-

nity, and others were German Jews who had escaped to the Middle East and from there to Britain to join the RAF. The planes were a part of the bomber stream jamming German night-fighter communication. They carried a regular bomb load and flew as a part of the normal bomber stream. The squadron often flew when the group itself was not scheduled for a raid, and thus it took part in more raids than any other Lancaster squadron in No. 1 Group.

Jim's plane failed to return 23 March 1945 in an operation of No. 1 and 5 Groups against the railway bridges of Bremen. F/O Bomb Aimer W.H. Brooks, and F/O Pilot R.R. Little (an American) both RCAF, and four RAF members were also killed. F/O Jim Gen Lee is buried in Sage War Cemetery, Oldenburg, Germany.

F/O Jim Gen Lee

– CFB Ottawa PL 22242

P/Os G. Aldworth, W.A. Elliott, Tom Ritchie, Joseph Hong, C.J. "Buzz" Bezaire, F/O R.M. McKenzie
10 November 1943

F/O Navigator Joseph Hong, J.37185, from Windsor, while training at No. 24 OTU, was shot down over Alençon, France, 23 May 1944, on his first flight dropping propaganda leaflets (a nickel raid). The leaflet flights were often carried out by OTU pupil crews; they were despatched on a short sortie to a target in northern France before completing the training course. F/O Pilot D.W. Goodwin, F/O Bomb Aimer C.B. Wykoff, WO Air Gunner J.G. Jacques, Sgt. AGs J. Hopper and W.G. Harris were also killed. F/O Joseph Hong was aged 23 and is buried with the others at Bretteville-sur-Laize Canadian War Cemetery, France. Joseph's brother, George, was killed in Italy a few months later.

LAC William Lem, R.251549, from Oshawa, Ont, joined the RCAF in 1943. After training at No. 1 Technical Training School, St. Thomas, Ont, Bill graduated as aero engine mechanic. He went overseas in October 1944 and was posted to Croft, Yorks, where he ser-viced the Lancasters of No. 431 (Iroquois) Squadron. No. 434 (Bluenose) Squadron was also located at Croft. After VE-Day, Bill volunteered for Tiger Force and was repatriated in July 1945. With war at an end in the Pacific, the squadron was disbanded in September at Dartmouth, NS, and Bill was released in Toronto the same month.

Arthur Ernest Jung, J.35156, from Victoria, joined the RCAF late in 1942 or early 1943. He was posted to No. 5 EFTS, High River, Alta, in March 1943, and in May to No. 7 SFTS at MacLeod as LAC. Arthur was rated as an above average pilot and received the highest standing in his class.

In England by the first of 1944, P/O Arthur Jung was posted to No. 7 EFTS at Desford, Leics, and in March he was attached to No. 10 OTU at Abingdon, Berks, for just over a week. Later in March, he was sent to No. 6 Advanced Flying Unit, Little Kissing-

Arthur E. Jung

– CFB Ottawa PL 42617

ton, Glos, and a month later to No. 1516 Battle Flight, Pershore, Worcs. His next posting on 1 June was to No. 14 OTU, Market Harbourgh, Leics, for training on Wellingtons and at the end of August to No. 1654 Heavy Conversion Unit at Wigsley, Lincs, for training on Stirlings.

By this stage of the war, there were too many pilots in the stream, and they were kept occupied in England by training and retraining; there were many other aircrew collecting at the Personnel Reception Centre in Bournemouth. Many of these men failed to receive their operational training and posting to squadrons before the war ended.

F/O Arthur Jung received another posting 16 October 1944 to No. 5 Lancaster Finishing School at Syerston, Notts, for training on Lancasters; he had been promoted to flying officer. On 1 November 1944 Arthur received his final posting to No. 50 Squadron in No. 5 Group RAF, based at Skellingthorpe, Lincs.

Arthur Jung flew his first night raid against the Mittelland Canal along with 235 other Lancasters and seven Mosquitoes on 6/7[13] November. He dropped fourteen 1,000 lb. bombs at 10,250 feet. The objective was to cut the Canal at its meeting with the

Dortmund-Ems Canal at Gravenhorst. There was a complex of linking canals in this area; the Rhine-Herne Canal connected Duisburg with Dortmund and from Dortmund, the Ems Canal carried the link to Emden, a port on the North Sea. The crew of the marking force dropped their marker so accurately that it fell into the water. Only 31 aircraft bombed and the Master Bomber ordered abandonment but not before ten Lancasters were lost. Arthur flew in six more raids on the Mittelland and the Dortmund-Ems Canals, the last two being daylight raids 24 February and 12 March 1945.

The Rhenania-Ossag oil refinery at Harburg, which had already been attacked by American day bombers, was raided 11/12 November 1944 by No. 5 Group, leaving damage mainly in the industrial and residential areas; and at Rositz (near Leipzig) 14/15 February 1945 leaving part of the plant damaged. No. 5 Group made several other raids on oil refineries, including the synthetic refineries at Politz (near Stettin) leaving the plant badly damaged 21/22 December 1944 and again 8/9 February 1945. After this final raid the plant produced no further oil during the war. The synthetic oil refinery at Lutzkendorf also received moderate damage in a bombing raid 14/15 March 1945 by No. 5 Group. The refinery was accurately bombed but 18 Lancasters were lost. Arthur participated in all these attacks.

Art Jung also took part in the attack on Wesel 23/24 March 1945 when Nos. 5 and 8 Groups bombed the city, which was left an almost total ruin having suffered many raids during the war. Regiments of the 21st Army Group were to cross the Rhine the following day.

Other raids were made in support of the Allied armies especially at Duren, Julich, and Heinsburg to cut communications behind German lines. Arthur took part in the bombing of Duren in a daylight attack but in spite of this support, there were heavy infantry losses. Duren itself suffered over 3,000 casualties. During the German Ardennes offensive, No. 5 Group bombed Houffallize 5/6 January 1945. This bottleneck in the German supply system was attacked with great accuracy.

The German garrison at Royan, at the mouth of the Gironde River, was the target 4/5 January 1945 by No. 5 Group in order to give the Allies the port facility of Bordeaux. The French Resistance, numbering some 12,000 men under Free French officers, besieged the town in which there were some 2,000 civilians. The Resistance lacked artillery. In the course of discussions with Americans the suggestion was made that bombers might soften up the town. The order was given by SHAEF to destroy the town and a reputed late cancellation did not reach Bomber Command in time to stop it.

Over 1,500 tons of high explosive bombs, including 185 "blockbusters," (a 4,000 lb. bomb) were dropped in two waves. The town was virtually destroyed; 500 to 800 civilians were killed but only 35 to 50 Germans. A ten-day truce prevailed while a search for survivors was made. The Germans did not surrender the port until 18 April.

The raids on Dresden 13/14 February 1945 were part of Operation *Thunderclap,* an effort to knock out Germany by raiding its cities to sow confusion and break down its war capability now that military conditions warranted such action and to prevent the transfer of German troops to the Russian front.

Dresden was a communications and transportation centre facing the Russians, who had crossed the eastern frontier of Germany 12 January. Air Marshal Harris, Commander in Chief of Bomber Command, was instructed on 27 January to put *Thunderclap* into effect, second to the primary target of oil. The weather often determined the area to be attacked so that Harris was left some discretion in the order in which raids were mounted. Dresden was selected out of four vital communications and supply cities (the others considered were Berlin, Leipzig, and Chemnitz) behind German lines facing the Russians. All four cities were filled with the wounded and with refugees fleeing the Russian armies. It was also believed that devastation of Dresden would crush morale and the Germans would surrender. The breaking of German morale had been a feature of the bombing strategy almost from the beginning. But the primary purpose of the attack was to prevent the Germans from moving troops from the Western front to the East. The *Thunderclap* directive was issued by the Air Ministry with Churchill's approval and conformed with Stalin's request for such assistance in the final planning at the Yalta Conference.

The leading American raid was cancelled because of bad weather, but the following two waves of Lancasters and Mosquitoes dropped 1,478 tons of high explosive bombs and 1,182 tons of incendiaries. Two hundred and forty-four Lancasters of No. 5 Group carried out the first attack, using their own low-level marking techniques and dropping 800 tons of bombs. There was cloud cover and the raid was only partially successful. The second raid three hours later of 529 Lancasters of No. 1, 3, 6, and 8 Groups, with 8 Group Pathfinder marking, and clear weather, dropped 1,800 tons of bombs accurately. The result was a firestorm and an estimated 40-50,000 (or up to 150,000 in some sources) people died. Six Lancasters were lost and two crashed in France and one in England.

Three hundred and eleven US B-17s dropped 771 tons of bombs the next day, aiming at the railway yards. The Mustang fighter escort was ordered to strafe the roads leading out of the city. The USAAF bombed the city again on 15 February and 2 March. The bombing of Dresden seemed to have no effect on the German will to wage war, but it did prevent the movement of German troops eastward.

No. 5 Group also attacked ports and U-boat pens. The raid on the pens at Trondheim in Norway was cancelled because the target was hidden by a smoke-screen. Shipping in Verle Bay, near Oslo, was attacked but apparently without success. The port of Gdynia on the Baltic was bombed 18/19 December 1944 causing damage to shipping and port installations.

Another daylight raid was made on Farge, a port on the River Weser, north of Bremen, on 27 March 1945. At this port No. 5 Group dropped their bombs on the oil-storage depot and on the U-boat shelter. No. 617 Squadron, the 'Dam Busters,' tackled the 23 foot reinforced concrete roof of the shelter dropping two *Grand Slams,* the new 22,000 lb. bomb, and several *Tallboys.* The roof was penetrated and the shelter made unusable. Like the 12,000 lb. *Tallboy,* the *Grand Slam* was a special bomb invented by Barnes Wallis, who had also developed the special spinning bombs used in the 'Dams Raid.' Normally, the Wallis bombs were used to produce 'small' earthquakes at the base of a structure, especially bridges and viaducts; occasionally they were used as in the destruction of the U-boat shelter at Farge. The Lancasters in 617 Squadron were reinforced and their bombays enlarged to carry the *Tallboys;* the aircraft were further modified to carry the *Grand Slam.*

The last Lancaster raid was made 25/26 April 1945 when submarine fuel stores were attacked at Tonsberg. Although 107 Lancasters and 12 Mosquitoes of No. 5 Group made the attack, Arthur Jung's plane was not among them. One Lancaster from this raid landed in neutral Sweden and its crew was interned until the end of the war—a matter of days.

From 26 April to 7 May (the war officially ended on the 8th) the Lancasters of Bomber Command flew to Brussels and other European airfields to repatriate British POWs now liberated from camps. Nos. 1, 5, 6, and 8 Groups took part in Operation *Exodus,* making 469 flights before the end of the war; about 75,000 POWs were transported to England by this means. Arthur took part in *Exodus* from Brussels on 6 May and from Juvincourt on the 8th. Three days later he was in Brussels to service *Exodus* aircraft. He completed his tour of 30 sorties over enemy territory, plus three in the *Exodus* repatriation, and five in mine-laying and dropping propaganda leaflets in the long OTU programme.

F/Lt. Arthur Jung was repatriated to Canada on 25 July 1945; he volunteered for the Pacific War, and was posted to No. 5 OTU, Boundary Bay. On 11 August he was posted to the instructors' course at the Central Flying School at Trenton. With war at an end in the Pacific, he returned to No. 5 OTU on 27 August and on 14 September was released at No. 9 Release Centre, Boundary Bay.

In 1947, Arthur Jung became a commercial pilot. He was killed in 1973 in a flying accident just outside Edmonton, when his plane hit the overhead wires on the highway leading from the airport into the city.

Also from Victoria, Kam Len Douglas Sam, J.86388, born 6 April 1918, tried to enlist in the RCAF in 1940 but was advised, as others had been, that volunteers must be of pure European descent. He was also advised that a request had been made to Ottawa for removal of the restriction. When the new *Regulations* were issued in 1942, he was informed by Ottawa.

Douglas Sam enlisted and was posted to No. 3 Manning Depot, Edmonton, and was then sent to No. 8 Bombing & Gunnery School at Lethbridge. Then came guard duties for three months until there was space at No. 9 Pre-Aircrew Educational Detachment at McGill University, Montreal. After this time at No. 1 Air Gunner Ground Training School at Quebec City, he was then posted to No. 9 B&GS Mont Joli, Que. for aerial gunnery training. Here he earned his wings 23 July 1943 and was promoted to sergeant.

– CFB Ottawa PL 85211
K.L. Douglas Sam

Sgt. Douglas Sam sailed from Halifax on 27 August 1943, and arrived at Greenock, Scotland, 2 September. From No. 3 Personnel Reception Centre at Bournemouth, he was posted to No. 22 OTU, RAF station, at Wellesbourne, Warks, where crews were formed of pilot, navigator, bomb aimer, wireless operator, and air gunner.

Before training had started Douglas Sam flew in one of the three Vickers Wellingtons in a search and rescue operation 2 October looking for downed airmen in the North Sea. Before the training ended 26 November, Douglas flew in one of the six Wellingtons that dropped leaflets over Angers, France. Most aircraft used in training had already been phased out of operational squadrons and casualties were often high; one crew out of the six in his group was lost in training. From No. 22 OTU, the five crews were posted to No. 6 Battle School at Thirsk, Yorks, for Commando training and lessons in

escape and evasion. On 1 January 1944, Douglas was posted to No. 426 (Thunderbird) Squadron of No. 6 Bomber Group.

There were seven operational bases in No. 6 Canadian Bomber Group all located in Yorkshire, with 14 squadrons, each squadron equipped with about 20 aircraft. No. 6 Group had been formed at Linton-on-Ouse 25 October 1942 and declared operational 1 January 1943. Douglas joined the group a year after it began operations.

Douglas Sam's first raid was on Germany's main ball-bearing plant at Schweinfurt, 24/25 February 1944. Total aircraft losses were 33 out of 734. This was also Bomber Command's first raid on this target although the USAAF had raided the factories the day before. The following night, Augsburg was successfully bombed. The Germans called it terror bombing because the historical central portion was destroyed. There were over 3,000 casualties. Some industrial destruction also occurred from the 2,000 tons of bombs dropped on this target, including a factory producing aircraft parts,

Frankfurt was the target 18/19 March and bombs were dropped accurately, again destroying many cultural buildings and the medieval section. Douglas Sam's first raid on Berlin took place 24/25 March but strong winds forced the bombers south and they were scattered. Some 72 aircraft out of over 800 were lost. More than 100 small towns outside Berlin were bombed. In Berlin, many buildings were destroyed, including five military centres. This was the last raid in the Battle of Berlin, a battle that had begun the previous August, although small Mosquito raids continued to the end.

In the Ruhr, Douglas flew 26/27 March in the 705 aircraft raid on the Krupps Works at Essen; only nine aircraft were lost. It was a successful attack leaving many industrial buildings damaged and over 1,700 homes destroyed. The city suffered about 460 casualties.

The Nuremberg raid of 30/31 March saw the loss of 95 bombers or almost 12 percent of the 795 aircraft despatched. The raid was a failure because of heavy cloud and strong winds. There was little damage in the city. The strong winds had carried the Pathfinders too far east and the winds had also caused the bombing of Schweinfurt by over 100 aircraft.

No. 426 Squadron was being re-equipped with Halifax III aircraft but two more raids were made before the changeover was completed, on Cologne and St. Ghislain, Belgium. Douglas Sam flew his last raid on a German target when Cologne was bombed on the night of 20/21 April. Heavy damage occurred in the industrial area including several railway stations and yards; much residential housing, churches, and other public buildings were destroyed or burned out.

P/O Douglas Sam was promoted at the same time as Group 6 settled into pre-invasion bombing. The squadrons of Groups 6 and 8 on 1/2 May bombed the railway yards at St. Ghislain with the loss of only two aircraft. The accuracy of this attack was carried through to the heavy gun positions in the Pas-de-Calais area on 9/10 May, flying in the Halifax III. The following night, railway targets in Ghent, Belgium, were the target. There were nearly 100 civilian casualties. In Louvain, Belgium, the target was again the railway yards but most of the bombs hit the railway workshops and storage sheds. From 19/20 to 31 May, bombs were dropped on some 13 other pre-invasion targets: the gun positions at Mereville, the railway yards at Le Mans, the military camp at Bourg-Leopold, and a coastal wireless transmitting station at Au Fevre.

After D-Day, their first bombing target was a daylight raid 12 June on the railways at Cambrai, Belgium. Many bombs fell in the town but the target was hit. Railways were again the target at St. Pol, France, but they were obscured by cloud. The attack on German ships at Boulogne caused extensive destruction to the port and surrounding area with about 200 people killed.

A night raid on a flying bomb site at Oisemont, near Abbeville, followed by a daylight raid on railways at St. Martins-l'Hortier, France, 21 June, were not successful because of cloud. There were several other bombing missions to attack flying bomb sites. Before his last sortie, Douglas Sam had flown 25 missions plus two flown while at No. 22 OTU.

P/O Douglas Sam's final sortie was on the railway yards at Metz, France, 28/29 June, to prevent supplies reaching the German line. When the Halifax III reached the turning point at Rheims to begin its final bombing run against the target, the aircraft was hit by Ju88 night fighters and the starboard wing tank burst into flame. The load of sixteen 500 lb. bombs and marker flares was jettisoned and the crew members were ordered to bail out by pilot F/O Bill Gerard. Mid-upper Gunner T.A. Rogers had been killed in the fighter attack but the rest of the crew landed in widely scattered areas around the German fighter base. The survivors all became evaders.

Douglas managed to link up with the local French Resistance who contacted MI 9 in London to verify his identity and status. Under the direction of MI 9, Douglas joined the local Free French network. He was rescued by the US 3rd Army when it entered Rheims on 3 September after he had organized and led the local Resistance forces to repel a German attack. Evaders in the area were then collected together, including Gerard's navigator, F/O Bill Lastuk, and evacuated to England. For his services to France, Douglas Sam was awarded the *Croix de Guerre avec Etoile d'Argent*.

Repatriated to Canada on the *Nieuw Amsterdam* 6 October 1944, Douglas arrived in Victoria on the 26th. He then volunteered for Tiger Force and attended the S-20 Japanese Language School in Vancouver. He graduated from the one-year course in March 1946, receiving a permanent commission in the RCAF the same year with the rank of flying officer. Douglas Sam felt that the Canadian Army discriminated against Chinese Canadians all through the war but in all his years in the air force, he "never experienced one single incident of racial discrimination."

After training by MI 6, from July 1950 to July 1951, Douglas Sam served as intelligence officer, RAF Far East Air Force HQs, RAF Singapore, the Federation of Malaya Police, at the time of the Malayan Emergency.

His comment on this episode was that "the guerrillas had been trained too well." In July 1951, Douglas was back in Ottawa at Air Force HQs, Directorate of Intelligence, as intelligence staff officer.

Douglas served with distinction for 25 years, retiring as squadron leader in 1967. He remained on the Primary Reserve list and was honourably released from service 14 March 1978 in the rank of lieutenant-colonel. In 1967 he joined Canada Manpower and Immigration, Pacific Region, based in Vancouver, serving as chief intelligence officer from 1968 to 1983. For this work Douglas Sam received a citation from the RCMP, the only civilian so honoured.

P/O Quan Jil Louie, J.38242, from Vancouver, enlisted in the RCAF in November 1942. Quan had been a good soccer and basketball player while attending UBC. At No. 3 Manning Depot, Edmonton, he met Douglas Sam and Allan Bing, both of whom

had begun their basic training about the same time. Quan went on to ITS, and B&GS, and then to No. 7 AOS at Portage La Prairie, Man, where he met Vic Aro. He graduated 12 November 1943, was awarded bomb aimer's wings, and commissioned as pilot officer. P/O Quan Jil Louie sailed from Halifax for England 5 March 1944 on the troopship *Andes* and arrived in Liverpool 14 March.

No. 7 AFTU at Bishops Court, County Down, was followed by No. 22 OTU at Wellesbourne, at which time air crews were formed. Quan's crew consisted of F/O Pilot E.W. (Bill) Watson, a navigator, P/O Bomb Aimer Quan Louie, P/O Wireless Airgunner W.J. Partridge, and another air gunner. An additional air gunner and flight engineer were added later. After completing his conversion training from two to four engine Halifax III A bombers, at Dishforth, Yorks, from 9 August to 12 September, and promotion to flying officer, Quan Jil Louie was posted to No. 6

– CFB Ottawa PL 40686

F/Os Bill Watson and Quan Jil Louie - 5 December 1944

Group RAF Bomber Command, No. 420 (Snowy Owl) Squadron, at Tholthorpe. No. 425 (Alouette) Squadron was also located here.

At this time 30 trips constituted a tour and Quan was on a mission just short of his 30th when the aircraft was hit by flak and blew up over Madgeburg, 16/17 January 1945. Seventeen out of the 371 aircraft of Groups 4, 6, and 8 sent on this raid were lost. Two Canadians, F/Sgts. Jacobi and Lynch, bailed out and became prisoners of war. F/Lt. Watson, F/O Quan Jil Louie, P/O W.J. Partridge, and two RAF crew members were killed. Quan, aged 23, is buried in Collective Grave No. 5 in the Berlin 1939-1945 War Cemetery, Charlottenberg, Germany. His brother, K.W. (Ernie) Louie, was dropped into Malaya later in 1945.

The last raid of the war was made by 16 Mosquitoes of No. 8 Group and 37 Mosquitoes of No. 100 Group when they attacked airfields at Kiel. One Mosquito was lost and two support Halifaxes. This raid was made 2/3 May to prevent the German Army escaping to Norway. British and Canadian troops entered Kiel a day and a half later.

This bombing campaign against Germany was one of the longest battles of the war; it was a part, and only a part, of the total war that raged from September 1939 to August 1945. The bombing began tentatively with attacks on enemy ships that were well away from shore so that civilians would not be killed; it progressed to destruction of entire cities and their inhabitants. The Canadian price was high: 9,980 young RCAF airmen died in Bomber Command alone. A total of 17,047 fatal casualties occurred in the RCAF as a whole.

Fighter Reconnaissance

Tommy Hoan, from Hamilton, R.256205, photographic interpreter, enlisted in May 1943 and trained in both ground and aerial courses for three months in the Photographic School at Rockcliffe, Ont. He went overseas in March 1944 and was posted to No. 430 (Sudbury) Squadron. This squadron had been formed in England in January 1943 as an Army Cooperation unit and was redesignated as Fighter Reconnaissance in June 1943. The unit flew Mustangs until re-equipped with Spitfires in November 1944. The Spitfires flew both high and low missions with the high-flying Spitfires being nicknamed "Bluebirds." They carried no armaments.

The squadron was grouped with Nos. 400 and 414 in No. 39 (RCAF) Wing and affiliated with No. 1 Canadian Army Air Photographic Interpretation Section (APIS). Photographs included pre-invasion work as well as before and after pictures of attacks on V-1 flying bomb launching sites.

The squadron was located at Odiham, Hants, from April to June 1944. It then moved to Normandy at the end of June following the army to Diest, Belgium, by 20 September, and on into the Netherlands at Eindhoven from October to March 1945. It moved back to Belgium until April 1945, and then finally moved into Germany where it was disbanded 7 August 1945. The squadron provided tactical photo reconnaissance for the armies throughout the campaign in Northwest Europe. The last mission was flown 5 May 1945 when two Spitfires from Soltau in Germany made a tactical reconnaissance survey over an airfield at Kiel.

When the European war ended in May and the squadron was disbanded in August, Tommy Hoan "had a long wait for repatriation to Canada which did not occur until January 1946"; he was then released immediately.

Coastal Command

Cpl. Edward Lee, R.187538, from Windsor, Ont, an aero engine fitter mechanic, served in No. 404 Coastal Command (Buffalo) Squadron, covering the area from the Shetlands to Land's End.

No. 404 Squadron had been formed at Thorney Island, Hants, 15 April 1941. The squadron flew Blenheims, Beaufighters, and Mosquitoes along the Dutch and Norwegian coasts on the lookout for enemy shipping; they provided long-range fighter escort for anti-submarine aircraft in the Bay of Biscay.

Coastal Command had both land and sea bases in England. The aircraft ranged from single to multi-engine bombers, and from fighters to flying boats. Catalinas and Sunderlands, Liberators, and Fortresses searched the far distances for submarines; Wellingtons and Hudsons searched areas closer to the British Isles; and Blenheims and Beaufighters served both the reconnaissance and close escort functions. Coastal Command protected Allied shipping and destroyed enemy ships, escorted Allied convoys and hunted for submarines, and attacked enemy convoys and bombed harbours where ships and submarines sheltered.

During the D-Day landings 6 June, 14 Beaufighters of No. 404 Squadron intercepted three German destroyers headed for the invasion fleet in the Channel; its rocket-firing Beaufighters joined a strike force in the attack. Ships of the RCN claim to have sunk one destroyer and beached and disabled the second. The third escaped.

The last mission was made 4 May on an anti-shipping sweep of the Kattegat near Kiel. The squadron claimed credit for one vessel probably destroyed and seven damaged. No. 404 Squadron was disbanded at Banff in Scotland on 25 May 1945; Edward Lee was then repatriated to Canada and released.

2nd Tactical Air Force

Direction of Bomber Command had formally passed to the Supreme Allied Commander, General Eisenhower, 14 April 1944, whose authority was exercised through AM Arthur W. Tedder, Deputy Supreme Allied Commander; it continued under control of SHAEF until 14 September 1944. Tedder had been appointed 21 January 1944; he controlled not only strategic bomber assistance to *Overlord* but exercised ultimate control of all air operations on the continent, including the 2nd TAF.

Bomber Command operated by groups and squadrons. The 2nd TAF, like Fighter Command, operated by groups, wings, squadrons, and sometimes flights.

Commanded by A/VM Sir Arthur Coningham, the 2nd TAF was formed 1 June 1943, composed of No. 2 Group from Bomber Command, and Nos. 83 and 84 Groups from Fighter Command. The Transport Groups, Nos. 38 and 46, were added later. For *Overlord* all air support came under the strategic control of A/CM Sir Trafford Leigh-Mallory. The headquarters association with the 21st Army Group for 2nd TAF was in the same manner as the heavy bombers; that is, all requests for assistance went through SHAEF.

Nos. 83 and 84 Groups were composed of Fighter, Reconnaissance, and Fighter Bomber Wings; these two groups gave direct support to the 21st Army Group. Army co-operation had been arranged by the artillery use of coloured marker shells in order to give close support; this close support was usually provided by the Typhoons and Spitfires of No. 83 and 84 Groups. Headquarters of these two groups moved to the continent with Army Headquarters early in June 1944. No. 84 Group gave direct support to the 1st Canadian Army. No. 85 (Base) Group was added for protection of European airfields.

The two Canadian transport squadrons from India, Nos. 435 and 436, became a part of No. 46 Group, 2nd TAF, in September 1945, joining No. 437 in No. 120 (RCAF) Wing. They continued to transport men, material, and supplies from England to Belgium, France, Germany, Poland, and Italy supporting Canadian units of the Occupation Force. There had been many replacements after the squadrons arrived in England. Over 60 percent were replacements from Transport OTUs in Canada; only 20 percent had been with the squadrons in Burma. The two squadrons were disbanded in England in the spring and early summer of 1946.

The transport squadrons dropped the parachutists for the D-Day assault in Normandy, for Operation *Market-Garden,* both under the control of Leigh-Mallory, and they dropped them again on the Rhine crossing when 2nd TAF had reverted to Coningham's command.

No. 98 Squadron, 2nd TAF, flying the B-25 Mitchell medium bomber, was in 139 Wing of No. 2 Group located at Dunsfold, Surrey. Also in No. 139 Wing were Nos. 180 and 320 (Netherlands) Squadrons (RAF), with which No. 98 was closely associated. No. 137

(Fighter) Wing operated in close support of No. 139. Each squadron was established for a total of 20 aircraft.

There were four wings in No. 2 Group when the 2nd TAF was established. By war's end, there were five wings each of fifteen squadrons of Bostons and Mitchells, with two additional Mosquito squadrons being added towards the end of 1944 and early 1945. It was not a static organization.

The B-25 Mitchell was a twin-engine bomber and was the first twin-engine aircraft to take off from an aircraft carrier in the Pacific to make the one-way raid on Tokyo in April 1942. The Mitchell was a land-based aircraft and President Roosevelt publicly declared that they had left from "Shangri-La." After dropping their bombs on the city, the aircraft were to land in Nationalist China but some ran out of fuel and the crews bailed out or they crash landed. Eight men were caught by the Japanese; three were beheaded as 'war criminals.' All the others managed to reach China and Vladivostok except four who drowned and one who died before he landed. Five were interned by the Russians.

In American service, the B-25 carried a crew of six or seven; in the RAF, only four aircrew were used. Double duties were performed by the navigator/bomb aimer and the air gunners.

Training in night operations began in February 1944. No. 98 Squadron was trained to drop flares for the bombing of enemy road and rail movement. After D-Day, the Mosquito squadrons often performed this function for themselves.

Spitfire fighter escort for the light bombers of No. 2 Group was provided from No. 137 Wing of 2nd TAF. The fighters cleared the way with forward or carpet support, gave close escort and sometimes cover for the bombers, and rear support when others were low on fuel and ammunition. From their bases in England, the bombers and fighters met at a designated location on the Channel coast and flew together to the target.

Enemy flak rather than fighters was the main problem by D-Day 1944. The Germans invariably increased anti-aircraft batteries at any location they deemed vital. Flying bomb sites, railways, bridges, road junctions, enemy army concentrations, road convoys, and ammunition and POL (petrol, oil, lubricant) dumps were all successfully attacked. The bombing of ammunition dumps was so accurate that little remained for the salvage crews of the Royal Canadian Ordnance Corps when they arrived on the scene.

Added to the pre-invasion bombing of the transportation system and other designated areas, raids were made on the V-1 flying bomb sites that the 2nd TAF and the US Tactical Air Force, as well as the heavy bombers, had been attacking from the previous December. Another threat appeared with the V-2 rocket sites shortly after D-Day. By August/September 1944 the remaining V-1 sites had been overrun by the army, but the V-2s were launched from the Netherlands beginning in September and the bombs continued to be launched from this country through to April 1945.

One of the Canadian members of the 2nd TAF was WO2 Fred Bing, R.242504, who enlisted in October 1942 at the age of 17, in Calgary. Fred had been a member of No. 11 Air Cadet Squadron in Lethbridge while in high school. He took his basic at No. 3 Manning Depot, Edmonton, and was selected for pilot training. When Fred learned that he would have to wait *a whole year* to begin his training as a pilot, he immediately took the next course that opened; he "wanted to get overseas as soon as possible." After completing No. 2 Wireless School at Calgary and aerial gunnery at No. 8 B&G at Lethbridge, Fred received his Wireless Airgunner badge in September 1943.

At Pennfield Ridge, NB, when they were being tested on the Ventura, the 'widow-maker,' Bing received the highest mark in the class. Also at Pennfield Ridge, while clearing a gun jam, Fred caught his arm underneath the two guns and was hospitalized for a short period.

They were formed into teams at No. 34 OTU, Pennfield, for the Mitchell medium bomber: Pilot Cy Poissant, Navigator/Bomb Aimer Peter (Doc) Ryan, Wireless Air Gunner

WO2 Bowmaster and Sgt. Fred Bing

Fred Bing, and the second Airgunner, Olsen, who joined them part way through their tour in England. They sailed on the *Louis Pasteur* for England.

They were posted to OTU at RAF Finenere for conversion to the B-25 Mitchell bomber. After completing the escape and evasion course in Northumberland, a Commando course for senior NCOs at the RAF Regiment School (British Marines), they were posted to No. 98 Squadron, 2nd TAF, RAF, at Dunsfold. There were six aircraft in their flight, with none in reserve.

The crews wore khaki, not air force blue. Since they were mobile and could "move the whole squadron for deployment anywhere to the continent, etc., the British thought that we should be in Khaki to distinguish us from the Germans who wore the drab grey colour uniforms. If we were engaged in conflict and shot down, the RAF blue could be mistaken for the German grey and we could be shot by our own troops." They wore the Canadian battledress until it wore out, then they had to switch to the British quartermaster stores for replacement. The most important

Pilot Cy Poissant, Obs. Peter (Doc) Ryan, WAG Fred Bing, and AG Olsen

part of their uniform was the CANADA badge; with this badge they were welcome everywhere.

Fred's first operation was 12 July 1944 in support of the British Army when the first stage of the invasion was complete. The aircraft had received identification markings the night of 6 June. "These three broad white stripes were recognition signals in order to prevent being fired upon by our own anti-aircraft batteries."

Activity was so intense that at its peak the three Dunsfold Squadrons in No. 139 Wing in one day flew over 100 sorties with only 21 minutes turn-around time.

The Mitchell used by No. 98 Squadron during Fred Bing's tour had .50 calibre guns located in the belly and tail turrets, the upper bubble, and the nose. The nose position was not usually manned but could be brought into play by the navigator if needed. Since the corkscrew maneuver was of little use in a Mitchell, the practice was to turn into an attack to meet German fighters head on so that all guns could be brought to bear on the enemy aircraft.

In addition to keeping the guns and turrets in readiness, the gunners kept a constant watch on the skies around the aircraft. Fred's gun position depended upon which one of the six possible box positions they flew. If they were in number four position, that is, in the middle, he would act as lookout from the top bubble directing the incoming attack to the air gunner. If they were flying in number five or six position, in the rear of their flight, Fred might crawl to the tail, and assess bomb damage on the target after bombs had been dropped. His normal position was in the belly turret with the twin .50s; here he kept a lookout for flak so that the pilot might take evasive action. He also dropped leaflets and sometimes bales of tinfoil (Window) to interfere with German radar detection.

The WAG was responsible for wireless communications although radio silence was maintained over enemy territory, except for emergencies. The Free French crews in their Boston squadrons were exuberant over the target, breaking silence to sing the French National Anthem. This action would bring up the fighters and the flak.

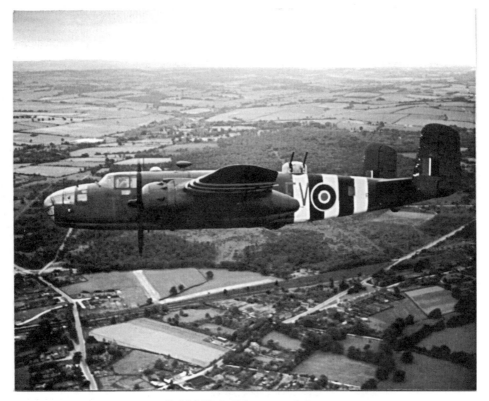

B-25 Mitchell in war colours

Le général Eisenhower s'adresse
aux peuples des Pays Occupés

PEUPLES DE L'EUROPE OCCIDENTALE:

Les troupes des Forces Expéditionnaires Alliées ont débarqué sur les côtes de France.

Ce débarquement fait partie du plan concerté par les Nations Unies, conjointement avec nos grands alliés Russes, pour la libération de l'Europe.

C'est à vous tous que j'adresse ce message. Même si le premier assaut n'a pas eu lieu sur votre territoire, l'heure de votre libération approche.

Tous les patriotes, hommes ou femmes, jeunes ou vieux, ont un rôle à jouer dans notre marche vers la victoire finale. Aux membres des mouvements de Résistance dirigés de l'intérieur ou de l'extérieur, je dis : '' Suivez les instructions que vous avez reçues ! '' Aux patriotes qui ne sont point membres de groupes de Résistance organisés, je dis : '' Continuez votre résistance auxiliaire, mais n'exposez pas vos vies inutilement ; attendez l'heure où je vous donnerai le signal de vous dresser et de frapper l'ennemi. Le jour viendra où j'aurai besoin de votre force unic.'' Jusqu'à ce jour, je compte sur vous pour vous plier à la dure obligation d'une discipline impassible.

CITOYENS FRANÇAIS:

Je suis fier de commander une fois de plus les vaillants soldats de France. Luttant côte à côte avec leurs Alliées, ils s'apprêtent à prendre leur pleine part dans la libération de leur Patrie natale.

Parce que le premier débarquement a eu lieu sur votre territoire, je répète pour vous, avec une insistance encore plus grande, mon message aux peuples des autres pays occupés de l'Europe Occidentale. Suivez les instructions de vos chefs. Un soulèvement prématuré de tous les Français risque de vous empêcher, quand l'heure décisive aura sonné, de mieux servir encore votre pays. Ne vous énervez pas, et restez en alerte !

Comme Commandant Suprême des Forces Expéditionnaires Alliées, j'ai le devoir et la responsabilité de prendre toutes les mesures necessaires à la conduite de la guerre. Je sais que je puis compter sur vous pour obeir aux ordres que je serai appelé à promulguer.

L'administration civile de la France doit effectivement être assurée par des Français. Chacun doit demeurer à son poste, à moins qu'il ne reçoive des instructions contraires. Ceux qui ont fait cause commune avec l'ennemi, et qui ont ainsi trahi leur patrie, seront révoqués. Quand la France sera libérée de ses oppresseurs, vous choisirez vous-mêmes vos représentants ainsi que le Gouvernement sous l'autorité duquel vous voudrez vivre.

Au cours de cette campagne qui a pour but l'écrasement définitif de l'ennemi, peut-être aurez-vous à subir encore des pertes et des destructions. Mais, si tragiques que soient ces épreuves, elles font partie du prix qu'exige la victoire. Je vous garantis que je ferai tout en mon pouvoir pour atténuer vos épreuves. Je sais que je puis compter sur votre fermeté, qui n'est pas moins grande aujourd'hui que par le passé. Les héroïques exploits des Français qui ont continué la lutte contre les Nazis et contre leurs satellites de Vichy, en France, en Italie et dans l'Empire français, ont été pour nous tous un modèle et une inspiration.

Ce débarquement ne fait que commencer la campagne d'Europe Occidentale. Nous sommes à la veille de grandes batailles. Je demande à tous les hommes qui aiment la liberté d'être des nôtres. Que rien n'ébranle votre foi — rien non plus n'arrêtera nos coups — ENSEMBLE, NOUS VAINCRONS.

Dwight D Eisenhower

DWIGHT D. EISENHOWER,
Commandant Suprême des
Forces Expéditionnaires Alliées

Z. F. 1.

LES ARMEES ALLIEES DEBARQUENT

The wing or wings were flown in an organized, compact formation, under the direction of a visible leader, accompanied by a wing or more of fighter escort. Between 24 to 98 aircraft might be involved on a particular operation with the leading aircraft, usually the wing commander and his navigator, heading the formation. By dropping their bombs precisely over the target, they gave the signal for those following to bomb as well. The wing commander would then reverse the process, leading the group safely back to England.

During early August, No. 98 Squadron was involved in the destruction of German tank, vehicle and equipment concentrations, fuel and ammunition dumps, and marshalling yards. After one trip in mid-August, Fred Bing counted 96 holes in the aircraft from flak received over the marshalling yards at Igoville. The controls had been damaged and on the return, the plane iced up and fell 12,000 feet, with control regained only at about 2,000 feet. The Mitchell was an exceptionally reliable aircraft able to endure both flak and fighters but still capable of reaching base and landing in safety even without wheels.

When receiving their briefing for a series of operations near Rouen against the fuel dump, marshalling yard, and enemy concentrations, they were warned not to bomb the cathedral. On 28 August, they bombed the south bank of the Seine at the Duclair ferry point where the Germans were backed up against the river and unable to get across. Bridges across the Seine had been destroyed and several thousand vehicles were packed together jamming the roads leading to the quays. The Mitchells attacked during the day and Mosquito squadrons added their quota to the destruction in the area that same night.

They gave support to the Canadian Army in taking Boulogne on 9 September; this town and the surrounding area were heavily fortified and their bombs, consisting of eight 500 lb. bombs, the normal load, were ineffective. They returned here several times to bomb gun positions during September. Flak was sometimes very heavy. They were in effect acting as long-range artillery for the army.

In early October, No. 98 Squadron made two trips to bomb enemy concentrations near Arnhem but it was too cloudy to see the target and they did not bomb. On the first operation at the Scheldt, at Breskens where the ferry crossed to the harbour at Flushing (an operation in support of the Canadian Army in its efforts to open the port of Antwerp), they were unable to drop their bombs because of a short circuit in the mechanism. They returned at night to the same location to drop flares.

As the armies advanced the 2nd TAF began to move to the continent. No. 139 Wing moved to the European theatre of operations in October 1944; it was located at Melsbroek, near Brussels, Belgium. This move brought them closer to their targets and eliminated the long Channel crossing.

November weather was so poor that very little flying could be done but some raids took place. On an operation on the rail centre at Reydt, Germany, on 25 November, Fred Bing's aircraft was hit by flak, knocking a hole in the perspex about the size of a baseball. The powdered sugar-like material hit the pilot but he regained control of the aircraft; they flew back to Belgium, however, at a very low level. This was the last flight for the team. Fred Bing flew 40 missions and earned his operational wings.

Repatriated late in 1944, he spent some time at Deer Lodge Hospital in Winnipeg undergoing a sinus operation; he had apparently frozen his forehead when the aircraft was damaged. He served as an instructor at No. 7 AOS, Portage la Prairie, and was then posted to No. 1 ANS, Rivers, Man, which operated as the Central Navigation School until September 1945.

Fred Bing was released after VJ-Day in 1945, but re-enlisted in the air force in 1955. He served in a variety of Canadian postings followed by four years in Germany, 1961 through 1965, then back to Ottawa. He was part of the Canadian contingent of the United Nations Peace Keeping Force in Cyprus; during his time on the island, PPCLI rotated with the Royal 22e every six months. Fred Bing returned to Ottawa and again retired as sergeant in July 1974.

Home Defence

There were many others in the RCAF who served in Home Defence. Fred Bing's brother, Cpl. Allan Bing, R.267351, from Lethbridge, enlisted in September 1942 and served as equipment supply specialist for two years in Pacific Command until his release in 1945. Allan took his basic training at No. 3 Manning Depot, Edmonton, and served at RCAF Station, Patricia Bay, then was posted to No. 2 AOS in Edmonton, and was finally posted to the RCAF station, Whitehorse, Yukon.

LAC Herbert (Herby)[14] Chan, R.166288, from Victoria, enlisted in May 1942 in Winnipeg. Herby had tried to enlist in 1941 but had been refused. After completing his pre-aircrew course in Winnipeg in June 1942, he was posted to No. 3 Manning Depot, Edmonton, for basic training. In September

Herby Chan

he was posted to No. 4 SFTS in Saskatoon for tarmac and guard duties, with introduction to Morse code, and then to No. 7 ITS also at Saskatoon. Here a strict routine of classes in aeronautics, basic mathematics, marching, cleaning, and physical training was maintained.

The Selection Board determined the aptitudes of the trainees and recommended what type of school they should be sent to next. In January 1943, Herby was posted to No. 3 Wireless School in Winnipeg where he obtained 20 words a minute in Morse, learned to operate several transmitter and receiver sets, and flew as the wireless operator on one flight. He graduated in August 1943 and was posted to No. 7 B&GS in Paulson (nine miles north of Dauphin), Man. Here he learned aircraft recognition, was taught to fire from turret on ground and aircraft using deflection firing at a drogue in flight, and learned to dismantle and assemble the .303 machine gun.

Finally, after graduation in September, half the class went on to air observer schools and half was retained for Home Defence duties. Herby remained at No. 7 ITS Ground Instruction School. In addition to assisting WAG trainees in their Morse code, Herby was the wireless operator on navigation training, and for the bomb aimer trainees flying on a triangle course on low flying exercises.

In May 1945 Herby was posted to Grande Prairie, Alta, Northwest Air Command, with Headquarters in Edmonton, as wireless operator and teletype operator with occasional turns doing night shift work in the radio station. While posted here, Herby and a group of musicians at the base sometimes played for station dances in the evenings; they also played at Grande Prairie's radio station.

LAC Herby Chan returned to Winnipeg in December 1945, was released 4 January 1946 at Winnipeg Release Centre, and was transferred to RCAF Reserve "E." Sergeant Bandsman Herby Chan served in the Royal Winnipeg Rifles from 1955 to 1975. Herby is the brother of Roy, Paul, and Ira Chan, who volunteered for special duty with SOE.

Two others from Vancouver who served in Canada were LAC Herbert Yep, an aero

Wilson Lee and Kim Yuen Lee

to No. 5 AOS, Winnipeg, and graduated as navigator. Kim was transferred to the (Reserve) General Section Class "E" in February 1945 and released 16 August 1946. As already noted, Kim Yuen Lee was flying with Albert Mah when their plane crashed at Terrebonne, 15 February 1946.

George Lee, R. 215888, born in Blaine Lake, Sask, enlisted in Kenora at the same time as his brother, Ernie Thomas Lee. Their parents had worked in several Ontario and Prairie cities and as already noted Ernie was born in Windsor. After No. 1 Manning Depot, Toronto, George was sent to No. 1 TTS, St. Thomas, and graduated as instrument technician.

He was then posted temporarily to the RAF at Dorval Airport (Ferry Command), and for a time to YW Halifax, NS. In 1943 he was attached to Gander, No. 19 Sub-Repair Depot, working out of Torbay. He remained at Torbay until 1945 in the Mobile Salvage Unit "picking up wrecks around the island." After May 1945, George was posted to No. 1 General Reconnaissance School, Summerside, PEI, then to No. 36 OTU at Greenwood, NS, originally an RAF school, on service work, then back to Summerside. He was released in Winnipeg early in 1946.

There were two who came from Cranbrook (or Kimberley), BC. AW1 Jean Suey Zee Lee was the only Chinese Canadian woman in the RCAF (Women's Division). She was stationed at RCAF depot, Eastern Air Command, Rockcliffe, Ont. Her brother, P/O Wilson John Lee, J.50015, served in the training command on Ansons at Fort MacLeod.

– CFB Ottawa PL 17045

AW1 Jean Lee, Daughter of Lee Chow Man, Cranbrooke, BC, and Miss Lucy Tou

– CFB Ottawa PL 17046

Prime Minister Mackenzie King, Flight Officer V.H. Webb, and AW1 Jean Lee at No. 7 Manning Depot, RCAF, Rockcliffe, 15 June 1943

Air Transport Command

The military transport service of the RCAF grew out of supplying Ferry Command at Goose Bay, Labrador. From one transport flight in June 1940, the Air Transport Command expanded to about nine squadrons by war's end. No. 168 Heavy Transport Squadron was formed at Rockcliffe in October 1943. This squadron supplied mail services to the Canadian forces, flying Liberators, Fortresses, and Dakotas. The squadron covered North Africa, Italy, Gibraltar, and Northwest Europe.

Cpl. Daniel Lee, R.170973, from New Westminster, joined the RCAF in June 1942

Cpl. Daniel Lee

and received his basic training at No. 5 Manning Depot, Lachine. He graduated from No. 1 TTS, St. Thomas, as aero engine mechanic. He serviced Ansons at No. 15 SFTS, Claresholm, Alta, and Ansons at No. 18 SFTS, Gimli, Man. He was then detached for four months training at No. 301 Composite Unit at Dorval, the RAF Ferry Command headquarters. He spent a few weeks at Goose Bay, Labrador. In November 1944, Daniel Lee was posted to No. 168 Heavy Transport Squadron at Rockcliffe. From Ottawa, he flew overseas and served from mid-1945 at Biggin Hill, Kent, as aero engine mechanic with the squadron's detachment. Cpl. Daniel Lee returned to Canada at the end of 1945 and was released March 1946. The squadron was disbanded 21 April 1946.

Ferry Command

With orders for aircraft in the United States amounting to over 26,000, and monthly delivery of 1,000, and with sea transportation uncertain and time-consuming, Great Britain sought an alternative delivery programme. The only option to ocean delivery was to fly the aircraft across the Atlantic, which was considered a very bold venture at the time. The number of successful flights across the Atlantic Ocean up to 1940 were very few indeed. Commercial flights began only in 1939 when Imperial Airways (name soon changed to British Overseas Airways Corporation) and Pan American Airways began flying boat services.

The British Ministry of Aircraft Production, in cooperation with the Canadian Pacific Railway, set up ferrying headquarters in Montreal. CPR hired all ground personnel, obtained supplies, and administered the Command. BMAP supplied aviation executives and aircrew and repaid CPR for expenses. Montreal and the St. Hubert airfield, east of Montreal, were the first centres.

The Department of Transport constructed a larger airfield at Dorval, west of

– courtesy Peter Wong
Ferry Command Crest

Montreal, which later became the headquarters. The DOT supplied radio operators, which totalled about 200 by 1944; it also provided meteorologists.

The agreement with CPR ended in May 1941 and BMAP assumed direct control of the Atlantic Ferry Organization when it was officially known as ATFERO for a short period. The RAF took over the organization 10 July 1941 but employees, both service and civilian, always referred to the organization as Ferry Command.

With the number of planes to deliver, there was difficulty in finding enough civilian pilots even though the numbers were increased by aircrew from BOAC and from the Air Transport Auxiliary in England. Many also came from the BCATP, the RCAF, and the RAF, and the RCAF recruited aircrew volunteers from the United States through the Clayton Knight Committee. Eventually, American pilots in the Air Transport Command delivered the planes to Canada, and Ferry Command pilots flew them across the Atlantic. The Air Transport Auxiliary then picked up the planes at Prestwick and delivered them to Maintenance Units and squadrons.

After a year of service, in 1941, there were slightly more than 200 civilians and about 400 aircrew at Dorval headquarters. The air crew included pilots, navigators, wireless operators, and flight engineers—a mixture of civilians and servicemen. BCATP graduates were being used by the end of 1941 in order to give long-range flying experience to those headed for Coastal Command in England. They were trained at No. 31 General Reconnaissance School, Charlottetown, PEI, and the RAF No. 31 OTU at Debert, NS, as well as at Dorval itself. Use was also made of the RCAF station at North Bay, Ont, which became a flying training unit for ensuring that BCATP graduates were at Ferry Command standards.

Many pilots, navigators, and wireless operators flew once or twice ferrying planes before posting to squadrons. Other RCAF crews, many from Eastern Air Command, also delivered aircraft before taking up postings.

Some civilian pilots from air observer schools, after completing a year or two with BCATP, accepted employment with Ferry Command. Because they were barred from enlistment in the RCAF in the early years, a few Chinese Canadians volunteered for Ferry Command as both air and ground crew.

Although pilots were paid $1000 a month, which contrasted sharply with service pay, a civilian pilot paid for his own room, meals, medical bills, and all the other incidentals that were supplied to servicemen. There were no pension or other benefits.

Ferry Command began operations in November 1940 when the first flight left Newfoundland for Aldergrove, Northern Ireland. There was only one navigator in the flight of seven Lockheed Hudsons and it was fortunate that all planes arrived safely since only three remained with the leader. By the following month, navigators, graduates of BCATP and with additional training, flew with each plane.

In the beginning, Ferry Command operated from St. Hubert through Gander. Later, when the airfield was constructed at Dorval, this location became the headquarters of the Ferry service, and a second route using Goose Bay, Labrador, with bases in Greenland and Iceland, was added in 1941. Two other routes to Britain for flying boats were based at Boucherville, Que, and Bermuda.

The Ferry Command ran a southern route as well, and by 1943 as many aircraft as in the north at the Dorval base were being ferried across the Atlantic. This southern route used Nashville, Tennessee (until the centre was moved to Nassau in the Bahamas in February 1943), with stops at Trinidad, Brazil, Ascension Island, and on to Accra in Africa, which was supposed to be the terminus but personnel of No. 216 Group RAF were not always available so flights continued to Cairo, and where required from Khartoum to Karachi in India.

The North Atlantic Return Ferry Service was begun in May 1941 to bring the aircrew back to St. Hubert in the first instance, then to Dorval, replacing a hit and miss hitch-hiking system and the slow sea-passage. Seven

Liberators were converted and used for this purpose. Use was also made of any aircraft returning to North America. Inevitably, urgent freight, mail, and passengers were added. After the RAF took over Ferry Command at the end of July 1941, BOAC aircrew operated the RFS, and soon it was operating on a daily basis. The southern RFS also became permanent after the initial ammunition delivery was made. The RFS from Australia reversed the delivery route from San Diego, California, passing through Honolulu, Canton Island, Fiji, Auckland, to Sydney, and Brisbane.

Accidents occurred on the RFS; three Liberators with nearly 50 Ferry Command aircrew as well as other passengers were lost in 1941 alone. Altogether some 225 flight crew were killed in the Ferry service; about 75 aircraft were lost.

In addition to passengers and other urgent items, aircraft were also ferried back across the Atlantic: the Lancaster for the Victory Aircraft factory at Malton, near Toronto, as a production model; the Hampdens to Patricia Bay for training purposes; the Halifax VI also for training; and finally the return of Mitchells on VJ-Day.

Hudsons, Liberators, Flying Fortresses, Catalinas, Mosquitoes, Lancasters, Mitchells, Venturas, Bostons, Marauders, and of course the Dakotas, both the DC-3 and the C-47, were the names of some of the types ferried across the Atlantic. Some of these, like the Catalinas and Dakotas, were ferried on to Africa. Over the Pacific route to Australia, nine Catalinas were ferried in 1942. Only one Waco glider delivery to Great Britain was attempted.

The North African campaign necessitated rushing a supply of anti-tank ammunition to the British 8th Army. Some 18 Liberators ferried the supplies for this emergency, picking up the ammunition at Long Island, New York, and later at Miami, Florida, and flying it to Cairo.

Ferry Command became No. 45 (Atlantic Transport) Group in RAF Transport Command in March 1943; but the old name continued to be used by its employees. Ferry Command also retained its own badges. The change did not affect the civilian air and ground crew; they continued as before. However, the three main routes were divided into Wings with No. 112 at Dorval covering the North Atlantic; No. 113 Wing at Nassau for the southern route; and No. 280 Wing operated in the Pacific.

With the end of the war in Europe, Dorval training ended in May, the South Atlantic route was closed in June, and Boucherville closed in October 1945. Civilian aircrew started to leave in July and service members began to apply for release. The Dorval operation was wound down early in 1946.

Wilbur Bruce Wong from Montreal, joined Ferry Command in December 1941 as a mechanic in ground maintenance. Eventually he became crew chief, and then flight engineer. A flight engineer was necessary on the Catalina, B-25 Mitchell, the Liberator, Fortress, Lancaster, and the Dakotas, to name a few. He carried out preflight inspections, checking the engines, fuel, and auxiliary power systems. The undercarriage lowering system and the fuel cocks were his special responsibility and, during landings and take-offs, he handled the throttles. He was also responsible for electrical, fuel, and hydraulic systems. Flight engineer training was similar to that for a pilot.

Wilbur's first ferrying mission as a flight engineer was in October 1943, after Ferry Command had become a part of No. 45 Group in RAF Transport Command in March of the same year. He flew at least 25 aircraft on overseas flights to India, North Africa, the Middle East, and Great Britain. There were at least two flight routes to India: one was from Florida, Brazil, Ascension Island, Accra, Khartoum, to India; and the other from New York to Gander, the Azores, Casablanca, Tripoli, Cairo, Iraq, Abadan in Iran, Karachi, Delhi and Agra to Calcutta.

Before making his first flight to the United States, Wilbur was required to obtain a special certificate from the Immigration Branch of the Department of Mines and

Resources to qualify for an exemption under American immigration restrictions. The American Exclusion Act of 1881 had been replaced by a quota system and by 1943, 105 Chinese were allowed to enter the country annually as immigrants. Although Wilbur was not entering the country as an immigrant, he was not allowed to enter without a certificate. It was necessary that he do so to perform the initial testing of some aircraft that were to be ferried overseas.

Wilbur Wong remained a civilian throughout the war period. It will be noted from his photograph that he is in uniform; any aircrew leaving Canada were issued with uniforms as a form of protection should they be captured by the enemy. The uniform was dark blue, much like the ATA uniform. Peter Wong, however, wore civilian clothing throughout his years at Dorval. Aircrew also received a colour-coded star to indicate the number of deliveries they had made; a new one was issued for every five planes delivered.

Wilbur's elder brother, George D. Wong, served in the RCN. His younger brother Howard (Gus) Wong also served in Ferry Command from 1941 to 1945 in the ground service crew. After the war Gus worked for 38 years in public relations for the Bank of Nova Scotia, retiring in 1981.

Peter S. Wong, also from Montreal, served as flight engineer at Dorval from 1941 to 1946. Peter had received his pilot licence from Curtis-Reid Flying School in Montreal in 1939. He received additional training at Ferry Command while working there, starting as mechanic and working his way to flight engineer performing pre-flight inspections.

Wilbur Bruce Wong

Peter was pilot on three or four flights and performed pre-flight inspection on Sir Winston Churchill's Liberator, AL504, the *Commando*. This aircraft, originally known as *Liberator AL504*, received the name *Commando* after its initial flight to Britain carrying Lord Louis Mountbatten, head of Combined Operations. The Commandos were a part of his organization. After the Liberator had been used by the British Prime Minister on his trips to the Middle East and Moscow, the aircraft was returned to the United States for refurbishing and updating of the interior in 1943. The aircraft continued to be used to carry important passengers until it was lost over the Atlantic in March 1945. There were no survivors.

Air Transport Auxiliary

Samaul Fong from Newcastle, NB, received his pilot licence at Leavens Flying School, Barker Airport, Toronto. Sammy was an instructor at No. 10 AOS, Chatham, NB, before moving on to Ferry Command in 1942. He made two or three delivery trips to England, finally remaining there in the Air Transport Auxiliary.

Air Transport Auxiliary

Pilots of the ATA ferried the aircraft from the receiving point in Great Britain, usually Prestwick in Scotland, to the Maintenance Units and squadrons, mainly in England, but also to Northwest Europe after D-Day. ATA also employed women in its delivery programme, and they were able to handle the large bombers as competently as their opposite numbers. About 200 different types for a total of 308,567 aircraft were safely delivered.

ATA was formed in September 1939 and disbanded in November 1945. Some 16 Ferry Pilots Pools operated throughout England and Scotland. Some of the stations were located at Bristol, on the Severn River; No. 1 at White Waltham, Berks, just west of London at Maidenhead (where Lord Beaverbrook officially closed down the service in 1945); and at Lyneham near Swindon, where the 50th anniversary of the station was held in 1990.

The service was set up originally to deliver aircraft from manufacturers to about 29 Maintenance Units in No. 41 Group for inspection and modification (armament and radio); to seven MUs in No. 43 Group (repairs); and to five Royal Navy Repair Yards

Samaul Fong

**Air Transport Auxiliary
Flying Wing**

and three additional Royal Navy Receipt and Despatch Units. Aircraft were also handed over by Ferry Command for dispersal by ATA at No. 4 Ferry Pool at Prestwick. If the Prestwick airport were closed because of weather conditions, alternative airports at Aldergrove in Northern Ireland, Siloth on the Isle of Man, and Blackpool were used.

Flying boat deliveries were added, both the Short Sunderland and the PBY Catalina, the latter received via Ferry Command. The Catalinas were picked up at Beaumaris, Angelsey, and delivered to the Shetlands, the Orkneys, and also to Ireland, as well as other coastal areas.

Sammy Fong appears to have been the only Chinese Canadian in the ATA. The men and women came from a variety of Allied nations; frequently they had not been accepted in the regular air forces for a variety of reasons. They were all tested and trained with medical fitness suitable for their duties attested to by the ATA medical programme. In addition to those from Great Britain (including Ireland), many were from European countries, and from Down Under, from both North and South America, and some came from South Africa, with at least one each from India, Ceylon, Siam, and Mauritius. Many American pilots were recruited through the Clayton Knight Committee; about 200 had been taken on strength, but when the United States entered the war, most of them returned to their own services. A few remained in ATA to the end of the war. Many pilots were recruited from BOAC as was the man who founded and

commanded ATA throughout the war years, Commodore Gerard d'Erlanger.

There were over 600 pilots in 1943, increased from the 26 with which the Auxiliary began, of whom 90 were women. The peak was reached in 1944/45 when 700 pilots (including instructors and pupils) were employed. In addition there were 150 flight engineers, and 2,786 ground staff.

No. 9 Ferry Pool was stationed in France to give support to the 2nd TAF in Northwest Europe as the armies fought their way through to Germany. Ferrying damaged planes back to England for repair was also undertaken by ATA. Mitchells and Bostons were delivered to Melsbroek, Belgium, to No. 139 Wing of 2nd TAF when it was stationed there, and to other stations in France and Holland. In 1944 alone 16,609 aircraft were delivered to Northwest Europe by 64 pilots.

Flying fatalities in the ATA totalled 153, which included one Nursing Sister and one Air Training Corps Cadet; these accidents occurred mainly as a result of weather conditions.

Sammy Fong remained with ATA until the end of the war and then made his home in Montreal; he had made fast friends there during his Ferry Command days.

Once the racial requirement had been removed from the *Regulations,* Chinese Canadians were allowed to enlist in the RCAF on an equal basis with other Canadians. The RCN also removed the requirement that a candidate must be of "the white race," but only a few Chinese Canadians appear to have joined this service.

NOTES

Unless the quotations and sources of information have been given in a note, the personal and service information in this chapter has come primarily from participants and relatives; these references are not all separately given. Some information has been extracted from the papers of K.L. Douglas Sam.

1. Order signed by AM L.S. Breadner, CAS, 1 Oct. 1942, in NAC, RG 24, Vol.17,800, File 828-21, Vol.14; and Order in Council PC 79/11160 in RG 2, Vol.1784, approved 9 Dec. 1942. This PC reference courtesy Glenn Wright, NAC.

2. Letters contained in NAC, RG 24, accession 83-84/049, Box 1624, File S-304-117. Reference courtesy Glenn Wright, NAC.

3. Note for External Files 27 April 1943 in NAC, RG 25, Vol. 2818, File 1154-40.

4. Commonwealth Air Training Plan Museum, *They Shall Grow not Old: A Book of Remembrance* (Brandon, 1992), Appendix I.

5. *The Star Weekly,* 11 Sept. 1954, p.6.

6. *The Daily News,* Prince Rupert, BC, 10 Aug. 1984.

7. *Vancouver Sun,* 15 Feb. 1946; and "Flying the Hump" and "Search and Rescue" in *Concordia University Magazine,* Vol.5, No.1, 1981/82.

8. Letter dated 13 March 1964, from K.W. Stuart, for Chief, Admissions Division, to Albert Mah (copy in author's possession).

9. *Vancouver Sun,* 15 Feb. 1946; and *The Star Weekly,* Toronto, 11 Sept. 1954, p. 6.

10. Interviews with Albert Mah and Tommy Wong in Montreal and correspondence with Albert and Cedric Mah; see also NAC, RG 27, V.1496, File 2B-184.

11. Letters from Harold Chinn and William Lore.

12. See articles by F/O David Martin, D.Hist. 77/267, "Determined to Deliver: the Story of the Chinthe Squadron"; and D.Hist. R S7 436, "The Flying Elephants: No. 436 Squadron." Interview with Hong Yuen Tso 1 March 1991, whose book *Canucks Unlimited: the Record in Story and Picture of the History, Life and Experiences of the Men of 436 R.C.A.F. Squadron, Burma 1944-1945* (Toronto, nd) was very helpful.

13. When two consecutive dates are written with a slash between, the raid was made during the night.

14. Herby Chan's birth certificate shows his name as 'Herby'; during school days and when he enlisted he used 'Herbert' because it was automatically assumed that 'Herby' was the short form of 'Herbert.'

Chapter V

THE ALLIED NAVIES

In the Royal Canadian Navy, as in the Royal Canadian Air Force, the *Regulations* specified that a recruit must be a British subject and of the white race. A Chinese Canadian Sea Cadet born in London, Ont, tried to enlist in the RCN in 1940, but was refused on the grounds that he was not white.

Blacks who were British subjects were allowed to enlist in the RCN in February of 1943, but Indians (native and Asian) from British Columbia in 1942 and Canadian born Japanese in 1945 were not enlisted in the navy. There is no explanation given in the official history as to why these particular years were mentioned, and the history makes no mention at all of Chinese Canadians.

In addition to the racial qualification, recruits could be refused on other grounds. If the parents of the prospective recruit were living in enemy territory or if the parents were naturalized and their loyalty might be doubted upon investigation by the RCMP, a recruit could also be denied acceptance.[1]

At an inter-departmental meeting in April 1943 the Navy had stated that its policy was to "accept any British subjects, but not aliens. Consequently, Canadian Chinese or Chinese born in Hong Kong may enlist in the Navy if they wish and are acceptable."[2] Order in Council PC 1986, dated 12 March 1943, removed all racial restrictions and specified only that the recruit must be a British subject.[3]

Not more than about ten Chinese Canadians enlisted in the RCN, with William Lore preceding the order in council by a month or so. A similar delay between the October enlistment date of Chinese Canadian volunteers and the official December sanction by order in council had occurred in the RCAF.

William King Lowd Lore, born 28 February 1909 in Victoria, had been the first Canadian Chinese to be accepted as a perma-nent civil servant in Canada in 1939. He was employed as radio operator with the Department of Transport, Radio Division, Marine Branch and Air Services Branch, and posted to Port Menier, Anticosti Island. The SOS signal from SS *Athenia,* torpedoed by a German submarine in the North Atlantic, was intercepted and relayed to DOT, Ottawa, on 2/3 September 1939, when he was stationed here.

In mid-September, Bill Lore received a summons to report to the RCAF Recruiting Station at Montreal and leave was requested from Ottawa. Ottawa advised that transfer would have to wait until navigation in the St. Lawrence closed for the winter which occurred mid-December.

When December came, he was instructed by DOT to transfer to the Air Services Branch for duty at St. Hubert Airport. Since this was an essential service, he was prohibited from transferring to the RCAF as officer in charge of the wireless school of the British Commonwealth Air Training Plan.

From December 1939 to 1941, Bill remained with DOT at St. Hubert Airport, handling radio range weather broadcasts and air ground radio voice communications. This involved voice transmissions for Northeast Airlines and Colonial Airlines; trans-Atlantic coded transmissions of weather reports to Shannon Airport; voice communications with Gander Airport in Newfoundland and later at Goose Bay in Labrador for trans-Atlantic flights, including Ferry Command; and D/F (direction/finding) station for location of German submarines.

When Ferry Command was transferred to Dorval Airport, Bill also was posted there until early 1943. He served as radio electrician and shift supervisor in close liaison with Ferry Command. During bad weather, a shift could last straight through from eight in the morning to four in the afternoon without a break and with the officer in charge assisting in logging all contacts.

In January 1943, William Lore, O-42700, joined the RCN at the personal request of V/Adm. Percy F. Nelles, Chief of Naval Staff. He took a few weeks preliminary training at HMCS *Montreal*.[4] he was then posted to HMCS *Cornwallis,* at Deep Brook on the Bay of Fundy, halfway between Digby and Annapolis, for emergency officer training. The first buildings at this new location had been completed in April 1943 although an advance party had been located there from January.

– DND/NAC PA-178852

S/Lt. William K.L. Lore 1944

Bill Lore was the first Canadian born Chinese in the RCN and the first officer of Chinese descent in "the whole of the British Commonwealth Navies." He graduated from the Officer Training Course and was appointed temporary sub-lieutenant (SB) RCN(VR) in June 1943. Special Branch or (SB) used after a naval rank indicated an officer with duties in technical areas or other extraordinary duties not common to all of that rank.

In July Bill was assigned to the Operational Intelligence Centre, Naval Service Headquarters, Ottawa. He immediately set out to inspect equipments and lecture staffs at various Radio Interception Centres. From October to December 1943 he was appointed officer in charge of the Naval Radio Interception Centre at Gordon Head, Victoria, and then as RCN liaison officer to the US 13th Naval District's radio intelligence establishment at Bainbridge Island in the State of Washington to May 1944.

Bill was recalled to NSHQ on D-Day and was detached for duty with the newly established Combined Services Radio Intelligence Unit at Guigues Street headed by Col. Ed Drake of the army, Lt.-Cmdr. Algy Noad of the navy, and S/Ldr. Chester A. Ronning of the air force. At the same time Bill was promoted to lieutenant (SB) RCN(VR).

By September 1944, orders were received for him to proceed overseas on loan to the Royal Navy for advanced HF/DF (high frequency/direction finding) training at HMS *Mercury*. He reported to HMCS *Peregrine* in Halifax, the newly created RCN Depot set up at a former BCATP facility, for pre-embarkation training, equipments, and medical inoculations.

Bill sailed for England on the unescorted, fast troopship *Andes* and arrived in Liverpool late in October. Upon inspection of the troops aboard the ship by a British major, Bill was told " I would not be allowed to land because I was Chinese and did not have a visa." This problem was soon overcome with the help and encouragement of the others on board ship, and he proceeded to London where he remained until December.

Because Bill was able to "read and interpret two lines of a Chinese epigram on a screen . . . [he] suddenly became a Japanese intelligence officer," and was one of a two-man officer team in Combined Services Detailed Intelligence Corps for duty in Burma.

From late December 1944 to late January 1945, after embarking at Liverpool and in a large RN Task Force, they sailed around Northern Ireland into the Atlantic, via Gibraltar, the Suez Canal, and the Indian Ocean to Colombo, Ceylon. Here for the next three months, after reporting to HMS *Lanka,* Bill took up quarters at *Mayina,* a large RN transit camp where he was pre-empted to work on *Dracula,* the plan to retake Rangoon.

By the end of March 1945, with the Rangoon plan completed, Bill was transferred to the British Pacific Fleet. He embarked on HMS *Adamant,* a submarine depot ship, and sailed from Colombo to Freemantle, Western Australia, then by train from Perth to Kalgoorlie, Adelaide, Melbourne, and Sydney arriving at the BPF shore station HMS *Golden Hind.*

He was then detached from BPF and attached to the US 7th Fleet, and further detached for duty with G-2 (American Intelligence) Allied Command Headquarters located near Brisbane, Queensland. It was here that Bill learned of the presence of Capt. Roger Cheng and the other Chinese Canadians but was unable to meet with any of them since the officer commanding at the camp was outraged that he should know anything at all about such a secret organization as SOE.

Shortly after VE-Day, Allied HQs moved forward on its way to the Philippines, landing at Hollandia, secured by Australian forces on the New Guinea coast in April 1944. Although the close of the New Guinea campaign was announced towards the end of May, it was well on into August 1944 before the Japanese were defeated at Biak and the campaign finally closed on the mainland.

Allied HQs went on to Leyte Island, where the successful campaign for the reconquest of the Philippines had opened late in 1944. After Manila had been retaken, battles continued in the northern part of Luzon until June 1945. General MacArthur had announced the liberation of the whole of the Philippines in July 1945, but Gen. Yamashita Tomoyuki, the conqueror of Malaya and now in command of the troops on Luzon, did not surrender until 3 September 1945.

Headquarters G-2 arrived at Manila Bay to find an obstacle course of sunken Japanese ships. The naval officers of G-2 were quartered in tents at the Santa Ana Race Course. Occasionally, Japanese stragglers would appear firing their weapons; it was assumed they preferred to be killed in action rather than be taken prisoner by the Filipinos. The US Chiefs of Staff had wanted BPF to support the attack on Borneo, but Admiral Nimitz had sanctioned their remaining in the main battle.

By mid-August most of the islands approaching Japan had been secured, and the atomic bombs had been dropped on Hiroshima and Nagasaki; Hirohito in his radio broadcast had accepted unconditional surrender. G-2 received orders to proceed to Manus Island in the Admiralty Group, north of New Guinea, for re-attachment to BPF. Manus had been used as a US naval base after they had fought the usual vicious battle for its possession between March and May 1944. R/Adm. Cecil Harcourt, commanding officer of the 11th Aircraft Carrier Squadron of the BPF, arrived a few days later at Manus on board his flagship, HMS *Venerable,* which Lieut. Bill Lore was to join as "the Admiral's Lieutenant."

The admiral's lieutenant was a position with functions completely unknown to Bill. Admiral Harcourt's Secretary, Commander Trythall, guided Bill in his duties, advising him that he was "the Admiral's eyes, ears, and legs and was supposed to be at the Admiral's side at all times possible AND be able to answer any query put to him." Commander Trythall very kindly coached Bill in this role but could not anticipate the questions since each admiral asked different ones. One vital fact the commander stressed was that Bill should "study up all references to Japanese naval vessels in *Jane's Fighting Ships.*"

On the trip to Leyte and up to Subic Bay, Bill followed this sound advice and became knowledgeable in matters concerning the Japanese fleet. Admiral Harcourt transferred his flag at Leyte Island to HMS *Indomitable,* a fleet carrier; several ships arrived from Australia, including HMCS *Prince Robert,* to join the Task Force.

Prince Robert, under the command of Capt. Wallace B. Creery of Vancouver, had left Esquimalt 5 July and arrived in Sydney 10 August. Before leaving Canada, Captain Creery had harangued the crew who had then voted to volunteer for the Pacific War.

All Canadians who served in the Pacific theatre after the capitulation in Europe 8 May were volunteers specifically for that theatre. Prime Minister Mackenzie King had announced in the House of Commons 7 April, to the dismay of National Defence, that those fighting in the Pacific War would be volunteers for the Pacific and only after thirty days' leave.

The crew of one Canadian ship, the cruiser HMCS *Uganda,* voted themselves out of the war. The *Uganda* arrived in Hawaii in July and sailed from Pearl Harbor 4 August; they reached Esquimalt on the 10th. The *Uganda* had been in action against Okinawa from early April after joining British Task Force 57 operating under the command of the US 5th Fleet. During July, after action at Truk, *Uganda* and the British Pacific Fleet had joined the US 3rd Fleet for action in Japanese home waters before the ship sailed back to Esquimalt.

Capt. F.G. Hart, RCN, had commanded the *Prince Robert* when that ship had escorted HMT *Awatea* to carry the two battalions, the Winnipeg Grenadiers and the Royal Rifles of Canada, to Hong Kong in 1941; the American ship *Don Jose*

carried the vehicles and equipment but this ship was re-routed to the Philippines and the material never reached Hong Kong. Despite announcement of the official Japanese surrender on 15 August, *Prince Robert* under the command of Captain Creery sailed from Sydney "according to her original schedule with a British Task Force."[5]

Returned to Subic Bay, an American base north of Manila, the fleet waited the

– NAC R-49742

Royal Rifles of Canada and Winnipeg Grenadiers marching up Nathan Road in Kowloon on way to Sham Shui Po Barracks.

decision as to which country would re-occupy Hong Kong: the American, the British, or the Chinese. Hong Kong was in an American theatre. The Americans, of course, refused to have anything to do with the retaking of former colonies. The fleet was split into squadrons for expected operations in the waters of Hong Kong, Singapore, and Shanghai.

On August 26th or 27th, Admiral Harcourt received orders from Admiral Sir Bruce Fraser, who had joined the BPF on the *Duke of York* on 19 August, to occupy Hong Kong Island and Kowloon and to leave the New Territories for occupation by the Chinese. Several ships proceeded to Yeiling, Formosa, and Shanghai, with R/Adm. R. M. Servaes taking surrender in Shanghai. A squadron under Admiral Walker on *Nelson* set out for Malaya arriving off Penang 2 September; Admiral Power on *Cleopatra* headed for the Singapore base the following day. Rabaul and Batavia each received several ships as well.

The remainder set out for Hong Kong where the capital ships arrived 28 August. While still outside the port, "a signal from the senior 'Hellcats Patrol' arrived reporting the sighting of a group of 30-odd speed boats in formation travelling in the direction of the Fleet [and] estimated to intercept the Fleet that evening." The Admiral asked Bill for identification of the boats; he was able to report that they were "suicide boats" from his reading of *Jane's Fighting Ships*. Harcourt immediately gave the order to sink them.

The Task Force remained outside the harbour and a cruiser was used by Harcourt to enter the port 30 August where he completed negotiations with the Japanese. The ships, accompanied by two converted corvettes of the Australian 21st Minesweeper Squadron, tied up at HMS *Tamar*, the RN shore station at Victoria on the Island. At the same time *Prince Robert* tied up at Holt's Wharf at Tsimshatsui, on the Kowloon or mainland side. The *Prince Robert* was "the first ship in the task force to dock in occupied territory and the first ship to put a landing party ashore."[6]

Lieut. William Lore was one of the first ashore. August 30th was "Liberation Day" for Hong Kong but it was a quiet day because "the Japanese had declared a curfew that morning and anyone discovered at the waterfront would be shot." In addition to this announcement, over one million Chinese had left or been expelled from the colony after the British capitulated and in May 1945 only 650,000 of the 1,729,000 remained, which also accounted for the relative calm.

There did not appear to be any contact in the initial period between those in the Task Force and Colonial Secretary Gimson who had struggled valiantly to set up an interim government. The only assistance he had had were the few half-starved officers from the POW camps.

Then came the relief and liberation of the men at Sham Shui Po where about 246 officers and 134 ORs (other ranks) were imprisoned. On 31 August, Lieut. Bill Lore led a three-man naval team to the former barracks.

After initial difficulty in overcoming the reluctance of the guards to admit them, they entered the camp. The three were taken to the area where the officers were housed, one building for the Canadians and across the way, one for the British. The English sub-lieutenant entered the British building, while Bill attended to the Canadian side where, on the ground floor, he found some ten Canadians. Once he was recognized as a Canadian, another 20 to 30 men rushed down from the upper floor. Tears flowed unashamedly.

They were able to unearth a tattered Union Jack that had been hidden away in the camp by one of the British officers. The Japanese were ordered to lower the Rising Sun and the Union Jack was raised to snap in the wind for another 52 years.

Admiral Harcourt made provision for "food and medical and other facilities from RN ships in harbour" as did the captain and crew of *Prince Robert*. The picture shows Cmdr. Peter MacRitchie, RCN(VR) (SB), of *Prince Robert*, the chief public relations

Cmdr. MacRitchie autographing for POWs at Sham Shui Po Camp

– NAC PA 145983

officer overseas, signing autographs for the POWs in the Camp.

Newly commissioned HMCS *Ontario* joined the Task Force 13 September. Peace terms were signed 16 September and, in the meantime, the Japanese cooperated in helping to maintain order.

Prince Robert assisted Australian minesweepers to transport civilian internees from Stanley Camp to the Canadian Pacific *Empress of Australia*. On 9 September the *Empress* carried most of the POWs to Manila where the Canadian Repatriation of Prisoners of War group was located. Those POWs who had been used as forced labour in Japan were removed on an American hospital ship, also to Manila. After the signing ceremony 16 September, *Prince Robert* sailed for Manila on the 26th to embark about 50 Canadian POWs for return to Canada.

Bill Lore remained on loan to the RN based at Hong Kong as staff lieutenant to Admiral Harcourt. Bill was a member of the Naval Intelligence Unit, the Joint Intelligence Unit, and liaison officer to China, until November 1946. He continued as naval member of the Joint Intelligence Unit until recalled to the RCN in February 1947. He arrived back in Ottawa on the converted UST *General Meigs* via Guam, Honolulu, and San

Francisco in April 1947 accompanied by his wife, Molly, the only war bride of a Canadian Chinese from Hong Kong.

It was a shock when William Lore arrived in Ottawa April 1947 to find that NSHQ, the DOT, and the Civil Service Commission records "showed that I was 'killed in action, sometime in 1945, somewhere in the South Pacific.'" By June 1947 after "several visits to Ottawa and desperate arguments I was finally resurrected by NSHQ" who at last admitted that he was indeed William King Lowd Lore, and had not died as reported, so that he was able to receive his pay.

After demobilization Bill was transferred to HMCS *Donnacona* at Montreal as lieutenant (SB) RCN(R) Active List "with a grudging admission that Admiralty had given me a high commendation for my services whilst on loan with the R.N.I." In 1952 he was promoted to lieutenant commander RCN(R) Retired List at HMCS *Donnacona*. He reached compulsory retirement age in 1969.

Bill was re-employed by DOT until February 1949 when he was granted leave to the RCN for duty on board HMCS *Crescent* for a trip to Shanghai to evacuate Canadian personnel. This trip to Hong Kong and Shanghai saw the conclusion of the civil war in China, which began with the overthrow of the Manchus in 1911/12; the Japanese incursions and the Second World War were interruptions only.

The *Crescent,* under Lt.-Cmdr. D.W. Groos, left Esquimalt 2 February 1949, crossed the Pacific and travelled up the Yangtze River as far as Woosung, where they anchored 25 February. A pilot guided the ship up the Whangpoo to Shanghai the next day. After a series of visits to and from officials ashore, the *Crescent* returned to Woosung 10 March.

They then travelled up the Yangtze to Kiang-Chang where arrangements had been made "between the Communists and Nationalist for ships to anchor safely overnight." They arrived at Nanking after an uneventful passage 11 March and anchored alongside HMS *Cossack.* They left for Shanghai on the 14 March and arrived the same day. Again calls were made to and from officials ashore.

HMCS *Crescent* was relieved by *Cossack* 23 March and the Chinese pilot guided the ship to Kiangyin and again "the ship's company settled down to enjoy the spectacle of sporadic starshell, flares and gunfire from the opposing factions some five miles away," as the Communists and Nationalists hammered it out. The ship proceeded to Woosung the following day.

They dropped their passengers at Woosung for Shanghai. None of the Canadians in Shanghai or Nanking wished to be evacuated; they considered that as business and professional men, and as missionaries and school teachers, with no political leanings, the Communists would not pose a danger to them so they remained in China.

The *Crescent* arrived in Hong Kong 27 March and remained there carrying out exercises with the land forces. A ship's party of 13 officers and 127 men, including a ceremonial guard, laid wreaths on Canadian graves at the Chai Wan Military Cemetery. The "Canadian flag was flying for the day" and sentries were posted in the Canadian section of the grounds. At the same time, another small party laid a wreath at Stanley Cemetery. Bill Lore still tries to attend these small remembrance

ceremonies each year as they occur; he welcomed the Canadian contingent for the 50th anniversary ceremonies in 1991.

HMCS *Crescent* remained on the China station performing incidental duties. One of the tasks performed was to assist HMS *Belfast* on her voyage to Shanghai; the *Belfast* had been recommissioned just a week before and needed her armament and equipment worked up.

Although the *Crescent* had already set out on the voyage home on 4 May, they were advised to remain on station until the Shanghai situation had cleared. They anchored in Alacrity Anchorage on 5 May. The Canadian and British Consulates requested the ship to send American funds; only American and Hong Kong dollars were of any value in Shanghai. The amount sent would tide them over until the Nationalists had departed and the Communists arrived. HMCS *Crescent* was ordered back to Canada 9 May and she left the China Station on that date for Esquimalt.[7]

At the request of the Department of Justice (RCMP), William Lore transferred to the Immigration Department for duty as immigration officer in Hong Kong for anti-corruption investigations from 1950 to 1953. This was during the initial period of investigation into the illegal Chinese immigration into Canada. The investigation was concluded with amnesty granted to over 12,000 Chinese who had entered Canada illegally before 1960. The Chinese Adjustment Statement Programme continued to regularize these immigrants until the programme ended in 1973.

William Lore continued as immigration officer in Montreal in 1953 and early in 1954 went to London, England, for consultation with government officials. From 1954 to 1957 he was on leave to the Admiralty as admiralty civilian officer for duty in London, then in Singapore, and finally in Combined Services Headquarters in Hong Kong.

Bill resigned from the Canadian Civil Service in 1957, and from 1957 to 1961 took up law studies in Hong Kong and London, England. In August 1962, he passed solicitors final examination in London. In October he was admitted as solicitor of the Supreme Court of Hong Kong, and in December 1967 he was admitted to practice as solicitor of the Supreme Court of England. From 1962 to the present (May 1993), he has practised as a solicitor in Hong Kong. Bill Lore introduced legal aid in Hong Kong, a programme that has proved to be very successful.

Lieut. (Temp.) William Mar, also from Victoria, enlisted at the Navy Recruiting Centre on Douglas Street in April 1943. He received his training at HMCS *Naden* and was then posted to HMCS *Protector* in Sydney, NS. He received additional training at HMCS *Cornwallis* at Deep Brook.

At *Cornwallis* Bill volunteered for the Fleet Air Arm and was waiting for one of the two light fleet carriers being built at Belfast to be commissioned. The war came to an end before this occurred, and he was released. Bill Mar's uncle, Richard Mar, served in the 1st Canadian Parachute Battalion in Northwest Europe.

Others who joined the RCN(VR) were Willie Yuen, David Lee, and Victor Hum, all from Montreal. Victor served on HMCS *Iroquois,* a tribal class destroyer commissioned 30 November 1942. Pay Lieut. (Temp.) Doug G. Wong from Brantford, Ont, served at NSHQ in Ottawa; he had been commissioned 16 August 1944. Radio Artificer Jean Raymond Marcel Wong, from Montreal, served on the high seas and ended with a posting to HMCS *Micmac,* a Canadian-built tribal class destroyer. This ship was not commissioned until 9 December 1945, but Marcel had joined the Navy much earlier.

After graduating from McGill University, Lieut. George D. Wong, also from Montreal, served in the Pay Department at NSHQ. George had joined the navy in the early spring of 1943 a few weeks after Bill Lore. He was the brother of Wilbur and Gus Wong, both of whom served in Ferry Command.

While serving in the RCN or in the RN, 1,787 Canadians were killed during the war, 319 were wounded, and 95 became POWs.

Merchant Marine

The merchant marine was a paranaval organization controlled in the case of Canada by NSHQ Ottawa, in Britain by the Admiralty, and by the Maritime Commission in Washington. The merchant navy carried fighting men and essential supplies to England to enable the Allies to fight. The efforts of the Canadian Navy were all directed to this end: the safe arrival of convoys and individual fast ships to England.

Sea transportation as well as inland routings to the sea, particularly railways and ports, were controlled in all Allied countries by their respective governments; the RCN's specialties were Canadian ports and the routing of merchant ships through the Naval Control Service. Coastal trade was included within the control system. In effect all transportation facilities were controlled by the government.

On 26 August 1939, all Canadian-registered and Commonwealth vessels within the Western Atlantic as far south as Savannah came under the Naval Control Service. Canada had about forty ocean-going ships, most of them government owned through Crown corporations. Eventually, with the construction of new ships, over 200 were controlled by the Naval Control Service.

This Service not only routed the convoys, it also saw that they were prepared for sea and this involved the repair and manning of ships, discipline of the sailors, controlling ships in ports, the inspection and restriction of cargoes, and setting up trade policy. The Director of Naval Intelligence in Ottawa, Capt. Eric Brand, an RN commander on loan to the RCN, controlled the activities of the Naval Control Service officers in Canadian ports. American ports were controlled by their own organization in a similar fashion.

Arranging the repair of ships and the timing and routing of convoys was followed by providing escorts against submarine attack. The matter of crews for the ships next had to be dealt with, for service in the merchant navy appeared to be a thankless job. The chances of survival from a torpedoed ship were small;

there were no recreational or other facilities for merchant seamen when they reached port; and their pay was low. Canadian merchant seamen earned $75 to $100 a month with a war risk bonus of $44.50. Because of the poor conditions under which they laboured, there was often 'crew trouble.'

There were 1,148 Canadian merchant seamen lost at sea going down in 68 Canadian ships during the Second World War; in the British merchant service the loss was more than 31,000.[8]

Crew trouble delayed the sailing of convoys and thus the navy became involved through the Naval Control Service officers, particularly through the efforts of Lieut. E.F.H. Watt, RCN(VR), in Halifax. The ideas generated in Halifax spread to other ports from St. John's to Vancouver and Prince Rupert; Britain became interested in his methods as well.

An early but weak Canadian order in council was strengthened by a subsequent one in 1941 and finalized in December 1942, which provided punishment for recalcitrant alien seamen. Manning pools were established to provide seamen with accommodation and pay while ashore and thus supplied the vessels with a pool of seamen; recreational facilities were set up; and a director of merchant seamen was appointed. An offender could be detained for three months and then released to a ship or further detained for another six months.

Only a few Chinese Canadians who served in the merchant marine have been located, and one of these was Andrew Wong, from Victoria, who joined the US Merchant Marine early in 1945. Andy had received his seaman's training on the BC coast and joined a US Liberty ship in Vancouver that was taking on ordinary seamen. The ship sailed through the Panama Canal to France and returned to Mobile, Alabama, where the port representative, a former Canadian, helped him to obtain his American seaman's papers. Andy made additional trips across the Atlantic, to South America, and on into the Pacific, including Hawaii. He was released in 1947.

Another was George Lem from Oshawa, Ont, who joined the Canadian Merchant Marine in 1942 and worked from the west coast to Australia and New Zealand as well as South America. George is the brother of William Lem who served in the RCAF.

As was noted in an earlier chapter, Lyman Quon was assistant to his father, catering superintendent to Canadian Pacific Steamship Lines in Hong Kong. Lyman was a member of the HKVDC, in the same unit as George Chow, but just before the Japanese attacked the colony, he had been sent to Singapore to investigate conditions on board one of the company's ships evacuating refugees. Lyman did not return to Hong Kong but continued to serve in the Canadian Merchant Marine. He helped man the anti-aircraft units on board ship while in England. Lyman returned to the Canadian Steamship Office in Montreal at the end of the war.

Two Chinese, one born in Canton and the other in Hong Kong, were also employed by the Hong Kong office of the Canadian Steamship Lines. George Chin (**Chin** Toy) and Paul K. Shein (**Sin** Kam) served from 1938, first on the *Empress of Japan,* later renamed *Empress of Canada.* The troopship left Hong Kong for Singapore, then picked up soldiers in Australia and New Zealand, and delivered the troops to Egypt. The *Empress* then delivered soldiers to England from Egypt before returning to Hong Kong.

Their next trip on SS *Cyclops,* a cargo ship, took them again to Singapore but this time back into the Atlantic through the Panama Canal. The ship was torpedoed 11/12 January 1941 some 160 miles south of Halifax.

The sinking of the *Cyclops* signalled a new threat in the war at sea; this was the first appearance of U-Boats in North American waters. From May of 1942, they entered the St. Lawrence River and sank two merchant ships; four more were sunk in July. Convoys were formed for protection of shipping between Quebec City and Sydney, NS. Convoys were later extended to Halifax and down into the West Indies.

George and Paul spent 24 hours in the icy waters after their ship was lost. An aircraft found them and signalled a destroyer, which picked them up. Seventy-five of the crew survived, but 180 died. The two men were taken to a hospital in Halifax for several weeks, and then to the Seamen's Club for two weeks. They had both signed a contract in Hong Kong ensuring that they could stay in any British colony should it become necessary, and in this case, the colony turned out to be Canada. They remained ashore, refusing to go to sea again. They both still suffer with leg problems that they attribute to the sojourn in the icy waters of the Atlantic. George is now a naturalized Canadian and Paul is still in the process of becoming one.

Although these two men were not Canadians when the war began, one was already a British subject according to the RCN definition; they entered Canada and became Canadians in a way that appears to be unique. The Exclusion Act was not repealed until 1947 and they did not enter the country in any of the categories as outlined in that Act.

Merchant seamen are now covered, however, under the Merchant Navy Veterans Bill, which amends the Pension Act, the War Veterans Allowance Act, and other legislation, to extend full veterans' services to high-sea merchant seamen, effective 18 June 1992. As of March 1992, some 3,500 out of 12,000 Canadian merchant seaman still survive.[9]

The RCN removal of the racial restriction allowed Chinese Canadians to enlist in this service; there were no similar regulations that applied in the merchant navy. Whether only a few Chinese Canadians wanted to enlist in the navy, or whether the navy wanted only a few Chinese Canadians, cannot be determined. Those who enlisted in the navy appear not to have encountered any problems, unlike the Canadian Army that never seemed to resolve the conflict between a Cabinet War Committee decision and the regulations.

NOTES

Quotations that are not identified in a note are from conversations or correspondence with participants and families.

1. Gilbert Norman Tucker, *The Naval Service of Canada: Its Official History*, vol. 2, *Activities on Shore during the Second World War* (Ottawa, 1952), pp. 268-9.
2. Note for External Files, 27 April 1943, in NAC, RG 25, Vol. 2818, File 1154-40.
3. NAC, RG 2, Vol.178, File March 12, 1943, Reel T5152; this reference courtesy Glenn Wright, NAC.
4. HMCS *Montreal*, the English language division, was merged with the French language division and together they became HMCS *Donnacona*.
5. D.Hist. H.M.C.S. *Prince Robert*, Vol. 1,8000.
6. D.Hist. *Prince Robert;* and see also Fraser M. McKee, "Princes Three: Canada's use of Armed Merchant Cruisers during World War II," *RCN in Retrospect 1910-1968,* ed. by James A. Boutilier (Vancouver, 1982), pp. 117-137.
7. D.Hist. H.M.C.S. *Crescent,* (Reports of Proceedings 1949-1957) 8000; all quotations concerning the *Crescent* trip to Shanghai are from this source.
8. Tucker, p. 375, n. 24.
9. See article by Elaine Flaherty, *Southam News* reprinted in *The London Free Press,* 27 March 1992; and *Legion* Magazine July/August 1992, p. 35.

Chapter VI

THE CANADIAN ARMY

The RCN and the RCAF were composed entirely of volunteers; men were never conscripted for these services. In the Canadian Army, the men were either volunteers (general service or active) who could be sent overseas, or they had been called up under NRMA of June 1940 and could be used in Home Defence only. Government policy allowing Chinese Canadians to enlist in the Canadian Army varied across Canada. From September 1939 Chinese Canadians could usually enlist voluntarily in any of the provinces but officially they were not called up under NRMA until September 1944.

Initially, they were not called up in British Columbia because Prime Minister Mackenzie King had acted on the request of Premier T.D. Pattullo not to call up Chinese and Japanese Canadians. If, said Pattullo, the Chinese and Japanese are "called up for service, there will be a demand that they be given the franchise, which we in this Province can never tolerate."[1] These instructions from the federal government were confirmed in September and October 1940; although some had been called for medical examination, Chinese and Japanese would not be sent to military training centres.[2]

At this point, October 1940, the federal government restriction applied only to British Columbia. Saskatchewan was the only other province to bar the Chinese from voting; there is no record of a similar protest from this province. The federal vote was dependent upon the provincial franchise. Provincially and federally there were only two provinces in which Chinese Canadians could not vote, but from January 1941 the extension of this call up ban by the Cabinet War Committee applied to all of Canada.

Chinese Canadians in Victoria were quite aware that there was a connection between compulsory military service and the franchise. A few months following the enactment of NRMA, they petitioned the Minister of National War Services in Ottawa, pointing out that Chinese Canadians would be more than willing "to give whatever service should be expected of Canadian citizens" in connection with compulsory military training, but that in turn they "should receive complete recognition as Canadian citizens and should have all the privileges of citizenship," and "particularly the right to vote."[3] Since practice in the professions such as law, pharmacy, and accounting depended upon being on the voters' lists, the right to vote was more important than just the act of casting one's ballot.

There were many civil servants and army officials, including some from British Columbia, who did not agree with government policy. One of these was Dr. Hugh L. Keenleyside of External Affairs who made a plea for fair treatment of Orientals in British Columbia. He considered the action of the CWC "both unjust and unwise"; instead he insisted that if the federal government would take a stand to ensure decent treatment for Canadians of Oriental origin, a large part of the opposition would collapse.[4] Also by 1943, there developed a very strong dislike in some quarters at the secret manner in which "the present cooked-up arrangements" had been made.[5] A public announcement of the ban on compulsory military service for Chinese Canadians was never made.

There were also many meetings consuming a great many man hours at the highest levels, both in Ottawa and Victoria (in Vancouver when Pacific Command HQs moved to that city), concerning the Oriental problem throughout the course of the war. None of these meetings had any influence on the cabinet decision. On the other hand, many officials looked on both the Chinese and Japanese as 'aliens' in the sense of 'non-white,' so that many of the meetings, although seemingly dealing with the Japanese, or the East Indians, affected the Chinese as well.

Pacific Command, which included British Columbia, Alberta, the Yukon, and adjacent parts of the Northwest Territories, was formed at the time the Special Committee on Orientals in British Columbia was appointed by the CWC in October 1940 to investigate the Japanese and Chinese in that province. The terms of reference for this Special Committee included internal security and military training. Japanese Canadians were well represented at the hearings, but there was not a single spokesman for Chinese Canadians although the committee had felt it was necessary to have a Chinese interpreter present!

According to the "Report and Recommendations of the Special Committee on Orientals in British Columbia December 1940," persons of Chinese racial origin in British Columbia presented little problem since there was no immigration, the numbers were decreasing, and they were distributed widely and more or less evenly in the province with the exception of Vancouver. There was, however, a sizable number of enemy aliens in the province: over 18,000 Germans[6] and nearly 15,000 Italians. The Japanese population was estimated at 23,000 and the Chinese at 21,760. The figures quoted in any of the Ottawa material never appear to be very accurate; the actual figure for Chinese in British Columbia according to the 1941 census was 18,619 or 53.8 percent of the total in Canada. It was popularly believed then and remains a strong myth today that virtually all Canadian Chinese lived in British Columbia. In spite of the fact that Chinese Canadians

presented no problem since "they accept discriminatory treatment with a minimum of expressed resentment," eight out of the ten recommendations in the "1940 Report" applied to Chinese Canadians as well as the Japanese. The two recommendations that did not apply were that Japanese were not allowed to enlist even voluntarily in the armed forces, and they were to register. The Chinese had already registered under the earlier Exclusion Act of 1923. The CWC on 20 January 1941 included a ban on compulsory military service for Chinese as well as Japanese Canadians all across Canada not just in British Columbia.[7] Possibly because all of this was handled so secretly, notice of the ban was slow to trickle down to the local mobilization boards.

Nine months after the CWC had made this decision, the Toronto chairman of NWS was not aware that Chinese Canadians were not to be called up under NRMA; he had been equally puzzled when the RCAF would not accept a qualified Chinese Canadian pilot in any category. Only now was the chairman informed that Japanese and Chinese Canadians were not presently to be called for military training all across Canada, not just in British Columbia. In spite of this information, Chinese Canadians continued to be called up under NRMA from the first call of 1940, especially in Ontario and Quebec.[8]

Pattullo altered his stand on 22 November 1941 with regard to Japanese Canadian voluntary enlistment provided they were sent out of the province as early as possible after they were accepted in the armed forces. On the provincial level, the link was between compulsory military service and the franchise and did not, therefore, affect voluntary enlistment.[9]

Two days before Pattullo's letter "Memorandum (Secret No. 1)" was issued to divisional registrars and chairmen instructing them not to call up "Canadians of Japanese and Chinese races" for military training. Rather than restrict this ban to the two provinces where the franchise was in question, it applied to the whole of Canada in line with the CWC decision.[10] This memorandum remained in effect until the CWC reversed its decision in the summer of 1944. The Canadian Army attempted several times in the intervening period by means of inter-departmental meetings (army, navy, air force, External Affairs, RCMP, and others) to bring about a change, and the Minister of National Defence supported it, but no reversal occurred. Although Pattullo left the premier-ship in December 1941, there were federal politicians from British Columbia adamantly opposed to such recognition of Orientals; one of these was a federal cabinet member who had the ear of Mackenzie King.

Before Pattullo's approval could be acted upon, on 7 December 1941, Japan attacked the United States at Pearl Harbor and at the same time attacked Britain at Hong Kong and Malaya. Canada was prompt to declare war against Japan on the day the attack was made and a day before the United States and Great Britain did so. Canada had been tardy to declare war against Germany in 1939 in order to demonstrate that the declaration of war was an independent sovereign decision. The two Canadian battalions in Hong Kong may have fostered the quick deci-sion on the declaration of war against Japan. For the declaration of war against Germany, Mackenzie King had canvassed the cabinet 24 August, and the cabinet had decided that Canada would participate, but war against Germany was not publicly declared in parliament until 10 September 1939.[11]

Following the declaration of war with Japan, an attempt was made to settle the issue of racial equality in the services; Canada was now allied with China and India and the war with Japan was not on a "colour line basis."[12]

The colour bar in the RCAF and the RCN was openly declared in the *Regulations:* a "pure European descent" and "pure white race" rule applied in these two services. The colour bar in the Canadian Army was much more subtle. At an inter-departmental meeting in January 1942 of the three Defence Depart-ments, RCMP, NWS, and External Affairs, to eliminate the charge of discrimination, it was decided that Chinese, Japanese, and East Indians should be called up under NRMA but that British Columbia would likely object,

although voluntary enlistment would not affect the franchise issue. It was also decided that there should be no discrimination on the basis of "race or colour" but there might be difficulties if races were mixed. This latent fear of mixing races was often evident in both the Ottawa and Vancouver meetings. It was further agreed that if a commanding officer refused to accept an Oriental or East Indian recruit in his unit he should suggest an alternative service.[13]

These decisions had no influence on the cabinet decision in any way, and the com-pulsory military service of these groups did not occur as a result. But the decision that no unit had to accept them appears to be one that remained in effect throughout the war period and accounts for some of the strange patterns that appear. During the reinforcement crises of late 1944 and early 1945, many Chinese Canadian soldiers who were general service were still being retained in Canada, or taken off overseas drafts, yet NRMA men were being sent overseas. Lieut. Wilfred Seto was rejected in Italy because of his race and the brigadier suggested to him that his services would be of more use in Pacific Command. The principle that there should be no discri-mination was effectively cancelled by the statement that no unit had to accept them.

Another unfounded fear raised at this meeting was that Canada's treatment of Canadian Japanese would have an affect on Canadian POWs in Japanese hands. Concern was also expressed on humanitarian grounds since their removal was a "barbarous contra-diction of all Canadian and Allied professions of justice and humanity."[14] The Japanese had been moved from the coastal areas of British Columbia and sent to internment camps in the interior or allowed to go east to the Prairie farms and some were moved on into Ontario; all their property had been transferred to the Custodian of Enemy Alien Property leaving them with only the little they could carry with them. It was about this time that Chinese Canadians in Vancouver began wearing a lapel pin saying 'I'm Chinese,' since Caucasians often were unable to distinguish between the two nationalities.

Canada's treatment of her Japanese citizens does not appear to have had any direct influence on conditions in any of the Prisoner of War and Internee camps where Canadians were imprisoned. Prisoners of other Allied countries were treated just as inhumanely. The Japanese had not ratified and did not pretend to adhere to the Geneva Convention for the treatment of POWs. Canada's treatment of these minorities, however, did have an affect on some of her own public servants; occasionally objections were raised or attempts made to alter things.

One proposal in the spring of 1942 was the formation of a Chinese Canadian Battalion in Pacific Command. In his attempts to obtain officer training, Wilfred Seto saw clearly that unless a separate battalion were formed, he was unlikely to see active service, and there were other supporters. Sgt. Frank Ho Lem from Calgary raised the same issue in September 1942.[15] These supporters may have considered a separate unit another form of discrimination, just as some Japanese Canadians apparently did,[16] but there is no record of such a view.

In response to the battalion suggestion, National Defence calculated that with 42,716 male Chinese residents in Canada (the 1941 census gave a total figure of both sexes of 34,627), about 2,300 would be available, which would be "enough for one Battalion," but 92.7 percent of the 42,716 remained Chinese nationals and there would be a language problem. The figure cited in a report for the Privy Council of 26 January 1941 gave 551 Chinese nationals. NDHQ never seemed to have a clear grasp of the numbers, the language capability, nor the nationality of the young Chinese Canadian men available for military service. Since the young men all spoke English, the Consul General for China in Pacific Command argued, English would be the battalion language.[17]

In addition to the three categories of Canadian born, naturalized (both British subjects), and Chinese nationals (alien), Chinese Canadians were also in 'special category' in the military. When Wilfred Seto learned of this, he made a strong plea that they be "trained in your various establishments as ordinary candidates." Queried about commissioning for Seto, Ottawa replied that Canadian Chinese were eligible for appointment to commissioned rank provided they were naturalized British subjects.[18] Wilfred Seto was a Canadian born British subject. Perhaps because National Defence thought applicants would nearly all be Chinese nationals, as indicated with regard to the Chinese Battalion, very few would qualify. There the matter rested but the idea of a Chinese Battalion was revived from time to time.

Other misunderstandings of the CWC and NDHQ are explained in part by information designed to produce a negative affect on the decision makers. It was reported that Orientals, especially the Japanese, although they "may appear to be good Canadian citizens . . . do, however, bear the appearance and characteristics of another race, which immediately sets them apart from the average Canadian," and that "adoption of Western manners and customs may be only a thin veneer." If Japanese Canadians were allowed to enlist in the army "racial hatreds may result in the swerving of loyalty." It was recommended to the CWC that any Japanese in the army should be discharged.

On the other hand, in May 1942, External Affairs recommended the enlistment of a few selected Japanese, in part because "the restrictions imposed on Canadians of Japanese race have gone so far beyond the demand of military necessity." External was against the proposal of NDHQ that no more Japanese be allowed to enlist and to dismiss the few already in the army.[19] As opposed to this NDHQ view on Japanese Canadian enlistment, Chinese Canadians had supporters in Pacific Command.

An officer in Corps Reserve, Royal Canadian Corps of Signals, recommended the formation of a Chinese Signal Unit. He in turn was supported by the staff officer (signals), Pacific Command, who confirmed that "Chinese are easily trained in technical services, and are particularly adaptable to Signals work." Using the previous argument from

National Defence (the small numbers, the language problem, and so forth) this proposal received no official support.[20]

Chinese, Japanese, and East Indian Canadians were not officially exempt from compulsory military service under NWS or National Selective Service regulations. The transfer of NRMA administration from NWS to the Department of Labour was made 1 December 1942 when the NSS Mobilization Regulations were issued by Order in Council PC 10924 and the NWS Regulations of 1940 were revoked. One of the regulations stated that no adult British male subject could leave Canada without permission from the chairman of the Mobilization Board. Just who would be classed as a British subject was a problem soon to be tackled by the army; as noted above, National Defence had come to the conclusion that almost 93 percent of Chinese Canadians were Chinese nationals.[21]

As a result of the new NSS Mobilization Regulations, a new Secret Circular Memorandum No. 25, "Ordering out of aliens under the Regulations," was issued 13 January 1943. Alien was now defined as including "all non-British subjects residing in Canada" and they were placed in Enemy, Allied, and Neutral categories. China was not included as one of the Allied countries; instead, Secret Memorandum No. 1 issued by NWS on 10 November 1941, which banned the call up of Chinese and Japanese Canadians under NRMA all across Canada, was still in effect.[22] China had been an Ally of Canada since war was declared on Japan in December 1941 and nearly all the Chinese Canadians of military age were Canadian born. External Affairs tried to correct some of these misunderstandings.

Although the reference was to East Indians who were "'not non-Canadian British Subjects,' but were Canadians," External seemed to be under the impression that British Columbia had given the vote to all servicemen after the Great War. This was not so for the Chinese nor the East Indians, and Japanese veterans had not received the franchise until 1931. External felt that it might be appro-

priate to ask the BC government if it "would adhere to past practice and enfranchise those individuals who actually serve in the war and survive."[23] If this were done, compulsory military service could naturally follow. Because the real point at issue was not the franchise, there was no action taken along these lines. However, another supporter of Chinese Canadians in Vancouver now began his own campaign with Ottawa.

The Vancouver Mobilization Board Chairman, The Honourable Mr. Justice A.M. Manson, was quite sympathetic towards Chinese Canadian enrollment under NRMA and wrote frequent letters to Ottawa, sometimes quite critical of government policy, in an attempt to change the situation. The secrecy with which all this had been handled meant that initially, like the Toronto chairman, he was unaware of all that had gone before. Instructions accompanying these secret memoranda were to keep the documents under lock and key.

The NSS Mobilization Boards had replaced the NWS Boards late in 1942. The boards, with a judge presiding, ruled on applications for postponement of military service. Chinese Canadians were in the 'catch-22' situation where they were not exempt from military service under the Regulations; on the other hand, although they would not be called up, they had to apply for postponements to defer compulsory military service!

Manson asked why the large number of Canadian Chinese had not been called for military training; they were English-speaking and there were enough to form one or two companies in which Chinese Canadian COTC officers could be used. Since the board was now short of men, and China was an Ally, he thought a lot of good might result from it. He gave as examples some NCOs and a number of very excellent men in the Reserve Army; in a recent shooting competition Chinese Cadets "walked off with the prize against all competitors" and he singled out Sgt. Frank Ho Lem in particular who was "on the Bisley team several times."[24]

It appears that very few Chinese Canadians in BC enlisted directly into active

– courtesy Bill Lowe

Members of 16th Canadian Scottish (Reserve)
Back l to r: Harry Lowe, John Ko Bong, Lloyd Chan, Roy Mah
Front l to r: Harry Lim, Bill Lowe, Roy Chan, Cecil Lam

units, although a few were able to. About a dozen enlisted in the 16th Canadian Scottish (Reserve) Battalion in 1942, most of whom 'turned active' and transferred out of the province. Others had enlisted in the Rocky Mountain Rangers, a militia regiment, and had also transferred to units outside the province. Manson did not receive a favourable response to his suggestion, but National Defence tried to come to terms with enrollment policy and NRMA.

The difficulty of enrolling individuals for compulsory military training who were denied the franchise appeared to be an insurmountable hurdle. On 26 March 1943, at another inter-departmental meeting, the Canadian Army decided to call up naturalized Chinese (relying on their own interpretation of 'naturalized' as given in the Chinese Battalion

suggestion) under NRMA as it was experiencing difficulty in obtaining adequate manpower. External Affairs would review the call up of Chinese nationals.

There was a flurry of meetings and correspondence over the decisions taken at this meeting, and the Minister of National Defence advised Vancouver that naturalized Chinese were to be called up under NRMA, but there was no change in the CWC decision.[25]

A completely opposite view on the call up of Chinese Canadians under NRMA was taken in Ottawa just a month later: neither naturalized nor alien Chinese would be called up. The Minister of National Defence, a member of the CWC, either had not carried the matter to the cabinet or had been unable to alter its stand.

Yet another meeting took place the following day. At this inter-departmental meeting on the question of Chinese aliens, the army representative indicated that an estimated 1,500 Chinese, alien or Canadian, should perhaps now be called up for compulsory military service. Aliens were "subject to examination of background, credentials, etc." The army member noted, however, that it had "difficulty in connection with the position of Chinese who were brought into the forces." In other words, it was difficult to know how to employ them, which was especially true of officers.[26] All Chinese Canadians were gradually slipping into the 'alien' category although the army representative at this meeting still allowed for two classes. The army, however, appeared to be undecided and no changes were actually proposed.

When Manson wrote to NSS at the end of April 1943, he expressed strong disagreement over Ottawa's description of Chinese Canadians as "naturalized." Chinese of callable years in British Columbia were nearly all born in Canada. Manson had understood that the intention was to call "both Canadian born and naturalized Chinese" and that External was to review the call up of alien Chinese.[27]

In May, Manson repeated this theme to the Department of Labour saying that mobilization boards were concerned only with men of callable years; there were very few naturalized Canadians of Chinese origin and very few Chinese nationals of callable years. There were, however, a great many Canadian born Chinese. Col. J.L. Ralston's letter of 13 April indicated that the army had decided to call up naturalized Chinese but the question of alien Chinese would be reviewed by External Affairs. Manson asked if the meeting discussed Secret Memorandum No. 1, which instructed divisional registrars not to call Canadians of Chinese racial origin.[28] This reminder of the CWC decision ended the question of compulsory military service for Chinese Canadians for the time.

However, since the Chinese in Canada were not exempt under mobilization regulations, the suggestion was made that they be called for alternative service. There was objection to this since "it would be unfair to apply the restrictions of alternative service to a person who has not been given another choice"; it would be resented because it would mean "that they have refused to fight or have refused to work."[29]

Ignoring the question of call up under NRMA, since it had been unable to affect the issue, during the summer of 1943 the Canadian Army began to formulate its own rules for 'aliens' including Chinese Canadians.

The adjutant general advised in June 1943 in a circular letter titled "Aliens and Canadians of Foreign Origin" that Canadian citizens of Chinese origin and Chinese nationals could enlist voluntarily but they would not be called up under NRMA. These terms were repeated in the adjutant general's memo of 12 July. Each man's documents were to be classified and marked in red showing the categories in which he was permitted to serve. The categories were all non-sensitive and only one of the five included overseas service. The Attestation Form, Particulars of Family, and Particulars of Family under NRMA were all to be completed after investigation by Military Intelligence and the RCMP,[30] which was what 'vetting' in this context meant. The secret nature of these decisions meant that instructions were not always understood or did not reach lower levels. It is possible that there was some other secret arrangement since Chinese Canadians were being called up outside Pacific Command.

In October 1943 a Chinese Canadian from Montreal raised another issue when he claimed exemption from the NRMA call up by reason of *The Chinese Immigration Act 1923*,[31] an Act generally referred to as the Exclusion Act. This Act had defined the Chinese both as Canadian citizens and as aliens; they had no legal status in the country. He was advised to take the matter up with the divisional registrar in Montreal without any mention that he should not have been called up.

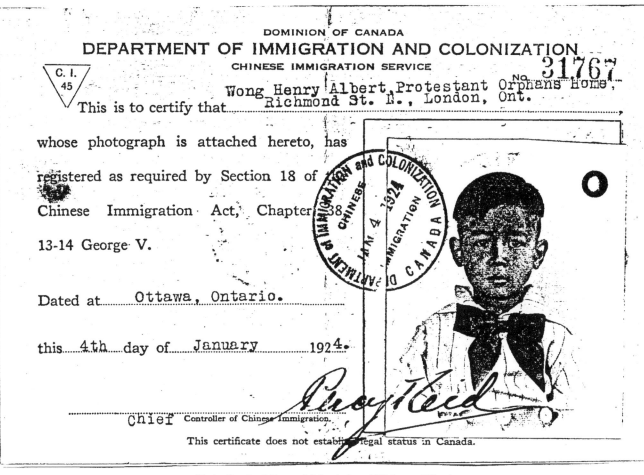

Note the last line which states: "This certificate does not establish legal status in Canada."

Chinese Canadians had been termed 'Registered Aliens' when this act, which set out the requirements for registering, was passed in 1923. In Section 18 of 13-14 George V "An Act Respecting Chinese Immigration,"[32] "every person of Chinese origin or descent in Canada, irrespective of allegiance or citizenship, shall register . . . and obtain a certificate." According to Section 2(e), in mixed marriages, the child took the nationality of the father. Interspersed throughout the Act were references to Canadian citizenship. There was no definition as to just what Canadian citizenship meant; certainly in this context it seemed to have little or no meaning. A Chinese Canadian could be a Canadian citizen and an alien at one and the same time; the same was true in the army.

The army never referred to the Exclusion Act and seems to have arrived at the term 'alien' for Chinese Canadian soldiers on a basis of its own. As late as 5 August 1944, Manson questioned the board's use of the word 'alien' because "about 60% of the men who are shown as aliens on their registration cards are not aliens at all."[33]

The Canadian Army, however, issued a consolidated circular letter on "aliens" 30 November 1943 in which Chinese Canadians for the first time were included in the list of Allied Aliens instead of appearing as a separate category. In this circular letter, it was stated that Chinese might enlist voluntarily but they would not be enrolled under NRMA.

All Allied Aliens, the circular continued, with the exception of American citizens, were subject to investigation and report, or vetting. The rules were always softened for American citizens serving in Canada; this is in sharp contrast to the rules developed for Canadian citizens of Chinese ancestry. American citizens could enlist in the same manner as Canadians of European descent, that is without vetting, and if the air force pattern were followed, they would take an oath of obedience to superior officers not the oath of allegiance.

For all other Allied Aliens, full particulars were to be submitted through Command or District Intelligence to NDHQ (MI 3) using Personal History Form (Alien) and accompanied by the Army Examiner's Report. If any Allied Alien was considered to be undesirable, he was to be discharged as "service no longer required" but on NDHQ authority only. All Allied Aliens, after vetting and if approved, would be "allowed to serve in any location, including Overseas, except in most secret assignments." Most secret assignments were described as Cipher, RDF (radar direction finding), Secret Assignments, Canadian Intelligence Corps, and Confidential Duties in all Headquarters. In addition Allied aliens could be employed in both sensitive and non-sensitive areas. Such assignment restrictions were "SECRET" and no soldier so restricted was to learn of them. Again the forms were to be marked with the classification.

A few Chinese Canadians were employed in some of these secret assignment and sensitive areas, but most had enlisted before November 1943. Other general service soldiers were removed from overseas drafts, which seems to conflict with the secret instructions. The short biographical sketches below illustrate many of these points. The only ones discharged as "services no longer required" appear to have been Chinese nationals.

Finally "for the purpose of these instructions," service in Canada included service in Newfoundland (including Labrador), Bermuda, Bahamas, Jamaica, British Guiana, and the United States of America (including Alaska).[34] Those Canadians who took part in the Kiska invasion, an island in the Aleutians, were not considered to have served 'overseas.'

This long and involved circular letter should have solved the problem of how to treat "aliens" as defined. NSS, however, was still uneasy over the problem of postponements issued to those who were not exempt under the regulations. At one point, NSS requested a secret order in council to cover the situation. The order was prepared but no action was taken on the request.

Rather than issue postponements, especially when these should not have been issued to British subjects who were not acceptable for military training although they were not exempt under the regulations, the decision was made by NSS in January 1944 to turn this problem over to the army and henceforth a rejection certificate was to be issued by the commanding or district officer.[35]

This NSS decision thus placed the burden back in the hands of the army to deal with. Partly as a result of this shuffling about of responsibility, many Chinese Canadians remained in the labour market and, possibly because of postponements and rejection certificates, were finding employment opportunities hitherto denied them. This change in British Columbia was felt to be unfair to 'white' Canadians because on layoffs in shipyards, "the Canadian on deferment is the first to go, while the Chinaman is allowed to remain in his employment." The complaint, similar to the one from the RCAF on the advantages enjoyed by Chinese Canadians in British Columbia because they were not called up under NRMA, was sent on to NSS and does not appear to have elicited any comment from Ottawa.[36]

The most important change in military service for Chinese Canadians occurred in the spring of 1944 when an NSS memo noted that "fifteen Canadian Chinese [are] wanted for dangerous duties." The interest in Chinese Canadians for special duty with SOE had begun late in 1943 when F.W. Kendall first approached Ottawa. Kendall, on the advice of British Security Coordination since the first recruits for SOE from Canada had been civilian Yugoslavs, at first had tried to recruit civilian Chinese, and Ottawa had also made this attempt to locate civilians through NSS files. The memo refers to the first group Kendall recruited; they were located by the Director of Military Intelligence already in the Canadian Army. It was not long before Kendall reported to London on the calibre of these men and the British War Office exerted pressure on Ottawa to make more of these special men available.[37]

Meanwhile in May 1944, unaware of these secret arrangements, Manson continued his campaign. Since there was now a shortage of men for the army, and many Chinese Canadians were requesting permits to allow them to enlist in United States forces, he wondered if the CWC might now reconsider the calling of Canadians of Chinese racial origin. Manson referred again to the formation of a Chinese Battalion, which might provide the answer to some of these hesitations. He knew the question of the franchise would have to be dealt with when they came back, if they were called up, but since men were needed, a change should be made.[38] Only a few of the men who enlisted in American forces have been located; certainly they did not enlist in the United States in anything like the numbers suggested by Manson. NDHQ now thought that perhaps the time had come to call up Canadian Chinese and asked for the views of NSS, which was in agreement.[39]

Although it appears that Manson, NSS, and the Canadian Army were instrumental in bringing about the change in enrollment of Chinese Canadians under NRMA, this change could not come about until the CWC altered its stand, as the Minister of National Defence had found. This change was not based on pressure from below but pressure from across the Atlantic. Sometime during May the CWC reversed its decision not to call up Chinese Canadians under NRMA.[40] It is interesting to note that the memo with regard to the 15 Chinese Canadians "wanted for dangerous duties" is in the same file as Manson's correspondence.

The army advised NSS on 8 June 1944 to amend Secret Memorandum No. 1; the Canadian Army was changing its instructions so that all Chinese regardless of nationality could be enlisted and all but Chinese nationals enrolled under NRMA.[41]

Canadian Chinese were still included in the Allied Alien category in the army's circular letter of 5 July 1944. They were still to be vetted, and the sensitive areas remained as originally described. In addition they were not to be accepted for any civil or military course leading to a commission without reference to NDHQ (DMI) for the usual security check and approval. Royal Canadian Electrical and Mechanical Engineers was added 24 July as a restricted area "in the handling and repair of secret equipment only." Another update 30 September 1944 included Employment with Civil Affairs as a sensitive or restricted area.[42]

The question of the franchise had not been lost sight of. A partial letter (signature page missing) dated 21 August to Maj.-Gen. George R. Pearkes, GOCinC, Pacific Command, regarding the call up of Canadian Chinese, referred to the fact that the "franchise is not being granted to the Chinese in this province, and there is a section of the Chinese who are anxious to take this chance to stir up action against government legislation."[43] The note is provocative but appeared not to be a valid comment on the situation; the Chinese Canadian Association in Vancouver was actively campaigning on the franchise issue, but this was handled in the usual manner of the Chinese in that speeches to gain support were given to church groups and service organizations.[44]

During August 1944, Pacific Command again raised the issue of forming a separate Chinese unit that could be employed in the Pacific with "special Canadian Units such as No. 1 Special Wireless Company, with British or Australian Armies, or with such special outfits as Kendall's." At a meeting held 2 September 1944, agreement was reached that the best way to handle the men was in a special training centre and pool, which would be a good way to use Chinese Canadian officers. Two days later Pacific Command was advised that these men were being recruited for the War Office.[45]

The idea of a separate training centre was rejected by National Defence in spite of suggested "difficulties arising from racial characteristics and language considerations." Only those who spoke and understood English should be accepted into the army. Pearkes knew very well that all but about three or four of the 13 Chinese Canadians trained in the Okanagan had received Cantonese lessons because English was their normal language. He had visited the camp one July weekend. There was no clarification of what the "racial characteristics" were that might require a separate training centre.

National Defence felt that Chinese Canadians should not be "treated in a different way from the normal soldier serving in the Canadian Army." Those already in the Canadian Army and in the RCAF "have had no difficulty in taking the training and have been treated the same as other soldiers in being selected for NCO and officer training." There was no need to consider them a "special class," and on a national basis it would "be a good thing to mix them with their fellow Canadians." The estimated number available was now lowered to about 500 in the "Vancouver Division."[46]

Chinese Canadians had been trained in regular training camps and with other Canadians from 1939. The new groups destined for India and Australia were also trained in the regular camps before setting out for their destinations. There is no record of any 'incidents'; rather, there is at least one instructor who still remembers them with warm regard.

Events did not change much in 1945. The army re-issued earlier consolidations regarding aliens as late as 20 January, but there was no change in the enlistment and enrollment of Chinese Canadians. The soldier was still not advised that he was an alien nor of his status.[47] In the spring of 1945 the BC legislature did, however, grant the franchise to Chinese Canadians then in the services and to those still surviving from the Great War.

Chinese Canadians do not appear to have moved out of the 'Allied Alien' and 'special categories,' as far as the Canadian

Army was concerned, throughout the war years. Their full legal status as Canadians was not adjusted until the Canadian Citizenship Act of 1947.

Japanese Canadians had not been deprived of their legal status by an Exclusion Act, but the CWC did not relax its views on military service for this group until the War Office requested Japanese linguists.

Both Australia and the British War Office had requested Japanese linguists in 1944 but the CWC refused to approve their enlistment in the Canadian Army; instead, in October 1944 they stated "that such personnel might be enlisted in Canada in the Armed Forces of other United Nations." In January 1945 the chief of general staff again recommended their enlistment for this purpose and finally, 17 January, NDHQ was authorized to accept 100. There was a request for additional linguists in April and an additional 150 were authorized by the CWC. Well over 100 were recruited for Southeast Asia and the Pacific in 1945 as language specialists. Among them were one or two Chinese Canadians who were also Japanese linguists.

And in spite of the great many secret memoranda stating that neither Chinese Canadians nor Chinese nationals were to be called up all across Canada, not just in British Columbia, they were called up under NRMA in all but the western provinces from the first call of 1940. Evidence for this came from many of the men interviewed who were enrolled under NRMA, and from letters in the files.[48]

Whether general service or called up under NRMA, several Chinese Canadians served in Newfoundland in the anti-aircraft batteries; no order in council appears to have been issued for their employment in this British colony. Some NRMA men were members of regiments escorting German POWs from New York to Canada and an order in council was issued. For the regiments that took part in the Kiska invasion in 1943, an order in council was issued, possibly because about half of the members were NRMA men. In spite of the definition of these areas as being within Home Defence by NDHQ,

Ottawa approached the matter cautiously when Canadian soldiers ventured onto American soil.

The original intent of NRMA was to give all eligible males 30 days military training; this training was extended in 1941 to four months and the men remained in the army in Home Defence. The 30-day men were also recalled.

During the late fall of 1944 and early 1945, with the infantry reinforcement position in Italy and Northwest Europe reaching crises proportions, all NRMA men were subject to compulsory military service 'overseas.' The Act had been amended for this purpose in August 1942, but the authority had not been exercised until this time. Nearly 13,000 NRMA men of the 16,000 approved were actually sent overseas in early 1945, under order in council of November 1944. Almost 2,500 were taken on strength of various units; 69 were killed in action.[49] At this time there were many Chinese Canadian soldiers who were general service but posted to Home Defence units; some, who were NRMA soldiers, turned active and volunteered for the Pacific war after Germany had been defeated.

Compulsory military service was resented by some Canadian Chinese but appears to have been based on the lack of civil rights, especially in the case of those from British Columbia, on having paid the Head Tax for those naturalized, and on being refused when they volunteered for service in the RCAF and the RCN. Some were refused when they volunteered for the Canadian Army as well since instructions from National Defence were not always very clear. Being refused when they volunteered appears to have produced the greatest sense of injustice. As one young candidate who had been refused for the air force put it: "A dead German pilot won't know the race of the person who shot him down."

Payment of the Head Tax was considered an injustice whether they were naturalized or Chinese nationals. A young Chinese national from Belleville, Ont, wrote to the mobilization board in Kingston in February 1945, saying that in return for the refund of the $500 Head Tax, he would be "only too glad to enlist in the Canadian Army." He had checked with the Chinese Consulate and had been advised that Chinese nationals were not liable for military service. Further, he felt that Canada "exacts from us Chinese the highest price for admission in comparison to other countries" and payment of the Head Tax had greatly contributed to inequality in this country.[50]

In spite of all the restrictions, Chinese Canadians saw service in several Canadian units in the European theatre as well as in Home Defence, and very rarely did two serve in the same unit. Because they were so scattered, it is not possible to discuss them as a group. A few, therefore, have been selected and a brief account of some of their activities and the units in which they served are related below. Some of their post-war occupations are also detailed to show how far they had moved from the traditional occupations of pre-war days. It also shows that discrimination was not based on ability.

Royal Canadian Army Medical Corps

Capt. Ross Jung from Victoria, enlisted 23 July 1942, after graduating from the University of Toronto in 1937 and internship followed by surgical residency at the Casualty

– The Journal Courier Jan. 13/76
Dr. Ross Jung

Hospital in Washington, DC. He went to England early in 1943 and served in North Africa from June of that year. He returned to England in 1945 and was able to meet his brother, Arthur, at Skellingthorpe before returning to Canada where he was demobilized.

Maj. Ross Jung then joined the US Army Medical Corps serving in Shanghai. He was on detached assignment with the Central Intelligence Agency as a physician in classified duties, and during the Korean War, he was recalled by the US Army to serve on special medical duties. Released to the CIA in 1953, Ross served overseas with this agency until 1959. He practiced in Washington until his death in 1976.

Armand Wong, RCAMC, from Montreal, went overseas as stretcher bearer; he took part in the Normandy D-Day landings, serving to the end of the war in Northwest Europe. Armand is the brother of Marcel Wong, RCN(VR).

Capt. Wilson Lee from Montreal enlisted in the RCAMC in 1942 and went on active service after interning at the Montreal General Hospital in 1943. He completed officers' training at Brockville, and additional training at Camp Borden; he spent 1944 as medical officer for the 25th Anti-Aircraft Regiment, Royal Canadian Artillery, in Newfoundland in Atlantic Command. Wilson then went to England early in 1945 and served as medical officer attached to Canadian Infantry Training Centres.

On VE-Day, Wilson was at Aldershot. He then volunteered for the Pacific War in 'Tiger Force' in a hospital unit that was to link up with the US Army. VJ-Day came before this unit could be used in the Pacific, and Wilson returned to No. 4 Military District at Longueuil, Que, his home depot. He was posted for a short time to the Montreal Military Hospital, Queen Mary Road, and received his discharge in May 1946.

For the following three years, Wilson took post-graduate studies in paediatrics at the Children's Memorial Hospital, Montreal, and the Children's Hospital of Halifax. In 1950, Wilson moved to Chatham, Ont, as a consultant in paediatrics. He retired in 1986.

Theodore Chang, from Vancouver, enlisted in COTC in 1944 and at the age of 23 was an honours graduate from the University of Toronto in February 1946; he had also won the silver medal for general proficiency in the Faculty of Medicine. He was too late to be an active participant in the war. Ted's brother, Robert, served in the army, and three uncles enlisted in the RCAF.[51]

Born in Kwangtung Province, China, 10 July 1915, Capt. So Won Leung came to Canada in the 1920s. His family first settled in Edmonton, then moved to Vancouver. Dr. Leung graduated in medicine from the University of Toronto. He was commissioned 11 January 1944 and served in various postings in Canada to the end of the war.

Capt. Henry Lore, originally from Victoria, enlisted in COTC while attending the University of Toronto. He was rejected for active duty by both the Canadian Army and RCAF because he was married and had several small children. Dr. Lore practiced in Toronto and was active in the Chinese Freemasons in that city. Henry was the brother of William K.L. Lore who served in the RCN.

Capt. William Andrew Wong from London, Ont, enlisted in 1943 in the COTC at

Dr. William A. Wong

the University of Western Ontario, and received his commission 1 March 1944. After specialist psychiatric training, Bill served in the Canadian Army, first at Gordon Head, and then Regina.

Royal Canadian Artillery

Peter Lee, A.61469, from Windsor, Ont, served in the 24th Light Anti-Aircraft Battery. In England, he became a chemical warfare instructor. Peter is the brother of Ben (Perth Regiment) and Edward (No. 404 Squadron, RCAF).

Pte. William Yee, from Toronto, took his basic training at Petawawa and then was posted to the 14th Field Regiment, RCA, in the 3rd Infantry Division. Like many others, Willie had been asked to switch to mess duties but he declined.

On D-Day, the 14th Field and the 19th Army Field Regiment took part in the Normandy assault at Bernière-sur-Mer, three LCTs (landing craft tank) abreast with three in staggered formation behind in support of the 8th Infantry Brigade at 7:30 am on 6 June when the self-propelled 105s opened up. After shelling the beach for 30 minutes, the LCTs then put out to sea again while the infantry stormed ashore; guns of the 14th Field landed at 9:25.

The self-propelled 105 was a 105 mm gun howitzer mounted on a tank chassis, carrying a heavy machine gun in a pulpit-shaped top mounting. It was called a 'Priest.' After the beaches were secured and the army moved inland, the SP guns were exchanged for 25-pounders. For Operation *Totalize* in August 1944, Lt.-Gen. G.G. Simmonds used the 'Priests,' withdrawn from the 3rd Canadian Division, as personnel carriers. The guns were removed and protective armour-plate added to the openings. These armoured personnel carriers were called "Kangaroos" using the name of the Advanced Workshop Detachment, which had worked extended hours to prepare them. They were also informally called 'Unfrocked Priests.'

The 14th Field Regiment gave active support throughout the cmpaign in Northwest Europe to the end of the war.

Some years after the war, Willie Yee helped to raise money to erect a tank of the 1st Hussars into a monument to the infantrymen of the 8th Brigade, which the 14th Field Regiment had supported on D-Day. The tank was discovered in 1970 or 1971 when it became tangled in a fisherman's net off the Normandy beaches.

Gunner Robert Yuen, D.147175, from Montreal, served in the RCA in the 2nd Infantry Division. The regiment was equipped with 25-pounders. Artillery of the 2nd Division arrived in Normandy the first week of July 1944 and engaged its first target on the 13th near Carpiquet. Caen was next and Canadian guns formed a half circle around the area.

The Canadian aspect of operation *Goodwood, Atlantic,* was to carry the attack on to Verrières Ridge commanding the Caen-Falaise road. *Goodwood* ended 21 July, but the artillery continued in support of the infantry repulsing German counter-attacks. Robert remained with the 2nd Division Artillery until the war officially ended 8 May. He was then repatriated and demobilized.

From Victoria, Gunner George Chow, K.25810, enlisted in August 1940 as gunner with the 16th AA Battery, in the 3rd LAA Regiment. In Vancouver, the unit manned the guns at Stanley Park and Yorke Island. This island, located to the north of Hardwicke Island, barred entry to Vancouver through the Johnstone Strait. The 17th LAA Battery from Calgary, the 15th from Winnipeg, and the 16th, made up the 3rd LAA Regiment.

In December, the regiment was sent to Windsor and from there to Debert, NS. In February of the following year, they arrived in England. They were posted successively to a variety of sites in the south but they were mainly concentrated around Colchester. Although short of 40 mm Bofors guns, they soon qualified by sharing those available among the batteries and regiments. In August 1941, a troop from the 16th shot down a Junkers Ju88 fighter bomber on the Essex coast. In Wales, George took commando training in 1943 as well as additional training in firing 5.5 howitzers.

As a unit of the 2nd Infantry Division, the 3rd LAA Regiment landed in Normandy on D+30 and fired its first round at Caen in air defence of the corps gun area at Carpiquet, joined by the 4th and 6th LAA Regiments. In this action, 15 enemy planes were shot down. A few days later, the 3rd LAA Regiment and a Bren gunner of the 4th Medium AA Regiment also shot down two Spitfires that were strafing the area. 'Friendly' fire and bombing were not uncommon. The turmoil around Caen-Falaise made it difficult for aircrew to identify bodies of troops on the ground. After firing directional tracer on 8 August, seven members of the 16th Battery were killed in bombing by Fortresses in Operation *Totalize*.

In September, a troop of the 3rd LAA with their 40 mm Bofors in a ground role, plus a 17-pounder of the 2nd Anti-Tank Regiment, killed the crew of a camouflaged gun position, and then fired through slits of the command post in 15 foot concrete walls to force the German surrender at Nieuport on the Channel coast.

At the Albert Canal, for the beginning of the Battle of the Scheldt on 1 October, the 3rd LAA gave support to the 8th Reconnaissance Regiment (14th Canadian Hussars). One battery and troop of the 3rd LAA succeeded in silencing both an 88 and an infantry gun. The 88 was a dual purpose German anti-aircraft, anti-tank gun; it became famous as an anti-tank gun in North Africa, Russia, and Northwest Europe. At the Reichswald on 8 February 1945, the 3rd and 4th LAA Regiments contributed their quota to the massive barrage before the crossing of the Rhine.

From Cleve, Germany, George Chow went on leave to England and was there on 8 May 1945, VE-Day, but after returning to the continent, he volunteered for Tiger Force. He had just returned to England when VJ-Day was proclaimed; he was repatriated to Canada 31 August 1945 and was demobilized in October. George enlisted in the Reserve in 1953 in the 43rd Heavy AA Regiment based in Vancouver, and served until 1965, retiring as battery sergeant major.

Simon Yuen, from Montreal, served in the 2nd Medium Regiment, RCA (Reserve), C Battery. After VE-Day, he transferred to the Chinese Army in New York City where an interpreter who spoke good English was needed. Mr. K.C. Lee of Universal Trading Corporation (1933) telephoned Simon, who had dual citizenship,[52] to handle logistics.

Stanley Chong, M.3815, was born 24 May 1914 in Vancouver. He returned to China for some of his schooling and then back to Vancouver and school again. He attended high school in Edmonton and remained there, enlisting in Edmonton 24 February 1941.

Stanley Chong

Stanley was posted to the 44th Field Battery of the 13th Field Regiment in the 3rd Infantry Division. The regiment had been formed at Shilo 14 October 1940 from the 22nd (Gleichen), the 44th (Prince Albert), and

Stanley Chong,

2nd from right

the 78th (Red Deer) Batteries all of Alberta. The regiment reached Debert, NS, by February 1941, and practiced on the ranges at Tracadie, NB. On to England by November, they were stationed in central Sussex.

For *Overlord,* the regiment trained at Billingshurst, near Horsham, and in Scotland, with gunners firing their 25-pounders on land targets from moving craft, each battery with two LCTs and one troop on each craft with

four guns lashed to the deck. The 25-pounder was a gun howitzer used as the standard British field artillery piece. Canadian and British weapons and equipment were usually interchangeable.

The regiment returned to the Bournemouth area to undergo assault training by brigade groups with the RAF and Force "J", the naval contingent. Practice assaults continued to the last week of April 1944. The RCA

Stanley Chong,

2nd from right

was to fire the beach barrage from the LCTs. During the invasion, they were to use SP 105 mm howitzers. The unit was bombed by German aircraft 19 May; a direct hit resulted in equipment losses.

Because of ill health, Stanley Chong was unable to proceed with the regiment on D-Day and was repatriated to Canada and demobilized in Calgary 1 November 1944. Stanley's "Discharge Certificate" notes a scar on his forehead. It is not known whether he was wounded during the German attack on 19 May; the regimental history states only that there were no fatal casualties.

From Calgary, Bombardier Frank Lung M.4328, enlisted in 1944 and was posted to the RCA. He was sent to Nova Scotia for his training and was stationed at Elkins Barrack. At the same camp but in a different troop was Willie Chong, also in the

artillery. Frank was on overseas drafts three times, but each time his name was removed with no explanation given. Before his discharge, Frank was transferred as clerk to the quartermaster stores. Frank's brother, Alex, M.4868, served in the Infantry Corps in Home Defence.

Alex Lung

Royal Canadian Electrical and Mechanical Engineers

Born in Vancouver 16 May 1919, but raised at Alert Bay, Cpl. Fong Bing (Frank) Wong, K.45536, enlisted the end of May 1942. After basic training at Vernon, he was posted to Barriefield. He spent two months in Ottawa in 1943 and was trained as storeman with RCEME. In February 1943, Frank Wong sailed to Greenock, Scotland, and joined the reinforcement unit at Aldershot. He was posted to the 1st Army Troops Workshop, RCEME, at Chatham, Surrey.

Frank Lung

In late July 1944, the unit crossed to Normandy and from Caen moved forward behind the artillery units providing repairs to artillery pieces (the 5.5" and 7.2") and vehicles, then crossed the Seine to Ghent, Belgium, and on to Arnhem and Nijmegen in Holland. In February 1945 they crossed the Rhine for four weeks in Germany, then returned to Nijmegen.

Frank welcomed his leave in Paris and was there on VE-Day, 8 May. While still on leave, he learned that his buddy had been killed when he stepped on a land mine two days after the war had ended. Frank returned to England in the fall of 1945 and was repatriated to Canada in January 1946, arriving in New York on the *Queen Elizabeth*. He was demobilized in Vancouver in April 1946.

Frank's younger brother Bing Chew Wong, K.5323, called up in 1944, received his training at Gordon Head. Bing volunteered for Tiger Force but before this force could be used, the war ended in the Pacific. The army counsellor suggested teaching as a career but at 5'4" and 110 pounds, Bing did not think he could cope with 6' students. Bing took an accounting course instead, and out of the 30 graduates, he was the only one not hired by the end of the summer. The counsellor finally located a job for him, and Bing says he is "very grateful to the Army for all the help they gave me." Bing now owns his own accounting firm on Pender Street in Vancouver, situated within a block of his birthplace.

Harry S. Woo, born in Montreal, was called up under NRMA in 1942 and was posted to RCEME; he turned active early in 1944. In the fall of 1944 he was sent overseas and was in England about a week before being rushed over to the continent by fast boat because of the Ardennes offensive. His group landed at Ostend and were rushed forward to guard the bridge at Nijmegen. When the danger ended because the German tanks ran out of gasoline and were unable to capture Allied supplies, Harry continued with the recovery work in Belgium and Holland.

Two days after VE-Day, Harry volunteered for Tiger Force and two or three weeks later, returned to Canada with the US 82nd Airborne on the *Queen Mary,* which docked in New York. When the war in the Pacific ended in August, Harry received his discharge and later moved to the United States where he still resides.

Frank Lee, also from Montreal, joined the RCCS (Reserve) a year or two before the war began, while he was living in Ottawa. Frank had taken a course in radio communications given by the signal corps and was well qualified. In September 1939 Frank tried to enlist as an NCO in the army and then in the RCN as petty officer, relying on his "years of reserve training in the Royal Canadian Corps of Signals." Frank was turned down in both cases "with no offer to accept me without non-commissioned officer status." Instead, he was advised that "the Army and Navy did not accept Chinese." Frank wrote a letter of protest to Mackenzie King, who avoided an outright statement or decision in his reply.

Frank Lee then attended Queen's University in Kingston, winning nine scholarships during his undergraduate years, including three for public speaking. He enlisted in the COTC and graduated from Queen's with first-class honours in May 1945. After commissioning as 2nd lieutenant in RCEME, Lieut. Frank Lee was selected as one of a team of 14 or 15 top students "from universities across Canada for elite RCEME assignment to Far East theatre of war." Training followed at Barriefield, but war in the Pacific ended before training finished and Frank was demobilized 17 October 1945.

Frank taught for a year at Queen's as an electrical engineering instructor. In 1946-47, he worked at General Electric in Schenectady, New York, as test engineer associated with the research and development labs before going on to the Massachusetts Institute of Technology to obtain his master's degree while still employed as an electrical engineering instructor. From 1949 to 1955, Frank worked in Halifax as assistant chief engineer at Cossor (Canada) Limited. He then joined Canadian Aviation Electronics in Montreal as manager of the Engineering Research Department, as project engineer for a flight simulator model, as chief project engineer for military simulators, and as programme manager for all military simulators.

On loan to the Boeing Company, in 1959-60 Frank moved to Seattle in charge of the CAE Missile Engineering Group. He joined Lockheed Aircraft Corporation in Burbank, California, in 1966, working on a variety of projects, including development of avionics for the Lockheed L-1011 aircraft, and work on flight controls for classified military projects. Frank retired in 1984 and still lives in California.[53]

Sgt. James Lee, B.548346, from Brantford, Ont, was called up in 1942 and took his advanced training at Barriefield. Jim was posted to RCOC as armourer until 1944 when he was transferred to RCEME; he served as armourer from 1944 to 1945 in RCEME, stationed in Newfoundland and Halifax.

– courtesy George Kwong

Back l to r
   2nd - Richard Mar, 1st Cdn. Para. Btn.
   6th - On Lim, CAC
   7th - George Y. Kwong, RCASC/CIC
   8th - 'Mech' Lee
   12th - Billy Der

Front l to r
   1st - Hank Hum, RCASC
   4th - Tom Wong, West Novas & C&Y
   5th - Frank Lee, RCEME
   6th - Edward Lee (uncle of Bobby Lee, QOR)

Photo was taken in the summer of 1945 in Toronto

1st Canadian Parachute Battalion

Cpl. Richard Mar from Victoria was the only Chinese Canadian to serve in the 1st Canadian Parachute Battalion. He enlisted in 1942. Richard received his parachute wings at Fort Benning, Georgia, on 10 February 1943.

The battalion arrived in England in July 1943 and formed part of the 6th British Airborne Division. The 6th Airborne was dropped in Normandy on the eve of D-Day, and dropped again during the Rhine crossing. Richard was unable to jump on D-Day, but was with his battalion in the aggressive patrolling during the Ardennes offensive from 2 January 1945. Richard also took part in the drop for the Rhine crossing on 23/24 March, in the 6th British Airborne Division which functioned with the US 17th Airborne Division.

After the armies had crossed the Rhine, the 6th Airborne passed under the command of the 8th British Corps, 2nd Army. The battalion crossed the Dortmund-Ems Canal, suffering several casualties before they reached Minden. One hundred reinforcements, many from First Special Service Force (disbanded 5 December 1944), were absorbed 1 and 2 April. Members of the 1st Canadian Special Service Battalion had been the Canadian contingent of the US-Canada Force and together, the forces of the two countries were called First Special Service Force or the "North Americans."[54]

Still with the Grenadier Guards, they passed through Minden, took the village of Kutenhausen, where more reinforcements and much needed supplies arrived, and went on to Wolpinghausen with the 4th Battalion Grenadier Guards. At Wunsdorf and crossing the Leine River at Ricklingen there was heavy fighting. They rested at Luthe and then went on to Celle on 14 April; they reached Eschede the following day. Three days later, transported by 6th British Tank Brigade, they arrived at Riestedt and assisted in taking the town. They crossed the Elbe at Boisenburg 29 April, again encountering fierce fighting. On 1 May, command of the division passed to the US 18th Airborne Corps under 2nd British Army.

Their last objective was to reach Wismar on the Baltic Sea before the Russians, and to prevent a German withdrawal into Denmark and Norway to join the army already there. This move would allow the Germans to surrender to the British rather than the Russians, a move the Germans considered desirable. The Danish government had banned the Communist party in 1941 and it had also signed the Anti-Comintern Pact. It was necessary, therefore, to prevent the Russians from entering the country.

Speed was essential and the race began. Boisenburg was taken; joined by the Scots Greys, they took Wittenberg with little opposition. German troops, fully armed, lined the roads as the tanks drove through the crowds. The number of Germans steadily increased but no real opposition appeared until a roadblock was met just outside Wismar. The city was entered cautiously and the battalion established itself; its main problem was receiving Germans who were fleeing the Russians.

The battalion met the Russians 2 and 3 May, and while negotiations were in progress, a cease-fire was called on the 4th for the following day. The war officially ended on the 8th. The 1st Canadian Parachute Battalion had gone the deepest into Germany, and Wismar was the most easterly city reached by any Canadian troops. Withdrawn to England, the battalion sailed on the *Ile de France* for Halifax in June. Richard arrived in Victoria 29 June 1945 where he was demobilized.

Royal Canadian Corps of Signals

Marshall Chow, M.6337, from Edmonton, enlisted in October 1941. After basic training at Camrose, and wireless training at Calgary, Edmonton, and Kingston (Vimy Barracks), he sailed for Europe. He served as wireless operator between 2nd Armoured Brigade Headquarters and the regiments during the European campaign. Marshall Chow was repatriated in October 1945 and demobilized in Calgary in January 1946.

L/Cpl. Diamond Quon, M.9074, from Calgary, also served in RCCS "with the 1st AA Brigade Signals" in the 1st Canadian Corps under commanding officer Maj. B. Lake. They were stationed at Kingston for basic training. After they arrived in England, additional training took place in Sussex, where they were billeted in a private home.

– courtesy Dora Foo

L/Cpl Diamond Quon

Diamond went to Italy with the 1st Canadian Corps in the fall of 1943 and served throughout the Italian campaign. The 1st Corps left Italy 13 February 1945, travelling nearly 700 miles through Marseilles to Belgium. The Corps became operational just north of Nijmegen on 15 March. Diamond Quon was killed 12 March 1945; he was 23 years old and is buried in the Nederweert War Cemetery, Holland.[55]

Canadian Infantry Corps

Pte. Benny Lee, A.117827, from Windsor, brother of Edward and Peter, enlisted directly out of high school, received 30 days basic training, and was sent directly to The Perth Regiment in Italy. The Perths formed part of the 11th Infantry Brigade in the 5th Armoured Division, which had arrived in the theatre late in 1943. The brigade saw action in January 1944 before the rest of the division had been fully equipped.

After a year's campaigning in Italy, by 4 February 1945, the 5th Armoured received notice of the move to Northwest Europe. Operation *Goldflake* began 13 February. The Canadians from Italy continued to arrive in Belgium from mid-March on. By the end of March the 5th Armoured re-entered the line south of Arnhem to drive north to seal off western Holland at the IJsselmeer (Zuider Zee). Ben Lee fought with the regiment to the end of the war. He was demobilized on his return to Canada.

Young Wing Hay, K.57403, from Port Alberni, enlisted in 1940, and served with the 1st Battalion, The Canadian Scottish Regiment (Princess Mary's). While waiting to go overseas in 1941, Wing won the light-weight championship of the 3rd Division at Debert. He was also a professional featherweight boxer, ranking third on the Pacific coast. Wing was belligerent not only in the ring and would accept no slight, real or imagined, as to his racial origin. He was promoted and demoted regularly because of unprovoked brawling. In spite of this, Wing was regarded as a good soldier and was popular in his regiment.

The Canadian Scottish arrived in England in 1941 brigaded with The Royal Winnipeg Rifles and The Regina Rifle Regiment to form the 7th Infantry Brigade in the 3rd Infantry Division. Wing landed with the regiment at Juno Beach on D-Day and fought through all the battles until VE-Day. In a village near Caen, he captured twelve Germans single-handed. Wing Hay **Young** was wounded 12 October 1944. He returned to Port Alberni after the war where he was later killed in an automobile accident.

Pte. Ivan G. Lee, D.143578, from Montreal, served with The South Saskatchewan Regiment. The 1st SSR formed a part of the 6th Brigade of the 2nd Infantry Division. Ivan Lee was killed in action 27 September 1944, and is buried in Schoonselhof Cemetery, Antwerp, Belgium.

Also with the South Saskatchewans was Lieut. S. Fraser Lee, from Regina, born 24 February 1922. He joined the 1st SSR in Normandy on 8 July 1944 as reinforcement lieutenant.

Fraser Lee had enlisted in January 1941 and worked in the recruiting end as a medical orderly "because I could type" until 1943. He then took officer training at Three Rivers, Que, before going to England as a reinforcement. Posted to the Saskatchewans, Fraser joined the battalion in Normandy arriving after the first attack outside Caen. He was in charge of D Company during the brutal battle at Forêt de la Londe.[56] The regiment fought in the Channel Ports area, at the Antwerp-Turnhout Canal, Lochtenboerg, the Scheldt, South Beveland, and in *Blockbuster* in the Rhineland.

Maj. Fraser Lee fought with the battalion to the end of the war "except for six weeks when I was training NCOs for the division." He was confirmed as major 15 October 1944, having been commissioned as captain only five weeks before. After demobilization, he attended university using his war gratuities, and retired in 1987 as vice president of Saskatchewan Tele-communications.

Wilfred Bing Tong Seto, from Vancouver. joined COTC at UBC and enlisted for active service. He took his basic training at Camp Gordon Head only after being advised that he was in 'special category.' Wilfred had been a strong supporter of a Chinese Battalion but, in spite of encouragement from various elements in British Columbia, Ottawa rejected the proposal.

Lieutenant Seto went to Italy as reinforcement officer for The Seaforth Highlanders. He arrived in Philippeville, Algeria, in October 1943, in the same convoy carrying Harry Lim and Bill Lowe but they did not meet. He went on to Italy to join the Seaforths, brigaded with Princess Patricia's Canadian Light Infantry and The Loyal Edmonton Regiment in the 2nd Infantry Brigade, but the brigadier would not accept him. He was told that he was not only a reinforcement but he was Chinese and the men would not follow him. The brigadier suggested he return to Canada where he would be of more use in Pacific Command.

After returning to Canada, Wilfred attended the S-20 Japanese Language School in Vancouver. After the war, Wilfred helped organize Pacific Unit 280 of the Army, Navy, and Air Force Veterans in Canada, the only Chinese Canadian Veterans' unit in Canada.

Pte. George Hong, A.117703, from Windsor, served with The West Nova Scotia Regiment. He was killed in Italy, 8 September 1944, and is buried at Ancona War Cemetery, on the Adriatic. George was 18 years old. His older brother, Joseph, had been shot down over France in May of the same year.

– *NAC PA 180435*
Major S. Fraser Lee

Pte. George Yet Kwong, K.1813, from Revelstoke, born 15 February 1924, enlisted late 1943 at Camp Little Mountain in Vancouver. He received his basic and advanced training at Camrose and Red Deer. In November a troop train picked up men from across Canada at Red Deer, Edmonton, Saskatoon, Kenora, and arrived in Debert.

They sailed from Halifax on the *Nieuw Amsterdam,* arriving in England the first week of July 1944. George was briefly posted to The Algonquin Regiment (five days) while at Aldershot. He took further training in Yorkshire for three weeks and was then posted to the Royal Canadian Army Service Corps. He served in Group 83 in France and Belgium, handling gasoline and 40 mm shells.

When infantry reinforcements became acute in September 1944, "officers and NCOs went through the rank and file behind the lines looking for surplus personnel." Many potential infantry recruits were gleaned from anti-aircraft batteries since the German Air Force was not as powerful as it had been. Some of the Army Service Corps members, including George, volunteered for the infantry early in October 1944.

Posted to the South Saskatchewans, George lasted as an infantryman for less than a week. He was badly wounded in Belgium, 21 October, and received medical attention at the No. 1 Advanced Dressing Station on the outskirts of Bruges, as well as treatment at a second Field Dressing Station. Taken by ambulance to the airport, George was too late to catch the plane just leaving, which was fortunate for him; that plane crashed killing all aboard.

George was evacuated on the second DC-3 and landed at Folkestone. He spent one week at a British Army Hospital, No. 2 Field Dressing Station. He was then moved to No. 9 Canadian General Hospital at Horsham, and later to No. 1 Roman Way, Convalescent Hospital, Colchester, for the next two months. Transferred to No. 21 Canadian General Hospital, just north of London, George met his future wife, Janet Grant, through S/Sgt. Lai Sham (Sammy) Mee. This hospital was operated by a medical team from New Westminster.

George was repatriated to Canada 25 May 1945 on the hospital ship SS *Laetitia.* He then volunteered for Tiger Force, but "even my PULHEMS says I'm eligible for immediate discharge." PULHEMS was a medical classification system introduced in 1941; the word stood for Physique, Upper and Lower extremities, Hearing, Eyes, Mental capacity and Stability. The category for a general duty infantryman originally was 1111221 but category changes were made as the war progressed.

In spite of his classification, George was accepted, shipped to Toronto in July 1945 and spent some time at Camp Borden. When the Pacific War ended in August 1945, it took some time for the authorities to bring the files and George together. During this waiting period, George took additional treatment at

George Y. Kwong

Sunnybrook Hospital in Toronto. When the files reached Vancouver in January 1946, George was located in Toronto and received his discharge 18 February 1946. He then spent seven months as an out-patient at the veterans' hospital in Vancouver.

George's wife, Janet Grant, was born in China, sold by her mother, ran away from the couple who had mistreated her, and was adopted by Richard William Grant, MC, and his wife. Grant was the high commissioner of Malaya at Labuan Island during 1925-26. Janet, educated in England, was a nurse at a London children's hospital when Sammy Mee introduced her to George. Despite her British passport, Janet could not enter Canada to marry George until after her adoptive father intervened on her behalf, and she was allowed into the country 31 August 1947.

Tom Wong, B.131675, originally from Victoria, was called up in Toronto in late 1942 and turned active. Shipped to England, Tom was immediately sent on to Philippeville, Algeria, as a reinforcement.

Posted to The West Nova Scotia Regiment, they "started at the toe of Italy" in September 1943 and began "working our way up the country." In the attack before Castel Di Sangro, at Point 1009, on the Upper Sangro, 22 November 1943, Tom was captured when Heidrich's 1st Parachute Division let his platoon climb into the area before the Bernhard Line (which runs north of the Winter Line to south of Ortona) and then fired killing the platoon commander and four others before capturing the rest. With 15 others, Tom was a POW from November 1943 to late April 1945. He was released to The Carleton & York Regiment two days before the war ended in Italy. Back in England by 5 May, Tom was repatriated to Canada and demobilized,

Pte. Fred Ho, B.37564, served with The Irish Regiment of Canada in the 11th Infantry Brigade. Fred died as a result of wounds 29 January 1944 at Orsogna, Italy (just west of Ortona), and is buried in Moro River Cemetery, Italy.

Lin Fat **Ho**, from Vancouver, enlisted 3 September 1939, aged 16, under the name Fred Howe or Hoe. His father had been the caretaker of the Chinese opera theatre located on Columbia Street. Fred went overseas with the Seaforth Highlanders in the summer of 1940. The Seaforths took part in operation *Husky,* the invasion of Sicily, 10 July 1943. Fred was with the regiment through to Ortona where the Canadians took the city 21-27 December. Fred was killed in this action and is buried in Ortona (Moro River) Cemetery. Although Fred is known in Vancouver, no other information concerning him is available and his grave is not verified by the Commonwealth War Graves Commission, probably because the name he used is uncertain; this may have been Fred Ho of the Irish Regiment. His name does not appear on the Nominal Roll for the Seaforths.

Pte. William Fong, a French-speaking Chinese Canadian from Mont Joli, Que, joined the Royal 22e Régiment at Avellino, Italy, in January 1944, as a reinforcement. He was wounded after the battle for Ortona. He was later joined by his younger brother, Pte. Jim Lee Fong, E.601397, when the regiment reached Germany, where William was again wounded. After the war, Willie made soldiering his career and rejoined the Royal 22e. William Fong was killed in Korea 23 June 1952.

Raymond Jang, B.145543, originally from Vancouver, enlisted in Toronto and was a reinforcement for The Royal Canadian Regiment. Raymond was wounded at the Remi River, near Bulgaria, Italy, 14 October 1944.

D Company of the RCRs had succeeded in capturing eight Germans near the Villa Gnaldo and had dug in for the night. They were, however, sitting in the middle of a minefield which they did not discover until Lieut. R. Falardeau was seriously wounded by the detonation of the Schü mine he stepped on. Total casualties were eleven and members of the platoon attempted to carry out the wounded men. Raymond was carrying Falardeau but his own foot was blown off and Raymond was unable to move throughout the night. He was successfully recovered the following morning after a Pioneer Platoon cleared a corridor to D Company. Falardeau did not survive the night. Raymond was repatriated and after demobilization, worked for the War Amputees in Toronto until his death in 1986.

Canadian Armoured Corps

Tpr. William Soo, B.135498, from Oshawa, Ont, served in The Governor General's Horse Guards. The Guards was formed 11 February 1941, and renamed the 3rd Armoured Reconnaissance Regiment 1 January 1943. As part of the 5th Armoured Division, the regiment arrived in Italy late in 1943 where the inevitable delay in being equipped was experienced. The Horse Guards received the first two Shermans to reach the division.

When the 1st Canadian Corps HQs and Corps Troops and the 5th Armoured Division were sent to Italy, because of lack of shipping, the Corps and Division did not take their equipment with them except for personal arms, Bren guns and mortars; they were to use the equipment of the 30th Corps HQs and Troops and the 7th Armoured Division that was being transferred to Britain. Most of this equipment had seen long service in North Africa and was quite unsuited to the mountainous terrain in Italy, especially the two-wheel drive vehicles. Many were also unserviceable and new vehicles had to be supplied from England. The tanks were also slow in arriving and it was the end of January before the Armoured Division was equipped; the tanks, however, were Shermans with 75 mm guns. Guns for the artillery were even slower to materialize and it took from late February to early May before these units were properly equipped. Signals equipment was also slow to appear.

The Horse Guards fought throughout the Italian campaign, taking part in the fighting in the Liri Valley, the Gothic Line, and in the Romagna in Cumberland Force and in Porter Force. After the move to Northwest Europe, the regiment took part in the fighting at the IJsselmeer. Bill was then repatriated to Canada and demobilized.

King Lewis **Chow** Hong, B.80078, from Sault Ste. Marie, had tried to enlist in the RCAF before he was called up under NRMA in 1940 for thirty days training. He was recalled in 1941 and took basic training at Camp Borden.

King was posted to the Kent Regiment and turned general service when the regiment was sent to New Westminster. After receiving clerical training, he was posted to the 5th Armoured Division HQs as military staff clerk. The division arrived in Italy late in 1943.

After seeing action in the Liri Valley, the Conca River, Coriano Ridge, in Cumberland Force, at Cervia, and the Lamone crossing, operations were completed by the 5th Armoured at the Valli di Commachio on the Adriatic (Sant'Alberto).

Early in 1945 the division left Italy, travelled north through France, and arrived in Belgium towards the end of February. With the British 49th Division, the 5th Armoured cleared the 'island' south of Arnhem up to the Neder Rijn to the west of the city in Operation *Destroyer*. The British 49th Division captured Arnhem and cleared the city by 14 April. Headquarters of 5 Armoured was "in Germany only to take Arnhem from Emmerich." It was located in the Didam-Doetinchem area, after passing through Emmerich, the only bridge over the Rhine.

The 5th Armoured then passed through the 49th in Arnhem to capture and fight the "battle of Otterloo." The HQs of the division, located in Otterloo, was in the path of about 800 or more Germans trying to escape to the safety of the Grebbe Line. With a motley collection of infantry, tanks, and artillery, Maj.-Gen. B.M. Hoffmeister's HQs drove the attackers back, inflicting about 300 casualties on the Germans. The division proceeded on to Barneveld, Voorthuizen, and Putten in Operation *Cleanser*. They then moved to the Groningen area to relieve the 3rd Infantry Division. The 5th Armoured captured and cleared Delfzijl by 1 May.

King Chow volunteered for Tiger Force and was repatriated 10 August 1945, but with war at an end in the Pacific on the 15th, he was demobilized.

Pu On Lim was born in China but brought up in Victoria. He enlisted early in the war and took his basic training in Vernon, followed by tank gunner training at Camp Borden. He was then posted to The British Columbia Dragoons in February 1941. The regiment had been moved to Camp Borden the end of May.

They sailed for England in November on the *Andes* where the BC Dragoons was designated the 9th Armoured Regiment in the 5th Armoured Division. The 5th Armoured arrived at Naples late in 1943, and settled at Matera.

The regiment did not see action in Italy until it was re-equipped with Sherman tanks at the end of January 1944. They were sent to the front with Lord Strathcona's Horse (Royal Canadians) on 4 February. The Dragoons remained in reserve until March when they moved to Casalavecchio. They then trained with the Irish Regiment of Canada at Caserta.

During the May spring offensive in the Liri Valley, the Dragoons took part in breaking through between Pontecorvo and Forme d'Aquino. From 26 May to the end of the month, the Dragoons fought their way across the Melfa River and took Ceprano. Two days later, Pofi was attacked with a squadron of the GG Horse Guards under command. Eleven days later, the BC Dragoons went into reserve, north of Caserta.

At the Gothic Line action, the BC Dragoons fought without infantry support leaving them with only 18 running tanks at the end of the day. Their colonel was killed during this action. They were later relieved by the Perths and Lord Strathcona's Horse.

The Dragoons next set out for the Romagna, an area forming the southeastern part of the Lombard Plain. But first Rimini and its approaches had to be taken. Here the Dragoons assisted the infantry using their tank guns as artillery. At the Fiumicino River, the Dragoons came under the command of the infantry; they then performed the same support service for The Lanark and Renfrew Scottish, the 4th Princess Louise Dragoon Guards, and finally the New Zealanders on 4 and 5 October. Cumberland Force was supported for 18 days with one or two troops of tanks at a time on request of the infantry. Porter Force replaced Cumberland and the 5th Armoured went into reserve at Cervia 13 miles south of Ravenna 28 October. Additional reinforcements were added to the regiment to bring all ranks up to 695.

By 5 December the Dragoons had crossed the Montone and, unable to enter the town because the bridge had been blown, gave support to the infantry and the Italian Partisans in capturing Ravenna. On the 10th they proceeded towards the Senio and two days later crossed Fosso Vecchio. At the Naviglio Canale they supported the 1st Infantry Brigade to beat off 13 German counterattacks. They reached the Senio River and crossed 22 December; it had taken three weeks to travel ten miles. From September on ammunition had been limited and there were no trained reinforcements.

During January the BC Dragoons supported the infantry in Operation *Syria,* the push from Mezzano to Sant'Alberto on the Bay of Comacchio. Eight tanks of B Squadron and a Perth Company reached Mandriole and the coast of the Bay of Comacchio on 4/5 January—the most northern Canadian regiment in Italy. There had been 49 casualties and 14 tank losses.

Withdrawn from battle on 6 February, the Dragoons moved to Harrod's No. 1 Camp, between Pisa and Leghorn, in preparation for the move to Northwest Europe. They landed in the south of France and travelled north to Roulers, Belgium. From this new base, Pu On Lim and the others were given nine-day furloughs to England.

Into Holland by 1 April, the BC Dragoons crossed the Rhine at Emmerich in a holding role. They took part in Operation *Cleanser* in the village of Terlet, and beyond to Otterloo, cleared Voorthuizen and went on to the IJsselmeer. At Ermelo, B Squadron helped Perth Company clear the town, but A Squadron was unable to sink the boats with escaping Germans and had to call on aircraft to do the job. *Cleanser* ended 18 April and the regiment was ordered into rest.

In clearing the Delfzijl Pocket on 23 April the BC Dragoons relieved the 3rd

Infantry Division. The 11th Infantry Brigade was to capture Delfzijl with BC Dragoons and other armoured elements in support. Delfzijl surrendered 2 May, just before the official end of the war.

Pu On served throughout as a tank gunner with the exception of two weeks when he became a cook. The British Columbia Dragoons was disbanded 31 Janaury 1946 and Pu On was repatriated and demobilized.

Guardsman Ted Darling, K.89870, enlisted in the Rocky Mountain Rangers, aged 16, and was then posted to the Halifax Rifles. He went to England with the Rifles and there the unit was broken up. Ted was one of those posted to The Canadian Grenadier Guards; the Guards became the 22nd Armoured Regiment when the 4th Armoured Brigade was formed in January 1943 in the 4th Armoured Division. He was in the Humber Car Reconnaissance Troop.

The Grenadiers landed in Normandy 14/15 July on Juno Beach in four landing craft loads. They set out immediately for Caen to relieve The Fort Garry Horse at Grentheville. With The Lake Superior Regiment (Motor), the 96th Anti-Tank Battery, and with Flails to lead (Halpenny Force), the 22nd Armoured took part in Operation *Totalize* from 8 to 10 August. In *Tractable,* they worked with The Governor General's Foot Guards, and the operation ended 16 August within three miles of Falaise. The Recce Troop blocked the road from Trun to Hordouseaux 17/18 August. The Grenadiers continued to Point 262 to assist the Polish Division, cut off from supplies. The Grenadiers fought on to the Seine, the Somme, and the Leopold Canal from 23 August to 12 October.

The regiment took part in the fighting at Antwerp, the Scheldt, and the Maas from 12 October to 22 February 1945; it then fought in the Rhineland from 24 February to 11 March. Beyond the Kusten Canal on 20 April 1945, they advanced towards Oldenburg in support of the infantry, continuing north until on the 26th, supporting the Lake Superiors, the Grenadiers reached Querenstede, about two miles from Bad Zwischenahn, but the bridge was blown as they arrived. Two days later they reached high ground on the edge of Bad Zwischenahn. The Germans evacuated. Pushing on toward Varel, the Lake Superiors and the Grenadier Guards captured Rastede and reached Beckhausen, about ten miles north of Oldenburg. In the evening of 4 May, orders for the cease-fire were announced effective the 5th, and the official German capitulation occurred on the 8th, VE-Day.

Ted Darling, 1943

The United Nations Rehabilitation and Relief Association purchased about 1,500 Canadian Army trucks that were to be turned over to Czechoslovakia and Poland to enable these countries to move their crops. When a request for driver volunteers was issued to deliver the trucks to Czechoslovakia in September, Ted left the regiment to act as a driver, returning to Aldershot in December. Ted noted that "there wasn't much in the way of crops to move."

The Canadian Grenadier Guards was repatriated on the *Ile de France* to Halifax and by train to Montreal 28 January 1946; Ted Darling returned on the *Queen Elizabeth,* arriving in New York the same month. The Grenadier Guards was disbanded in February 1946 and at the same time Ted was demobilized.

Royal Canadian Army Service Corps

F.C. (Alfred) Jong, C.130969, originally from Vancouver but living in Montreal from 1939, enlisted in Cornwall, Ont, at the end of 1940. After instruction in RCASC Motor Mechanics at Orillia, Ont, Alfred also took trade school training in Hamilton, and advanced training at Aldershot, NS. As his group was preparing to leave camp to board ship for overseas, Alfred was refused permission to proceed and was sent back to Aldershot where he became an instructor until demobilized in 1945.

Manuel Dan, K.76963, from Kamloops, born 29 March 1919, enlisted 25 March 1942. Manuel served in France and Germany in the 69th Transport Unit. This unit landed in Normandy 3 August after Caen had fallen and the 2nd Infantry Division was just about to launch *Totalize.* The traffic congestion was aggravated by the enemy shells and air attacks. The 69th Transport Unit helped to dump the ammunition, petrol, and rations behind the forward positions.

Operation *Tractable* followed and the 69th Transport Unit wheeled their vehicles through the same conditions to replenish the new dump. The two 'friendly' bombing incidents, one by the RAF and the other by the

USAAF, occurred during these two operations; many Canadian and Polish troops were killed and injured. Manuel Dan served throughout the campaign in Northwest Europe; he was repatriated to Canada and demobilized 8 February 1946.

S/Sgt. John Rose Chinn, SK.53628, served in RCASC from 4 April 1941. He was attached to The Seaforth Highlanders and served in Sicily and Italy from 1943 to the spring of 1945 when the Canadian Corps moved to Northwest Europe. John Chinn served continuously as a member of the Regular Force from 1940 to 1964.

CSM (WO2) Harry Hang, from Toronto, served with No. 1 Canadian Base Reinforcement Group HQs in Avellino, Italy. This group was one of the last to leave Italy through France to Holland in 1945. Harry was in charge of the Trianon Club at Luilen Hospital of the Canadian Army in Holland. After VE-Day, Harry moved to England and took charge of catering at the 21 Canadian General Hospital in Oldham in which one wing was staffed by army personnel from New Westminster. Harry received a Mention in Despatches.

RSM Harry Bing Mon Lim, K.16400, and Pte. William Hong Yuen Lowe, K.16401, both from Victoria, had enlisted together in the 16th Canadian Scottish (Reserve) in February 1942. They turned active 21 January 1943, took their basic training at Vernon and advanced training at Calgary.

In the summer of 1943, they were sent to Britain as reinforcements, and from there to The Loyal Edmonton Regiment in Italy. On the way to North Africa in the fall of 1943, the convoy was attacked by torpedo bombers (three ships were sunk). Harry and Bill reached the No. 1 Base Reinforcement Depot at Philippeville the morning of 7 November 1943.

After seven weeks infantry training in North Africa, on New Year's Day 1944, Harry Lim and Bill Lowe arrived at Naples. From Naples they were sent on to Avellino, to the No. 1 Canadian Base Reinforcement Group, where they met CSM Harry Hang, who persuaded them to join the Army Service Corps.

– courtesy Bill Lowe
l to r - Harry Lim, Bill Lowe, Harry Hang

The Catering Wing had been established in 1942 in England, under the Directorate of Supplies and Transport, so that obtaining, delivering, and cooking of all food came under one command. All cooks were now trained by RCASC; they were tested, promoted, and posted to various units. George Wong served as cook, for a short time in France, but mostly in Belgium. He was repatriated and demobilized by early 1946.

George E. Wong

Bill Lowe served in the junior officers' mess and Harry Lim in the brigadier's mess.

Early in 1945, Bill Lowe was repatriated to Canada on compassionate grounds. Harry Lim was one of the last to leave Italy, along with Harry Hang; Harry Lim served as cook until repatriated to Canada in February 1946. After reaching Vancouver 6 March 1946, he was demobilized at Little Mountain on the 30th.

L/Cpl. George Edward Wong, A.104597, from London, Ont, enlisted in 1943. Because George's family owned and operated a well-known restaurant where Guy Lombardo and his Royal Canadians once played before the band's rise to fame, he was immediately posted to the RCASC as cook although he had little or no cooking experience. He was soon trained by the army.

CSM Lai Sham (Sammy) Mee, K.74279, from Revelstoke, was one of the first to enlist in September 1939; he joined the Rocky Mountain Rangers. Sam had been employed as a cook at a hotel in Revelstoke before he enlisted. He turned active in August 1940 and took his basic training at Vernon. After advanced tank training at Camp Borden, Sam was posted to The British Columbia Dragoons. They sailed for England on the *Andes* in November 1941, arriving at Liverpool. In England, the BC Dragoons was designated the 9th Armoured Regiment. Sam trained as 75 mm tank gunner in Wales.

On 14 November 1943 Sammy Mee was detached from his regiment and posted to the Industrial Imperial School in London where he trained as a cook. Success from the past had caught up with him. Sam graduated

Lai Sham (Sammy) Mee - England 1941

from the school with a grade of 96 percent, but the mark was lowered in part because the lieutenant-colonel in charge didn't think it fitting that he should be topped by a student, and also because Sam failed in cooking rice. The English method of cooking rice is 'wet,' that is all kinds of water is used and the rice is stirred during cooking; the Chinese method is 'dry,' where the correct proportion of water to rice leaves the kernels individually intact and chewable. Sam accepted the lower grade and received promotion to staff sergeant. This rank was confirmed but not the acting CSM rank. Sam was on course when his regiment was sent to Italy, so he "missed this end of the war."

Sam was NCO in charge of the Western Command School of Catering at Farnborough; he went on to Colchester Convalescent Hospital in Sussex. He instructed cooks and inspected camps on the continent making one trip to Italy where he advised the cooks on how to set up make-shift stoves, and other trips to Belgium.

Sam Mee was repatriated to Canada in December 1945 and demobilized in January 1946. Sammy continued in his catering and cooking career in peacetime; in 1972 he was selected by the BC Chefs' Association as Chef of the Year.

Pte. James Chin, B.135924, from Lucknow, Ont, joined the army in November 1942, aged 19. He received his training at Camp Simcoe, Ont, at Calgary and Red Deer, and was posted to the support group unit, supplies company, RCASC, of the 4th Armoured Brigade in the 4th Armoured Division.

James Chin

James sailed to England with the division in December 1943. The unit landed in Normandy 7 July 1944. He served with the brigade until the surrender handling "foods and ammunition supplies." James was in Germany when VE-Day was declared 8 May. He was repatriated 26 January 1946 and demobilized 12 March. James worked for the post office for 29 years after the war.

Born in Wingham, Ont, Cpl. Jim Lee, A.66726, enlisted in London 11 September 1941. Jim was posted to the RCASC unit attached to the 19th Field Regiment. Arriving in England in July 1943, the unit was designated the 19th Army Field Regiment, 2nd Army Group, RCA. The 19th took part in the D-Day assault along with the 14th Field Regiment, and was in action at Carpiquet, and Caen. Jim served with the regiment until he was repatriated to Canada and demobilized in April 1946. While in Holland, Jim married a Dutch girl; his bride appears to have had no

problems in entering Canada. The law had changed in the mid 1930s so that a wife no longer took the nationality of her husband.

Home Defence

Pte. Percy F. Hem, 19872, from Saint John, NB, another general service soldier, was prevented from going overseas because of illness. He remained in Canada serving in Home Defence. Percy's regimental number is incomplete; "G" was the letter used for those troops raised in New Brunswick. The picture shows Percy in the Tank Corps at Camp

– courtesy William Seto
Percy Hem

Borden with Louey King and Norman Low, two members of Mike Kendall's first group. It is possible that Kendall had selected Percy for the operation into China but he had been pre-

– courtesy William Seto

Percy Hem, Louey King, Norman Low

vented from joining them in the Okanagan because of illness.

Lieut. Frank Ho Lem, born in Canton, China, shortly after 1900, came to Canada with his mother about 1905 or 1906. His father had been the first Chinese to establish a business in Calgary around 1903. While a high school student, Frank joined the Canadian Reserve Army as a cadet, with the 13th Canadian Machine Gun Corps, and reached the rank of sergeant.

During the '20s and '30s Frank excelled at the rifle ranges and represented the Alberta team many times at the Canadian Championships held at Long Branch Ranges, Toronto. Frank's picture appeared in the *Toronto Daily Star* 11 August 1928, when he obtained the highest aggregate in the 54th annual meet of the Ontario Rifle Association at Long Branch. He was awarded the ORA silver medal and $25 for his excellent score of 317 out of a possible 330.

At the British Empire shoot offs at Bisley, near Aldershot, England, Frank came in fourth in the British Empire Grand Aggregate. Sergeant Ho Lem scored 23 consecutive bulls eyes in a shoot off with Sgt. T.A. Jensen of the 15th Canadian Light Horse, Innisfail, in the Wayne Coal Industries match at the Alberta Provincial Rifle Association, 16 July 1935. The Calgary *Herald* of 6 May 1940 reported that Sgt. Frank Ho Lem of the Calgary Regiment scored ten straight bulls eyes at the 200 yards outdoor range at the rifle shoot held at Sarcee camp. He competed in competitions at distances from 100 to 1,000 yards.

Frank was one of the first to join the army in 1939; he was assigned to A-16 Currie Barracks, Calgary, as small arms instructor, with the 1st Calgary Tank Regiment. He took officer's training at Gordon Head and was a strong supporter of the Chinese Canadian Battalion proposed in Pacific Command.

– courtesy Alvin Ho Lem

Lieut. Frank Ho Lem

In 1944 Lieut. Frank Ho Lem attended the S-20 Japanese Language School in Vancouver, graduating in 1945, but he had not received a posting before the war ended. Frank was demobilized in 1946. He immediately set out as leader of the drive to the federal government to obtain Canadian citizenship status for all Chinese in Canada. The drive was successful, and Canadian born and naturalized Chinese in Canada became full-fledged Canadian citizens in 1947.

Three brothers from Montreal, William, Samuel, and Robert Lee, also served in the Canadian Army. William and Robert joined the COTC while at McGill University.

– courtesy Arthur Lee

William Lee, front 1st on left

– courtesy Arthur Lee

Samuel Lee, back 3rd from left

William Lee graduated in May 1945 and received his commission. When the war ended in both Europe and the Pacific, William was demobilized. He worked for the National Research Council at Chalk River, and later died from radiation exposure.

Pte. Samuel Lee, D.189647, trained at St. Jean, Que. Training was complete and his group was ready for shipment overseas when the war in Europe ended, 8 May 1945. He volunteered for Tiger Force but war ended in the Pacific as well 15 August before training with American forces had got under way. The Pacific was a United States theatre of war and Canadian forces had to be trained in the American pattern and with US equipment in order to operate effectively in the theatre. William, Samuel, and Robert were the brothers of Arthur Lee who spent the war years in Hong Kong.

Pte. Henry Louie, K.1788, from Vancouver, enlisted in December 1944. Henry took his basic training at Wetaskiwin where he met On Lim, Wally Mah from Victoria, and Ken Der of Vancouver. He took his advanced training at Currie Barracks. Henry was posted to the POW camp at Seebee, Alta, the only Chinese Canadian in camp. He was demobilized August 1946.

Pte. On Wah Lim, K.10766, during most of the war years was employed as an aircraft engineer by Boeing, the first Chinese Canadian employed by this company. By late 1944, aircraft production was greatly reduced and On Lim was called up. He took his basic training at Wetaskiwin (where he met Francis Lum) and armoured training at Camp Borden (George Mah and George Mar were also at Borden). He was then posted to Winnipeg but by then the war was over and he received his discharge.

Born in Radville, Sask, Pte. Larry George Wong, K.7986, was called up under NRMA 12 October 1944, and turned active on the 17th. He was sent to Nova Scotia for basic training. Larry was then posted to the Edmonton Fusiliers in 1944 as infantry signaller 'C' serving in Newfoundland. Larry was demobilized 6 June 1946.

Sgt. Art Ten (Henry) Hum, E.100068, from Montreal, enlisted in 1942 at Military District No. 5, Quebec City. He was attached to the Royal Rifles, 2nd Battalion, and then

Sgt. A.T. (Hank) Hum

posted to the Royal 22e Régiment where he gave instruction in both French and English to new recruits. Hank Hum also performed guard duties for POWs and conducted men from Quebec City to Kingston. He was demobilized in 1945.

Born in China 16 September 1921, Pte. Alfred Quinn Lee, H.28434, enlisted 18 November 1944 in Winnipeg. Alfred was another general service soldier retained in Canada. He was released from service on compassionate grounds 9 November 1945.

Rfm. Robert Lee (Bandsman)

– courtesy Mrs. Alfred Gin
Pte. Alfred Quinn Lee

There were musicians in the army bands, some of whom were general service. One of these was Rifleman Robert Lee, B.168081, who enlisted in The Queen's Own Rifles of Canada in Toronto in 1944. After basic training he was transferred to No. 2 Headquarters Department, Army Band. Bandsman Robert Lee was demobilized in September 1946. Music was Bob's second name and he continued to play into the 1990s in the Kamloops orchestra. Bob's father, Y.C. Lee, served in the Great War.

Canadian Intelligence Corps

Donald Sung, M.36555, served in the No. 6 Canadian Field Security Section in Pacific Command at Prince George. He volunteered for special duty and went to India in 1945 to join Force 136, where he received field promotion to WO 2 in the Army Intelligence Corps.

Douglas Jung was on staff at Pacific Command until he began studies at the S-20 Japanese Language School in April 1944. He volunteered for Mike Kendall's China operation. Douglas is the brother of Arthur (Air Force) and Ross (RCAMC).

Others in the army recruited by Kendall, and those called up in 1944 and recruited by Maj. H.J. Legg, are discussed in later chapters.

Canadian Women's Army Corps

The Canadian Women's Army Corps began accepting volunteers in September 1941.

Pte. Edna Silaine Lowe, W.11703, of Victoria, the sister of Bill and Stanley Lowe, enlisted in July 1942. She took her basic training at Vermillion, Alta. Edna was posted to Work Point Barracks at Esquimalt as cipher clerk with RCCS. She received her discharge in November 1943.

Cpl. Lila Wong, W.111494, of Nanaimo, BC, also joined the CWACs as did Pte. Mary Laura Mah, W.111243, of Victoria (born Salmon Arm, BC), who enlisted in Vancouver. Pte. Mah was employed as teletype keyboard operator at 29 Admin. Corps from 13 May 1944 to 6 July 1945. Pte. Mary Ko Bong, W. 115036, also of Victoria, served in the CWACs as well. Mary is the sister of John, Peter and Andrew Ko Bong who also served in the Canadian armed forces. Pte. Helen Hoe, W.100858, served in No. 40 Admin. Unit, Ottawa.

That all these Chinese Canadians were able to serve without any of the 'incidents' so feared by Ottawa is a tribute to them and to other Canadians with whom they served. A few were officers and many were NCOs and gave orders to those under their charge; there was no problem. Only one Chinese Canadian veteran, a sergeant, has commented on an occasion when he was called a "Chink" but he just considered that the man using the term was ignorant. Wing Hay Young was also sensitive to racial slurs but again nothing serious came of it.

Three of the men whose careers are given above attended the Japanese Language School: Wilfred Seto, Frank Ho Lem, and Douglas Jung. A few other Chinese Canadians attended this school as well.

NOTES

The personal and service information has come primarily from participants and relatives; these references are not separately given. A few extracts have been made from the papers of K.L. Douglas Sam.

1. NAC, MG 26J1, Vol. 293, pp. 247684-248556, Reel C.4573.
2. NAC, MG 26J1, File 290, pp. 244976-245782, Reel C.4570.
3. NAC, RG 25, Vol.2818, File 1154-40, 20 September 1940.
4. "Memorandum against Canadians of Oriental Racial Origin in Military Training Scheme," to Dr. O.D. Skelton, Under Secretary of State for External Affairs, in NAC, RG 25, Vol. 2818, File 1154-40, 20 Sept. 1940. Hugh L. Keenleyside was promoted to Assistant Under Secretary as was Mike Pearson in 1941 after the death of Dr. Skelton in January and Norman Robertson was promoted to Undersecretary of State for External Affairs.
5. Maj.-Gen. H.J. Riley, Armed Services Division, NSS, to A. MacNamara, Deputy Minister of Labour, 31 May 1943, in NAC, RG 27, Vol. 998, File 2-114, pt. 15.
6. It should be noted that in the *Vancouver Sun* of 5 October 1939, German "enemy aliens" were required to register in British Columbia. Enemy aliens were those Germans who had not been naturalized.
7. The "Report and Recommendations of the Special Committee on Orientals in British Columbia December 1940" in NAC, RG 27, Vol.1500, File 2-K-184, N.W.S. Oriental B.C.
8. L.R. LaFlèche, Associate Deputy Minister, NWS, to External Affairs, 6 Oct.; Keenleyside reply, 9 Oct.; LaFlèche to The Hon. Mr. Justice J.G. Gillanders, Toronto, 10 Oct. 1941, in NAC, RG 27, Vol.1489, File 2-184, NWS Orientals.
9. Pattullo to Alexander 22 Nov. 1941, quoted in Robertson's letter to Deputy Minister of NWS, 15 Dec. 1941, in NAC, RG 27, Vol. 1486, File 2-162-9, and Pattullo to Ralston 6 Dec. 1941, in RG 25, Vol. 2818, File 1154-40.
10. LaFlèche memo 20 Nov. 1941, "Men of Oriental Racial Origin," in NAC, RG 27, Vol. 998, File 2-114-6.
11. Col. C.P. Stacey, *Arms, Men and Governments: The War Policies of Canada 1939-1945* (Ottawa, 1970), pp. 7-8.
12. Memo dated 19 Dec. 1941 of 18 Dec. meeting "Military Service for Canadians of Oriental Race," prepared by H.F. Angus of External, Chairman of the meeting, in NAC, RG 25, Vol. 2818, File 1154-40.

13. Minutes of 13 Jan. 1942 in NAC, RG 27, Vol.1486, File 2-162-9; and RG 25, Vol. 2818, File 1154-40.

14. Draft Report titled "The Conference endorses the following principles . . . ." in NAC, RG 27, Vol. 1486, File 2-162-9.

15. Letters from Seto to Alexander 15 April 1942 in D.Hist. 322.009, (D814), and from Ho Lem 6 Dec. 1942 to Pearkes, who had succeeded Alexander as GOCinC 1942 in D.Hist. 322.009, (D478).

16. Patricia E. Roy, "The Soldiers Canada Didn't Want," *CHR,* LIX, 3 (1978), pp. 345-6, quoting *The New Canadian,* 29 November 1940.

17. Murchie to Alexander 13 April 1942; Dr. C.Y. Hsie to Alexander 21 April 1942; Seto to Wills 27 April 1942, all in D.Hist. 322.009, (D814); and "Memo on Compulsory Military Service as applied to Aliens and other Exempt Groups" prepared for Council in NAC, RG 27, Vol. 985, File 10.

18. Seto to Wills 27 April 1942 and Adjutant General telegram 13 May 1942 in D.Hist. 322.009, (D814).

19. Memo prepared for CWC, Document No. 167, and another for Norman Robertson, "Men of Japanese Racial Origin in the Army," 23 May, 1942, both in NAC, RG 25, Vol. 2818, File 1154-40.

20. D.Hist. 322.009, (D814) and D.Hist. 322.009, (D478) contain letters from McCallum of 19 June and 2 July 1942, and from St. Louis of 25 June 1942.

21. Covering letter dated 9 Dec. 1942 from Maj.-Gen. H.F.G. Letson, AG, in D.Hist. 321.009, (D102).

22. Supervisor of Mobilization, NSS, to Chairmen and Registrars in NAC, RG 27, Vol. 1489, File 1-184.

23. Unsigned memo prepared for Hume Wrong 13 February 1943 "Military Service of Sikhs in British Columbia," in NAC, RG 25, Vol. 2818, File 1154-40.

24. Manson to Riley, 26 February 1943, in NAC, RG 27, Vol. 998, File 2-114, pt.15. Although James Morton in *In the Sea of Sterile Mountains,* p. 238, claims that Manson had a long history of anti-Chinese sentiment, this view is not reflected in the NRMA wartime correspondence; rather Manson is supportive of their efforts.

25. Minutes of meeting in office of Brig. R.D. Sutherland, 26 March 1943 in NAC, RG 27, Vol. 998, File 2-114, pt.15.

26. Note for External Files 27 April 1943, in NAC, RG 25, Vol. 2818, File 1154-40.

27. Manson to Riley 18 May 1943, 30 April 1943 in NAC, RG 27, Vol. 998, File 2-114, pt. 15.

28. Manson to MacNamara 27 May in NAC, RG 27, Vol. 998, File 2-114, pt. 15.

29. MacNamara to Riley; Riley response 31 May 1943 in NAC, RG 27, Vol. 998, File 2-114, pt. 15.

30. Maj.-Gen. H.F.G. Letson, 14 June 1943, "Employment of Aliens and Naturalized Citizens of Enemy Origin in the Canadian Army" in NAC, RG 27, Vol. 998, File 2-114, pt. 15, and in D.Hist.

112.3S2009, (D35); Letson, 3, 12, 23, July 1943, "Aliens and Canadians of Foreign Origin - Service in the Canadian Army," and 14 July 1943, "Employment of Aliens and Naturalized Citizens of Enemy origin in the Canadian Army," and 30 Nov. 1943, 5 July 1944, 24 July 1944, 30 Sept. 1944, "Enlistment (Enrollment) and Employment of Aliens and Naturalized Canadian Citizens in the Canadian Army" all in D.Hist. 006.066, (D5).

31. Letter in NAC, RG 27, Vol. 998, File 2-114, pt. 15.

32. *Statutes of Canada,* 1923, Vol. I-II.

33. Manson to Assistant Director, Mobilization in NAC, RG 27, Vol. 997, File 2-114, pt. 5.

34. "Enlistment (Enrolment) and Employment of Aliens and Naturalized Canadian Citizens in the Canadian Army" in D.Hist. 006.066, (D5); and NAC, RG 27, Vol. 1486, File 2-162-9.

35. Associate Director of Mobilization to Brig. A.N. Nash, 29 Jan. 1944 in NAC, RG 27, Vol. 1486, File 2-162-9.

36. Pacific Regional Director 28 February 1944 to NSS Advisory Board in NAC, RG 27, Vol. 998, File 2-114-15.

37. McLaren to MacNamara 25 April 1944 in NAC, RG 27, Vol. 3004; and Report from SOE Adviser, Foreign & Commonwealth Office.

38. Manson letter 3 May 1944 in NAC, RG 27, Vol. 998, File 2-114, pt. 15.

39. Letson to MacNamara 8 May 1944 and MacNamara reply in NAC, RG 27, Vol. 998, File 2-114, pt. 15.

40. Meeting 24 May 1944 in office of Brig. J.A. de LaLanne in NAC, RG 27, Vol. 3004, Chinese.

41. AG memo in NAC, RG 27, Vol. 998, File 2-114-15.

42. Circular letter in D.Hist. 006.066, (D5), Aliens - Policy.

43. Letter in D.Hist. 322.009, (D478).

44. The *Vancouver Sun* of Oct. 16, 1944, p. 13, comments on Reverend Andrew Lam's campaign for the franchise.

45. Pearkes to Gibson; "The Disposal of Men of Chinese Racial Origin called up for Service under N.R.M.A." in D.Hist. 322.009, (D478).

46. Draft letter 20 Sept. in D.Hist. 112.21009, (D185), and signed copy 23 Sept. from Murchie to Pearkes in D.Hist. 322.009, (D478).

47. Maj-Gen. A.E. Walford, AG, in NAC, RG 24, Vol. 2661, File HQS-3488-3, v.3.

48. See letters in NAC, RG 27, Vol.998, File 2-114-15; RG 27, Vol.1500, File 2K-184; RG 27, Vol. 1500, File 2K-138.5; RG 27, Vol.1489, File 2-184, NWS Orientals; RG 27, Vol. 1489, File 2-184; and RG 27, Vol.1496, File 28-184.

49. Col. C.P. Stacey, *Official History of the Canadian Army in the Second World War.* Vol. I. *Six Years of War,* (Ottawa, 1955), pp. 82, 118-123; and p. 479; see also D.Hist. 315.009, (D20).

50. Letter in NAC, RG 27, Vol. 998, File 2-114-15.

51. *Vancouver Sun,* 25 February 1946.

52. Although the Chinese Government claimed all Chinese no matter where they were born as Chinese nationals, those born in Canada could opt for either Chinese or Canadian citizenship at the time they turned 21. See legal opinion in letter from MacDougall, Macfarlane, Scott & Hugessen dated 14 Nov. 1941 in NAC, RG 27, Vol.1489, File 2.184, NWS Orientals. The reader will note that this opinion does not agree with the terms of the Exclusion Act of 1923.

53. Frank's daughter, Carol F. Lee, is the author of "The Road to Enfranchisement."

54. There was only one Canadian Parachute Battalion properly so-called. For security reasons, the Canadian members of the First Special Service Force were called the 2nd Canadian Parachute Battalion from June 1942 to May 1943. The name was then changed to 1st Canadian Special Service Battalion for administrative purposes only; Canadians were scattered throughout the Force. American uniforms and rank badges were worn by Canadian members.

55. Clarence Murphy wrote to tell me that he knew Diamond Quon from 1st Canadian Corps Signals in England and in Italy and that "I didn't only know him, he was my friend and a good friend. When I was wounded it was Quon who wrote to my girl friend, now my wife."

56. For this action see Col. C.P. Stacey, *Official History of the Canadian Army in the Second World War.* Vol.III. *The Victory Campaign* (Ottawa, 1966), p. 292, and footnote.

Chapter VII

S-20 JAPANESE LANGUAGE SCHOOL

Several Chinese Canadians attended the S-20 Japanese Language School in Vancouver, a unit of the Canadian Army Intelligence Corps. Graduates were posted to Washington and Ottawa. Graduates, including Japanese Canadians, were also volunteers as language specialists in Southeast Asia Command on loan to the British Army.

The volunteers were employed in the South East Asia Translators and Interpreters Corps (SEATIC) in SEAC. In August of 1944 over 600 linguists had been requested by SEAC and Australia; others were required for the Pacific Force when it was being formed in 1945. Unfortunately, government action came too late to supply demands and only about 130 graduated from the school as language interpreters.

In Ottawa, linguists were attached to No. 1 Discrimination Unit, a branch of Military Intelligence, formed in 1943 to translate Japanese intercepts and act as a pool of linguists. Some of the material handled by this unit was received at *Hydra,* the radio station at Camp X in Oshawa, Ont. From Oshawa, these intercepts were distributed to Ottawa and Washington for translation. In Washington, graduates were employed in Pacific Military Intelligence Research Section (PACMIRS) to translate Japanese documents captured during the campaigns in the Pacific as well as wireless intercepts.

The language school was established in the summer of 1943 under the direction of Lt.-Col. Arthur P. McKenzie, who commanded from October 1943. McKenzie had been born in Tokyo in 1889 and had been a school teacher in Japan from 1920 to 1941. The idea of training Japanese linguists was that of Lt.-

Col. B.R. Mullaly, intelligence officer, Pacific Command.

Mullaly had been British Military Attaché to Tokyo from 1939 to 1941; before this he had been an officer in the Indian Army. Mullaly would have been familiar with the School of Oriental and African Studies at London University, which turned out highly qualified linguists. Four *Nisei* (second generation Japanese Canadians) were employed at this school from 1942; they had all succeeded in joining the Canadian Army before December 1941.

The S-20 Japanese Language School operated from various facilities. From the Vancouver Vocational School where it began courses in 1943, it was moved to Ambleside Camp in West Vancouver in November 1945. From Pacific Command School in January 1944, it was placed on Active Service and renamed the S-20 Japanese Language School 1 October 1944. The school was closed 15 July 1945.

Canadians at the language school at Camp Savage, Minnesota, were withdrawn in 1943 and most of them entered the first course at the new school. After completing a preliminary written and spoken course, students received another six months of instruction in military doctrine, organization, tactics and terminology, in interrogation techniques relating to prisoners of war, and lessons in geography. The aim of the school was to produce interpreters as quickly as possible.

There were four language courses given, with about 232 students enrolled between August 1943 and July 1945. The first course began in August as soon as the school was opened, and the last began in April 1945 with students graduating in 1946.

Of the 232 students who attended the school, 137 successfully completed the full course and qualified as Japanese language interpreters. Some students were sent to postings without having completed the full course. Sixteen were sent to the No. 1 Special Wireless Group in Australia; this number included three Japanese Canadians who had attended the school.

Japanese Canadians, like many Chinese Canadians, were not always fluent in their mother tongue, and some did not speak the language at all. Many had never learned to read and write anything but English. This fact always came as a surprise to Caucasians.

The students were from diverse backgrounds; 56 were Japanese Canadians, about half a dozen were Chinese Canadians, and the rest were Caucasians. The Chinese Canadians included: K.C. (Charlie) Lowe (Washington and SEAC), S.J. (Danny) Chin (SEAC), Frank Ho Lem (unassigned), Wilfred B. Seto (No. 1 Discrimination Unit), and K.L. Douglas Sam, RCAF, who graduated in the last class.

Sgt. K. Chee (Charlie) Lowe, 1046585, one of the first graduates of S-20, served for nine months in PACMIRS, Washington, from November 1943, after completing an intensive course in Japanese at the Military Language School at Camp Savage. Some of the Japanese documents he translated were later introduced as evidence during the war crimes trials. From warrant officer class 2 on his return in June 1944, he was promoted to 2nd lieutenant and became an instructor at the school.

In September 1945 Charlie Lowe received high praise when McKenzie recommended his employment in SEAC. McKenzie maintained that he was "probably most highly qualified translator in Cdn. Army."[1] He was seconded to SEAC and sailed for England with six other officers and 15 Japanese Canadians; they flew from England to New Delhi, India.

Charlie Lowe served in the SEATIC detachment in the Singapore War Crimes Trials, and later in the Joint Intelligence Unit in Hong Kong in the rank of captain. He returned to Canada in August 1947 and was demobilized. He had been one of the first Canadian Chinese to join the army in 1939, at the age of 39, and he was also one of the first Canadian Chinese scholars.

K.L. Douglas Sam, after being shot down over Rheims in France and rescued by the Allied armies in 1944, returned to Canada and attended the one-year course at S-20. He graduated in March 1946, too late to be employed as a Japanese linguist.

S.J. (Danny) Chin, K.7956, from Vancouver, trained at Gordon Head after attending S-20. He was posted to SEAC in 1945 as a Japanese linguist along with a group of twelve Nisei who had originally been destined for Australia.

Some members of this group, including Danny Chin, were redirected to the Singapore War Crimes Committee. In 1945, a few went on to the War Crimes Trials in Hong Kong. Here Danny served in the SEATIC detachment under Capt. Charlie Lowe who was working with the Joint Intelligence Unit. Courtroom attendance was often gruelling, especially when Japanese lawyers questioned the work of the translators. Danny survived the experience and returned to Canada in 1947.

Cpl. Douglas Jung had begun instruction at S-20 but did not progress very far in the Japanese language course before volunteering for special duty with SOE.

After Lieut. Wilfred B.T. Seto returned from Italy, he attended S-20 and completed the course in 1945. He was employed in the rank of captain at the No. 1 Discrimination Unit in Ottawa, translating some of the radio interceptions of Japanese wireless traffic in the Pacific.

Lieut. Frank Ho Lem, from Calgary, also completed the course and was employed as instructor at the school; he had not yet received an assignment when the war ended.

Written Japanese is derivative from written Chinese and although the two have diverged considerably over time, the basic written character, or *kanji,* is still very similar. Thus, some Chinese Canadians, if they had received instruction in Chinese as children, had an advantage in the Japanese language course. Many, but not all, had received lessons in both English and Chinese schools, or they had private tutors. The Chinese Canadians were also well-educated in the Canadian pattern. Wilfred Seto had graduated from UBC before enlisting in the Canadian Army.

British Security Coordination assisted in recruiting Japanese linguists for work in SEAC and Australia. These linguists were not trained for clandestine operations but were needed for their translation and interpretation skills. BSC also recruited the Chinese Canadians for Special Operations Executive employed in SEAC and the Southwest Pacific.

NOTES

1. Maj. A.P. McKenzie Report in NAC, RG 24, Vol.2641, File HQS-348-3, Vol. 4.

Chapter VIII

SPECIAL OPERATIONS EXECUTIVE

Special Operations Executive

SOE was a secret organization formed in 1940. Until long after the war had ended and the usual first person accounts began to appear in print, very little was known about what it did and how it functioned. Most of those employed by SOE were generally aware of only their own minute part in it. Most of the story has now appeared in print, but many are still unaware of just what this irregular organization was and what it was intended to do.

After the British Expeditionary Force had been driven from the continent, Britain had no foothold in Europe. Most of the army had been saved at Dunkirk but the equipment had been abandoned. Denmark, Norway, Holland, and Belgium had all been over run; France accepted terms with Germany. The Secret Intelligence Service and its Section D (Z Organization allied with SIS's Passport Control Office) had all been driven out, except for a few agents who were able to remain in Switzerland, Spain, Portugal and Sweden. These four countries guarded their neutrality jealously, but diplomats, journalists, and businessmen were able to move about and work freely. These men in the occupations named were not always what they appeared to be.

SOE, an unusual means for an unusual situation, was devised to at least infiltrate agents with specific objectives: sabotage, subversion, guerrilla warfare. In Europe, SOE provided liaison officers to assist in training and arming the Resistance; in Asia, SOE operatives took an active part not only in training guerrillas but in leading them against the enemy.

SOE was created by the civil authority, not the military, and action was instituted from London, not by the commanders in the field. There was, however, coordination with the military commander in each theatre.

SOE was formed in July 1940 and wound up as an independent body in January 1946. It was originally composed of three organizations. The first was Section D or Z Organization, which undertook sabotage and non-military attack and was then under Foreign Office (SIS) cover. The second was Military Intelligence (Research), a branch of the War Office, which developed guerrilla warfare. And finally, the third element was Electra House handling propaganda, also under the Foreign Office.

The British Chiefs of Staff supported this new organization since at the time there was no alternative, initially to create turmoil in occupied Europe; and when the war threatened to become worldwide with the Japanese attitude in the Far East, SOE was expanded into Southeast Asia and the Southwest Pacific areas.

Section D (SIS) had been set up in March 1938 under the Foreign Office; it was to investigate attacking enemies other than by the use of regular military forces. Z Force in Hong Kong was set up under Section D. F.W. Kendall was recruited into this organization in Hong Kong in 1939, and he in turn recruited D.R. Holmes and others.

MI(R), set up in November 1938, was formerly General Staff (Research) at the War Office. MI(R) investigated the training and use of guerrillas, the necessary evasive tactics, and the achievement of high mobility; it also developed the appropriate light equipment. Escape and evasion, which became MI 9, and deception of the enemy, as well as the Independent Companies which were soon renamed Commandos, were also developed by MI(R). In India, escape and evasion was called E Group, to which the British Army Aid Group in China belonged. Australia retained the name Independent Companies for its Commando units.

Electra House had been set up in 1938 to study propaganda and remained with SOE just a little over a year when it became the Political Warfare Executive. SOE operatives periodically helped PWE agents.

SOE absorbed the Industrial Intelligence Centre, another branch of SIS. William Stephenson, head of British Security Co-ordination in New York, had carried out numerous intelligence duties for the Centre before the war began.

Control of the new organization was assigned to the Ministry of Economic Warfare. MEW was a civilian department conducting economic blockade of the continent. The Minister of Economic Warfare was not a member of the War Cabinet nor Defence Committee, yet SOE had to rely on the army, the air force, and the navy for transportation, supplies, and for many of its operatives.

Strategic direction came from the British Chiefs of Staff but all other aspects were controlled by SOE itself. Lacking bombers for a strategic offensive against Germany, the Chiefs of Staff concluded that rebellion engineered and controlled from Britain was the only method available until more bombers were on hand and the army had built up its strength after Dunkirk.

This independent arrangement enabled SOE to work and train its people on paramilitary lines rather than as soldiers. They received Commando training, but they were not Commandos who operated in uniform. They normally used military rank but they were not a part of any military unit. They received training on a variety of small boats but they were not Combined Operations Pilotage Parties, Special Boat Sections, or any

of the other small boat units that flourished during the period. They were trained as parachutists but they were not intended for a parachute battalion nor for Special Air Services. SOE began with regular army equipment but much specialized equipment was developed during the war especially for this group.

SOE agents were not 'spies,' although military intelligence was necessary for their own operations. This military intelligence was relayed to headquarters and passed on to the appropriate authorities. The Secret Intelligence Service operated intelligence networks and needed quiet conditions under which to work. Sometimes there was conflict between these two groups.

SOE missions were generally long term and, through a form of military organization, the agents recruited, armed, and trained willing locals in the countries where they worked. These internal armies raised by SOE operatives were to work closely with the regular forces when an invasion should be undertaken. Commando actions, on the other hand, were usually short raids with one specific objective and generally did not involve working with local populations.

The organization was also able to employ people of various nationalities either born in the country in which they were to operate or descendants of people from that country. Canada was the recruiting ground for various European nationalities as well as for the Chinese Canadian agents recruited by Kendall and for those recruited for Force 136 by Major Legg. Japanese Canadian linguists also were recruited and trained in Canada for duties in the Far East and Southwest Pacific; they did not operate as agents but as language specialists.

Because these SOE agents in Europe were civilians, or individuals from the military masquerading as civilians and did not wear regular uniforms, when caught they could be shot immediately rather than treated as defeated soldiers. They could still be shot, whether in or out of uniform, after Hitler issued his Commando Order in October 1942. In Malaya and Sarawak uniforms of a kind were worn, but Europeans in these countries were not able to pose as native inhabitants.

In European operations, SOE invariably obtained commissioned rank for the operatives so that they might have some protection if captured; they were posted to Military Intelligence or the General List. Canadian volunteers appear to have all been posted to Military Intelligence. Commissioning was frowned upon by the Department of National Defence in Ottawa. DND even hesitated to confirm the rank of corporal, at least insofar as Chinese Canadians were concerned.

From late 1943, SOE came under closer control of the military. Special agent training of small numbers of men was replaced by training leaders in large groups for partisan or guerrilla warfare who were to work closely with invading Allied forces. The Jedburgh teams were an instance of this shift in focus; the Jedburgh teams operated in uniform. The military emphasis became increasingly apparent as the war progressed, especially in the Far East, where the military insisted that, from its point of view, intelligence ought to be the main function of this clandestine body.

India had been militarily oriented from the beginning with the necessary approval for any action coming from the Commander in Chief, India, or the Viceroy, until 1943 when South East Asia Command was formed. From the time SEAC was established, all clandestine operations had to be cleared through P Division, which was set up to coordinate activities of the dozen clandestine bodies active in that theatre.

In Australia, SOE was set up before the Allied Intelligence Bureau was formed. SOE came under AIB, which coordinated the activities of both the 'M' organization and the 'Z' Special Unit of the Services Reconnaissance Department. The gathering of military intelligence was also stressed in this theatre.

SOE was not an intelligence gathering organization but, because of the position of its operatives, military intelligence was incidentally gathered. The intelligence function was often misunderstood, as was the fact that SOE was strictly operational in character. Even the upper echelons of SOE were not always consistent about its proper role. Force 136 teams in Malaya and 'Z' Special Unit operatives in Sarawak served the army intelligence function at the same time as they trained and armed guerrillas and led them against the Japanese.

The crucial role of a friendly population was demonstrated in Portuguese Timor, when guerrilla leaders were forced to pull out because the local population was turning against them under pressure of Japanese reprisals. The operatives in Borneo were able to function only because of the cooperation and friendly reception of the native tribes. One can't say the Chinese Communists were 'friendly' in Malaya but at least they tolerated Force 136 agents and cooperated with them until the surrender. The political implications of training and support for the Chinese Communists in Malaya by Force 136 would have to be held in abeyance until the war was over, as had been the practice in European countries. There was no similar local movement in Sarawak among the Dyaks.

In London there was a director in charge of overseas groups and missions, including the Far East. There was no change in the terms of reference for operations in the Far East from those originally produced for operations in Europe. London never seemed to acknowledge the immense distances that had to be covered in any operation in the Far East. All insertions had to be made by submarine; long-range aircraft did not become available until late 1944 and early 1945. Economic differences gave European countries an industrial base suitable for sabotage, but the agricultural base of most Asian countries meant there was very little if anything to destroy. There were no 'safe' houses; operatives in Malaya and Sarawak were forced to make their own shelters in an alien, often hostile, jungle environment. Tropical diseases took a heavy toll of men, and their equipment rapidly deteriorated.

Overseas groups and missions included Special Training School No. 101, whose personnel moved to India after the fall of Singapore; Haifa in Palestine, STS No. 102, trained operatives for the Mediterranean area; Whitby, Ont, STS No. 103, where training of agents for various European countries occurred; as well as others scattered world wide primarily in North Africa, Australia, Ceylon, and India. Military Establishment 100 appears to have been the equivalent in Australia. There is no significance in the alternate use of STS and ME—they have the same meaning. Similar military establishments in India were numbered below 100.

Training in Great Britain took place in special training schools spread throughout the Kingdom. Preliminary training consisted of two or three weeks of physical training, map-reading, and basic weapons training. Many recruits were weeded out at this stage as unsuitable.

Graduates of this course then advanced to one of the Group A Schools at Arisaig at Inverness for three or four weeks of intensive training in small arms, silent killing, demolition, sabotage, fieldcraft, and Morse code. These aggressive aspects of training were offensive in nature, as opposed to the defensive instruction given in the final Group B Schools.

The finishing schools at Beaulieu in the New Forest provided the polish for those who were able to stay the course. Knowledge of the police and military, and of the language of the country where the agents were headed, interrogation, security, cover, disguise, agent-recruiting, communications, codes and ciphers, and propaganda techniques were taught. Practical exercises in the techniques they had learned were held for graduates of the various courses.

Some of this had to be changed for different conditions in Southeast Asia and the Southwest Pacific but many European techniques were still being taught even though the methods did not apply. For example, the Ringwood Special Intelligence School in Australia taught operatives going into Sarawak the need to remain inconspicuous when frequenting coffee shops, that is "to avoid regular visits to the same cafe but in the event of an unavoidable repeat, do not sit at

the same location."[1] There were no coffee shops on the Rejang.

Changes in training did occur, however, and stress was laid on jungle survival, especially in learning the thousand and one uses for bamboo, identification of edible foods, and the need to purify water. Heavy emphasis was placed on hygiene; even a small cut or leech bite could lead to a tropical ulcer which could eat its way to the bone in a very short time.

There were no resistance movements in Asia similar to those in Europe, and local populations had to be carefully approached. Inhabitants in the Far East often saw their freedom equally balanced between the colonial British and the conquering Japanese without much choice between them. Sarawak was an exception since the Ibans, Kayans, Kenyahs, and other native tribes were quite happy with their rajah and welcomed the return of the white men.

Parachute training was another part of the programme which took place at Ringway in England. Departures were made from Tempsford from 1942, using the Whitley, Halifax, Lysander and Hudson. The Stirling was added in 1943/4. Although having a relatively short range, these aircraft were suitable for the purpose of dropping agents and stores in nearby European countries. When Liberators and Dakotas of American Special Duty Squadrons were added early in 1944, more distant areas were within range.

In India, parachute training was moved from Chaklala near Rawalpindi to Jessore in January 1944; here the training of aircrew in the special duty squadrons for dropping members of the clandestine organizations and their supplies was concentrated. Operatives were dropped into Burma from Dakotas but only long-range Liberators had the necessary range for Malaya. The Catalina Flying Boat had the range but the boat had to land to deliver its passengers, and the noise of take-off proved hazardous.

In Australia, long-range aircraft became available in early 1945 when Special Duties Flight 200 RAAF was assigned to the Allied Intelligence Bureau by the Americans.

Three of the original six aircraft in this flight were lost soon after its formation. Five additional aircraft were then released to the organization but it took two or three months before they finally began appearing as part of the flight. Training was given on Dakotas at Richmond, near Sydney, but was later moved to Leyburn, near Brisbane, where the SD Flight of Liberators was located.

Previously, clandestine parties had to be landed by submarine from both India and Australia, with submarine captains more anxious to sink enemy shipping than to carry and despatch clandestine agents.

Those who completed the courses in these schools, and who were considered to be suitable psychologically and physically, were then sent to holding schools to await their call. Like some of the training schools, these holding schools were often segregated into language and country areas. For operations into Malaya, holding camps were located in Ceylon. By 1945, the holding camp for operations in Sarawak was located at Morotai in the Halmaheras, just off the northwest tip of New Guinea.

Secrecy and SOE were synonymous; the very fact of its existence was a long-maintained secret. Cover names were used to hide its identity and this may account in part for some of the uncertainty surrounding the organization and its relations with the rest of the secret community and the military. The name used in India was Force 136 after the headquarters moved to Ceylon. In Australia its most secret name known to only a few was Special Operations Australia, but it was normally called the Services Reconnaissance Department. Some knew it only as 'Z' Special Unit.

STS 101, based in Singapore from May 1941, operated under the name of the Far Eastern Office of the Ministry of Economic Warfare which ironically is exactly what it was. By early 1942 STS 101 had managed to infiltrate eight 'leave behind' parties, each made up of 45 men. Although the Japanese prevented these parties from taking up northern positions in Malaya, they were able to infiltrate into nearby areas. A few Chinese Communists had been trained at No. 101 and 163 of them were also in position by January in seven arms and food depots. Many but not all of the British 'leave behind' parties were captured; some were successfully evacuated along with thousands of other personnel including troops. Headquarters personnel from STS 101 escaped when the British capitulated, some to Australia, and others to India. An escape route, set up and supplied by SOE, was instrumental in assisting many of these refugees.

STS 101 signals group from Singapore set up its station in the grounds of the British Consulate in Kunming, China, when they reached that city. Then some went on to Chungking where they set up another station, and finally a few reached Calcutta where a third station was established to maintain links with the scattered stations.

British Security Coordination

Canadians from a variety of national backgrounds were recruited into SOE by British Security Coordination, housed on the 6th Floor, Rockefeller Centre on Fifth Avenue in New York City.

The head of SIS appointed William Stephenson to the post of Passport Control Officer in the United States. PCO was a cover name for his actual work of intelligence agent, but passport duties were also handled by his office. The 'Z' organization, set up as a companion to the Passport Control Office, became part of SOE when it was formed in 1940. In his role as British Security Coordinator, Stephenson was responsible for all sections of British Intelligence. In addition to MI 6 (SIS functions), and MI 5 (the internal and overseas security service), SOE was added after December 1940, and later still, responsibility for communications.

MI 6 and SOE operated in Canada from Camp X, STS No. 103, on a farm between Whitby and Oshawa, Ont. The school was set up in December 1941 by BSC. The radio station, *Hydra*, had already been established here.

This school was used to give preliminary training for operatives for the European theatre, as well as initially to train OSS agents. It was not a complete training such as obtained in England, although it did have many instructors from those schools, but it was a short, intensive, preliminary training designed to weed out those who were not considered capable of the work so that they would not be sent overseas. The school was also used to impress and help the Americans, serving as their initial training school until their own camps were established. Training at STS 103 ceased in the spring of 1944.

With Stephenson's help and guidance, Gen. William Donovan set up the Office of Strategic Services, the American equivalent. OSS opened its own schools in Virginia and Maryland from mid-1942 with a few of the STS 103 personnel as instructors. Donovan added the collection of intelligence to that of operations in the OSS mandate, unlike the two distinct organizations of the British—SOE and SIS.

The Canadian representative of BSC was T.G. Drew-Brook, a Toronto stockbroker. Drew-Brook received the assistance of the Minister of National Defence, the Undersecretary of State for External Affairs, and the secretary to the cabinet. The Department of External Affairs was the main link between Ottawa and New York. F/Lt. Herbert Sichel of the BSC New York office visited Ottawa on a monthly basis, and Camp X; he visited the Okanagan Camp once or twice during the summer of 1944.

In addition to National Defence and External Affairs, the RCMP assisted in locating personnel for the New York and Toronto offices of BSC. The RCMP also screened agents for overseas duties, as did Military Intelligence.

Those recruited by BSC for special duty were not all in the services. Civilian Yugoslavs and other Europeans were recruited through names in RCMP files and ethnic newspapers. After being interviewed by a BSC recruiting team, volunteers were enlisted into the army at Military District No. 2 in Toronto and sent on to Camp X for training.

When the request for Japanese Canadians was made by both India and Australia, this again was handled by BSC. Clearances were given by the RCMP, but the Cabinet War Committee offered alternatives to their enlistment in the Canadian Army, such as allowing any United Nations country including Britain to enlist them directly. As there was no guarantee that the volunteers would be allowed to return to Canada, the Japanese Canadians already enlisted withdrew. When this issue was finally cleared, they were enlisted in the Canadian Army and given some basic training before being sent to England for the Asian theatre.[2]

According to Military Intelligence, volunteers originally were discharged from the Canadian Army and enlisted into SOE, but by 1942, volunteers were on loan to the British for six months at a time with extensions as required. In May of 1944, Canada paid the European volunteers, but items such as 'danger pay' were made by SOE or BSC itself. These additional items were not recorded on the volunteer's Canadian army record.[3]

The original group of 13 men recruited by Kendall in 1944 were paid by BSC with allowances and gratuities paid by the Canadian Government. It would appear that, for Chinese Canadians at least, a new agreement was worked out for Kendall's first group that differed from that of European recruits and those Chinese Canadians recruited for India by Major Legg. For this first group, although their cheques were issued by the Canadian government in the normal way, the cheques were passed on to Drew-Brook to be forwarded to the men, and recovery was made from BSC on behalf of the War Office. Kendall's second group of 15 and those in Force 136 were paid by Canada except for rations and quarters.

STS 103 was one of about 60 schools scattered around the world and the only one in North America. The Okanagan Camp was not a numbered training school in the sense of No. 103; it was a tented camp set up for the purpose of training Chinese Canadians for Operation *Oblivion* and no further use was made of the site. No. 103, on the other hand, was one of the regular but unusual schools for

SOE in that all training took place at the one location.

In other countries there were usually at least three locations denoting the preliminary, the offensive, and the defensive aspects of training, with the holding schools making a fourth location. Parachute training was usually handled by the air force base near which the school was located; parachute training was not undertaken at STS 103 but some exercises were arranged with the RCAF. Communications along with codes (words) and ciphers (numbers) using the one-time pad were taught. The courses at No. 103 were also of short duration, taking about a third of the time for the same courses in other schools.

Many of the courses throughout the world varied according to the local situation. The special camp in the Okanagan adjusted the training to suit conditions in China; availability of food in the Canton-Hong Kong area and language became of prime importance. In Australia and India, a very short hygiene and medical programme was added where time permitted, since the agents not only had to treat themselves but had to care for the guerrillas and other members of the community.

In the June 1942 London agreement between OSS and SOE, OSS came under the control of the Joint Chiefs of Staff and was granted primacy in Australia, China, the South and Southwest Pacific, North Africa, Finland, and the Atlantic Islands. SOE's sphere continued in India, East and West Africa, and Western Europe. Shared zones included Burma, Siam, Malaya, Sumatra, Germany, Italy, Sweden, Switzerland, Portugal and Spain.

Malaya appears to have been shared between SOE and OSS but the retaking of the peninsula was undertaken by SEAC and did not involve American troops. Australia in the Southwest Pacific theatre was assigned to the United States. General MacArthur refused to have anything to do with either SOE or OSS, yet the Allied Intelligence Bureau (which he set up in Australia) continued to harbour SOE. Any SOE operation mounted from Australia, that would take place outside the Southwest

Pacific theatre and that did not receive the approval and funding of AIB, was handled by Force 136.

Hydra, the wireless facility, remained at the camp when SOE closed the school in September 1944; it was expanded and operated by the Canadian Army into the 1960s. Japanese ship-to-ship and ship-to-shore transmissions were intercepted in the Far East. Darwin was a receiving centre for this work. Intercepts were then relayed via Ceylon to London; from London they were transmitted to *Hydra* and sent on to Canadian and American authorities for translation and analysis. The No. 1 Discrimination Unit in Ottawa handled some of this traffic. The Discrimination Unit, a branch of Military Intelligence, had been set up in 1943 as a translation centre and linguist pool, and was disbanded 31 August 1946.

There were about 336 Royal Canadian Corps of Signals wireless operators in Australia, including 45 in an Intelligence Section, as well as three Canadian Japanese linguists, who monitored all Japanese wireless traffic received. The Japanese used a phonetic system for the transmission of wireless messages. Members of the RCCS were employed at Darwin in the Northern Territory from the spring of 1945 through to the capitulation.

STS No. 103, or Camp X, gave preliminary training for European agents only. Some of the equipment was shipped west for use by Kendall in the spring of 1944, and two of the sergeant instructors were made available for similar duties in training the first group of Chinese Canadians in the Okanagan. This first group was selected and trained by Kendall.

Francis Woodley (Mike) Kendall
F. W. (Mike) Kendall, (1907-1976), a Canadian mining engineer working in China, before 1939 had spent some three and a half years carrying out relief work for the Hong Kong government. Because of the commendable manner in which he handled the leper convoys, Kendall was recommended for the OBE. Throughout this period he

– courtesy John Ko Bong

F.W. (Mike) and Betty Kendall

contributed military intelligence to the Hong Kong garrison.

Recruited by MI 6 (Z Organization) in an intelligence network along the South China coast, in July 1939 Kendall was requested by Gen. A.E. Grasett, general officer commanding in Hong Kong, to form a unit with the code name 'Z' Force, an irregular sabotage group under SIS. Z Force was later called the Reconnaissance Unit. While in command of this unit in July 1941, Kendall left for training at STS No. 101, Singapore; he returned to Hong Kong as an officer in SOE.

Kendall recruited and started to train Chinese agents in the crown colony for sabotage work in Canton, Amoy, Swatow, and Hainan. Weapons were being packed for shipment to these areas when the Japanese attacked 8 December and the programme had to be abandoned.

Kendall had enlisted at least half a dozen others, including D.R. (Ronald) Holmes (a civil servant), along with four other civilians, including Monia Talan. They prepared hidden food and ammunition dumps in the New Territories for 'leave behind' parties if this should prove necessary.

Most of these military titles were courtesy titles. Kendall was always a civilian and never inducted into the army. When he first approached National Defence in Ottawa, he was known as Mr. Kendall. Kendall had been instructed by London to take on military rank so, in Vancouver when he was buying a uniform at the Hudson's Bay Company before meeting with the senior officers of Pacific Command, he decided that he might as well be a major as a captain.[4] As one of those employed from the early days has stated in his own case, he was a major twice and a lieutenant-colonel three times in a nine-month period in 1943.[5]

SOE was not a part of the regular military organization; when a civilian was employed he was given a suitable rank in one of the three services. This did not mean that he became a member of a unit having a War Establishment. If the agent was already in the military, his rank might be retained, increased, or lowered, as in the case of Maj. W.L.P. Sochon who accepted the rank of captain when he volunteered for special duty with SRD in Australia. Problems arose, of course, when those in the military returned to their units, especially if they had received promotions.

With another civilian member, Monia Talan (later Major), Kendall succeeded in attacking ships in the harbour at the request of Maj.-Gen. C.M. Maltby, who had replaced Grasett. The first ship of about 3,000 tons was carrying enemy observers. Kendall attached limpet mines, "which he took out to the vessel at night by sampan." He had arranged "covering fire for his party by machine gun. The limpets were fired by three hour fuses but the job was well done." A second freighter with larger tonnage was similarly sunk off Stone Cutters Island.[6]

A plan to smuggle machine guns, ammunition, and hand grenades to independent Chinese guerrillas operating in the Hong Kong vicinity proved impracticable. Kendall then handled Fifth Column control work and some 43 enemy agents were arrested and executed. He continued Reconnaissance Unit work at the same time. Other members of the group caused some harassment to the Japanese but a few members were forced to surrender when Hong Kong fell.

A week before Hong Kong capitulated, 18 December, General Maltby, the commodore, and the General Staff Officer (GSO1) met with Kendall to request that he take charge of an organized escape of key government and military personnel if this should become necessary. Five motor torpedo boats were prepared with stores and arms for escape.

When the time came, Kendall refused to leave until Admiral Chan Chak, who had lost a leg in a naval action against the Japanese on the Yangtze River, and Maj.-Gen. S.K. Yee, who represented the Chinese Secret Service, could accompany them. The admiral had set up a mission in Hong Kong for Chiang Kai-Shek. Chan Chak was later decorated by the British government and after the war became mayor of Canton as Admiral Sir Chan Chak, KCB. These two men could not be left behind without jeopardizing all future British relations in China.

By 25 December, Lt.-Cmdr. G.H. Gandy had sheltered his boats against Japanese artillery to the west of Aberdeen Island. Kendall insisted that they must rescue the two Chinese officials. Meanwhile, Admiral Chan and General Yee had teemed up with several British officers and others and commandeered a small boat which they loaded with food and fuel. When they set off, heavy machine gun fire killed General Yee and several others; the remainder, including Admiral Chan, jumped into the water.

Rescued by Gandy's motor torpedo boats, they headed northwest of Hong Kong to Mirs Bay on the advice of the admiral, since that area was controlled by Chinese guerrillas. They anchored near Peng Chau Island and contacted local resistance. The ships were scuttled. The British numbered 62.

The guerrillas led them north and they reached Waichow 30 December. The party then separated with the army group going on to Chungking and the rest to Kunming where they hired new lorries to take them on to Rangoon, 600 miles away.

Kendall did not continue with these groups but remained in China and worked with BAAG from January to July 1942, operating in Kwangtung Province. Kendall rescued his wife, Betty, from Hong Kong about three months after his own escape.[7]

Kendall then went on to Poona, India (near Bombay), where he became commandant in July 1942 at Singarh Fort and 2 i/c of the Eastern Warfare School. D.R. Holmes and Vincent Yeung continued to work for BAAG until the Chinese Canadian operation was ready for insertion in mid-December 1944.

After the United States entered the war, China came almost completely within its sphere of influence and the most effective organization Britain had in China was BAAG. A BAAG radio station operated at Chungking. Britain was further cut off from China by the division of the China-Burma-India theatre into China-Burma under Wedemeyer, and India-Burma under Mountbatten, late in 1944.

In July 1943, Kendall left India for London, England, where the proposed operation into China, now called *Oblivion,* was approved. He then travelled to Washington for American approval, but the Americans opposed it on political grounds, that is, the group would be working with the Communists.

Notwithstanding this decision, Kendall went on to New York in November 1943 to obtain the services of BSC to recruit Chinese Canadians for service in China. Ottawa came next and Kendall and Drew-Brook met with National Defence and External Affairs officials to obtain approval for their recruitment.

Kendall at first tried to interest civilian Chinese Canadians in Vancouver but without success. This had been the pattern used by BSC to recruit for SOE, particularly for operatives in Eastern Europe, such as Yugoslavia.

In his home province of British Columbia, Kendall found that Chinese Canadians were discriminated against in every imaginable way. Although they could enlist voluntarily, they were not called up for military service. Many of those who had not already voluntarily enlisted were not eager to volunteer for dangerous duties on behalf of the British Empire. An attempt to locate volunteers through NSS files was not followed up.[8]

The only alternative was to look to those in the army, and the first group of Chinese Canadians were already Canadian soldiers when they were approached initially by Canadian Military Intelligence for an interview with Kendall. The RCMP vetted the candidates as well as CMI.

Mike Kendall is important to Chinese Canadians in both the Canadian military and civil contexts. Without his request for volunteers for the China operation, and the exceptional quality of the 13 he initially recruited, and the subsequent British War Office request for additional volunteers on his recommendation, it is doubtful whether they would ever have been called up in British Columbia. Because they were called up under NRMA in 1944, there was a strong obligation on the part of the BC government to grant them the franchise.

And, despite the fact that they were called up in British Columbia under NRMA in 1944, all those recruited by Major Legg were volunteers before they again volunteered for special duty. If they had been called up for service in the Canadian Army only a very few of these men would have seen active service since many who had previously enlisted voluntarily, or had been called up under NRMA outside Pacific Command and had then turned active, were still serving in Home Defence when the war ended.

NOTES

1. Keith Barrie, "Some Personal & Training Background and Recollections of the Semut Operations, Borneo 1945," 24 April 1991 (unpublished MS in author's possession).
2. Summary of requests for Nisei and their enlistment prepared by Maj. Murray Biggar in NAC, RG 24, Vol. 2641, HQS-3488-3, Vol. 3.
3. Maj. S.R. Elliot, *Scarlet to Green; a History of Intelligence in the Canadian Army 1903-1963* (pp, 1981), p.387.
4. Reginald H. Roy, transcript of tape interview with F.W. Kendall 16 July 1968, University of British Columbia Special Collections, G.R. Pearkes Collection, p. 9.
5. Bickham Sweet-Escott, *Baker Street Irregular* (London, 1965), p.254.
6. SOE Adviser, Foreign & Commonwealth Office.
7. Roy/Kendall transcript, p.18.
8. MacNamara letter to S.H. McLaren, dated 25 April 1944 in NAC, RG 27, Vol.3004, File 'Chinese.'

Chapter IX

RECRUITMENT AND TRAINING – CANADA AND AUSTRALIA

Ottawa advised Pacific Command on 24 March 1944 that the British government was setting up a special training school in that command to be operated by British Security Coordination, an agent of the War Office. There does not appear to have been any direct contact between Ottawa and SOE; BSC handled all matters in Canada having to do with this organization. Because this was so, when the four sergeants were recommended for the Military Medal for their work in Sarawak, it was to BSC in New York that National Defence first turned for verification.

Special accommodation for the trainees, Ottawa continued, would not be necessary since tents would be used both for the men and equipment. The camp would operate for no more than three months, to train a maximum of 15 students. The men, all Chinese Canadian volunteers, would be selected by BSC in cooperation with Canadian Military Intelligence. BSC would pay for all assistance, as well as the cost of equipment and materials. Vouchers would be sent to Ottawa, passed on to BSC, and payment would be made monthly by BSC direct to the treasury officer.

The students, Ottawa added, would be recruited from the Canadian Army or from suitable civilians. If civilians were recruited, they would be enlisted at Military District No. 11 and placed on loan to the British Army. If the Whitby pattern were followed, they would be struck-off-strength Canadian Army and enlisted in the British Army when their course was complete and they moved overseas. Any obligation on the part of the Canadian government would then cease. This, of course, applied to civilians recruited into the army for training only; the men recruited by Kendall were already members of the Canadian Army and the procedure was changed.

Major-General Pearkes, GOCinC, Pacific Command, appointed Col. Hugh Allan, his aide-de-camp, as liaison officer to work with the new school; Col. A.R. St. Louis, signals officer Pacific Command, was also helpful. The commandant of the school, Mr. F.W. Kendall (as he was known in Ottawa at this time), after interviewing each candidate, notified Colonel Allan of the names of those accepted and Allan in turn advised Ottawa; arrangements were then made to complete the loan. The men selected by Kendall reported to Allan, who directed them to the school.

The First Group

The first Chinese Canadian group recruited for SOE consisted of 13 men selected from the 35 originally requested and the 15 actually located by Military Intelligence. Kendall insisted that he had originally requested 35 but Ottawa later disputed the number agreed upon. Some of these men were given preliminary interviews at MD No. 11 in Pacific Command and others at MD No. 2 in Toronto. They were also vetted by the RCMP.

Throughout the summer the students would continue to receive their pay from the Canadian government; allowances also would be continued. Cheques would be forwarded to T.G. Drew-Brook, the Canadian representative of BSC, who was responsible for ensuring each man received his pay; in the event of casualties, it was also his responsibility to notify the paymaster general.

By 31 March it was decided that the two instructors from Special Training School No. 103 would be exempt from the requirement of being placed on loan to the British while in Canada and would remain members of the Canadian Army. Training at STS 103 had ceased in April and all other activity at that school came to an end by 15 September 1944.

Drew-Brook visited Pacific Command to consult with Pearkes, and to work out the details of arrangements for this new school. Some equipment (over 100 cases) from STS 103 was shipped to the west addressed to Kendall, who met with Colonel Allan 17 April, along with S/Ldr. Herbert M. Sichel from BSC, New York.

About ten miles north of Penticton, in the Okanagan Valley, Kendall selected a camp site and tents were erected in May. The Canadian Army built a rather substantial dock and gave the camp special protection. The camp was located on a small cove on land originally known as Dunrobin's.

The *Oblivion* group called the cove Goose Bay. The name Commando Bay was officially given to the site because of a misunderstanding of the exact function the men were called on to perform. The land surrounding the Bay is now officially a heritage site, Okanagan Mountain Provincial Park, in honour of the men who trained there.

In September 1988 a bronze plaque was erected at Commando Bay commemorating the services of the 13 Chinese Canadians, omitting the name of Maj. H.J. Legg but including "Lt-Col. F.W. Kendall, O.C." Maj. Victor Wilson, MC, of Paradise Ranch, was instrumental in having the site named and designated.[1]

Upon volunteering for special duty, each man signed a copy of the Official Secrets Act at the conclusion of the interview. Each man also received a code number in the 600 series but no one now remembers what that number was after nearly 50 years.

Kendall attempted to obtain commissioned rank for the twelve trainees, but Ottawa refused. This request was made after it was learned that candidates could not be obtained among civilians but only through Canadian Army sources.

Kendall also requested that the men remain Canadian soldiers and not be enlisted in the British Army as had been done for the SOE operatives in Europe trained at Camp X. He had a sound reason for doing this since they would be working in China, and the fact that they were Canadian soldiers rather than British, quite possibly might make the project favourable to the Americans. This request was not considered by Ottawa until the men were about to leave for Australia.

The two sergeant instructors from STS 103 were Andy McClure and Jack Clayton.

Andy McClure

Sgt. Andrew Wylie McClure, B.80261, RCE, taught demolition: how to attach limpets to vessels; how to conceal weapons and to move in the water without causing phosphorescence; how to blow up railway tracks; and how to disable communications and equipment. Andy volunteered for overseas service with SOE and accompanied part of the group to Australia.

Sgt. Jack K. Clayton, B.80451, RCE, taught unarmed combat, or silent killing, and gave instruction in small arms. Jack was unable to go overseas because of eye problems.

Maj. Hugh John Legg from SOE England gave wireless instruction to three or four of the men. Legg had served in the Merchant Navy Reserve in the Mediterranean Sea, the Indian, and the South Atlantic Oceans, and convoy duty in the North Atlantic from 1939. In October 1941 he was recruited by SOE. Until February 1942 Legg was involved in the Shetland Bus operations and in March 1942 in the invasion and take-over of Madagascar, completed in August. Legg continued to monitor enemy wireless stations in Durban, South Africa, for the next two years. Recalled to London in March 1944, he was sent to the Okanagan in April.

Jack Clayton

Major Hugh John Legg

While three or four of the men received intensive wireless training, the rest of the group concentrated on other aspects of guerrilla tactics taught by Clayton and McClure. Kendall taught some aspects of the training programme, such as how to move about the country at night in silence and unseen.

Because the camp, halfway between Penticton and Kelowna, was isolated and without road access, a boat was rented from Hugh Leir in Penticton, and Sgt. Côté from RCASC was assigned the task of its care and operation.

The men arrived at the bay at various times with five on 9 May through to one on 23 June. The early arrivals erected the tents and prepared the area for the newcomers. Kendall and one or two of the volunteers met Capt. Roger Cheng in Penticton with the boat under the control of Sergeant Côté; Roger was one of the last to arrive.

The members of the group were from a variety of backgrounds and only about four were fluent in Cantonese, one of whom was Jimmy Shiu; another was Roger Cheng. Cantonese lessons were essential both at the Okanagan camp and in Australia. It did not take long for memories to be sharpened for they had all spoken the language as children.

Capt. Roger Kee Cheng, born in Lillooet, BC, 16 May 1915, was the first Chinese Canadian recruited in Toronto, MD No. 2, by Kendall, after his initial interview by Military Intelligence in Ottawa for special duty in Asia. During the Toronto interview, Kendall advised him how to proceed and that he would be met in Penticton. There were no written orders. The only paper Roger received was one that showed how he would get his pay and a box number in Toronto for mail.[2]

Roger, who was not only fluent in Cantonese but was able to read and write Chinese, acted as Chinese censor in the camp both in the Okanagan and in Australia; he had been posted to MI before his interview with Kendall. Letters written in English were censored by Kendall and he found that one of the men, unfortunately, was completely lacking in any sense of security.

Influenced by Col. A.R. St. Louis, officer commanding signals, Pacific Command, Roger Cheng had gone to training centre and qualified. When qualified, St. Louis urged him to join the army. Roger did so, and graduated from Brockville officers training. He went on to Vimy Class A14 and graduated from there in 1942. Roger Cheng was a graduate of McGill University in electrical engineering and had served in the

Johnny Bong and Tommy Lock
– note dock and boat in background

Directorate of Electrical Communications and Design in Ottawa for two years. Roger took over command in Australia after the China mission was cancelled and Kendall left the groups.

Sgt. John **Ko** Bong (76 in 1988) was born in Victoria. He enlisted in the 16th Canadian Scottish (Reserve) in 1942 and turned active in 1943. John took his basic and anti-aircraft training at Vernon and was then posted to Gander, Newfoundland, for aerodrome defence in the 56th Heavy AA Battery for eight months. When his duties were finished here, he returned to Halifax and then Toronto. He then trained at Camp Borden for infantry tank support and was at Brampton when called for his interview in Toronto. John was already a sergeant when he joined the group. Johnny Bong[3] was "the perfect handyman. He could turn his hand to anything and even if he had never done it before he would always make a good job of it."[4] One of the things John turned his hand to was barbering and he became barber for the camp.

posted to Red Deer, then to the Tank Corps, Camp Borden, before his interview with Kendall. Roy's brothers Paul, Ira, and Herby, sons of Chan Dun whose Panama Cafe was a popular spot in Victoria, also served in the Canadian forces in the Second World War.

Edward Chow, born in Vancouver, 9 February 1919, moved to Toronto in his teens. Eddie had tried to enlist in the RCAF in Toronto but after sitting in the recruitment centre for two days watching others being called in for their interview, he was informed that the RCAF did not take Orientals. He was called up in 1940 and joined the RCAMC as a medical orderly. At this time Eddie was unwilling to turn active; he wasn't going to fight for "them." Eddie joined the Medical Corps band at Camp Borden and entered Major Bowes' talent contest, winning a trip to New York. He appeared on Bowes' radio programme with the song: "He's a bra, bra, Hieland laddie."

Eddie was sent to Toronto for his interview with Kendall and because he thought he had been ordered to volunteer, he did. As

Louey King and Norm Wong – note dock in background

Roy Sin Twe Chan, born in Victoria, 11 October 1916, enlisted in the 16th Canadian Scottish (Reserve) 2 February 1942, and went active in 1943. Roy took his basic training while in the Reserve. He was

Eddie maintained, in the army when you were ordered to do something, you did it without question. He entertained the group in the evenings at Commando Bay with his songs and gymnastics.

When the war ended and the men were returning from overseas, it was the practice in Toronto for someone from city hall to meet every incoming train carrying returning servicemen. Frequently it was the mayor who met the train. By January 1946 the great rush was over and it was Controller Innes who met one lone Canadian soldier at Toronto Union Station when the train pulled in from the West; it was Eddie Chow. They shook hands, and Controller Innes welcomed him home.

Cpl. Douglas Jung, from Victoria, had served in MI in Pacific Command and had just been accepted for the course at the S-20 Japanese Language School in Vancouver when summoned for an interview. Douglas became the first Chinese Canadian to be elected a member of Parliament in 1957, and is still a practising lawyer in Vancouver.

Louey King[5] was born in Didsbury, Alta, December 1923. Louey joined the army in Calgary and was in the Tank Corps at Camp Borden when he was called to Toronto for his interview. Louey was the youngest member of the group.

Sgt. George Thomas Lock, from Toronto, born 28 July 1916, enlisted 12 May 1942 in the Dental Corps but was discharged out of the Canadian Ordnance Corps (Active) 2 March 1946. Tommy was dental inspector for the group, using portable dental equipment. Tommy was already a sergeant when he transferred to the group, and retention of his stripes was one of the conditions upon which he volunteered.

Norman Mon Low, from Vancouver, was located at Camp Borden in the Tank Corps when summoned to Toronto for his interview. Norman was trained as a wireless operator and received additional training at Meerut before joining the others in Australia. He apparently had a bad landing on one of the parachute jumps and was never well after his return to Canada.

Raymond Young Lowe, born 29 October 1913, originally from Victoria, enlisted in Winnipeg, 10 July 1942; Raymond was another wireless operator who received additional training at Meerut.

James Shiu, born in Saskatoon, returned to Canada from his university studies in California to enlist in the Canadian Army. He was serving in the Tank Corps at Camp Borden when he received his summons to Toronto. He also received additional wireless training at Meerut. Major Legg considered Jimmy to "have the finest intellect of anybody in the camp, including the commanding officer."[6] After the war, Jimmy returned to his studies in California and upon graduation was employed in the aircraft industry. After retirement, he became an aeronautical consultant.

Cpl. Henry Albert (Hank) Wong was born 25 August 1920 in London, Ont. Hank enlisted in the Kent Regiment, Chatham, Ont, in 1940, after being refused for service in the RCN. He served with his regiment in Halifax, Niagara Falls, and in Pacific Command at Terrace as part of the 14th Canadian Infantry Brigade. Hank was infantry instructor in Commando type training, or battle drill as it was later called. Hank was on compassionate leave at his sister's restaurant in Palmerston, Ont, when he was approached by MI. His interview did not occur until he returned to British Columbia and it took place at the Vancouver Hotel, Army Headquarters in Pacific Command.

Sgt. Norman Donald Wong was born 6 February 1916, also in London, Ont. Like Eddie Chow, Norman had tried to enlist in the air force in 1941 without success. Although he was not refused by the recruiting office, there was a long waiting list. He was called up under NRMA in 1942 and was posted to the Canadian Fusiliers (City of London Regiment). It was a month after being accepted that he learned he was a 'Zombie' and promptly turned active. The Fusiliers escorted German POWs, captured in the African campaign, from New York to Calgary in 1942.

The Canadian Fusiliers was then attached to Pacific Command and formed a part of the combined operations with the Americans on the Kiska invasion in the Aleutians. They left Nanaimo 12 July 1943. When they landed in Kiska on 16 August, they found that the Japanese had evacuated two weeks before. The First Special Service Force (the North Americans) moving inland from a different beach had met the assault troops head on and they fired on each other until the mistake was recognized. There were a few Canadian casualties but these were mostly from Japanese booby-traps. The commanding officer of the Fusiliers had issued a notice to all troops that the Oriental with them was not Japanese but Chinese, just in case Norman should be mistaken for the enemy.

Japanese hut

Shinto Shrine

Kiska Winter Scene

Recalled from Kiska to Vernon in the advance party 21 November, Norman next took the jungle warfare course at Prince George. The rest of the battalion landed in Vancouver on 3 January 1944. The Canadian Fusiliers then formed a part of the 13th Canadian Infantry Brigade for overseas service. When the Brigade arrived in England the men were used as reinforcements and the officers as a training cadre for new arrivals.

Japanese anti-aircraft gun

About the time the regiment was to move overseas, his commanding officer informed Norman that because his PULHEMS showed 5 under the E he would not be going with them. There had been no change in his eyes from when he joined the Army. His personal file showed 4 under the E.

Instead of moving with his regiment, Norman was sent to Vancouver for an interview with Kendall. He was already a sergeant when he volunteered for special duty and became staff sergeant during training. Norman was the senior sergeant "who didn't speak much but when he did it was worth listening to—he had the gift of leadership—he was a born but quiet leader."[7]

Wing Lee Wong (87 in 1988) was the oldest member of the group and the others were inclined to call him 'Dad.' Wing came to Canada when he was about nine years old. He worked in missionary homes as house boy, and was sent to school for some education, which must have been difficult for him since he was so much older than the others. After several years as houseboy, Wing moved out to the Prairies and began to prosper, acquiring a farm and a restaurant. Then disasters struck; fire destroyed the restaurant, and the drought and the Depression destroyed the farm.

Like many other Canadians in similar circumstances, Wing enlisted in Regina in 1941. He took his basic training at Vernon. Initially sent to Barriefield for signals training, Wing requested a transfer to a signals unit in Vancouver. Before this could transpire, Wing was remustered into the artillery. Kendall and Major Legg together interviewed Wing in Vancouver. He was one of the last to join the group.

Of this group, Major Legg said, even those who were not intellectuals were "the sort of men you would like to have beside you in a real scrap."[8]

Sergeant Côté, who looked after the boat was "a complete loner: he lived, ate, cooked his own meals and kept himself completely apart from us. He was mad on boats," and Legg was sure that after the war that it would be his preferred way of living again—on a boat and alone.[9]

Training was continuous from May to September, seven days a week, from dawn to dark. The only relief was when they assisted Mrs. Wilson at Paradise Ranch to harvest cherries and peaches; Maj. Victor Wilson was overseas and help was impossible to get. Kendall and Legg were aware of the labour problems at the ranch because the mail was picked up nearby.

Although they all took some wireless training, the group was split, with eight concentrating on arms and demolition. Unarmed combat (silent killing), small arms, sabotage (incendiaries and explosives), boat work, both in attaching limpet mines and in manipulating two-man boats (folboats), swimming (especially underwater work), night operations, night landings from boats, and mountain climbing, were all a part of their training.

Hank Wong with mountain pack

Johnny Bong and Eddie Chow

At one time they set fire to the mountain and it was necessary to summon firefighters from Summerland across the lake to control it. This may have been at the time they were clearing the camp before they left since nothing was to remain behind and Kendall had instructed them to dispose of any remaining supplies.

At least six tents were erected at Commando Bay; two for the men, and one each for mess, the Kendalls, the instructors, and Major Legg. The old wooden hut that was already on the property when they arrived was used as storage. Major Legg also kept some of the equipment in his tent.

The cookhouse and stores were located on the shore, the living quarters about a thousand feet up the steep bank. They ran up and down this bank from first thing in the morning, when they all swam in the icy water, until they retired for the night.

The area was restricted by the Department of National Defence between defined limits. The regular army camp at Vernon took some of the pressure off the natural curiosity of the inhabitants of the valley, especially when demolition practice was in full swing. The rather substantial dock built by the army has completely disappeared, used for firewood by campers.

The small island just off the bay was used to keep hens; they could neither fly nor swim. It proved an ideal place for them until the smell proved too much when the wind blew across it and the idea had to be abandoned. They took turns preparing their meals.

Underwater work was also a part of their curriculum so the ability to swim was a necessary part of their training. Louey King was unable to learn to dive but the group thought they were teaching him to swim and this may have been one of the problems. The area was infested by rattle snakes and Louey very bravely allowed a snake to slither across his arms while lying in ambush; this particular snake was harmless.

Jack Clayton shot a bear when they were returning from Penticton on the supply boat. Apparently he always kept a rifle with him and from the boat he aimed and shot the bear in a tree. Landing on the shore, he started to approach the tree with his pistol to finish off the animal, when the bear fell. Jack thought the bear was still alive and raced back to the shore and the safety of the boat. Whether this was a grizzly bear is not known; apparently Kendall had agreed not to remove any grizzlies from the area and a marginal note on the record in London wanted to know if the grizzlies had offered to act in the same manner.

Major Legg remembers a deer being shot as well. When he enquired in Penticton about the legality of killing deer out of season, the official advised him that if the deer attacked them they could legally shoot it.

At the end of training, the group was taken on practice raids against military and industrial establishments. At Powell River, they attacked the flume carrying water to the pulp and paper mill. They tried to capture the three-inch batteries facing the sea at Yorke Island, in Johnstone Strait. They attacked an airfield in the same general area. They used folboats to paddle around the harbour, and attached dummy limpet mines to the ferries at Victoria. Next door, at the naval establishment in Esquimalt, they managed to reach the submarine nets before they were spotted; the navy boat, in spite of its searchlights, ran aground when it gave chase.

They were all instructed to have boots made for themselves and this is the only personal item that appears to have been supplied by BSC. The boots were made in Vancouver before they left Canada. Also at some time in their training, they were issued with what later became known as Commando knives; these knives were originally developed by and called Fairbairn/Sykes, two of the original SOE instructors.

The special training school in the Okanagan was officially closed in mid-September while the men received embarkation leave and stores and accounts were cleared up.

Now that training was complete, final arrangements had to be made for their trip to Australia. Ottawa decreed that each volunteer was to sign a declaration stating his willingness to be discharged from the Canadian Army and to be enlisted in the British Army before he left Canada. Discharge arrangements would be made along with transportation to Australia, the latter being handled by BSC.

When Kendall met with Ottawa officials in early August, he stressed the importance to the operation that the men remain in the Canadian rather than be transferred to the British Army. Operating in China, their Canadian nationality would help soothe the Americans who might not realize Operation *Oblivion* was British-sponsored since all, with the exception of Holmes and Yeung, were Canadians. Kendall flew on to England on the 17th.

A new draft form of agreement was drawn up since the one proposed by BSC had been designed for civilians recruited into the Canadian Army for training only. Although the transfer to the British Army was still the official stand, there had been problems associated with this policy. On 3 August, it was noted with alarm the lack of information available when any of the Canadians employed by SOE became casualties. Since there was little if any record of the man's activities in Ottawa, and SOE kept all records to a minimum, suitable information could not be passed on to the next of kin. It was felt that a better system should be developed.

On Kendall's return from England and New York on 24 August, the argument was put forward by Drew-Brook that the circumstances were such that the Canadian Army personnel going to Australia should remain Canadian soldiers. In order to obtain men of the required nationality and type, BSC was compelled to select Canadian citizens who were already members of the Canadian Army before selection. As such it would be unfair to deprive them of their rights as Canadian soldiers. Since pay and the cost of their maintenance and upkeep would be undertaken by BSC on behalf of the War Office, it would only be dependants' allowances, service gratuities, pensions, and so on that would be underwritten by the Canadian government. The men were undertaking a hazardous job in the war against Japan, Drew-Brook concluded, and should not be penalized for volunteering.

Ottawa accepted this argument and it was subsequently decided that instead of being enlisted in the British Army, they would be on loan only. Ottawa would continue to pay the men, the cheques would be sent to Drew-Brook, and the amount would be recovered from BSC for the War Office. BSC would also pay the cost of maintenance and upkeep. This new proposal was approved by the Minister of National Defence on 27 August. The Disposal Order was issued 2 October authorizing the temporary attachment of one officer and 13 other ranks; McClure makes the 13th OR.

The question of rank also came under discussion before the departure of the group. Captain Cheng was confirmed in his rank in September and all the others as sergeants with

N.D. Wong being confirmed as staff sergeant effective 1 October. Ottawa was reluctant to confirm these ranks and the proposal for staff sergeant was in lieu of the requested company sergeant major rank as put forth by Drew-Brook. Originally Ottawa had proposed that Roger Cheng relinquish his rank from the date that he joined the group and he was to sign a document indicating his willingness to do so. This request was also dropped.

Once the question of rank was resolved, the men were then posted to the Unattached List ("Q" List), NDHQ, on departure from Canada. This is one of the reasons many of them received their discharge from units in which they had not served. The military districts had no record of these men or their activities and appear to have picked any unit for demobilization. One from Toronto was demobilized in Hamilton, Ont.

Kendall and Sichel at the meeting in Ottawa 31 August also tried to recruit an additional 25 men, insisting that these had been promised originally. Ottawa had no recollection of such a promise and the 13 already approved and trained appeared to be the maximum.

However, by late October, the Disposal Order (PC 3464) stated that 25 all ranks were eligible for service on loan to British forces in the 'Pacific Theatre' for duty in India and Australia. An additional 15 were selected by Major Legg upon his return to Canada the end of 1944 for Kendall's second group, and they arrived in Australia in March 1945. A third group was to follow them.

These 15 were included in Disposal Order 100 authorizing the loan of 150 Chinese Canadians to the British (the Disposal Order for 25 had been cancelled). The total number of Chinese Canadians under Kendall's command in Australia rose to 28. The grand total of 150 did not include the first group nor individuals outside these two main groups.

General Pearkes, true to his promise to the trainees at Commando Bay on his visit to the camp one July weekend, when the call up for Chinese Canadians in British Columbia got under way in August 1944, wrote to Ottawa to stress that the lack of enthusiasm was directly related to the lack of the franchise. The question of the franchise had been discussed on his visit to the camp. Pearkes also raised the question of the status of the men on their return to Canada but no response on this matter was forthcoming.[10]

The call up of Chinese Canadians in British Columbia in August 1944 was brought about by pressure from the British War Office for additional recruits of this nationality. When Kendall had reported to London on the calibre of the men he was training, it was decided that here was the source of suitable members for similar work with Force 136 in India.[11]

Drew-Brook raised another point in Ottawa 29 September when he queried the status of Chinese wives should any of them marry while in Australia. Ever since 1923 Chinese immigrants were prohibited from entering Canada; wives were not included in the exceptions. A large imbalance between males and females in the Chinese Canadian population was the result and produced what became known as a 'bachelor society.' Many of these men might have wives in China but these wives could not enter Canada. National Defence promptly handed Drew-Brook's query on to External Affairs for its consideration without comment.

Meanwhile, conducted by Lieut. Gordon Thomson, Capt. Roger Cheng and Sgts. James Shiu, Norman Low, and Raymond Lowe, left Vancouver the first week of September 1944 by plane to Gander, on to England, North Africa, then to India, where they received specialized training in wireless, ciphers, and codes at Force 136 Meerut. They completed the trip to Australia accompanied by Kendall after he had conferred in London, England, and then consulted with Force 136 in India where he received his directive.

The *Oblivion* group was to arm and train anti-Japanese forces in China; attack Japanese communications; perform industrial and shipping sabotage in Hong Kong, the New Territories, and Canton areas; arm and man six Chinese junks to direct aerial attacks on ships; photograph landing places and beach and underwater defences; act as a Fifth

Chinese money for Operation *Oblivion*

Column; perform coast watching duties; and carry on anti-Japanese propaganda.[12] The second and third groups were to land at three-month intervals.

Together with Cheng and the three sergeants, Kendall joined the larger group in Australia on 22 November.[13] The Chinese Canadians recruited by Kendall spoke Cantonese and could operate only within the narrow range of Hong Kong. Canadian Chinese were selected because, according to Kendall, in India "we ran out of Chinese, and we couldn't get Cantonese speakers in that particular part of the world."[14] Holmes had received language lessons as a civil service cadet and spoke Mandarin and Cantonese, and Sgt. Vincent Yeung spoke Hakka, a dialect of the original boat people. It is not known whether Kendall spoke Cantonese, although members of the first group believed that he always understood what was said.

For their operation in China, Ottawa prescribed appropriate vitamin pills packaged to resist the climate in order to offset a diet of polished rice and fish; identification of local vegetation for supplementary vitamins was

A C K N O W L E D G M E N T

EXEMPTION. *19(1)*
ACCESS TO INFORMATION ACT   member of an active

unit of the Canadian Army, hereby acknowledge that I have

voluntarily expressed my willingness to be attached for

duty with the United Kingdom Forces serving in the Pacific

theatre of war. I understand that, during such attachment,

I shall be subject at all times to the Military law and

discipline applicable to the said United Kingdom Forces.

DATED at..*Vancouver*..this.......6..day of....*Oct*.......1944.

EXEMPTION. *19(1)*
~~TO INFORMATION ACT~~

Signature of Officer, Warrant
Officer, Non-commissioned
Officer or Other Rank.

WITNESS;

_____ *major*

149

WAR DEPARTMENT
The Adjutant General's Office   COPY NO. _____ 24
Washington 25, D. C.

AG 091.713(26 Sep 44)OB-S-E   LAP - 2B 939 Pentagon

                                               27 September 1944

SUBJECT: Invitational Travel Orders   ::::::::::::::::::::::
                                               :   S E C R E T   :
TO: The Commanding General,   :Auth: T. A. G.   :
          San Francisco Port of Embarkation   :Initials -RDV   :
       The Chief of Transportation,   :Date: 27 Sep 44 P
          Army Service Forces   ::::::::::::::::::::::

     1.   Upon call of the port commander, on or about 1 October 1944, the
following named Canadian Army personnel are hereby authorized and invited to
proceed by water transportation from the San Francisco Port of Embarkation to
Melbourne, Australia.

                          Major H. J. Legg
              B. 80261   Sgt. A. W. McClure
              K. 50956   Sgt. John Ko Bong
              K. 69908   Sgt. Roy Sin Twe Chan
              B. 91866   Sgt. Edward Chow
              K. 50902   Sgt. Douglas Jung
              K. 50207   Sgt. Loui King
              B. 113018   Sgt. George Thomas Lock
              A. 50317   Sgt. Henry Albert Wong
              A. 61714   Sgt. Norman Donald Wong
              L. 100443   Sgt. Wing Lee Wong

     2.   Prior to departure from the continental United States, they will be
required to have completed the prescribed immunizations in conformity with
current War Department instructions.

     3.   Baggage will not exceed one hundred seventy-five (175) pounds each
and must be shipped to the port of embarkation so as to arrive at least forty-
eight (48) hours prior to sailing time or be brought to the port in the physical
possession of the owner. Baggage shipped to the port will be marked with the
owner's full name and addressed as follows: .   ·

              TO: PORT TRANS O (PB)
                    SF P of E
                    SAN FRANCISCO, CALIF.
              FOR: (Port Commander will enter appropriate marking.)

Under no conditions will personal baggage be crated or boxed for shipment to
the port.

                                                       SECRET

also pointed out. The stores that accompanied the men travelling by train to San Francisco included small arms and grenades. Dental equipment valued at less than $100, and technical stores were also included. Six cases of incendiaries and one case containing an Adana printing press weighing 26 pounds were consigned to Special Operations Australia and shipped from West Saint John, NB. Most of these technical stores were used to continue their training in Australia; the printing press was for propaganda purposes in China.

Disciplinary regulations were spelled out in a letter from Canadian Military Headquarters, London, outlining the procedure for Canadian military personnel attached to United Kingdom forces. These regulations were to apply to both the Australia and India groups. Before they left Vancouver each man was required to sign an "Acknowledgment."

The Canadian Military Attaché in Australia, Col. L. Moore Cosgrave, was advised that the men would be arriving in Australia, as he had been advised for the 336 in the No.1 Special Wireless Group, RCCS,[15] and the 73 in the Radar Detachment.[16]

Although the move was made on behalf of BSC, for security reasons, orders ensured that no indication was made of this connection; the movement was made as if these were ordinary Canadian troops. Under the US War Department's "Invitational Travel Orders" dated 27 September 1944, nine of the group plus Andy McClure, conducted by Major Legg, left Vancouver 6 October, and travelled by train to San Francisco where they arrived two days later.

On the troopship SS *Lurline,* they set out from San Francisco on their passage across the Pacific. Before they reached their destination, the ship was rerouted to the Philippines by General MacArthur, who needed the American troops immediately. Major Legg prevailed on the captain to put them ashore in New Guinea.

They were deposited at an almost deserted American staging camp at Oro Bay, near Buna, the scene of a major battle between the Australians, Americans, and Japanese. Although New Guinea had been strategically

Oro Bay, New Guinea
Open air theatre

retaken by 28 May 1944, it was 23 August before the Biak and Noemfoor fighting ended. Debris from the Buna and Gona battles still littered the beach when the SS *Lurline* dropped them at Oro Bay.

Oro Bay, New Guinea
'outhouse'

The area had been a US Army holding camp for surplus military personnel, and had also been used as a repatriation station, and had contained a hospital. A five-mile walk up the beach on loose sand to an Australian signal post was necessary in order to get word through to Australian Army Headquarters, Melbourne, of their predicament.

The Australian liner *Duntroon,* a 2000 ton first-class luxury liner converted to war purposes, was sent to pick them up in New Guinea and take them to Townsville, Queensland, where they landed early November. They were loaded into coaches to make the trip to Melbourne, New South Wales, and Mornington Camp. Three station changes were necessary before they reached Melbourne because of triple gauge tracks. They arrived at the camp 12 November 1944.[17]

Canadian Army, was granted a commission in the British Army the end of December 1944. He became a member of 'Z' Special Unit in June 1945.

Kendall oversaw the brief Australian training, as he had done in the Okanagan. This additional training covered aspects that could not be handled at Commando Bay, such as familiarization with Japanese weapons, and knowledge of all aspects of the Japanese military including the *Kempei Tai* (military police). The group was not a part of the normal training stream of the Services Reconnaissance Department, but kept separate from other trainees.

**Training at Fraser Island
Mike Kendall and Norm Wong
with Japanese weapon**

Roy Chan, Hank Wong, and Andy McClure

While the 13 Canadians came under the command of British Security Co-ordination, Military Establishment 100, Sergeant McClure, after discharge from the

The men trained at Park Orchards, near Melbourne, at the School of Eastern Interpreters (another cover name), with a course probably very similar to the one at

Alam Bazaar near Calcutta, which was set up on the lines of the Beaulieu schools to provide agent and propaganda training. They were given continued instruction in Cantonese, which is duly commented upon in the Australian Archives. They went to Melbourne to practise tailing, and losing a tail, and other aspects of surveillance. There was constant movement up and down the coast and from Melbourne to Fraser Island. Frequently, they were able to hitch-hike by air.

At Fraser Island, Queensland, they trained in small boat work and Japanese equipment. Here too they underwent jungle training, and were given a medical course both for themselves and for others they would come in contact with. Medical assistance to

Hitchhiking trio:
Norm Wong, Tom Lock, and Hank Wong

Ready to board submarine
Back l to r - Doug Jung, Jim Shiu, Norm Wong, Hank Wong, Louey King
Front l to r - John Bong, Ed Chow, Roy Chan, Wing Wong (in front)
Norm Low, Roger Cheng, Tom Lock, Vincent Yeung, Ray Lowe

the Chinese was a programme begun by the British Army Aid Group and since they would be working in the BAAG area they would need to be skilled in medical treatment.

By mid-December training was complete, specialized stores were packed and they were ready to board the submarine for infiltration to China via Mirs or Bias Bay, northeast of Hong Kong.

Gen. Albert Wedemeyer, recently appointed commander of the China theatre, soon made strong objections. He insisted that all clandestine operations in China must have his approval. So far as this operation was concerned, he claimed it would be a waste of resources to land such a party on the coast from an Australian-based submarine, and they would be involved with the Communist party. He maintained this position even when there was no implication of communist contact in alternative suggestions.

After cancellation of the China operation, both Kendall and Holmes, the political adviser, tried to obtain volunteers for operations in Malaya, or Sumatra, or some of the other nearby islands, but the men were not agreeable to operating in these areas. Kendall remained with them until this operation and all other proposals were irrevocably cancelled. Maj. D.R. Holmes and Sgt. Vincent Yeung returned to BAAG to continue their work in China.

Kendall left the group when the operation was cancelled and continued instruction for SRD in Australia until "Just prior to the first atom bomb on Japan I was ordered back to the United States for liaison duties with the American O.S.F.[*sic*]."[18] Kendall left SOE 1 October 1945 and returned to Hong Kong.

The 13 took their parachute training at Richmond, just west of Sydney. Five from this group completed the conversion training at Leyburn by 6 April. The others did not withdraw their volunteer status but for various reasons were unable to complete the parachute training. Those who became qualified parachutists received additional parachute pay.

Sgt. Douglas Jung from the first group broke his ankle on a drop and spent several months in an Australian hospital, being discharged from hospital on 14 August, the day of Hirohito's surrender broadcast. Ironically enough, he dropped on an ambulance, which in its turn was trying to get out of his way. Sgt. Roy Chan wrenched his ankle badly on a drop but he bandaged it up and continued his training. Sgt. Norman Low had a bad drop and others received wrenched and torn muscles as well.

The Second Group

The second group for Australia, consisting of the 15 men selected by Major Legg, travelled via Vancouver-Seattle-Portland-Stockton to Pittsburg, California, on a through tourist sleeper with all meals. They were met by someone from Camp Stoneman where they stayed until embarkation. The US War Department's Invitational Travel Orders were sent by air mail. The men received enough American money for incidentals while they were in the United States. Cpl. Charlie J. Fong was conducting NCO. From San Francisco, they took passage 28 February 1945 on the UST *Fred Ainsworth* for Australia. They arrived at Brisbane 26 March.

Before they left Canada, on 1 February, the move of ten to Australia was cancelled, and they were to be included with those going to the UK. The following day it was confirmed that five would still be going to Australia. Then all 15 were reinstated. Kendall's proposed Operation *Oblivion* and all other proposals for the Hong Kong area had been cancelled during January but Australia had decided they could use the men.

They left Brisbane after two days at a staging camp and reached Maryborough, Queensland, by train. A landing barge took them to Fraser Island where they trained until July. They arrived too late to train for the China mission; their training was for an operation into Sarawak.

Training for the Sarawak operation consisted of "building stamina, demolition, unarmed combat, night maneuvers with compass only, the use of folboats and learning to speak Malay." They completed their training on the island with a stamina test consisting of

Back l to r - Ed Fong, Harden Lee, Henry Cheng, Jan Yuen
Front l to r - Doug Marr, Harry Eng, Dick Lam

– *courtesy Harden Lee*

Training at Fraser Island
Back: Harden Lee and Dick Lam
Front: Ed Fong and Georges Fong

AUSTRALIA

143

"swimming 500 yards fully clothed, leaving the water and removing the wet clothing and running five miles on loose sand back to camp, all within forty minutes."[19]

They next took parachute training at Richmond, consisting of seven jumps. Ten received their wings 7 July; the four others preferred submarine or other type of insertion.

Rupert Fong returned to Vancouver for medical reasons on 1 June. Rupert had broken his foot when a child and the fracture had not healed properly; he was unable to keep up with the others in running and other pro-longed and strenuous activities. Since he was unable to read and write Chinese, SRD had no position for him.

From Richmond, the group was supposed to travel to Brisbane but they were misdirected to Melbourne instead where they spent a week before reaching the desired goal. On 15 August, all leave was cancelled, and they were briefed to leave at 3:00 am the following morning as a part of Operation *Hippo*.

At eight o'clock that night they were informed that all orders had been cancelled and that the war was over. They were issued passes to go into Brisbane, where they cele-brated. They then moved into Camp Tabragalba where they met members of Kendall's first group, which would be about four at this time. Here, with the others, they waited for transportation home.

Repatriation of Canadian POWs

Seven members of the first group were transferred to No. 1 Special Wireless Group for rations and pay. Of this number, four con-tinued to live at Coolangatta (near Brisbane) and not far from Tabragalba where they also spent considerable time. The three others performed minor military tasks, such as testing ammunition in various weapons.

These three, John Ko Bong, Wing Wong, and Ray Lowe, were sent to Hong Kong by Colonel Cosgrave, for repatriation of Canadian Prisoner of War duties. They arrived at Leyte, PI, on 3 July via Morotai and Biak; on 6 July they embarked on an LCI (landing craft infantry) from Tacloban, Leyte,

to proceed to Manila with S/Sgt. H.A. Wright of the Radar Detachment and arrived at Manila Harbor the following day. They never reached Hong Kong although Wing Wong says he met his future wife, Moi, while interviewing the inhabitants of the colony regarding the treatment meted out to Canadian POWs. The three helped set up the tents at Manila for the former prisoners when these men should arrive at the centre.

Members of the Canadian Repatriation Team converged on Manila from Ottawa and from Australia. Personnel of the Canadian Intelligence Corps, a part of the No. 1 Special Wireless Group numbering about a dozen, arrived from Australia the end of August. Other repatriation team members continued to arrive in early September.

S/Sgt. Wright arrived 4 September at the Fifth Replacement Depot from Leyte via landing craft bringing the three Chinese Canadian interpreters, now attached to the Far East Liaison Group, SEAC.[20] The three apparently were not attached to the Canadian repatriation team.

Sometime during this period, the three sergeants had worked in Admiral Nimitz's headquarters in Guam checking the regimen-tal lists of the two Canadian battalions imprisoned after the fall of Hong Kong. Guam had been taken by the Americans in August 1944.

When they reached the repatriation centre in Manila, they helped to care for the POWs when they arrived. Some POWs were too ill to be moved from the ships that brought them in, and they were nursed on board. Sgts. John Ko Bong, Wing Wong, and Raymond Lowe returned to Canada in October on the *General Brewster*.

Australian War Brides

Meanwhile, during the summer, two marriages were authorized by Colonel Cosgrave. Sgt. H.A. Wong married Myrtle O'Hoy, in Bendigo, 4 August 1945; and Sgt. G.T. Lock married Joan Lim On, in Melbourne, 17 May 1945. Travelling on the SS *Monterey* from Australia, via Hawaii, the two war brides arrived in Canada in 1946.

They entered Canada at White Rock, BC, and did not pay the Head Tax. Their entry certificates were stamped "Head Tax Waived." Although one of the brides insists she made a small payment at the time, this may have been the entry certificate fee. Canada had paid the costs of their trip from Australia to their Canadian destination, as it did for European and English war brides. Undoubtedly an order in council would have been issued to cover their entry.

Between 1923 and 1947 there were no more than six to eight[21] Chinese admitted to Canada as immigrants; two of these were the merchant seamen who were torpedoed off Halifax in 1941, and two were the war brides from Australia in 1946; another may have been Molly Lore from Hong Kong, the bride of Lieut. William Lore, who entered Canada as a war bride in 1947. Janet Grant, who was allowed to enter Canada in 1947 before her marriage, may also have been one of the eight. Sgt. J.K. Bong met Ida Tang Sueyek of Innisfail, NQ, and returned to Australia to marry her the following year. Ida arrived in Canada in 1948 as a landed immigrant (she is still an Australian citizen). The Exclusion Act was no longer in effect so that Ida was able to enter the country as the wife of a citizen without encountering any problems. Wives and unmarried children of Chinese Canadians were now allowed to enter Canada.

The men had to find their own ships to return to Canada. Once they had secured passage, they then advised the No. 1 Signals who completed arrangements. Some returned on the *Kitsilano Park* as crew members, and received pay for their work, while others, including members of the *Hippo* party, travelled on the *English Prince*.

Five of the group, Capt. Cheng and Sgts. Low, Shiu, Chan, and King, had volunteered for operations with SRD, 'Z' Special Unit, and would soon be leading Operation *Hippo* in Sarawak. They immediately set about learning Malay.

Once he had safely delivered his charges to Australia, Major Legg returned to New York and Ottawa to recruit additional Chinese Canadians: the two additional parties for *Oblivion,* and the much larger group for India.

NOTES

Personal information, if not separately noted, is from conversations and correspondence with participants. Archival material is from NAC, RG24, C1 reel C-8383 (or old system DND HQS 8885, Vol. 1, File 70-163A, and Vol. 2 to Vol. 8, File 70-163B).

1. Maj. H.J. Legg, transcript of tape interview by Maj. Victor Wilson, 1975, in Penticton (R.N. Atkinson) Museum; and articles by Debra Fataguna in *The Okanagan Historical Society,* 41st Report 1977, and by Angeline Waterman of Penticton in *OHS,* 53rd Report 1989.
2. Maj. Roger Cheng, transcript of tape interview by Reginald H. Roy, 22 Feb.1971, in G.R. Pearkes Collection, Archives Box 16, University of British Columbia.
3. The name is 'Ko Bong' with 'Ko' being the surname and 'Bong' the generation name. John and his brother, Peter, became 'Bong' when they enlisted. Two other members of the family, Mary and Andrew, were able to retain the full name.
4. Legg/Wilson transcript, p. 26.
5. The surname is 'Yee' but when Louey was registered for school by his brother, 'King' alone was used; Louey later legally changed his surname to 'King.'
6. Legg/Wilson transcript, p. 27.
7. Legg/Wilson, p. 27.
8. Legg/Wilson, p. 27.
9. Legg/Wilson, p. 27.
10. Roy, *For Most Conspicuous Bravery,* p. 190.
11. SOE Adviser, Maj. H.J. Legg report.
12. Australian War Memorial, 3 DRL 6201, Brig. Sir Kenneth Wills, AIB 2 AIF 1939-45, p. 21.
13. Cheng/Roy transcript; SOE Adviser.
14. Kendall/Roy transcript, p. 7.
15. *Souvenir Booklet,* 1944-1945, CSWG (pp, n.d.).
16. Master File *Diary* "Canadian Radar Detachment on Loan to Australian Military Forces," copy sent to author courtesy Radar Detachment members Danny Arntsen and J. T. Haines.

17. "Daily Orders Part II by Lt.-Col. H.D.W. Wethey Commanding No. 1 Special Wireless Group, R.C. Sigs, CA (A), Order No. 73, 26 Nov. 45" (copy in author's possession), gives their arrival in Australia as 17 March 1945. This date, of course, is in error. For those concerned with badges, the No. 1 RCCS wore Australian insignia indicating they were members of advanced workshop units; it was a black circle on a red square. This large group was attached to the Australian Army for medicals and documentation, and they were "discharged" from that Army.

18. Kendall/Roy Transcript, p.18. "O.S.F." should read "O.S.S."

19. Letter from Harden Lee.

20. Radar Diary, pp. 42-47; the dates and itinerary sound most implausible but the men themselves do not remember.

21. Tan and Roy *Chinese in Canada,* p. 9, give 7 between 1926 and 1945.

Chapter X

RECRUITMENT AND TRAINING – CANADA AND INDIA

In the summer of 1944, the Cabinet War Committee reversed its stand on the enrollment of Chinese Canadians under the NRMA; they were now to be called up in Pacific Command in the normal way. At the request of the British War Office, these men were to be loaned to Britain for employment in Southeast Asia and the Southwest Pacific.

The original request to Ottawa from British Security Coordination, however, was to expand Kendall's group to the number he had originally requested. There is no mention of "Allied Alien" in any of the documents referring to this call up, although the Canadian Army continued to maintain the Allied alien category. Nor was there any suggestion that these men be used as reinforcements in the European theatre in spite of the problems in providing infantry replacements for that theatre.

The call up of Chinese Canadians under NRMA was played out against the background of the cabinet crisis, which in turn was brought on by the lack of trained infantry reinforcements in Italy and Northwest Europe. Insisting that conscription was necessary so that trained reinforcements could be provided, Col. J.L. Ralston, whose resignation of two years earlier over the same problem had remained in the Prime Minister's hands, was dismissed by Mackenzie King 1 November and Gen. A.G.L. McNaughton became Minister of National Defence. McNaughton and the district officers were unable to convince NRMA men that they should turn active so the 1942 change in the NRMA regulations was invoked and an order in council passed to send these men overseas as reinforcements. As a result of this change to a conscription policy from the previous voluntary basis, the Minister for Air, C.G. Power, resigned 27 November. The debate in parliament over conscription did not end until 8 December.

Arrangements for the loan of 25 Chinese Canadian soldiers for service in India and Australia "as wireless operators" were made as early as 27 September 1944, between National Defence and T.G. Drew-Brook, the BSC representative in Canada. The loan was approved by the Minister of National Defence in September and Drew-Brook received confirmation 18 October.

It took some time to work out the status of the men on loan and at first, the model used was that for the Kendall party. The government would continue full "responsibility for dependent's allowance, pensions, as well as war service gratuity, as if they had continued to serve in the Canadian Army." BSC would be responsible for pay and allowances and expenses from their departure from Canada and during the time they were on loan. Whether the special pay arrangements that had been made for the original group would apply to this second group was subject to further discussion. Under this method, cheques would be issued in Ottawa, passed to Drew-Brook for delivery to the men, and recovery made through BSC from the War Office.

All 25 Chinese Canadians were destined for Australia; the BSC request soon to follow would concern the men for India. These 25 were to follow at three-month intervals the first group of 13 into China in Operation *Oblivion*.

Arrangements were made by Ottawa through BSC to notify Special Operations Australia and the Canadian Military Attaché, Col. L. Moore Cosgrave, of the impending arrivals. Again, this arrangement was similar to that proposed in Drew-Brook's 18 September letter for Kendall's party.

Major Legg left Australia late November to report first to BSC in New York. Also in November, BSC requested that the number be increased to 150 from 25. The original loan for 25 was then cancelled and the new one for 150 took its place. Approval for the loan was requested 23 November, reached the CWC 9 December, and Drew-Brook received approval on the 15th.

In this new loan of 150 Chinese Canadian soldiers for special duty in India and Australia, the men would remain members of the Canadian Army, which would be responsible for pay and allowances and all other rights, privileges, and gratuities. Providing pay as well as allowances was a departure from the arrangement that prevailed for the original group. Pay arrangements were approved by the CWC on 13 December. As with the previous 13, BSC would select the personnel.

Pay could be made by any British or Allied paymaster on a recoverable basis from the Canadian government. Rations and quarters (or allowance) and travelling expenses were the responsibility of the British government. Provision was made for the disparity in rations where the Indian Code applied by a 12-1/2 percent supplement which would be paid by Canada under PC 83/8848 dated 22nd November 1944.

The original group of 13 continued to be paid according to the system worked out at the time they left Canada; the group to India and the second group to Australia were now to be paid in all respects by Canada except for rations and quarters. The personnel going to India would be carried on strength "Q" List, CMHQ, London; those to Australia on the "Unattached List," NDHQ, Ottawa.

Recruitment

When Major Legg arrived in Ottawa late 1944, he received permission from National Defence on Disposal Order No. 100, to begin recruiting general service Chinese Canadians already in the army. Contrary to all previous estimates, National Defence did not think there would be 150 men available.

Originally Legg searched for men who could be trained as wireless operators, liaison men, interpreters, translators, members of Jedburgh teams, and PWE operatives. Many men he did not assess but left the question of their employment open to Force 136.

Although nearly all the men had been called up under NRMA in Pacific Command, the men selected were general service and in addition were volunteers for special duty. Major Legg invariably greeted them with, "You boys are special," signifying that because of their language and their appearance they would be able to move about in an Asian context in a way that no Caucasian could.

Further, the recruits all agreed to the condition of further training and that in India their particular job would be decided when they arrived there. They were also advised that they would probably be involved in guerrilla warfare and so they must be prepared to operate behind enemy lines, if required to do so. All recruits were to have two months basic training.

The Chinese Canadians were attached as individuals to British Military Forces serving in the two theatres effective on embarkation; they were then subject to British service law. The British unit to which they were attached was to list them in Daily Orders Part II quoting Disposal Order No. 100. The age limit was set at not less than 19 and not more than 40.

Since the men were in various stages of training, further training would be given by British forces. The British commanding officer was authorized to grant promotions but they would be acting rank only until confirmed by Ottawa.

The volunteers were advised that mail was to be addressed to Force 136, Canadian Forces Posts, Bombay, India, apparently with no thought that this open acknowledgment of such an organization was a breach of security. All the volunteers signed an "Acknowledgment" worded exactly the same as that for the original group.

National Defence contacted the commanding officer of each Army Training

Centre at Wetaskiwin, Red Deer, Maple Creek, and Shilo, advising him that either Maj. H.J. Legg of the British Army Staff or T.G. Drew-Brook would visit each camp "to interview all Canadian-born Chinese soldiers to establish their suitability for loan to the British War Office." Major Legg also carried a letter of introduction to each commanding officer. He had with him Sgt. J. Thru of the British Army; Sgt. Harry Con of Vancouver also assisted. All volunteers were to be granted embarkation leave with additional leave to ensure ten days at home before proceeding to Ottawa.

Nominal roll of all soldiers of Chinese extraction serving in the Military Districts No. 1 (London), 2 (Toronto), 3 (Kingston), 10, 12, and 13 (the Prairies), was requested by the adjutant general on 3 January 1945. No. 11 of course was British Columbia and all Chinese Canadians had been counted here many times over so there was no need to again ask for lists. Kingston appears to be the most easterly district contacted. Quite possibly Montreal and Quebec City were excluded because Chinese Canadians in Quebec were usually tri-lingual, and French-speaking infantry were urgently needed for the French regiments in Europe. The Maritimes or Atlantic Command does not seem to have been canvassed at all in this connection, although many Chinese Canadians from other parts of Canada had been posted to this command.

Five were located in the Kingston area; Bowmanville and Brockville gave a nil return; there were five reported by Peterborough, with five in RCEME and three in RCCS at Barriefield. No. 40 Adm. Unit, Ottawa area (Kingston) came up with W.100858, Pte. Howe, "the only soldier Chinese extraction serving Ottawa area." This was CWAC Pte. Helen Hoe, and therefore, not eligible. At least two NRMA men also were rejected.

The director of staff duties in a letter to Drew-Brook of 9 January emphasized that: "these men cannot be loaned to, or serve with, other forces such as the Indian Army in the case of India, or the Australian Army in the case of Australia. In other words they must be posted to units of the British Army." He further stated that it was "the responsibility of the British Army to ensure that their training is completed to the level that will fit them adequately to serve in an operational theatre."

SOE did not operate as a unit of the British Army although the men in Force 136 and 'Z' Special Unit came under direct command of the British and Australian Armies for a period during their operations in Malaya and Sarawak. The five who went into Sarawak came under the command of the Australian Army for six weeks after the Japanese surrender; a similar army command situation developed during the period of Military Government in Malaya. Indian troops were the only troops available when the September invasion took place in Malaya. Force 136 in India complained about the stage of training so these instructions from the director of staff duties at Ottawa were apparently not passed on.

Twenty-five men selected for India were sent to Ottawa by 25 January and five selected for Australia were held at Chilliwack. On 8 February the five held at Chilliwack along with the other ten (nine from Camp Borden and one from Peterborough) were ordered to proceed directly to Melbourne, Australia. Of the 150 involved, the majority would pass through England.

By 26 January, Legg had interviewed and selected 136 men, but the final total on 16 February was 139. Of the 124[1] destined for India, eight or nine were rejected on medical grounds either in Canada or in England and the total passing through Aldershot in 1945 was 116. According to India records, 117 arrived there. The additional man had been stopped in England for medical reasons, but he recovered in time to join the others at Poona.

From Red Deer, Alta, out of six Chinese Canadians, five were selected by Major Legg and volunteered for special duty. The Chinese Canadian Association in Vancouver requested a delay in the return of four of these volunteers from embarkation leave so that they might attend "a reception held in honour of Chinese privates." An extension was granted. There had been rumblings of discontent when Chinese Canadians were called up in British Columbia. The Chinese Canadian Association, however, looked on their service in the Canadian Army as a forward step and approved it. The association was preparing to present its petition for the franchise to the BC legislature.

From Chilliwack, BC, Sgt. Harry Con, K.7534, and from Wetaskiwin, Alta, Sgt. Roy Q.Q. Mah, K.5358, suggested by BSC as conducting NCOs, collected men from Red Deer, Alta, Shilo, Man, and with men from Camp Borden and Barriefield, Ont, arrived in Ottawa on the 18th. Both Harry Con and Roy Mah had received promotions to acting/sergeant on the recommendation of Drew-Brook and National Defence gave its approval; "however, due to existing regulations, it will be impossible to grant confirmation in the rank of

Corporal." Rank could be confirmed by the British commanding officer if service merited it according to promotional policy in British Forces. This statement does not agree with the one above, but it does illustrate lack of consistency in Ottawa.

Movement orders for 30 ORs came through on 9 February for train travel to Ottawa from Wetaskiwin, to Red Deer, to Calgary. These men were met at the railway station, Ottawa, on the 18th and transported to Unit Quarters, No. 3 District Depot.

The men continued to arrive in Ottawa district over the next few weeks: five ORs from Barriefield and Peterborough arrived 13 February. Forty-eight men from Maple Creek were available to leave 6 February with L/Cpl. A.Y.P.[2] Chan, K.7429, as NCO in charge and, if the draft had to be divided, L/Cpl. M. (Jackie) Chiu, K.7511, would assist. BSC

– courtesy Charlie Q. Lee

**Front l to r - Albert Chang, Robert Chan Kent, Raymond Chan,
Sid Y. Wong, Hayward Kiway, George Fong KANG
Centre l to r - Lloyd Chow, Bing Lee, Paul Chan, Ernest Sing,
Peter Ko Bong, Harry Lowe, Jerry W. Wong Eng, Frank W. Eng,
Watts Lee, Ira Chan
Back l to r - Ronald Lee, Bill K. Lee, Charlie Q. Lee, Clarence Jang
Taken at Chilliwack, BC**

**Nearly 50 of the Chinese Canadians from Maple Creek being
entertained by Calgary restaurant owners before they left for
Ottawa 1945.**

approved the rank and duties of the two NCOs. They were ordered to arrive in Ottawa by 18 February. Before the group left Maple Creek, the Chinese restaurant owners in Calgary gave the men a farewell dinner. The group at Maple Creek was the largest from any of the Training Centres.

Pte. Chong Loy (John) Quan, K.7718, from Maple Creek, was added to the list 1 March 1945. Barriefield granted embarkation leave to John on 7 March but if he did not return before the draft left, he would "have to proceed on special duty by himself on his return from embarkation leave." John had gone to his home in California and would not be available until 26 March. He was able to make the last small draft on 10 April so was not forced to travel completely alone.

Two others were to be deleted: Pte. Quan Lai Chow, K.7560, and Pte. Wing Herbert Dong, K.7792, both from Maple Creek; they had been ordered to Ottawa from Camp Borden 22 March. One was in Rideau Military Hospital and the other had fractured a leg and was "walking on crutches at the Depot." Pte. Chow was to be deleted from the list and discharged; his PULHEMS had been reduced. He was included in Draft No. 3 from Regina to Ottawa of 1 February and reached England. Pte. Dong recovered in time to be included in the last draft to England 10 April.

A signalman in Barriefield turned active 23 March for special duty; he had not been interviewed by Major Legg so, on 12 April, he was turned down by BSC. Two days later Brigadier Armstrong of Kingston assured

National Defence that the signalman had turned general service before he expressed an interest in the "Chinese Special Duty Group." The director of staff duties wrote to Drew-Brook on his behalf as well. These pleas had no effect since the man had not been interviewed; he was returned to the reinforcement pool.

Some of the men were still in Canada when the BC legislature, yielding to local pressure, the petition from the Chinese Canadian Association, and perhaps keeping in mind the view already expressed by External Affairs that these men now merited the franchise, gave the vote to Chinese Canadian veterans of the First World War and to those serving in the Second. The provincial vote automatically gave them the federal franchise; it also threw open the doors to professional practice in the province for those veterans already university graduates or who completed post-secondary education when the war was over.

The first draft for India of 21 men left Ottawa 27 January; 25 were posted on 7 February to "Q" List, CMHQ, London, effective the 28th. The conducting officer was detailed by NDHQ. Four in hospital from this draft were picked up on Draft No. 2.

The first group sailed from Halifax to Greenock, Scotland, in the *Nieuw Amsterdam* and from there half took the SS *Canton* to Bombay, India; the other half flew to Karachi. The Burma Star and the Pacific Star were awarded to two brothers in this group, apparently on the same split basis. Other than their mode of travel to India, there was no difference in their service.

Major Legg had carefully interviewed these 25 men, discussing with them their interests and inclinations. He was favourably impressed when he selected 13 for wireless, since this was his own field, and he was thoroughly familiar with the requirements. The recruits were to have received elementary wireless training during their basic training, but this was not given. Instruction was begun as soon as they reached England but would take three to five months to complete.

A press release from the chief censor of publications on 22 February advised that 100 Canadian born Japanese linguists were being recruited. Their duties were "of a most secret military intelligence character" so there must be no publicity. A number of Chinese Canadian soldiers were also being trained "for special employment in the Far East" and no disclosure was to be made that they were being trained for this area or that they were to be specially employed. The media could, however, publish stories about normally employed Chinese Canadian soldiers.

London reported to BSC in New York that the initial group of men were "a fine lot." They were doing well in both signals training and on the rifle range. In a later report, London repeated that the men were first class.

The second draft of 87 men left Ottawa 24 February. Five of these men were removed from the draft or returned from England because of a variety of illnesses— one with mumps, another with bronchitis, and so on. Lieuts. John J. Harding and F.M. Sutcliffe were the conducting officers.

A third draft of eight men left Ottawa 18 March. Before the final small draft No. 4 of five men sailed from Halifax on 18 April, about 120 men had been despatched to Britain on the disposal order. They were assigned to No. 1 Canadian Group Reinforcement Unit, Canadian Army Overseas. Movement instructions made it clear that these men were *not* reinforcements at No. 1 CGRU.

Clothing was issued the same as for reinforcements overseas, that is, one suit of battledress and one beret per man, and in addition each man carried two suits of khaki drill with long trousers, two pair of khaki drill shorts, two khaki cotton shirts, and one pair of puttees.[3] They did not carry weapons. All other replacement clothing and equipment was provided by British forces.

They left for England and India in their Canadian battledress, and they returned in the same uniform wearing the Far East Asia patches which consisted of a white patch with a blue dragon below the CANADA badge. During training they wore the Canadian issue tropical kit or other casual clothing and the

– courtesy K.F. (Danny) Yip

at Poona, India

– courtesy K.F. (Danny) Yip

at Poona, India

ten who were dropped into Malaya wore the jungle green of Force 136.

Training in India

The Special Training Schools were established at various locations in India. At Kharakvasla, near Poona, the Guerrilla Training Unit had been set up in July 1942 by F.W. Kendall, the first commandant. This Basic Training School and Rehabilitation Camp became the Eastern Warfare School. Here began the basic paramilitary course of weapons training, map reading, fieldcraft, an elementary jungle course, and a short testing or filter course to assess students in training.

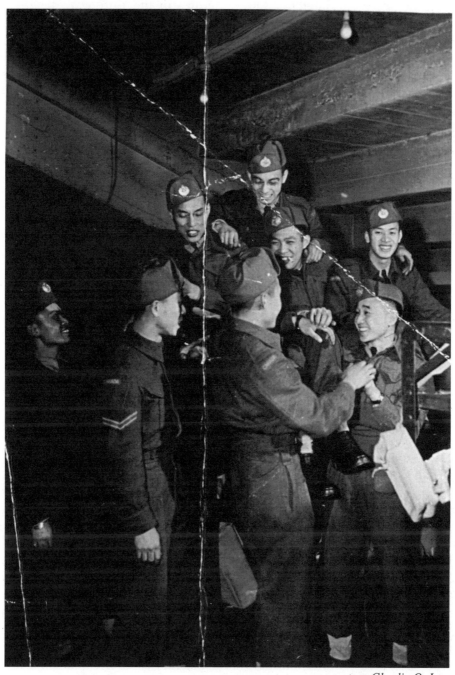

– courtesy Charlie Q. Lee

Clarence Jang
Ronald Lee, Bing Lee, Paul Chan
Sidney Wong, Cpl. Lloyd Chow, Charlie Q. Lee, Bill K. Lee

Those who passed the subjective ratings took further training of four or eight weeks at EWS(1) proper and became field operatives (eight weeks), or assistants such as interpreters (four weeks). Survival in the jungle, Japanese tactics, the multiple uses of bamboo (as weapons, food, and utensils), first aid both for themselves and the guerrillas they raised, and hygiene were all taught. On nearby Lake Fife, the handling of small boats and beach landings were practised in the Marine Course. Instruction in industrial sabotage was also given.

A basic wireless training wing functioned at Poona, taking three to four months. There was also overflow wireless training at Meerut and Meerut also gave a final month of operational training for those from Poona and from Trincomalee in Ceylon. Those who succeeded in these courses, and who volunteered for further training, went on to the Advanced Operations School at Trincomalee.

In spite of the favourable impression in London, India found many of the men unsuitable. Their "standard of training was not high," and over 40 were either medically unfit, or they did not volunteer for operations, or they were rejected as being unsuitable for the purpose. This harsh judgement on Chinese Canadians was similar to the assessment of Chinese from other countries that Force 136 had trained. India's suggestion that these 43 might be used in British OR vacancies was easily dismissed as unsatisfactory. Since there was no Canadian establishment in the theatre to which they could be posted, the only alternative was to return them to England and Canada.

On the other hand, seven were being trained as wireless operators, nine as coders, 19 as operational interpreters, and one sergeant for record duties in the Malaya Country Section. Another 18 were taking basic wireless training at Meerut and would form a reserve pool of operators and coders. Most of those noted as non-volunteers nonetheless continued their training. Two or three of these were at the PWE School at Alam Bazaar, near Calcutta.

In Legg's response to the criticism, he outlined the reasons for SOE enlisting Canadian Chinese. When Kendall recruited the *Oblivion* personnel, he had to make do with fewer than required because he could find so few already in the Canadian Army. Although Kendall and Legg may not have been aware of it, many were already in the army in the European theatre and in Home Defence, especially in Atlantic Command, which included Newfoundland. When Legg conducted his interviews only those remaining in Canada west of Montreal were available, most of whom had been called up in Pacific Command in August 1944.

Legg had conferred with Melbourne and Kendall on the type of men required. When he returned to Canada and selected the men, the total available was about 150. Canadian induction standards were high, particularly in mental and stability tests, and the M & S standard showed that "Canadian Chinese proved to be considerably higher than the average of white Canadians." All men interviewed had passed the Canadian Army Filter for physical condition, and mental and stability tests. The Canadian Army had insisted that all men were to complete their basic training course before being made available.

Since the rejections were not on medical grounds, and since the findings of the Filter Board in India were in conflict with the Canadian Army Filter and of Legg's own impressions when interviewing the men, he found it incomprehensible. He concluded that the explanation might lie in the outlook of the Filter Board in India with regard to "racial qualities and mentality." The Canadian Army Filter had dealt with a variety of European and Oriental nationalities "which the description 'Canadian' covers." Both Major Legg and Kendall had lived in the Far East and were aware that the initial caution and passivity soon disappeared when confidence had been established. Major Legg alone had selected and trained over 1,000 men for wireless and special work and he had considerable experience in the field. He further stated that India appeared to be training all the men as wireless operators, ignoring the categories for which they had been recruited.

Legg also pointed out the discrepancy between the Filter Board and the findings of its President; the difference was so great that it was almost impossible to believe that the same person was the subject of the two findings. Legg further pointed out that the India Filter appeared to want to find unsuitability and that the conclusions of the President reflected agreement with his own and the Canadian Army Filter findings.

Major Legg was not quite correct when he attributed immaturity to Canadian Chinese because, even though married and with children, some of the men had requested permission to consult their mothers before they volunteered for special duty. Cultural differences were often misunderstood, even by someone as knowledgeable as Legg. The eldest son in many Chinese families was and possibly still is indoctrinated from childhood with the belief that his first duty is to care for his parents. Family influences were very strong and whether the son should volunteer would be based on family rather than individual needs. A young man in Southwestern Ontario was not allowed by his family to volunteer for the army; he had to await his call up in 1942 so that he could remain in Home Defence. His younger brother was free to volunteer in the air force when he turned eighteen. When the author made an appointment to interview a Toronto veteran, his sister-in-law advised that the *family* had decided he should talk to the author.

London sent Legg's report to India on 6 April along with comments of their own. London had been favourably impressed with the first draft of 21 men. They had not gone through the Army Filter in England both because of the time and the fact that the War Office would be "only too pleased to get hold of Chinese speakers" and would have siphoned off a few. Although all might not qualify as operational personnel, India should be able to usefully employ all of them. Because of India's rejection of such a large number, BSC in New York would be advised to cease recruiting activities. Australia had not yet reported on the 15 men sent to them, but quite possibly that country would be willing to have some of those in India transferred.

India's response on 4 May upheld the findings of the Filter Board. India claimed that since 60 to 70 percent of those filtered at Poona were Asiatics, the Board was experienced in this matter. But 850 out of the 1500 trained at Poona were Europeans; only 650 were Asiatics, something like 40 percent.[4]

India further claimed that Chinese from other countries were at a disadvantage because of language but Canadian Chinese used English as their first language. Again, there was a misunderstanding here because the first language of Chinese Canadians was their mother tongue; they learned English usually when they started English schooling. If they lived in isolated towns, which many of them did, they lost fluency in their language because their school friends and all those with whom they came in contact were English speaking. They might still speak some Cantonese at home but they would not be fluent in the language. If they lived in Victoria, Vancouver, or Toronto where there were large Chinatowns, from which many of them came, then English was used in school and in contact with whites, but Chinese, usually Cantonese, was the normal language.

India claimed the Filter Board was using the same principles that had been used successfully with Indian ORs and they saw no need to change. And here, perhaps, lies the nub of the matter. These men were not Indian ORs but Canadians and in spite of the restrictions against them in this country their background and mental outlook more nearly matched the average Canadian than the average Indian.

In spite of their complaint about the type of recruit, India continued to send them into the training courses. The need was for wireless operators and so the early arrivals had been trained in this field. The reply from India indicated that no consideration had been given to Legg's comments on the suitability for various other roles.

Although the Canadian government had made provision for the discrepancy in rations in India, a dispute at Meerut had to be settled by the RCAF Headquarters in Bombay when the men vigorously complained on receiving their evening rations of one cup of raw rice per man, and there were no sports facilities. The RCAF ensured that sports equipment was made available and the food allowance improved.

An Ottawa summary made 20 April 1945 showed that of 135 to go to Great Britain, 121 had been sent, and five had been returned as medically unfit; 15 had gone to Australia. These figures do not include the original 13 nor the few from the S-20 Japanese Language School who also served in the Far East.

The decision announced in the House of Commons by Mackenzie King, 4 April 1945, that all those serving in the 'Pacific Theatre' would be volunteers only, apparently did not have any bearing on Chinese Canadians serving in India or Australia. Ottawa invariably included SEAC in the 'Pacific Theatre.' There is no record of their being canvassed in this connection, nor has anyone mentioned it as having occurred, although one or two of those in India have mentioned voting in the federal general election in June.

They were all in training and eight had entered the field by the time the Japanese capitulated in August 1945; the ninth was dropped after the surrender as was the tenth who was dropped as a member of E Group (Escape & Evasion). Many others had been teemed up ready for insertion, with about 30 in operational readiness at Horana in Ceylon.

Every recruit had to volunteer at each successive stage in training and parachuting was one area that stopped many; this had happened in Australia too. These men, however, could be used if insertion were by sea; many were slated to act as interpreters in the company of the invading British Army. Interpreters were always needed in a country where nearly half the population was Chinese.

Parachute training took place at Jessore, near Calcutta. In SEAC, a slide exit had been fitted on Liberators for parachutists; it was thought that because of the small size of some of the men, the effect of the slip-stream would cause them to tangle in their parachutes. They were able to exit from Dakota doorways, however, without mishap. The slide had to be positioned during flight, which was inconvenient and cut down on the room for packages; containers were carried in the bomb bay. There was one advantage to the slide in that a stick of six men could be dropped so that they landed fairly closely together. 'Stick' was a term applied to the dropping of six men or half a dozen bombs. Despatchers assisted in the quick exit of the men from the aircraft.

From India or Ceylon to Malaya and return could be a 22 or occasionally a 24 hour flight, depending upon the weather. Sometimes there was no reception committee and the aircraft had to return without dropping its load; sometimes the aircraft returned because of mechanical problems; rarely were enemy planes met. Only over Singapore was there any anti-aircraft activity.

During the build-up of guerrilla resistance in Malaya, from mid-May on, the weather was at its worst; the southwest monsoons made flying perilous. The dense jungle often hid the dropping zones so that they were almost impossible to locate. Frequently a river was the only visible landmark.

In addition to weapons and other military equipment, food was also a part of their supplies, whether taken with them or dropped once they were in place. In Malaya many people including the guerrillas were close to starvation by 1945; food drops were eagerly awaited by both Force 136 teams and the guerrillas.

The close cooperation between Force 136 and SRD in Australia resulted in Force 136 asking SRD to put a party ashore in eastern Malaya, which was easier and safer by submarine from Australia than from Calcutta or Trincomalee. SRD complied inserting *Carpenter* and *Mint* in South Johore. Also the *Oblivion* groups, promoted by Force 136, received final preparation for insertion by submarine at Mirs or Bias Bay on the South China Coast by SRD in Australia in order to circumvent Chiang Kai-Shek's ban on overland travel in China. *Jaywick* and *Rimau,* the raids on Singapore harbour, were also sponsored by India but mounted from Australia.

After the Japanese capitulation, many of the men returned to Canada on the *Monarch of Bermuda,* conducted by Lieut. John J. Harding, RCOC. Harding, whose parents were Canadian, was brought up in Shanghai and returned from Oakland, California, to join the Canadian Army. He conducted Chinese Canadians from Canada to India and also was conducting officer on their return on the *Mauritania* to Liverpool, 27 November, and to Halifax on the *Monarch of Bermuda.* A second large group arrived in Canada in January 1946.

Some of the members of this second group had been dropped into Malaya as interpreters and coders. Both the guerrilla groups armed and trained by Force 136 teams and the regular armed troops in Operation *Zipper* were to combine to bring about the Japanese defeat in Malaya.

– courtesy K.F. (Danny) Yip

Chinese group who served in India and Malaya and returned over a 7,000-mile route, Bombay to Liverpool in the *Mauretania* and Liverpool to Halifax on Monarch of *Bermuda*.

**Back l to r: L/Cpl. Robt. Yeasting, Cpl. James Wong, Sgt. Jack Chiu, Cpl. Robt. Lee, Sgt. Charles Hoy, all of Vancouver;
Front row: Sgt. Horace Lee, Vancouver, Pte. Joe Takashima, London, Ont, only Japanese-Canadian in group, CSM Donald Sung, Vancouver; Lieut. John Harding, Oakland, Cal., who had commanded the group of 60 since they left Canada; L/Cpl. Charles Lum, Vancouver.**

NOTES

Unless otherwise noted, personal information has come from conversations and correspondence with participants. Other information is from the SOE Adviser; and D.Hist. 163.009, (D25); D.Hist. 112.3S2009, (D191); and D.Hist. 360.2009, (D4).

1. Col. F.H. Walter, "Cloak and Dagger" gives 126 as the number who left Canada for service with Force 136, p. 26, in D.Hist. 760.013, (D1); Elliot in *Scarlet to Green,* lists the first group to Australia, p. 664, but omits the second group of 15; and on p. 656, lists 117 for India, but he includes one Japanese and fails to include Sgt. Harry Con.

2. His name is Allen Yee Poy Chan; A.E.R. Chan and A.L.R. Chan are sometimes shown for him in the records.

3. The two pictures from Danny Yip illustrate the casual type of clothing worn during training in India. Those dropped into Malaya wore jungle green; see picture of Capt. M. Levy and six of the Canadians at Kuala Lumpur in Chapter XI.

4. Charles Cruickshank, *SOE in the Far East* (Oxford, 1986), p. 19.

Chapter XI

MALAYA OPERATIONS

There was no Malaya nation to resist the Japanese during the 1941-1945 war and the Malays, Chinese, and Indian communities had no concept of loyalty to a country. It was only after the war that Malaysia as a state emerged.

The Japanese were unable to control the whole of the peninsula and when the persecuted Chinese went underground after the surrender, they were able to operate with comparative freedom in the jungle. The Chinese emerged as leaders in all the Malay states. Most were Communists and they set out to harass the Japanese in small guerrilla bands. Lack of weapons, ammunition, medicines, and food prevented them from being a serious menace.

The Malaya peninsula, about 700 miles long and 250 miles wide, consisted of a central mountainous region covered in dense jungle. In the fertile coastal regions much of the economic activity occurred. Here too were the roads, and the railway running through to Siam, and another through the central portion to the northeast coast. The jungle, so thick that in places it was almost impenetrable, sheltered the guerrillas and Force 136 teams when the time came for their insertion.

The Japanese did not promote a form of independence in the peninsula as they had done in Burma, the Dutch East Indies, and the Philippines. The Japanese were selective in their application of the Greater East Asia Co-Prosperity doctrine.

Europeans who had not escaped, government and other officials, planters, and the military, were executed or imprisoned. Special Training School 101 had infiltrated some operatives and Chinese Communists in the jungle, but approval for this effort had come too late to be of much value. Most of the European 'leave behind' parties who had not escaped were captured and executed although a few survived. About 130,000 British, Australian, Indian, and Malay troops became Prisoners of War.

POWs both at Changi and Outram Gaols in Singapore, Padu Gaol in Kuala Lumpur, and many other camps were used as labour battalions to build the Burma-Siam railway. Nearly 15,000 prisoners died in its construction. About 2,750 Australian and British POWs were taken to North Borneo to build military airstrips for the Japanese. Prisoners were used as labour battalions in Formosa and Japan and other Japanese controlled areas as well.

Some of the Indian Prisoners of War in Malaya were used by the Japanese to foment unrest against the British, both in India itself and by sponsoring the India National Army in Burma. A few of those captured in Hong Kong were also enticed into the INA. The majority of the men of the Indian Army who had surrendered at Singapore, although separated from their officers, refused to collaborate with the Japanese. They remained Prisoners of War.

There were twelve states making up the Malaya peninsula. In 1943, Japan ceded to Siam the northern Malay states of Perlis, Kedah, Kelantan, and Trenggenu containing 2,870,000 inhabitants, nearly half the population, possibly for its early cooperation and in return for the use of Siam as a throughway to Burma. Siam had also long laid claim to these four northern states.

SIAM

MALAYA

PERLIS

Kangar

Alor Star

KEDAH

Gurun

Sungai Patani

Grik

PENANG

Kota Bahru

Kuala Krai

PERAK

KELANTAN

TRENGGENU

Taiping

Ipoh

Gong Gajah

Kampar

Kuala Lipis

PAHANG

Tapah

Telok Anson

Slim River

Raub

K. Kubu Bahru

Benton

Mentakab

SELANGOR

Serendah

Kuala Lumpur

Ampang

Kajang

NEGRI

Kuala Pilah

Merlin

Seremban

SEMBILAN

Sepang

Gemas

Port Dixon

Tampin

MALACCA

JOHORE

Malacca

Kluang

Muar

Batu Pahat

Kota Tinggi

SUMATRA

Johore Bahru

SINGAPORE Changi

Singapore (city)

The Japanese directly controlled the governments in the crown colony of the Straits Settlements of Singapore, Malacca, and Penang (Labuan, Cocos, and Christmas Islands were also included in the Straits Settlements); they advised the local governments in Johore, Negri Sembilan, Selangor, Perak, and Pahang, the remaining Malay states.

The Japanese military police, the Kempei Tai, controlled the local police. Indians, Malays, Chinese, and Eurasians were also conscripted, as well as POWs, to work on the Burma-Siam railway. The inhabitants of the country were more or less willing conscripts since there was no employment for them and they faced starvation.

The shortage of food became progressively worse as the Japanese navy and merchant shipping declined throughout the war years. Without shipping, tin and rubber, the primary products of Malaya, could not be exported nor foodstuffs imported. Rice, the staple food in Malaya, was in very short supply since most of the requirements had been imported. Those living in towns were especially hard hit by food shortages. The Japanese made no provision for medical care or treatment; instead they destroyed the medical facilities that existed.

In addition to exploiting racial tensions between Malays and Chinese, the Japanese were able to openly attack their old enemies—the Chinese. The two countries had been fighting since the Japanese take over in Manchuria in 1931. Many Chinese were massacred, including about 20,000 who had been slaughtered and thrown into Singapore harbour on capitulation of the British in February 1942. Many of those who survived retreated into the central Malayan jungles and formed guerrilla groups in opposition to the Japanese; others set up shanty-towns on the edge of the jungle where they could grow food to support themselves. They also provided food for the guerrillas.

Authorized by Mountbatten, Col. John H.L. Davis of Force 136, inserted by submarine in a series of *Gustavus* operations, signed an agreement with the Malayan

Peoples' Anti-Japanese Army in November 1943. There was more than one Chinese communist guerrilla organization, as well as the groups who supported the Nationalist Chinese Government (Kuomintang) and, of course, there were independent bandits as well. One of the better known communist groups was the Anti-Japanese Union and Forces. These groups are not distinguished in this chapter and collectively are called MPAJA or guerrillas.

According to the terms of the agreement, SEAC was to provide money, arms, instructors, and medical supplies in return for MPAJA assistance against the common enemy. Until the British Army invaded, the guerrillas were to attack shipping whenever possible and to increase labour strife. The guerrillas also agreed to accept orders from SEAC and fight under its direction when the invasion occurred. This agreement was not approved by London until March 1945, in part because Davis was unable to contact Force 136 until February 1945.

John Davis was a former member of the Malaya Police Force. He was first inserted by submarine for a month in the summer of 1943 to discover whether or not the Chinese guerrillas had survived and, if so, whether they would support the Allies in defeating the Japanese. On his second trip, Davis was provided with a 450-pound wireless set, too heavy for them to carry to the camp. Even the submarine captain felt sorry for the men trying to manhandle this machine.

In November 1943, Lim Bo Seng, a Malayan born Chinese, was inserted by submarine; he brought with him two 45-pound wireless sets which were easily carried. They also had the range necessary to reach headquarters. The generator at first would not function but by improvisation, Davis, Richard Broome, and F.W. Spencer Chapman were finally able to contact Ceylon with news of the agreement in February 1945.[1]

Frederick W. Spencer Chapman had been a member of one of the 'leave behind' parties in January 1942 just before Singapore capitulated. He not only survived in the jungle but had already linked up with the guerrillas, over 100 of whom had been trained at STS 101, and had provided what training he could until he met up with John Davis and Capt. Richard Broome of the *Gustavus* submarine insertions on Christmas Day 1943. He was extracted by submarine 13 May 1945 and reached Colombo on the 19th.[2]

Extractions, or 'exfiltrations' as they were sometimes called, had to be made by submarine. There were no landing facilities for pick-up by aircraft nor aircraft with the necessary range until early 1945. Insertions by submarine, however, were much more complicated than drops from aircraft, and from early 1945, the latter was the method used as soon as long-range Liberators became readily available in the theatre.

In the very early build up, some teams were dropped 'blind'; there was no reception committee waiting to receive them, or to ensure that the dropping zone was a safe one. Since it took some time to reach the ground, it was possible for the Japanese to reach the dropping zone before the agent landed and immediately capture him if the drop had been made near an outpost. The agent could also be shot by the Japanese as his parachute carried him towards the ground. When the DZ had not been inspected for hazards, what looked like an abandoned *padi* (rice field) from the air could be studded with stumps and the agent be injured or killed on landing.

When there was a reception party, the DZ by pre-arrangement was indicated by the receiving party after consultation with the Malaya Country Section (Section B) in Colombo. The appropriate letter, 'L', 'T', 'V', and so on, was indicated by fires and the code letter flashed to the aircraft by flashlight; the aircrew had been briefed to search for the appropriate letter. Fires at night were clearly visible since drops were made during a full moon period; during daylight drops, smoke was the only indication with wind and the thick jungle canopy making the exact location uncertain. In addition to fire-signalling during daylight drops, three white panels could be spread out in the form of the code letter, some-times the letter signifying the particular item the land party required.

Eureka/Rebecca and the *S.Phone* were not available until towards the end of hostilities in SEAC. *Eureka,* a responder beacon on the ground, was activated by the airborne *Rebecca* interrogator radar equipment. The *S.Phone* was a secure, soundproof, radiotelephone system between the aircraft and ·ground. These aids were not always successful in SEAC and SWP theatres because of the mountains and the jungle. SEAC was usually at the bottom of the list for equipment and received most items only after the needs of other theatres had been satisfied.

There were three main aspects to Force 136 operations in Malaya: the first was to control the internal resistance movement made up of predominately Chinese, the MPAJA; the second was to do the same thing among the Malays; and the third was to drop independent support groups, the Gurkhas, as and when required. Early in 1945 for political reasons, Force 136 made a considerable effort to encourage Malay resistance and infiltrated several liaison teams to promote their active participation.

The Malays

The first Malay insertion was Operation *Oatmeal,* led by Capt. Ibrahim bin Ismail in October 1944. The noise of the Catalina flying boat alerted the Japanese and the party was soon captured. At this time, the Catalina was the only long-range aircraft available. By pretending to act as double agents, their lives were spared and they were able to deceive the Japanese as to the proposed landing areas of the invading British. Ibrahim successfully played the deception game with the Japanese under the direction of D Division at SEAC until after the Japanese surrendered; he was decorated by both sides.

The second attempt to recruit Malay guerrillas was Operation *Hebrides,* led by Capt. P.G.J. Dobree, a former Malaya official, who was dropped blind in north Perak just east of Grik in December 1944. This was the first Force 136 blind drop in Malaya and the first use of the long-range aircraft. The team was briefed to train Malay guerrillas, transmit military intelligence to Ceylon, and to set up an intelligence network in northern Kedah.

Dobree found the inhabitants lacked food, in spite of attempts to grow vegetables in jungle clearings, and they had no medicines even in hospitals so that diseases went untreated. Inflation was rampant; the Japanese "banana" money was printed and circulated without any attempt to give it value. When British Military Government began in September 1945, all Japanese money was declared valueless; there was no attempt to redeem it.

Bandits in Kelantan and north Perak were harassing the MPAJA and had to be dealt with by Dobree's team. By the end of February, however, the network was operating, they had trained about 100 men, and the team acted as the reception committee for other drops in the area.

Another group sent in to arm and train Malays was *Fighter,* led by Maj. G.A. Hasler[3] who operated in Kedah. When the Japanese surrendered, Hasler's team located and cared for a small camp of POWs at Gong Gajah.

The others were *Beacon,* under Maj. J.A. Richardson, dropped to the Dobree reception party near Kuala Lipis in Pahang, and *Multiple,* with Maj. Derek Headly, another former Malaya official, also in Pahang east of Raub.

Richardson's parachute canopy snagged on a tree with the lowest branches some 30 feet from the ground. He was helpless until a Malay with Dobree's reception party climbed a nearby smaller tree, and set it moving until it enabled him to grab the canopy. Richardson was thus able to transfer to the smaller tree and make his way safely to the ground.

In the jungles of Asia and on the Pacific islands there was always the danger of an isolated parachutist being unable to extricate himself from such a position. It was very important that men be dropped closely together, especially in a blind drop, so they could lend each other assistance.

Headly's instructions included investigation of rubber production, which was in short supply, and the train services, along with arming and training Malay guerrillas and, of course, military intelligence. Headly managed to raise and train nearly 250 Malays by the date of surrender. He began the practice of each agent taking a 60-foot line with him in case he should be caught up in a tree.

It was a simple matter for Headly to check the train services; the 200-mile stretch of railway track from Mentakab in Pahang to Kuala Krai in Kelantan of the whole line running between Gemas in Johore to Kota Bahru near the east coast, was torn up by the Japanese and used on the Burma-Siam railway. Another stretch of track, 18 miles of a branch line between Tapah and Telok Anson, was also sent north for use on the new line. The main line running from Singapore to Bangkok was left intact. After the Japanese surrender, Headly's team located a POW camp at Raub, news of which they wirelessed to headquarters.

Malayan Peoples Anti-Japanese Army

An early drop to the MPAJA guerrillas was led by Maj. G.R. Leonard, a pre-war game warden in Malaya, in Operation *Pontoon*. His team was dropped towards the end of February 1945 in west Pahang, east of Merapoh. They were to arm and train the 6th MPAJA Regiment. Inserted at the same time was an OSS team. Both teams were met by a reception party. Frederick Spencer Chapman returned to the jungle and joined Leonard as civil affairs officer about ten miles northwest of Batu Talam in Pahang towards the end of August.

Another of the early Force 136 drops to the guerrillas was that in the Operation *Funnel* series led by Maj. J.F. Hannah. Hannah was a former prospector who had spent three years in Malaya and the Netherlands East Indies. The team was dropped in Perak in the Grik Valley toward the end of February 1945. The 5th MPAJA Regiment operated in Perak and Perak was also the headquarters for the MPAJA. Here the Kuomintang guerrillas (or bandits) presented a problem and Hannah's team was briefed to deal with them. The team was met by the *Gustavus* reception party. With Hannah were Maj. Harry Harrison, his 2 i/c (second-in-command), two wireless operators, and a Chinese interpreter.

By 1945 the famous, or infamous, L capsules were no longer issued by the MCS. Section B in Ceylon stopped issuing them after Hannah objected and refused to accept one, since a suicide's wife would not receive a pension, according to *King's Regulations*. They had routinely been issued to volunteers going on operations both in Europe and in the Middle and Far East including Malaya and Sarawak in case of capture and torture by the enemy. It was felt that instant death was preferable to lingering torture and there would be no revelation of future or current plans. They continued to be issued to 'Z' Special Unit operatives going into Sarawak.

According to the agreement between the MPAJA and SEAC, the guerrillas agreed to receive a British Group Liaison Officer in each regiment with each patrol receiving a Patrol Liaison Team. They would come under the orders of the Allied commander in chief through the Liaison Officers. There were seven MPAJA guerrilla regiments headquartered at Perak; each regiment received a Group Liaison Officer with five Patrol Liaison Teams assigned to each regiment.

On 12 May 1945, Lt.-Col. D.R. Alexander, with three captains, was dropped to a reception committee headed by Davis and Hannah. This drop was one of the few times when the special duty Liberators were met by Japanese fighter planes but no harm resulted from the encounter. Only once more were Japanese fighters able to take to the air during insertions of Force 136 personnel and again there was no damage.

Another drop on 6 July brought in Maj. W.I.L. Travers, a wireless operator, and a Gurkha support group; they joined Hannah and entered Tapah after the atomic bomb was dropped.

After 15 August, Hannah's team was ordered to contact the local Japanese headquarters for a cease fire agreement but they were not to accept surrender. They were to locate POW camps and also airfields and assess their serviceability.

They journeyed to Tapah and the Japanese headquarters; the Japanese took them to Ipoh where they met the Japanese military governor of Perak and an agreement was concluded. The journey of 60 miles back to camp took them through Kampar. They had located a POW camp near Ipoh containing some 300 Indians and this information was immediately wirelessed to headquarters.

By the end of August, Hannah's team and the 5th Perak Regiment, operating between Taiping in the north and Slim River in the south, had twelve sections of 15 men each with 21 British officers plus cooks and quartermasters, making about 1,000 total. There was also a Gurkha support group and NCO wireless operators, and coders.

During the long wait, it was necessary to control the guerrillas and keep them from committing sabotage and from prematurely attacking the Japanese. For the moment, they were being trained and armed ready to fight, to block roads and disable the railways, and generally to hinder any action on the part of the Japanese when the British Army invasion began in September. A display of force too soon would have aroused the Japanese to take effective action and the whole infiltration process and invasion plans would have been jeopardized. The objective was to remain concealed so that when Operation *Zipper* was mounted, this armed force would be ready to go into action.

Some 6,500 guerrillas throughout Malaya were armed and ready when Operation *Zipper* was moved up from November to September. Six Gurkha support groups had been parachuted in as well, one of the earliest being under Maj. J.E. Heelis, 1st Gurkha Regiment, who was dropped in Selangor 21 July with his NCO, 18 ORs and a Punjabi wireless operator. It was intended that the Gurkhas would form the main resistance force operating with the GLTs and the guerrillas would be used as auxiliaries. There was a delay in providing these support groups, however, which meant that some of the teams were forced to rely exclusively on the guerrillas, at least in the initial stages.

There were five patrol liaison teams dropped in Selangor in Operation *Galvanic*. Five of the Chinese Canadians were dropped into Selangor in the *Galvanic* series, one operating in each of four PLTs and the fifth at headquarters. Sgt. Bing Chu Lee served at headquarters; Sgt. O. (Ted) Wong in *Galvanic Orange* at Serendah; Sgt. Bing Lee Chinn in *Galvanic Green* at Kerling; and Sgt. H.W. (Henry) Fung in *Galvanic Brown* at Kajang; the fifth was Sgt. R.W. (Bob) Lew in *Galvanic Slate* at Kachau. Interpreters often served as instructors as well, adding another dimension to their responsibilities.

The Liaison Officer operating with the 1st MPAJA Regiment in Selangor was Lt.-Col. D.K. Broadhurst, a former Malaya police officer. After he escaped from Singapore to Australia, Broadhurst had undertaken missions to Borneo, the Philippines, and Portuguese Timor, before going on to India where he was taken on by Force 136.

It is not possible to be precise about dates in either Malaya or Sarawak. Dates given in archival material are often inaccurate, in part because reports were usually prepared after the event. All insertion and other dates should be accepted with caution. The date given in Broadhurst's report is 24 July for *Brown* but one of the men in this team says it was June. The arrangement below shows the order in which they are discussed in Broadhurst's report and his date system has been retained.

Broadhurst's seven-man team set out from Jessore in two Liberators on 30 May; they were dropped blind at Serendah, about ten to fifteen miles northwest of Kuala Lumpur. The rest of his party was dropped some distance away at Ulu Yam owing to faulty navigation. Because of poor wireless communication and the slowness of the early courier system, it was 15 June before the two parties joined at Serendah, where headquarters was established. A representative of the MPAJA visited the party to confirm identities, and posted one of its members to the team.

Included in Broadhurst's headquarters group was Sgt. Bing Chu Lee, K.7405, from

– HMSO London
Bing Chu Lee

Vancouver. Bing's code name was *Pear* and he served as the coder for the headquarters team. He encoded all messages before they were transmitted to headquarters by the wireless operator, and then decoded all messages received. The one-time pad was in use by this time, which ensured excellent security. The system was easy and quick to learn and relatively error-free.

The *Galvanic Orange* PLT, with headquarters at Serendah, was formed by F/O J. Robertson who was dropped 31 May. Maj. P.T. Thompson-Walker took over when he was dropped on 10 July with a Chinese interpreter and Sgt. David John Richardson to a reception committee at Ulu Yam. Sgt. Richardson drowned when he landed in a stagnant pool that resembled solid ground. Because he was not expecting a water landing, Richardson did not press the button to release his parachute and was drowned within its wet folds. Enemy troops were present at Ulu Yam Bahru, probably due to an ISLD drop in the Rasa area two days before, and Broadhurst had not been advised. ISLD, OSS,[4] and Force 136 teams operated completely independently of each other, thus sometimes jeopardizing the activities of one of the other groups. Because of the presence of enemy troops, the Force 136 party had to disperse quickly so appropriate action could not be taken to save Richardson's life. After Broadhurst met with the ISLD party and discussed the matter with them, that party moved to a new area at Taik Hing tin mines.

Because of the tragedy at this location, a small DZ was located at Sungei Rusa. Ulu Yam was still sometimes used, but Sungei Rusa and the DZ at Serendah were the prime locations for the next few weeks for the receiving of additional personnel and stores for *Orange* and other members of the team.

Reinforcements for the GLT and *Orange* dropped to this team included Sgt. On (Ted) Wong, K.7425, from Vancouver,

– HMSO London
O. (Ted) Wong

interpreter, code named *Guava,* and a wireless operator to replace Richardson. They were to make their headquarters near Serendah. Interpreting could often be a tedious business, especially with both the MPAJA and Chinese members of the community. It took patience and skill to translate for both sides but Ted's command of English and Cantonese was excellent. Ted was also fortunate that

members of the MPAJA Regiment and the Chinese community in this area spoke Cantonese.

Broadhurst sent Maj. A.J. Hunter, as PLO in *Galvanic Blue* patrol, to the Ampang Gombak area to cover the Kuala Lumpur-Benton Road and to receive additional parties. The team·was unable to move until early July because it lacked a wireless. *Orange* resources had to be shared with *Blue.*

As already mentioned, Maj. John E. Heelis, 1st Gurkha Regiment, with his 20-man support group, arrived 21 July "in perfect weather conditions and without enemy interference although strong reinforcements had arrived in Rawang." Henceforth, the Gurkhas guarded the DZ during supply drops since the enemy could watch the parachutes as the stores descended. Although DZs were easily accessible and exposed, the Japanese action always came too late; no personnel or stores were ever lost to them. The Japanese usually waited for an hour or so before setting out to investigate and by the time they arrived at the DZ the stores had been disposed of and the men dispersed.

After the capitulation, the Gurkhas were also used to help keep the peace. Their reputation was enough to quell the guerrillas when the time came for disbanding the MPAJA Regiments; even the Japanese appeared to be awed by them. Broadhurst felt that both the Gurkhas and the liaison officers were too late in arriving and should have been sent in long before they were.

Galvanic Brown, led by Maj. Ian A. Macdonald, a rubber planter who spoke Malay, was dropped 24 July, with Capt. M.G. Levy[5] his 2 i/c. The wireless operator was Sgt. Tom R. Henney, and Sgt. Hinn Wing (Henry) Fung,[6] code named *Kale,* K.5224, from Vancouver, was the interpreter. Two members of E Group were included in this drop.

The plane started out on the 20th but the pilot was forced to return because of a malfunction. It took six hours flying to get rid of the gasoline that could not be jettisoned, before they could safely land. They started

– HMSO London
H.W. (Henry) Fung

out again on the 22nd and their drop was completed without further mishap.

The *Galvanic Brown* team was dropped to a *Blue* reception committee north of Kuala Lumpur. They set out for their camp near Kajang, a trip that took nearly a week. The camp was south of Kuala Lumpur close to the guerrilla regiment. They had no sooner set up camp than they were forced to move because of a Japanese patrol rapidly nearing their location and the guerrillas moved with them.

Food and medical drops were made and they set about giving what medical help they could. Macdonald was briefed to report on the rubber and tin situation.

After the surrender the group entered Kajang but the Japanese stationed here refused to discuss surrender until the British Army arrived.

The team was able to diffuse hostilities between the MPAJA and collaborators as well as to maintain control of the Japanese and ward off bandits until an Indian Army detachment arrived 9/10 September and the team moved into Kuala Lumpur. Macdonald was pleased with Henry Fung who was the first of the Chinese Canadians to volunteer for operations in Malaya. Henry was "a great success with the guerrillas and always cheerful to do any amount of work asked of him."

This particular team lived with the guerrillas and seem to have established an

Stores drop

excellent rapport with them. The wives and children of the MPAJA were also sheltered in the camp and made clothing for their men from bolts of cloth dropped by Force 136; most of the men were too small for standard issue clothing. It is possible that the three stars worn on his sleeve by Henry Fung indicates that this item also was made by one of the ladies in the camp.

Galvanic Green PLT was dropped 28 July to a reception party at Kerling in Selangor. Maj. C.E. Maxwell led the team with a lieutenant, a sergeant, and two Nationalist Chinese wireless operators, and Sgt. Bing Lee Chinn, K.5161, from Vancouver, code-named *Haricot*, the interpreter.

Maxwell was disappointed that Chinn was able to speak only the Cantonese dialect. The two Nationalist Chinese may have spoken Mandarin and little or no English so that communication with these two might have been difficult. Unlike the Cantonese-speaking Canadian Chinese, the Chinese in Malaya were not all from the same area in China, although most came from the southern provinces. As a result there were several distinct spoken dialects. In spite of language problems, Bing Lee Chinn was able to

– HMSO London
Bing Lee Chinn

interpret for most of the MPAJA without difficulty.

By the time Maxwell's group had set up camp, the Japanese had capitulated. The team immediately began providing medical assistance to the guerrillas who were suffering from beri-beri and skin ulcers and they also gave medical attention to those in Kuala Kubu

Chinese Nationalist Wireless Operator

Picking up Stores Container

Japanese work party

Bahru. They used work parties of Japanese in Kuala Kubu Bahru to clean up.

Galvanic Slate was dropped near Kuala Lumpur 28 July, under Capt. K. Robert

Japanese work party

Heine, his 2 i/c, Capt. Hugh Fraser, two wireless operators, and Sgt. Robert W. (Bob) Lew, K.5677, code-named *Maize,* interpreter,

– HMSO London
R.W. (Bob) Lew

as well as a tracker dog that was killed on landing.

Slate was dropped to a guerrilla reception committee near Kuala Lipis, about 30 miles north of Kuala Lumpur. It took five

days to reach their camp at Kachau, near Serendah. Again, because of a Japanese patrol, they had to quickly and quietly leave camp. There was tension and anxiety as they slipped away unseen and unheard while the Japanese approached. The Japanese, on the other hand, never seemed to mount a serious campaign to winkle them out.

Broadhurst had distributed three of his teams north of Kuala Lumpur and the two others, *Blue* and *Brown,* to the east and south. The teams were instructed to establish secure bases quickly so that there would not be long lines of communication. The patrols were to set up camps in places where they could develop quickly and be prepared to go into action immediately.

Enemy pressure steadily increased during late July and early August as the Japanese probed into their positions with a frontal penetration, repulsed by a section of the Gurkha support group. If the Japanese had attacked at this point, the whole Selangor organization would have been jeopardized. There was no further Japanese action until fighting erupted between the MPAJA and the Japanese at Serendah on 31 August.

The guerrillas at first had wanted *Slate* to be formed near *Orange* but lack of food in the area and increased enemy activity necessitated its move to the Kachau-Broga area, south of *Brown*. The move was not complete until after the Japanese capitulation.

On the Japanese surrender, Heine and Lew drove into Serendah; like Davis and Broadhurst at Kuala Lumpur, they were astonished to find a map on the walls of the garrison showing the location of most of the guerrilla camps.

The *Slate* team provided medical help to the Malays and the guerrillas who, like the inhabitants generally, were suffering from lack of medical treatment. Bob Lew then travelled to Kuala Lumpur to join the others.

It was not until 22 August that a medical team of Capt. John Holman and his medical orderly, Sergeant Goodyer, as well as a British sergeant wireless operator, were added to the Selangor teams; they were dropped to a reception committee at Serendah. It had been planned to complete the drop of additional Gurkha support groups during the August moon period but bodies were 'frozen' after the Japanese surrender.

John Davis moved from Perak to Selangor to join Broadhurst when the prospect of a Japanese surrender seemed imminent in mid-August. Bing Lee and Ted Wong were with Broadhurst when Davis joined the group.

When they moved to the headquarters camp near Serendah, Davis and Broadhurst learned that the Japanese commander in Singapore, Gen. Itagaki Seishiro, intended to continue fighting. There was a tedious period while they waited for news of the surrender. By 24 August, the Japanese still had not replied to the surrender; instead they attacked the guerrillas in Serendah. Also during this period, there was a guerrilla attack on a Japanese convoy in south Perak, which did not help the tension. The fighting was stopped in Serendah by the personal intervention of Davis and Broadhurst.

They then entered Kuala Lumpur and contacted the Japanese governor of Selangor with regard to the surrender. The Japanese officer in Kuala Lumpur, where some 6,000 Japanese troops were garrisoned, left some troops in Serendah to help keep the peace, but they insisted on waiting for the British Army to arrive before any formal surrender could occur.

On 31 August, Davis and Broadhurst moved into Kuala Lumpur to prevent further incidents. They established themselves in a Chinese house overlooking the race track where the guerrillas were encamped; they were thus able to keep watch over both the former enemy and their MPAJA allies.

Ugly situations developed: the guerrillas were hard to disband, and the Japanese refused to recognize the British connection with the guerrillas. Instructions had come from headquarters not to jeopardize the lives of prisoners by any kind of confrontation with the Japanese. Some 1,300 internees were located by the teams in a camp near Kachau in Selangor; wireless contact was immediately made with headquarters advising the number and location of this group. Since nothing further could be done in Kuala Lumpur, Davis and Broadhurst set out for Morib Beach for Operation *Zipper*.

At the time the British Army invaded on 9 September, the guerrillas were being used to prevent looting and lynchings and their health was improving with food supplies, transport, and quarters provided by the Japanese. Although General MacArthur had accepted the Japanese surrender on 2 September in Tokyo Bay, British troops did not reach Kuala Lumpur until 13 September, the day following Mountbatten's acceptance of the Japanese surrender of all troops in the SEAC theatre at Singapore.

By the end of September the British military authority and Force 136 teams were disbanding and disarming the guerrillas. Bing Lee coded messages to Ceylon concerning the situation in Selangor, including information on the POW camps they had found. Both he and Ted Wong helped supervise Japanese work parties and with the help of guerrillas maintained the peace between the Chinese and Malays. Assistance was also given to Australian Prisoners of War. At Serendah, the Japanese allowed the team to use the local police station and the hospital.

In Negri Sembilan the team was led by Maj. Claude Fenner, who was dropped the end of July with Capt. L.V.C. White near Seremban in *Humour Slate*. They were to arm and train the 2nd MPAJA Regiment. Fenner's wireless operator was not able to get on the air for a week after landing because the set had been dropped two miles away and it took days of tramping through dense jungle to recover it.

The Japanese were aware of the arrival of the *Humour* parties and made unsuccessful attempts to ambush them. Again the guerrillas and patrol teams had to tread cautiously, avoiding the Japanese. Fortunately, in another two weeks the war was over and like the other teams their tasks turned to keeping the peace.

There were four additional Patrol Liaison Teams dropped in Negri Sembilan. In the first week of August, the *Humour Orange* party, led by Allen Shaw, a Malaya police officer, with Captain Pepper, two wireless operators, and Sgt. Victor Joy Louie,[7] K.7785,

– HMSO London
Victor J.Y. Louie

from Victoria, interpreter, were dropped near Kuala Pila. Their territory extended from that village and Tampin close to the border of Malacca.

Although the 2nd MPAJA Regiment was headquartered in this state, the team was

dropped too late to become involved in training them. Drops of food, clothing, and medicines were received using the *S.Phone* to guide the aircraft in its approach.

Their main assignment was to keep the peace and restore civil administration. Shaw and Louie journeyed to the city of Malacca to negotiate the Japanese surrender. They then assisted in disbanding the 2nd MPAJA Regiment and left Malaya early in 1946. Shaw found Victor Louie "to be intelligent, keen and hard working, an NCO that can be trusted to carry out any order given him to the best of his ability."

In north Johore a series of *Tideway* operations under the command of Lt.-Col. A.C. Campbell-Miles was made to train the 3rd MPAJA Regiment. Another *Tideway* operation in Johore was led by Lt.-Col. Ian S. Wylie. Wylie later moved north to disband Hannah's 5th Perak Regiment.

The all-Canadian team of *Tideway Green* was dropped on 5 August to Campbell-Miles's reception committee in north Johore. The team was led by Maj. Joe H.A. Benoit, and included Sgt. Kim Wing (Ernie) Louie,

– HMSO London
K.W. (Ernie) Louie

K.5163,[8] interpreter, who spoke Cantonese. Ernie had completed his training when he joined the team at Horana. Benoit's 2 i/c,

Capt. John E. Hanna, who spoke Mandarin, and Capt. Roger M. Caza,[9] wireless operator, were dropped to the team two days later.

They remained at base for about five days and then set out on what was supposed to be a three-day trip through the jungle. Some of the equipment and kit had to be discarded to lighten their loads. The trip lasted a nightmarish seven days as they tramped 85 miles through swamps and dense jungle. It rained for three full days and their boots disintegrated. They were able to retain only items necessary for their survival because of lack of carriers.

Some of the guerrillas were accustomed to leading new arrivals through the thickest and swampiest jungle. Many teams never knew the precise locations of guerrilla camps, but the guerrillas were always aware of the team locations. The guerrillas often mounted skeleton guards on the patrol liaison team camps, ostensibly as protection against enemy attack. *Tideway Green* never learned the location of the guerrilla camp in their area.

A DZ adequate for food and stores was soon located but it was unsuitable for personnel. The food shortages both among the guerrillas and the Malays was very bad. On 17 August they were ordered to take no action and remain at their base. Then on the 20th, they were instructed to search out POW camps and report their condition to base.

The first drop of bulk food, including rice and dried fish, was received for the guerrillas. The wireless set then became unusable. Another drop of food and replacement parts for the wireless was made on 24 August, but this time the food was for members of the team.

At the end of the month, an Australian captain and corporal jumped to a reception committee of Ernie Louie and John Hanna. The two had searched out the DZ for the parachutists since the guerrillas had refused to help locate it. They had doggedly tramped through the area by compass marching and discovered a DZ they considered reasonably safe about six miles away.

The Japanese surrendered before there was need to go into action; the Benoit team was to have blocked the roads in the north Johore area for the *Zipper* invasion.

On 1 September the team moved to Batu Pahat and at nearby Kluang three days later, they found 900 POWs. In addition, twelve Indian escapees, as well as one British and three Australians, reported to the team. These former POWs were transferred to British military authorities in Singapore. For the POWs at Kluang, contact was made with the Japanese authorities and food and medicine drops were organized for their relief. Arrangements were then made for their repatriation between 12 and 14 September.

The guerrillas were becoming unwilling to cooperate now and the team had to deal with the inevitable conflict between the Malays and the Chinese. The team was forced to request help from the British Army at Singapore in order to restrain the Malays, who allegedly had killed two hundred Chinese at Batu Pahat. The Chinese requested immediate help since some killing was still going on and houses were being burned. Singapore headquarters sent a company of Punjabis but the team used the Japanese as well to patrol and maintain order.

In mid-September, Hanna and Louie were posted to Muar, and the team itself moved into the town on 21 September. After a month at Muar, on 18 October, they turned over control to a British officer but they continued their police and civil administration duties until they left Malaya 12 November. Ernie Louie travelled to Meerut, and the others went to Colombo.

There were two other operations in south Johore: *Carpenter,* led by Maj. W.P.S.B. Martin, an SOE operation to work with the 4th Regiment, and *Mint,* an ISLD team led by Maj. John V. Hart. *Carpenter* was infiltrated by submarine from Exmouth Gulf, Western Australia, on 28 October 1944. It was a Force 136 operation but because the approaches to South Johore were too dangerous for the submarine travelling from Ceylon, SRD Australia handled the insertion. In Martin's party were Maj. D.G. Reddish and Maj. D. Sime. They landed between Balau and Rampat in Johore. The ferry party remained with the team although it had been intended that it return with the submarine. Wireless contact was made with Colombo by 15 November and the team proceeded to send vital intelligence concerning the Japanese positions in south Johore.

In contact with John Davis, Martin relayed to Ceylon news of the survival of the *Gustavus* party. The team also began the usual instructional guerrilla training. Although Martin was killed by the Japanese when the team received a stores drop on 25 January, Major Sime took over and the intelligence service and training of the guerrillas was carried through to the surrender. When the Japanese capitulated, the *Carpenter* team cared for about 1,000 Indian POWs located in their area.

Maj. J.V. Hart, Capt. D.E. Trevaldwyn, and S/Maj. A. Norris were also landed by submarine in south Johore, with two Chinese wireless operators, to make up the ISLD *Mint* party. The team set up their camp between Tangja Tuloh and Kuala Papan and kept watch on the naval base from Johore Bahru. They gathered intelligence concerning the use being made of the base, and Hart included all dockyard activity in his reports.

Both groups were supplied by *Carpenter II* from Ceylon. In April, Hart wirelessed for clothing and rations to succour the crew of a B-29 shot down over the Singapore docks 11 January 1945. The items requested were promptly delivered by Liberator. Five members of the American crew of eleven had bailed out safely and had been sheltered by the guerrillas. Two of the survivors were unwilling to put their trust in the guerrillas; they were caught by the Japanese and beheaded. Three airmen were delivered to Hart by the guerrillas along with John Cross, an ISLD agent, and a jungle survivor since the fall of Singapore.

Hart arranged for a submarine to pick up all four and *Carpenter III* carried out the rescue. *Carpenter III* also landed 20 Royal Marines to take a beach south of Jason Bay, which was successfully accomplished. After the Japanese capitulated, the team located a POW camp of about 1,000 Indians.

In the northern state of Kedah, a series of *Sergeant* operations began with the *Sergeant Brown* team being dropped 14 July near Alor Star, the capital. The team was led by Maj. Pierre E. Chassé, with Derek Burr,

– HMSO London
Charlie Chung

wireless operator, and two other Canadians, Sgts. Charley Chung,[10] K.5487, and Fat Chung (Harry) Ho, M.7593, interpreters. They were to train the 7th MPAJA Regiment.

– HMSO London
F.C. (Harry) Ho

MPAJA Guerrilla Regiment

Chassé, a private from 1st Canadian Division in Italy, volunteered for special duty shortly after D-Day; he was trained and commissioned for the August *Dragoon* invasion in the Rhone Valley in southern France. Chassé had also served near Rangoon in Burma from early April to May.

A second team led by Roger Landes was dropped in the same area to a guerrilla reception committee also on 14 July. Landes, from the RCCS, had worked in France as radio operator in 1942. Back to England in January 1944, he returned in February to operate around Bordeaux.

After the Japanese surrender, Chassé and his four companions were ordered to Kangar, the capital of Perlis, to assume local government. Chassé's team separated from Landes and set out for Perlis, a two-week jungle trip. They had turned south before this to accept the surrender of the Japanese at Sungei Patani in south Kedah with Landes. On their return to Perlis, they were able to use the roads, reducing their travelling time considerably.

A Gurkha support group was promised but was late arriving; Chassé had to use the Japanese to keep order. Serious food shortages created additional problems. Some fanatical Japanese refused to surrender and fled into the jungle.[11] Siamese bandits, including a Siamese general who had administered the two border states, had to be controlled by Chassé's team and the Rajah of Perlis restored to his throne.

The *Sergeant Brown* team assisted in setting up civil government with the help of a British Army paymaster. When the Gurkhas arrived, the Japanese were repatriated and the Chinese guerrillas blocked in Siam.

Both Harry Ho and Charley Chung were diligent in their duties but sometimes the dialect spoken by the local Chinese in this northern part of Malaya was not a familiar one, as has already been noted.

Chassé was replaced by another Canadian in late October, Maj. Colin D. Munro, who had served as an artillery officer during the campaign in Northwest Europe.

At first, the MPAJA Regiment operating in Perlis was unwilling to surrender arms but was finally disbanded by Munro, who left Malaya in December.

Col. R. Musgrave and his Jedburgh teams of European veterans were also dropped in Malaya. They had to undergo extensive retraining in India. They were experienced operatives in the European theatre but would know nothing of jungle living or of other conditions in Malaya.

In Europe, a Jedburgh team was composed of American, British, and French members, or OSS, SOE, and one of the French partisan groups; they operated in uniform as liaison teams between the Resistance and the Maquis and London headquarters. In Malaya this combination was revised to reflect different conditions in the country and of Force 136 teams, that is, it was made up of an officer commanding, a second-in-command, a wireless operator, and an interpreter. The name 'Jedburgh' apparently came from the locality where they were first trained in Britain. The wireless equipment carried by these teams was known as a Jedburgh set.

When the Japanese were defeated, the Chinese Communists intended to replace both the Japanese and British as rulers of Malaya and generally were obstructive during the period of British Military Government. Law and order were maintained by Force 136 teams sometimes using the guerrillas and sometimes the defeated Japanese. The local police forces by now were considered suspect by both Malays and Chinese because they had cooperated with the Japanese. Many crimes were committed; violence and lawlessness were widespread. Food shortages and health problems, including epidemics and malaria, created an urgency to the situation.

British Military Government began in September 1945 and ended in March 1946. The MPAJA itself was disarmed and disbanded by Force 136 teams before the end of 1945, but the Communist Party went underground in February 1946 and proclaimed open rebellion in 1948. Although most MPAJA weapons had been turned in for a money consideration of $350 when ceremonial parades had been held during disbanding, a supply of arms and ammunition had been hidden in the jungle for future use. Over 6,000 guerrillas turned in weapons. Some of these weapons, both those turned in and those retained, had been salvaged after the British capitulation in 1942, or abandoned by the Japanese, while others had been pilfered from the supply drops regularly made to the group liaison teams.

After 15 August, serious clashes sometimes occurred between the Malays and Chinese; both sides apparently were executing collaborators. The role of the Force 136 teams suddenly changed from training and arming the guerrillas to negotiating working arrangements with the Japanese, to keeping the peace, and to searching out POW and internee camps.

When camps were found there was immediate wireless contact with headquarters giving their location and the number of prisoners; instructions were received from Ceylon or Calcutta as to how to proceed with rendering safe assistance.

After the Japanese surrendered, SOE personnel were re-assigned to keep the peace between the guerrillas and the Japanese and between the Malays and Chinese until Operation *Zipper* and the British Army arrived. They helped in repatriating the Japanese, in disarming and disbanding the guerrillas, and in restoring civil order. The SOE teams also assisted POWs suffering from disease and extreme malnutrition. On August 28, at the same time as preliminary surrender documents were being signed in Rangoon by Japanese envoys, Force 136 parties were instructed to move to the camps, to contact headquarters with lists of needs, and arrange for drops of supplies and medicines.

Colin Mackenzie, a civilian, but carrying the rank of lieutenant-general, headed Force 136 throughout the war. When he visited Malaya in October, his instructions to all liaison officers on the 23rd commended them for their control of the complex situation and requested their continued cooperation in disarming and re-settling the guerrillas.

Many of the 42,000 POWs in Changi and over 5,000 scattered in camps throughout the peninsula had worked on the 260 mile Burma-Siam railway. Some of these men had been moved south at the end of 1943 and several thousands had been selected for shipment to Japan and other areas as a labour force. Over 36,000 POWs were found in Singapore in early September 1945. Among

PERSONAL MESSAGE FROM THE COMMANDER FORCE 136.

To all Force 136 Liaison Officers with A.J.A.

I have the impression, as a result of my short visit to Malaya, that some Force 136 Liaison officers have a sense of frustration, and are impatient to be released.

I can well understand that Operational Officers who expected to be employed in the usual form of operational role are disappointed, and find their present work uncongenial. I wish to emphasise that the success of S.O.E. operations in any area must be considered as a whole. Wherever an indigenous resistance movement is organised, a problem is created which has to be resolved on the cessation of hostilities. This problem, whatever the local variations may be, consists essentially in the reabsorption of the resistance elements into the peacetime community.

In the case of foreign countries, this responsibility for solving the problem falls primarily on the nationals of the countries concerned, but even so, in cases where S.O.E. has taken a prominent role, they have been held responsible at least in part for the post-hostilities developments. So much so, that the value of the S.O.E. contribution has, rightly or wrongly, often been assessed finally on the results as a whole, including the liquidation of the resistance movement we have supported.

In the case of British territories, our responsibility is obviously much greater as the post war situation of these territories is a direct British interest, and we cannot to any large extent shift our responsibilities on to the local population. This being so, in Malaya the reabsorption of the members of the A.J.A. into civil life is of the greatest importance, and an integral part of the Force 136 task in this country, the earlier phase of which was the organising and supporting of resistance.

As you know, that resistance is mainly found in the A.J.A., an organisation which is inspired by Communism, and was earlier, Republican and Separatist in sympathy. The absorption of these elements into peacetime civil life would not in any case have been easy. With the present difficulties of finding civil employment for these men, and the present shortage of rice in the country, the problem becomes a great deal harder.

Owing primarily to the outstanding work and judgment of the late O.C. Malaya Country Section, Lt. Col. Innes Tremlett, and Col. J.L. Davis, D.S.O., we have so far achieved remarkable success. The organisation we built up gave an Intelligence yield of the utmost value, and if called upon would have shown itself at least equally valuable in action. But what I want to stress here is that we succeeded in winning over the A.J.A. to accept SEAC orders and the British connection. This automatically leads to co-operation with the B.M.A. You will appreciate that those leaders who had started with a Revolutionary Communist and anti-foreign bias have already come quite a long way in our direction, but this will only continue as long as following this course does not make the task of leadership too difficult for them. In other words, it is essential that the members of the A.J.A. should as far as possible be a contented body of men.

I would ask all officers, therefore, to put all they can into
these last six weeks.   Do everything you can to see that the men
reach the disbandment date in good fettle.   Make every effort to
see that during ensuing weeks they are given suitable employment
by the military authorities whereever possible.   Nothing can be
worse for their morale than that they should be left with nothing
to do.   Full details will be issued to G.L.O's and through them
to P.L.O's, covering the programme of disbandment, together with
the conditions which the men will receive.

I realise that this species of garrison duty without the
simplicity of direct command of your men may to some of you be
tedious and unattractive, but I feel justified in appealing to you
to give of your best during the coming six weeks, in view of the
great importance the work will have in relation to Force 136
performance as a whole in Malaya, and quite possibly to the more
immedate future of Malaya itself.   By a narrow margin we succeeded
in Burma in solving this problem.   We must succeed in Malaya, and
see to it that by sympathy, skill and attention to duty there is no
development here, even on a small scale, resembling those in
F.I.C. or N.E.I.

(Sgd). COLIN MACKENZIE.

Commander, Force 136.

Date: 23rd October, 1945.

them were twelve Canadians at Changi and Malai POW camps in Singapore and two others in Malaya whose precise location was unknown.[12]

The danger of the Japanese subjecting their prisoners to a general massacre before help could arrive was a very real one since plans existed at the Japanese Army headquarters in Saigon[13] to eliminate all prisoners and internees. The reason for such drastic action was to silence those who could testify against them at the War Crimes Trials that the Japanese knew would follow capitulation.

Many thousands of POWs were dispersed throughout the South East Asia and Dutch East Indies areas in over 225 camps. Since the men found in Singapore and throughout Malaya were part of the same army groups as were now dead at Sandakan/Ranau in British North Borneo, extreme caution had to be used in approaching a camp. Similar massacres had occurred at other camps both on the mainland and in the Pacific. Because of this, Mountbatten had forbidden approaching a camp until the situation had clarified.[22]

Lt.-Col. Arthur Stewart, another Canadian from Vancouver, who spoke both Cantonese and Mandarin, had been loaned to the War Office in January 1944. He saw duty in Burma with E Group before volunteering for Malaya. With his team of Captain Ross, RAMC, Major Clough his 2 i/c, and Sgt.

Billy Kong Lee

– HMSO London

Billy Kong Lee, K.7597, from Vancouver, they were dropped 24 August in the state of Johore in Operation *Snooper*.

At the end of August, Stewart and his team set out to cross the causeway to Singapore Island. They reached Japanese intelligence headquarters at Johore Bahru and were given directions and transportation to Changi Gaol. General Itagaki, commander of the 7th Japanese Army in Singapore, had finally decided to surrender.

The team arrived at Changi on 1 September but found that the prisoners had everything under control although they were suffering from malnutrition, malaria, and ulcers. There was also a group of POWs at Outram Gaol in Singapore city as well as in other prisons on the island.

Billy Lee coded, decoded, and transmitted messages to and from headquarters, detailing the camp conditions they found in Singapore and the availability of airfields. Medicine and food were dropped. Stewart used Japanese troops to control the city until the Royal Navy arrived 5 September. Repatriation of POWs made headway using both naval and air facilities.

Stewart went on to Sumatra, Java, and Borneo, with teams from Ceylon, again to see to the freeing of POWs and internees, leaving Billy Lee in Singapore. After his task was completed in early October, Billy set out for Kuala Lumpur and joined the five others with Captain Levy.

E Group handled the rescue operation with the help of Force 136 teams already in position; they began an active search for camps. Once a camp was located, wireless messages were immediately sent to Colombo and Calcutta. The air force dropped leaflets notifying Japanese guards that their country had surrendered; POWs and internees were also notified by leaflet drops on camps. The prisoners were requested to stay in their camps ready to receive medicines and food. With the food drops, relief teams were parachuted in.

Every plane available was pressed into service; the SD Squadrons were assisted by other Liberator squadrons in the theatre for dropping supplies when surrender came. These additional squadrons were limited to supply drops since their crews had not been trained for the dropping of personnel. There were many Canadian aircrew flying RAF aircraft, especially the Liberators, and they flew many SD sorties.

About 270,000 Asians from Malaya, including Chinese, Malays, and 60,000 Tamils, had also been lured by the promise of employment to work on the Burma-Siam railway; very few survived for their living and working conditions were even worse than what the POWs endured. There was extreme hardship among the families left behind in Malaya and a system of care for the widows and children was set up.

The British Indian Fleet set out for Malaya leaving three ships at Penang on 3 September. The much larger force with an Indian Division (the only troops available) and civil affairs officers arrived at Singapore on the 5th, three weeks after the surrender. British Military Administration began immediately. On 9 September 1945, Operation *Zipper* was proceeded with as the army landed unopposed on the beaches at Morib, Sepang (Lolang), and Port Dixon. The invasion operation had been cancelled at the conclusion of hostilities and then reinstated because of the chaotic and uncertain conditions in Malaya. Formal surrender was taken by Mountbatten at Singapore on 12 September.

In "Order of the Day," issued 12 September, Lord Louis Mountbatten acknowledged the surrender of the Japanese and issued instructions to all personnel with regard to their conduct toward the former enemy.

Operation *Mastiff* was launched by the Supreme Allied Command South East Asia for those on the ground to contact POWs, and for E Group to send in men and supplies. E Group used Force 136 Calcutta and Colombo headquarters to send in 400 tons of relief supplies from Calcutta and 250 tons from Colombo in the Relief of Allied Prisoners of War and Internees (RAWPI) operation.

Teams, which included a doctor wherever possible, were dropped in Siam, French Indo-China, Burma, and Malaya. Members of the Australian Parachute Battalion, trained to effect the rescue of the prisoners at Sandakan in Operation *Kingfisher,* and considered for the same purpose at Kuching, arrived at Singapore to assist members of the Australian 8th Division who were among the captives imprisoned there.

Fatal casualties in Group B, which included MCS, were Major Martin of *Carpenter,* killed by the Japanese; Sergeant Richardson, drowned; and when hostilities ceased, two officials from MCS just moved to Singapore when their aircraft crashed. Another fatality not usually included in the official casualty list was Lim Bo Seng, who had recruited Nationalist Chinese for the *Gustavus* insertions and had returned to Malaya himself to assist in setting up an intelligence network. Lim was captured by the Japanese and died in Batu Gaja prison 29 June 1944, aged 33. He had volunteered to return to Malaya 25 October 1943, apparently as a civilian, and was arrested by the Japanese in March 1944.

The Chinese in the Far East appear not to have been fully accepted members of the British and Australian organizations in Malaya and Sarawak; the usual term for them was 'civilian' or sometimes 'contact man.' Perhaps Canada was ahead of its times in accepting Chinese Canadians as full-fledged members of the Canadian Army, ambiguous as the acceptance was.

Six of the Canadians were collected in Kuala Lumpur by Capt. M.G. Levy and conducted from Penang on 7 December to Meerut where they stayed for three weeks before heading for Bombay. From Bombay they sailed for England on the *Moreton Bay* and arrived in Southampton on 28 March; they landed in Halifax from the *Ile de France* in late April.

By the time Mountbatten accepted surrender, 371 personnel had been infiltrated of whom 120 were British officers and 56 British ORs. There were 70 Asiatics, including the ten Chinese Canadians, and six Gurkha support groups. These ten Canadians

<u>ORDER OF THE DAY</u>
BY

The Supreme Allied Commander,
ADMIRAL THE LORD LOUIS MOUNTBATTEN, G.C.V.O., K.G.B.,
D.S.O., A.D.O.

The Order of the Day reproduced below for the information of all
personnel, has been issued by the Supreme Allied Commander on the occasion
of the surrender at Singapore:-

(Begins). "I have today received the surrender of the Supreme
Commander of the Japanese forces you have been fighting, and I have
accepted this surrender on behalf of all of you.

I wish you all to know the gratitude and the pride that I feel towards
every man and woman in the Command today. You beat the Japanese soldier in
battle, inflicting six times the amount of deaths that he was able to
inflict on you, and you chased him out of Burma.

The defeat of Japan last month is the first in her history. For
hundreds of years the Japanese have been ruled by a small set of
militarists, and they have been taught to look on themselves as a superior
race of divine origin. They have been encouraged to be arrogant to
foreigners, and to believe that treachery such as they practised at Pearl
Harbour is a virtue, so long as it results in a Japanese victory. They are
finding it very hard to accept defeat, and have not been too proud to try
and wriggle out of the terms of their surrender. Field Marshal Count
Terauchi, the Supreme Commander of the Japanese forces in this area, is at
the present time an ill man, having had a stroke last April; and I
therefore decided to accept this surrender through General Itagaki. But I
have ordered him to report to me in person as soon as he is strong enough
to travel; and you may all rest assured that I shall put up with no evasion
or trickery on the part of any defeated Japanese, however important or
divine he may consider himself.

I am telling you this because I wish to warn you of the situation you
may find when you proceed to liberate the other territories in the Command.
In the new areas you will be occupying, the Japanese have not been beaten
in battle; they are mostly composed either of troops who have never fought
us at all, and so never discovered for themselves that we could lick them;
or else of troops who took part in the early days, when we were not strong
enough to hold them. So there is every likelihood that they may feel they
could have bested us in battle, if their Emperor had not ordered them to
surrender.

You may well find, therefore, that those Japanese who have a fanatical
belief in their divine superiority, and who feel that we are too soft to
put them in their place, will try to behave arrogantly. You are to stand
no nonsense from those people. You will have my support in taking the
firmest measures against any attempt at obstinancy, impudence, or non-
cooperation.

On the other hand, you will find that there are many Japanese who are no more taken in by the preposterous claims of the militarists than you are yourselves. The Japanese, as a nation, had no say whatever in their own government, and were perhaps less responsible than any other people for their government's decision to go to war. Many of them therefore, have had little desire, for a long time now, to continue the fight, and are only too thankful that it is all over. Prisoners of this kind must be humanely treated, and I will not tolerate any case that is brought to my notice of taking it out on Japanese if they are prepared to be cooperative. In fact, I may even consider it necessary to protect them, perhaps by separating them, from the fanatics among their own countrymen.

It is possible that there will be hopeless cases, who may commit suicide, if they are prevented from behaving arrogantly and insultingly towards the Allied troops. This must be their own responsibility; for these are the people who can probably never be re-educated, and who have no contribution to make towards building the peaceable, civilised country which Japan must become if she is not to continue to threaten the peace of the world.

The Japanese prisoners, although they will number about half a million, will by no means be your only responsibility; there will be much more which will need doing. You will realize how much when I say that the enlarged South east Asia Command now includes 1-1/2 million square miles of land, with a population of 128 million people.

For some months to come, only SEAC will be in a position to undertake such vital tasks as repatriating our prisoners of war and civilian internees, who number more than one hundred thousand, and have the first claim on us. We shall also be removing the half-million Japanese, and we shall have to see about getting the millions of inhabitants in these vast areas properly fed, and given work, and brought back to peacetime conditions. All this will call for a great deal of planning, hard and practical work, initiative, and understanding.

I feel sure I can rely on you to do as well in peace as you did in war, and to get down to this gigantic task so that we can all of us return to our homes as soon as is humanly possible, feeling that we have done a good job. In the meantime, I know you will agree that our prisoners of war who have suffered for so long out here must have the first call on shipping space to take them home; but I shall do everything in my power to see that those of you who are due for release and repat. get home as fast as shipping and the rate of replacements permit." (Ends).

LOUIS MOUNTBATTEN
Supreme Allied Commander.

722/256/P.1
12th September, 1945.
Distribution: All Branches & Sections H.Q. Air Command.47

Back l to r - Unknown, Bing Lee, Ernie Louie, Harry Ho, Bill Lee
Seated l to r - Ted Wong, Nationalist Chinese Officer, Mike Levy, Henry Fung
Photo taken November 1945 at Kuala Lumpur, Malaya

gave invaluable service, often under conditions of very considerable personal danger; the indigenous population could easily mistake a Chinese Canadian for a Chinese Communist or bandit. There were 50 wireless sets operating. About 3,000 guerrillas had been armed and trained by Force 136, a figure that reached over 6,000 after 15 August, VJ-Day.

Most officers were temporary officers but with the help of their teams, who were also temporary soldiers, they instructed, trained, and led the guerrillas and then successfully disbanded them. They and their teams served as a buffer between the guerrillas and the general population, between the Malays and Chinese, and they controlled and used the

Japanese on policing and clean-up duties after surrender came. They brought help and hope to the prisoners of war and civilian internees.

Maj. H.J. Legg had selected the entire group for India, 15 in the second group for Australia, and had also trained three of the first group of 13 in wireless in the Okanagan camp from May to the end of August 1944. He had told the men as he interviewed them from Chilliwack, Wetaskiwin, Maple Creek, Red Deer, Shilo, Camp Borden, Barriefield, and Peterborough in late 1944 and early 1945 that they were 'special.'

Although only ten were sent into the field in Malaya, there were more than 30 in operational readiness at Horana. Others were still undergoing training at Poona and Meerut.

Had it not been for the atomic bombs and the sudden capitulation of Japan, many more would have been employed in the role for which they had been selected and trained.

Meanwhile, at the same time as these ten were operating in Malaya, five members of Kendall's first group had volunteered for operations in Borneo.

NOTES

The SOE Adviser has supplied several reports and summaries for the writing of this chapter; conversations with participants have provided added detail.

1. Broome, Davis, and Ivan Lyon, escaped from Singapore with others to Ceylon in February 1942.
2. Spencer Chapman, Seaforth Highlanders, had trained Commandos in Scotland (1939), Australia (1940), and had instructed at STS 101 Singapore (1941).
3. Maj. H.G. Hasler, Royal Marine, had been successful in a limpet mine raid on shipping in Bordeaux harbour in Dec. 1942, Operation *Frankton*.
4. ISLD, Inter-Services Liaison Department, SEAC name for MI 6, the Secret Intelligence Service. OSS combined the functions of MI 6 and SOE.
5. Levy escaped from Lung Wha internment camp in Shanghai and on his way to India met Arthur Stewart in Kunming, China. Levy was taken on by Force 136. He was Mentioned in Despatches for his work in Malaya. After the war Mike Levy emigrated to Canada; he enlisted in the Princess Patricia's Canadian Light Infantry, 2nd Battalion, and saw action in Korea. He retired in the rank of major in 1975.
6. Henry Fung returned to Canada from England about a month later than the others on the *Lady Nelson* hospital ship suffering from malaria and jaundice.
7. Victor Louie, first cousin to Ernie Louie, had spent 1931 to 1937 in China.
8. Ernie Louie was the brother of P/O Quan Jil Louie, killed when his plane was shot down over Madgeburg, Germany.

9. Benoit operated in France in 1944 and Burma in the Karenni region near Siam from April to May 1945; Hanna arrived in India November 1944 for seven months training; Caza operated in the Rhone Valley, southern France. He had injured his ankle and delayed the team from the scheduled July drop.
10. Sgt. Charley Chung donated his uniform to the Canadian War Museum, Ottawa.
11. The last two Japanese survivors came out of the jungle in 1990, 45 years after the war had ended; see *London Free Press,* 11 January 1990. Chin Peng, or Chen Ping, who had taken over leadership of the Communists in Malaya, and about 1,200 guerrillas, had surrendered in Siam in 1989; *see Toronto Star,* 3 December 1989. Chin Peng had been awarded the OBE for his support during World War II, although he did not actually receive the award. Chin Peng had emerged from the jungle in 1955 and met with John Davis and other officials at the Siam border, but this was only a truce and the war went on to 1960 and even into the 70s when the Communist Terrorists destroyed the National War Memorial in Kuala Lumpur.
12. NAC, RG 24, Vol. 59, File 650-92-54, telegram to Col. R.S. Malone then in Manila.
13. Clifford Kinvig, *Death Railway* (New York, 1973), p. 141; see also *The Knights of Bushido: A Short History of Japanese War Crimes* by Lord Russell of Liverpool (London, 1958), p.110; and Athol Moffitt *Project Kingfisher* (North Ryde, NSW, 1989), p.165.

Chapter XII

SARAWAK OPERATIONS

Services Reconnaissance Department began infiltrating 'Z' Special Unit agents into Borneo for the forthcoming Australian Army invasion about the time F.W. Kendall left the *Oblivion* groups. In early June, five of the original 13 and twelve of the second group of 15 Chinese Canadians had volunteered for special duty in Sarawak. By the 13th of the month, Capt. Roger Cheng, Sgts. Jimmy Shiu, Norman Low, Roy Chan, and Louey King were on their way to Morotai.

Sarawak, Brunei, British North Borneo, and Dutch Borneo fell to the Japanese in January 1942; Singapore surrendered the following month. Singapore Command, which at this time had military jurisdiction also in British Borneo, had instructed the small force in Sarawak to destroy the oil wells in the north at Miri in Sarawak, and Seria in Brunei.

Senior officials and most of the troops were evacuated by ship. Other members of the civil administration and remaining soldiers became prisoners of the Japanese, first at Labuan Island, then at Kuching.

In the Kuching area, the Japanese operated a group of compounds for Prisoners of War and Internees from North Borneo as well as Sarawak, and others rounded up by the Japanese throughout the island. Three compounds housed civilian internees, and there were two each for British, Australian, and Dutch POWs. These nine compounds were located about three miles from Kuching, the capital of Sarawak.

Sarawak contained about 600,000 inhabitants at the time of the Japanese invasion. A quarter of the population were Malays and another quarter Chinese, with Europeans, Indians, and Melanaus along with the interior tribes making up the rest. About half were pagans. The Malays, Melanaus, and Chinese lived along the coast; the pagans lived along the rivers in the interior. The Chinese also sometimes operated shops in the river towns.

The interior tribes were head hunters with the Ibans being considered the wickedest of all. Head hunting had been eliminated by administrators, with the exception of a period in the 1930s, until the Second World War released formal restraints and the pagans were again free to pursue their old pastime. The rajah declared an open season for Japanese head hunting early in 1942 and the Dyaks (Dyak is a generic term used for all the Borneo tribes) needed no second invitation since Japanese heads were the perfect shape and many of them had gold teeth, which considerably enhanced their value.

The Japanese Greater East Asia Co-prosperity Sphere did not extend to Borneo and the native tribes resented and detested the Japanese for their confiscation of rice and other produce, the forced hunting of game for their tables, and the loss of their shotguns. They were humiliated by the conquerors who expressed open contempt for them and their way of life as they had done to the Malays on the coast. There was no trade. Although the interior tribes required little of outside goods, they did appreciate a piece of cloth. They especially liked the parachute cloth when it first appeared in their midst, and bits of metal, which they fashioned into weapons and tools. They were also addicted to tobacco, which they grew themselves and rolled into cigars.

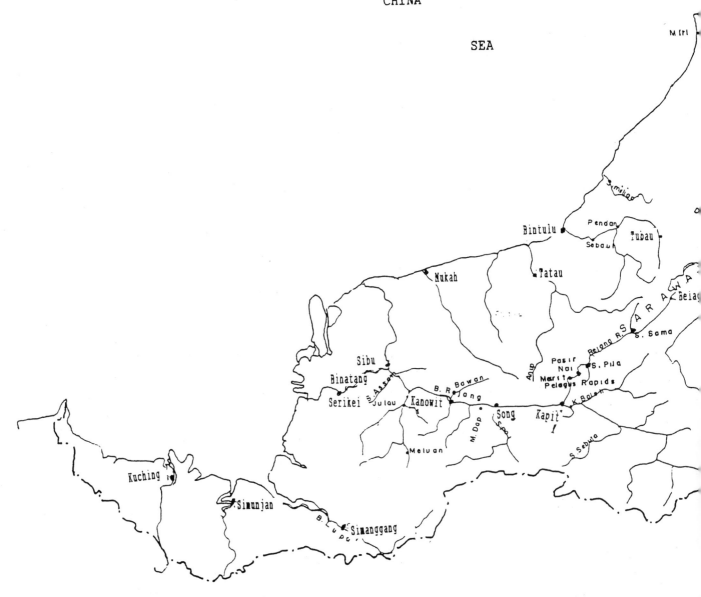

SOUTH

CHINA

SEA

Miri

Bintulu Pendan Tubau
Sebauh

Mukah Tatau Belag

SARAWA

Belong RS S. Sama

Sibu Anup Pasir
Nai S. Pila
Binatang Merit
S. Assam B. R. Bawan Pelagus Rapids
Serikei Sulau Kanowit Rajang K. Balen

Song Kapit
M. Dap Sapa
S. Sebla

Meluan

Kuching

Simunjan

B. L u p a Simanggang

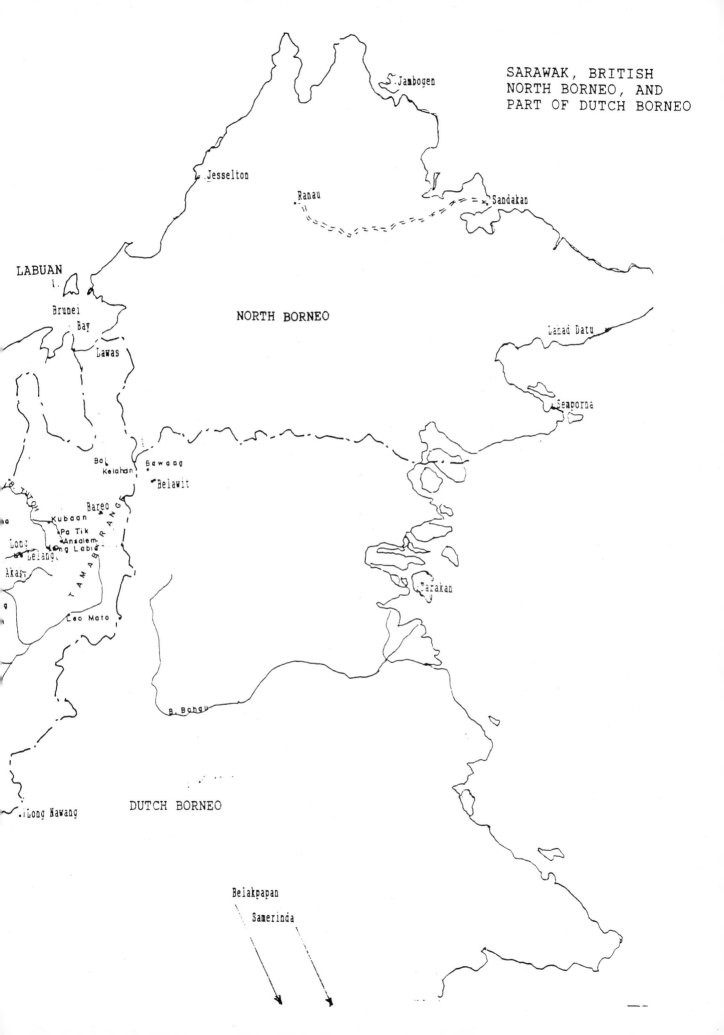

SARAWAK, BRITISH
NORTH BORNEO, AND
PART OF DUTCH BORNEO

S.Jambogen

.Jesselton

Ranau   Sandakan

LABUAN
I.

Brunei   NORTH BORNEO
Bay   Lahad Datu

Lawas

Semporna

Bol
Kelahan   Bawang
              Belawit

Bareo
Kubaan
Pa Tik
Ansalem
Long   ong Labid
Lelang
Akah

Tarakan

Leo Mato

B. Bangu

DUTCH BORNEO
.Long Nawang

Belakpapan

Samerinda

Borneo was not self-sufficient in food, except possibly for the interior tribes, and by late 1944 and early 1945, the food situation was becoming acute both for the inhabitants of the island and for the Japanese overlords. The losses in Japanese shipping restricted the amount of food that could be brought into the island. Rice was confiscated from the central tribes by the Japanese who sent patrols to escort the grain through the steaming jungle to the coastal garrisons. Occasionally a *rentis* (path) would be cut through the jungle to assist the passage of the carriers.

The rainfall was fairly evenly distributed throughout the year, unlike Burma and Malaya. Rain was an almost daily problem for the 'Z' Special Unit operatives, often restricting their movements, and causing deteriorating health to many.

The land was covered in thick jungle with clearings at towns and *kampongs* (villages) along the rivers where the longhouses were erected. Here the tribes grew their main crop of rice, building their longhouses in new locations as the soil became depleted.

The longhouse sometimes housed several hundred relatives in one extended building. The average longhouse sheltered about thirty families. Built on stilts, originally as protection, with steps cut into a log, the space beneath the longhouse was inhabited by the village pigs, dogs, and chickens fed on whatever dropped from the house above. As a result, pork had the taste and aroma of excreta when served as food since it was never completely cooked.

The Chinese rose against the Japanese at Jesselton in North Borneo in 1943. A force of about 200 Chinese had gathered in Jesselton and attacked on 9 October, killing about 50 Japanese. Within three months, the Japanese regained control, bombing and burning several villages as well as carrying out reprisals against the rest of the civilian population. In January 1944 alone, 176 were executed. The Suluk tribe on nearby islands, suspected of complicity in the uprising, was virtually wiped out. An estimate of the total number killed was at least 1,000. It was well over a year after this rising was subdued before any attempt to regain control in Borneo was made by the Allies.

There were two main operations in Borneo by SOE agents. The first was a series of operations code-named *Agas* (sandfly). Under Maj. F.G.L. Chester of the British Army and five others, including a wireless operator. *Agas I* was landed by submarine on the east coast of North Borneo 3 March 1945. *Agas II* under Maj. R.G.P.N. Combe with three others, including a Chinese medical officer, was dropped on 3 May to assist the original group.

The two parties established an agent network, trained the natives in guerrilla tactics, and wirelessed back to headquarters in Melbourne information concerning the number of Japanese and troop movements in the area. The Australian Army required such intelligence for its forthcoming invasion. The teams also ambushed outlying garrisons, and killed any small parties of Japanese they were able to catch on the move.

Operation *Agas* had been instructed to locate and report on the 2,500 Allied POWs at Sandakan. Of the original 2750 prisoners moved to Sandakan from Singapore by the Japanese to build military airstrips, about 300 officers and NCOs had been moved to Kuching. Before the end of May 1945, over 1,000 had already died at Sandakan.

Walking a distance of 165 jungle miles, acting as bearers for the Japanese, with little food and already in a weakened condition, many more prisoners died on the march to Ranau in the interior. Those who did not die of starvation, disease, or exhaustion were shot by the Japanese either on the march or after reaching camp. Many were killed after Japan had capitulated. Although preparations had been made to rescue these prisoners in Operation *Kingfisher,* Australia was advised that air and marine transport was not available.

The third *Agas* operation, inserted by submarine at Jambogen Island 23 June, was led by F/Lt. G.C. Ripley with Sgt. A.W.C.

Hywood (wireless operator) in an attempt to
rescue the POWs; they reached the Ranau area
in early August. By this time there were only
six survivors of the camps and the marches.
Through a native's help, Ripley picked up one
survivor on 10 August. This man, WO Bill
Sticpewich, escaped from Ranau 28 July; he
advised Ripley that four others had escaped in
early July from the same camp. There was
also a single escape. Four of the six died. The
second survivor reached the coast and, with
the help of natives, was picked up at sea by an
American torpedo boat.

Ripley advised Morotai headquarters
about 13 August of what he had found, a few
days after Capt. Roger Cheng and his *Hippo*
party of Sgts. James Shiu, Norman Low, Roy
Chan, and Louey King left for the Rejang.

Norman Mon Low

– HMSO London

Roy S.T. Chan

– HMSO London

Roger K. Cheng

– HMSO London

Louey King

– HMSO London

James Shiu

– HMSO London

Ripley requested that a doctor be included in
reinforcements; he was unable to obtain
accurate information about current conditions
in the camp at Ranau.

Three days after Hirohito's surrender
broadcast, on 18 August, five Australian Army
men with three 'Z' Special operatives, including a doctor, were dropped into the Ranau area
to assist Ripley. The Japanese in Borneo had
not surrendered.

One of the POWs who had been destined for the camp at Sandakan was Maj. Rex Blow, an Australian and a former official in North Borneo. On the eve of their transport to Sandakan, he escaped from Berhala Island, the harbour at Sandakan, along with four others on 4 June 1942. Another party of three, including Maj. Jock McLaren, also escaped at the same time. The assistance of local Chinese and natives, members of the underground, was crucial in sheltering the men and in obtaining *prahus* (boats). Major Blow reached the Philippines where he operated as a guerrilla leader before returning to Australia. Blow and McLaren were briefed for Operation *Kingfisher,* an attempt to rescue the POWs at Sandakan, but the operation never took place.

Blow volunteered to return to North Borneo on 14 July 1945; with three others they were inserted by motor launch at Semporna. Operation *Agas IV* was to report on Japanese troops for the whole of the Semporna peninsula. Just north of them was McLaren, who headed *Agas V* in the Lahad Datu area from 27 July.

With the exception of *Agas III,* the *Agas* operations were primarily in the coastal areas of North Borneo. Here is where the Australian Army would invade and where intelligence concerning enemy dispositions could be critical. The guerrilla teams could attack the Japanese only when there was a small group isolated from the main body, but the information concerning Japanese strength, movements, and general local conditions was invaluable.

For the Australian Army assaults at Tarakan, Labuan Island and Brunei Bay, and finally at Balikpapan, under the code name *Oboe,* SRD mounted operations from Morotai in support. The men performed a variety of functions: the gathering of intelligence, the checking of beaches and the surrounding areas, and the rescue of downed airmen. Lacking some of the esoteric organizations spawned in Europe, the Australian Army relied on SRD to perform many of these functions. There were also other smaller raids undertaken by SRD that would normally have been considered suitable for Commandos.

The First Australia Corps, 7th and 9th Divisions, began its offensive in Borneo on 1 May. The first landing was at Tarakan where fierce fighting delayed the island's capture. The second landing was 10 June at Labuan and the Brunei Bay area, unopposed and without casualties. The army landing at Labuan and the Bay was the signal for the native guerrillas under SRD leadership to attack the Japanese. The third landing was in Dutch Borneo at Balikpapan on 1 July where heavy navy and aerial bombardments led the assault. All three landings were successful and the Japanese were driven into the interior where the army did not follow them.

It was not part of the army's task to control the interior and the natives would have been left defenceless, but long before the army invaded from the coasts, SRD had begun infiltrating 'Z' Special Unit agents and wireless operators into the Sarawak interior. The Australian Army did not go much beyond the three coastal oil producing areas. The *Semut* (ant) operations, on the other hand, began in the interior and worked down the jungle trails and rivers attacking each strongpoint in turn until they reached the coast.

There were three main parties in the *Semut* operations, originally designed to work under the direction of Maj. G.S. Carter. Because of the size of the area to be covered, and the problems encountered with wireless communications due to the equipment and the mountains, the three parties ultimately operated independently. A fourth party was added after the capitulation.

Initially designated to act as reconnaissance party for the *Semut* operation, Capt. T.H. Harrisson (promoted to major in the field) headed the first group to be dropped. *Semut I* soon operated as an independent unit and its orders were changed so that it covered the area from Brunei Bay to the Bahau River including the Kelabit plateau and a section of Dutch Borneo.

The eight-man reconnaissance party flew from Leyburn the RAAF parachute training centre, to Darwin the signals centre, and on to Morotai which had just been captured and where some Japanese were still holding out. From Morotai they flew to San Jose Air Base on Mindoro Island in the southern Philippines. They were dropped blind at Bareo in the interior on Sunday, 25 March, from two Liberators of 200 (SD) Flight RAAF.

In addition to the six Liberators of the Special Duty Flight, and 113 Air Sea Rescue Flight Catalinas, there was an army coopera-tion unit of Austers used to evacuate recovered American pilots at Belawit. The Austers operated first from newly recaptured Tarakan, then moved to Labuan where the ASR unit was also located.

The first of the two planes, command-ed by S/Ldr. Graeme Pockley, disappeared on its return to base; as a result there was a "major disruption to the insertion and back-up plans for the operation,"[1] a disruption that reached serious proportions when two additional planes disappeared, one on reconnaissance over East Timor and the other supplying the *Agas* operation. At this time the three lost planes and crews constituted half of 200 RAAF Special Duties Flight.

In the first party accompanying Harrisson were Sgt. C.F. Sanderson (a language expert), S/Sgt. Doug Bower (wire-less), and Sgt. J. Keith Barrie[2] (surveyor). The second plane carried Harrisson's 2 i/c, Lieut. Eric Edmeades,[3] later captain, (senior para-chute instructor), WO Rod Cusack (stores), Sgts. Jack Tredrea (medical), and K.W. Hallam (wireless). Because of increasing cloud cover, the second drop was made half a day's walk away from the first group. The fear of a Japanese reception was soon dispelled and the second group met Harrisson at the Kelabit longhouse. Other members of Harrisson's team were out with the natives gathering up the stores.

Their first contact was with *Penghulu* (chief) Lawai Bisarai, of the Kelabit tribe, at Bareo. Lawai did not speak Malay and nego-tiations in sign language were conducted by Sanderson to obtain the Penghulu's help and cooperation, not only immediately to round up the stores dropped at the same time as the

Sgt. Keith Barrie, AIF

agents, but also for future operations against the Japanese. Radio contact was immediately made with Darwin.

Their official instructions were to gather intelligence, to organize, arm, train and lead native levies in general operations, to provide medical services to the natives, to pro-vide rehabilitation, and to distribute food.

These instructions were later modified and expanded by Harrisson to also include investigation of the route for Carter's and Sochon's parties, to ascertain the situation to the east in Dutch Borneo, in Brunei Bay to report on the Japanese dispositions, and finally to try to locate escaped POWs who had disappeared into the interior especially in the heights around Tarakan. With the Boston wireless set and its hand generator, contact was soon made with head-quarters and these extended terms of reference were accepted.

The party was split into three groups. Two members were to go into the Tarakan area in Dutch Borneo; Sanderson was to make for Brunei Bay; and Edmeades, Hallam, and Barrie were sent to Long Lelang on the upper Baram where *Semut II* was to operate. They would meet new tribes on the Baram—the Kenyah and Kayan tribes.

The Edmeades group set out 27 March with guide and porters on a gruelling six-day trip over the Tamabo Range, skirting the headwaters of the Tutoh River and passing through several Kelabit villages (Kubaan, Pa Tik, Ansalam, Long Labid) and spending two nights in the jungle. "It was days of steep climbing and torrential rains; we were continually sliding in the mud and attacked by a never ending army of large black leeches."[4] They arrived at Long Lelang 2 April.

At Long Lelang they located a DZ for stores and the possible insertion of personnel of *Semut II* and *III*. Edmeades left 4 April to return to Bareo. Because the natives had given them a traditional feast on their arrival, Edmeades reported to Harrisson that there was plenty of food. Except for some rice, the natives were suffering from serious food shortages. The food they had shared with their guests left them with very little in reserve.

Barrie and Hallam were without stores of any kind and a stores drop was delayed because of the search for Pockley and his crew. "All we had to keep us going was gluey rice crammed into bamboo pipes supplied by the villagers which was pretty much all they had also."[5] For three weeks they were also without wireless contact with Bareo. Hallam was unable to get the ATR4 wireless set to transmit to Bareo with 5,000-foot mountains intervening.

Since they were the advance party of Europeans returning to liberate Borneo, they were in a difficult position when the days lengthened into weeks without any signs of the promised food, arms, and ammunition. It was at this point that Keith Barrie and Kel Hallam requested transfer from *Semut I* to *II* in a letter sent to Harrisson by runner. Their request was granted. Barrie

went on to serve in *Semut III* but Hallam remained with *Semut II*.

They signalled an aircraft by the use of smoke canisters 16 April but the entire stores drop was made in the Tutoh area below Ansalam some miles away. Barrie and Hallam, with the help of the natives, located the stores and all were recovered except one storepedo and one package. Some Sarawak currency was among the items lost. There was still another week of waiting before anything further developed.

Two additional groups and stores set out from Morotai for San Jose on Mindoro Island; they were dropped 16 April from two Liberators with a third carrying stores. Maj. G.S. (Toby) Carter was to lead *Semut II* on the *Batang* (river) Baram, and Capt. W.L.P. (Bill) Sochon[6] (who soon was promoted to major) headed *Semut III* on the Batang Rejang. "Both Toby and Bill were 'old' - in their 40s - compared to the rest of us," said Barrie, and he himself was 31.[7]

Dropped with Sochon were Sgts. Abu bin Kassim (contact man), Bob Long, (wireless operator, who remained with *Semut I*), and WO D.L. Horsnell (small arms expert). With Carter were Capt. Ian A.N. (Dr) McCallum (who disagreed with Harrisson's bare foot policy and transferred to *Semut II*), Sgts. Teh Soen Hin (contact man), and C.W. Pare (wireless operator). Carter led this group until they were able to determine the reaction of the native tribes, then Sochon and two others left to establish *Semut III*.

They split the party to travel to Long Lelang so that natives would from the beginning see them as two separate groups and, perhaps, make it seem that more whites were on the ground than were actually present. Barrie and Hallam learned the reason for the delay—the loss of Pockley and his aircraft—when the parties arrived at Long Lelang.

Back at Bareo, Harrisson relocated his headquarters to the head of the Bawang River, west of Belawit and directly west of Tarakan in Dutch Borneo. There were additional drops of men and supplies for *Semut I,* one in May, five in June, and another on 10 August.

Harrisson's group covered the area from Brunei Bay to the Bahau River capturing 23 and killing 940 Japanese with 233 auxiliary casualties. Of their own group, 14 natives were killed.[8]

The Batang Baram is the main highway in the Fourth Division of Sarawak, with Miri the capital. Many Ibans lived along the lower Baram, while the Kayans and Kenyahs lived further up the river. Carter moved his headquarters to Long Akah.

There was a drop of men and supplies in May, followed by three further drops in June. Major Carter led his band of Kenyah and Kayan warriors down the Baram River, passing through Long Lama and Murudi, relocating his headquarters as he captured each town. They ambushed a heavy Japanese wireless station at Long Lama and succeeded in laying an ambush for the Japanese headquarters at Murudi. The *Semut II* party killed 258 of the enemy and took two POWs along with three auxiliary prisoners, losing five of their own native troops.[9]

Major Sochon led the third group, a final total of about 40 men, in the Kanowit area on the Rejang River in *Semut III*. This number included Captain Cheng's *Hippo*

– courtesy Mrs. Margaret Sochon
Major W.L.P. Sochon

party when it joined Sochon's group after the Japanese capitulated.

When Sochon was dropped at Bareo 16 April in the same drop as Carter, Sochon's parachute developed seven split panels when it opened initially, with 14 by the time he reached the ground. His fall was accelerated disastrously but he guided his parachute to a small padi marsh and landed in a foot of water without injury. The parachutes assigned to 'Z' Special Unit had already been used up to 100 times; since the agents' parachutes were not to be recovered, it was felt the use of newer ones would be a waste. This policy was soon changed.

Sochon's orders were to gather intelligence, organize native levies, perform general operations against the enemy, provide medical services to the natives along with rehabilitation and food distribution. "It was also considered necessary to control the river as far west as Kanowit before operation *Hippo* could commence the penetration of the Kuching area based on *Semut III*."[10] Captain Cheng and the four sergeants were held for over six weeks at Morotai from mid-June. Because of the number of internees as well as Prisoners

of War in the Kuching compounds, extreme caution would be needed in any attempt to approach the camps.

Maj. Bill Sochon, WO Don Horsnell, and Sgt. Abu bin Kassim set out from Bareo 17 April on the same track as Barrie and Hallam to Long Lelang which they reached on the 23rd. "They had been informed by Harrisson that few bearers were available, and no stores were necessary for the trip. As a result, the party had to carry their own equipment and personal stores."[11] The mud, the leeches, and the lack of food and carriers made it a difficult trip. It was impossible for white people to "live off the land," as Harrisson had insisted they should do, and remain capable of fighting.

On arrival Sochon found that Barrie and Hallam were "in not too good shape," and "very upset by treatment received from Harrisson."[12] With guides and boatmen, Sochon, Barrie and Abu Kassim set off down the Akah (through Long Lengaleh, Long Seniai, over the rapids and portages) to join Carter at Long Akah arriving 1 May. They moved into the *Kubu* (Fort) where they waited daily for stores drops. Without

– courtesy Keith Barrie from Toby Carter
Advance parties of Semut II and III at Long Akah Kubu,
May 1945
L to r - Iban ex-Sarawak constabulary member, Abu Bin Kassim,
Bill Sochon, Keith Barrie, Toby Carter, Wally Pare, Kel Hallam,
Teh Soen Hin, and Don Horsnell

wireless contact it was 16 May before they were advised by runner that a drop would be made between the 19 and 21 of May.

It was at Long Akah that they first contacted Tama Weng Ajang, supreme chief of the Kayans in the Baram. Penghulu Tama Weng Ajang lived at Long San some three miles above Long Akah. Penghulu Puso, Skapan chief (a minor Kayan clan), lived at Belaga on the Rejang about 100 miles from Kapit. These two tribes lived upriver in the interior with the largest part of the population being in Dutch Borneo. About 9,000 natives lived on the Baram. None of the natives in the *Semut* areas ever betrayed any of the 'Z' operatives, in spite of the reward offered by the Japanese.

Tama Weng arrived at Long Akah flying a large Union Jack at the stern of his prahu. Only the Japanese flag was permitted in Sarawak, so he was denying Japanese

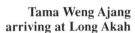

Tama Weng Ajang arriving at Long Akah

– courtesy Keith Barrie and G. Carter

Tama Weng drawing alongside

– courtesy Keith Barrie and G. Carter

authority and demonstrating his cooperation. After protracted discussions with Tama Weng and Puso, the usual native manner of doing business, it was finally agreed that the Kayans would supply auxiliaries.

During their stay at Long Akah, Don Horsnell, ex-machine gunner, instructed the natives on the use of weapons. "An

also by this means they learned that the European War had ended, and that the Australian Imperial Force 9th Division had invaded at Tarakan, followed by Labuan Island and the Brunei Bay area.

Harrisson advised them that there was a force of 1,000 Japanese approaching the *Ulu* (interior) Baram from Dutch Borneo. Sochon

– courtesy Keith Barrie and G. Carter
Kubu at Long Akah

improvised range was made in the general area of the Kubu, butts and firing mounds, where the training proceeded . . . at one period so great was the enthusiasm for firing the weapons, and so little was the experience of the riflemen, that one began to feel it was safer to be stationed at the butts rather than on the firing mounds."[13]

Radio contact was finally established with Bareo. In addition to the ATR4, Barrie had been issued an early type miniature MCR radio on which shortwave radio news broadcasts could be received. This kept the party informed of war news from the rest of the world and thus they were able to speak with conviction to the natives of the inevitability of the Japanese defeat. It was

and Barrie patrolled up the river with a party of Kayans as guides and prahu crew. They met with the local Kenyah Penghulu at *Sungei* (river) Mo, and the village constable in charge of the Kubu Lio Matu, and requested their help in closing the Japanese route from the Dutch side into the Ulu Baram. It had taken five days to reach Kubu Lio Matu on the Ulu Baram to find that it was a false alarm. Their trip back to Long Akah took just one day; they arrived 15 May.

After receiving a stores drop, Sochon, Barrie, and Abu bin Kassim began their journey on 21 May towards Batang Belaga and the Rejang going by way of the Tinjar and Ulu Dapoi across the Dulit Range. They were guided into Iban territory by an Iban ex-NCO

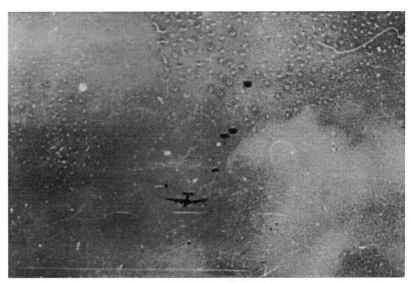

– courtesy Keith Barrie and G. Carter
Stores drop at Long Akah 1945

– courtesy Keith Barrie and G. Carter
Recovering Storepedoes

of the Sarawak Constabulary, known by Sochon from former days.

They travelled on foot, carrying their stores and equipment. The country was very hilly and the route included a lot of river-bed walking; they were not dry for six days. There was a ready welcome each time they stopped at a longhouse or kampong. The Kayans who accompanied them were reluctant to move out of their traditional territory, unlike the Ibans who cheerfully ventured into other tribal areas.

They travelled down river to *Kuala* (estuary) Sungei Pawan, through Long Pawan, Ulu Pawan, Dapoi and Ulu Dapoi and then upstream until the stream became impassable. When they reached Punan territory, they stayed overnight at Sungei

Nibong, a Punan house, and then went on to Kerangan. Here they found a new Japanese rest house built in a commanding position on the Batang Lobang.

The Punans with their blowpipes and poisoned darts were able to bring down monkeys out of the jungle canopy high above. The blowpipe was a hard wood rod, about eight feet long with its centre bored through. The hunter fitted a bamboo dart tipped with poison made from the sap of the ipoh tree, into one end of the weapon. Filling his cheeks with air, the hunter blew the arrow through the hollow shaft of the pipe. When the barbed dart buried itself in the flesh, the poison acted almost immediately. The Punan's aim was excellent and deadly accurate at twenty yards. It was a silent and effective method of killing.

– courtesy Keith Barrie and G. Carter
Punans with blowpipes

"They were unable to make contact with any headquarters, in spite of every effort being made to find a suitable site for successful transmission."[14] Sochon sent a runner to Carter saying he would reach Belaga by 1 June, and requested flying boat insertion between the 4th and 6th. They continued on the newly cut rentis, which was supposed to be for the purpose of carrying supplies from the Sibu area to Bintulu on the coast but the path was actually an escape route.

The Japanese had used forced Javanese labour to cut a man-made trail through the jungle. It had taken 1,000 Javanese three weeks to cut over eight miles of path. The log bridges with handrails, the steps cut into steep sidings and ridges also with handrails, and with occasional rough jungle benches sometimes with *atap* (thatched) shelters on the ridge tops, all contributed to the comparative ease of the journey. "Previous to this, path going from Kerangan to Maa was a 3-day trip—now can be done in 7 hours."[15]

After crossing the Dulit Range they reached Kuala Maa on Ulu Belaga. They found another Japanese station in disrepair as was the track they had just arrived on. The Punans took them down river where they met Jok Emut from *Tua Rumah* (head of household) Baling's house. They arrived at Sungei Paku, the start of the Bintulu rentis similar to the Tinjar one, with Belaga a short distance downstream.

Sgt. Abu bin Kassim and Wan Osman had been sent ahead to reconnoitre Belaga; the rest of the party reached the village 1 June. They were well received by Tua Rumah Baling on the left bank of Batang Belaga at its junction with the Batang Balui, by Penghulu Puso at Belaga further downstream on the right bank, and by the Chinese and Malay communities. They carried a letter to Penghulu Puso from John Fisher, pre-war resident in the Third Division, requesting personal assistance for the party. Fisher was greatly respected throughout the Rejang.

Belaga was a four-hour trip from Kapit on the Batang Rejang, over the Pelagus, Tekok and other rapids. It was a small administrative town in Kayan territory and one of the first to be occupied. As in all administrative centres of Rajah Brooke, there was a dominating fort, Fort Vyner. The Rejang continued into the interior to its source, another two or three week journey.

It was at Belaga that Sochon's party learned of the "massacre of Europeans, men, women and children, who had fled to Long Nawang from the coast, in an attempt to escape capture by the Japs." The Japanese had followed them into the interior.[16] Sochon was later to send one of the men to obtain accurate information on this massacre.

The ATR4 portable radio transmitter was still not functioning but Barrie signalled a flight of Liberators by emergency mirror on 7 June. Uncertain as to whether or not the message had been received, Sochon sent a runner to Carter at Long Akah with information of their predicament and proposed new location at Sungei Pila. Sochon, Barrie, and Abu Kassim moved by prahu to Kuala Sungei Pila further down the Rejang just above the rapids, which they reached 8 June.

At Sungei Pila, they set up camp in the jungle on the left bank of the Rejang, opposite Penghulu Sandai's longhouse, where they remained for the next three weeks. They were without food or adequate weapons or wireless communication. They were now in Iban territory and waited for the promised insertion of men and supplies.

Sochon arranged to meet with several Penghulus to obtain their support in offensive action against the Japanese. "Initially [they were] to ambush any Jap patrols which might venture out of the downstream forts heading up river. There was the added attraction of acquiring some heads." The Ibans were doubtful "as to how we three were going to rout the Japanese on our own as there did not seem to be any stores or arms forthcoming."[17]

Meanwhile, Abu bin Kassim was sent back to Belaga to hold that position and reassure the people. When the Ibans learned of the Baram insertions under Major Carter, there was an easing of tensions but still some nervousness. They were, with justification,

fearful of Japanese reprisals. At Belaga, Abu Kassim found that Puso and his Kayans had ambushed and killed two Japanese on the Bintulu-Paku rentis.

Another group of Ibans massacred five Japanese and 19 of their Chinese prisoners travelling up from Kapit at Pasir Nai, on the right bank of the Rejang above the Pelagus Rapids; there were times when the Ibans made no distinction between the two long-standing enemies. The Ibans were revelling in the glory of taking heads and were not too concerned as to the identity of the victims; it had been "many years since they had enjoyed such a windfall of heads."[18]

One of the Ibans, when excitedly reporting their deeds to Sochon's group, grabbed Barrie with one bloodstained right hand to greet him, and carried "in his other hand the fresh head of one of the victims which had been hollowed out, a bit like the melon heads we used to make up when I was a boy." All the Ibans had to tell of their prowess at the same time with great excitement and wild exaggeration. There was a celebration in Penghulu Sandai's house that night with a dance and ceremony of "feeding the heads before they were eventually smoked and hung up to adorn the various longhouses."[19]

Barrie was sent to investigate the site of the massacre because the Ibans were rather vague as to what had happened to the bodies. They were quite averse to discussing this aspect of the matter. If they had been thrown into the river, it would have presented a security risk when the bodies floated down stream. There was also uncertainty as to the number that had actually been killed since the Ibans were unable to count. Barrie returned to the site with a small party but the Ibans were reluctant to undertake the task of burial since this was beneath the dignity of warriors. An attempt at cremation fizzled out and nothing more could be done at the moment except to ensure that the bodies did not get into the river.

A Catalina of the RAAF ASR Squadron, now operating out of Labuan, finally arrived at Sungei Pila on 21 June bringing Capt. D.J. Kearny, Sgt. E.R. Spurling (experienced signaller with more powerful wireless equipment), Lieut. R.J. Baker, and food. For the first time in a month the party was able to make wireless contact with other *Semut* parties and with headquarters at Labuan. SRD "A" headquarters had moved from Morotai to Labuan and now the ATR4s were able to maintain contact with field headquarters. At last the long period of waiting was at an end.

Barrie arrived back on the 22nd, and two days later he left with Baker and ten native soldiers for Kapit. They reached Kapit in a couple of days where about 2,000 eager Ibans greeted them with the news that they had killed three Japanese two nights before. Sochon's orders had been for the Ibans to wait until the main body arrived but, since there was only a "limited number of Japanese heads available, their patience had run out."[20] Two more Japanese had been killed during a Spitfire fighter strike on 24 June. A lone Japanese arriving from Song was also killed. The small town of Kapit is about 180 miles from the mouth of the Rejang with Fort Sylvia in a commanding position overlooking the river.

The Ibans were eager to proceed to Song, but Baker and Barrie decided to organize the unruly mob into some form of cohesion. With news that a Japanese launch was expected, they planned to attack close to the landing stage with Baker and Barrie on each side of the path, supported by Tom Crocker and six Belaga volunteers. When the launch arrived, two Japanese were killed with another possible and the launch drifted downstream. With another launch expected and the guns jammed, the party withdrew.

The Catalina arrived with Capt. R.A. Astill and Lieut. P.W. Hume on 26 June; three days later Sochon moved to Sungei Sama, a short distance down stream from Sungei Pila. He had sent Kearny and Astill to Kuala Baleh to set up a defensive position to hold both the Batang Rejang and Baleh and prevent Japanese reprisals against the Dyaks in various regions in that locality.

Astill reported the overall position to Sochon at Sungei Sama on 2 July, then he and Baker set out again to join the party at Kuala Baleh in order to strengthen that area. The fort was built as usual in a commanding position so that both the Baleh and Rejang rivers were covered, but the Japanese could easily infiltrate the position and cut off the party. Eighty Japanese in two launches approached to within a mile and a half of the Kuala Baleh post to carry out reprisals against the Dyaks. They had machine gunned every longhouse and native they encountered on their trip up the river. The Japanese party withdrew after remaining about 18 hours in the Kapit area and joined the 100 already garrisoned at Song. Kearny left the fort at Kuala Baleh in the hands of Astill and Baker and returned to headquarters at Sungei Sama.

At Belaga, Barrie joined Abu bin Kassim on 5 July in order to organize the approaches from Bintulu to Long Nawang. A B-24 had dropped the first supply of arms and ammunition the day before. Another B-24 drop was received on the 8th containing stores and arms, half of which was sent to headquarters.

Now recruits already enlisted by Abu had to be trained and patrols sent out to the Tubau area to contact a party from *Semut II*. Other patrols were sent to Long Nawang to advise the locals that there were Europeans at Belaga, and to request their cooperation to fight against the Japanese.

At Sungei Sama the Catalina brought in Lieut. F.R. Oldham, Cpls. H.N. Fowler, R.M. Outhwaite, B.B. Walpole, R.J. Croton, and R.W. Bradbury on 5 July, with additional stores, equipment, and weapons. Many of these men had been on several missions before joining *Semut III*. Outhwaite and Walpole had been on three of the *Stallion* operations supporting the *Oboe* army assaults before volunteering for *Semut*.

Kearny went on to Belaga contacting local kampongs on his way and arranging native patrols for emergency measures. Sochon expected the enemy to infiltrate from Bintulu, crossing to Ulu Anak and Ulu Merit. Kearny was to contact local headmen in these areas and arrange for native patrols. He was also to collect stores and equipment to be dropped at Belaga and take them to headquarters.

Sochon visited Kuala Baleh and decided it was time to move into Kapit to give the natives forward protection. Kapit had been used as a headquarters by Japanese troops. Many buildings in the village were destroyed although Fort Sylvia survived in spite of the vicious fighting between Sochon's Ibans and the Japanese. He sent Oldham to set up a river block on Kapit at Sabatu, about two hours from Song, where the Japanese had now collected.

set up a block on the Japanese escape route through Bintulu and Tatau to Kapit. Abu Kassim in the Tubau area covered the escape route through Bintulu to Belaga, linking up with *Semut II*.

At Sabatu, Oldham and his patrol formed a river block on both sides of the Rejang on 10 July. With both Bren guns and Piats, Dyak blowpipes, and spotlights from Labuan, the Japanese would be unable to reach Kapit by night. Since the group was greatly outnumbered by the Japanese, there were tense moments when unfounded rumour among the Ibans made it necessary to guard against such a move by the enemy. During the

– courtesy Mrs. Margaret Sochon

Headhunters with blowpipes

Astill and Baker were sent to Belaga in mid-July to relieve Barrie, who advised Sochon that the Japanese party returning from Long Nawang had been killed just above the Kuala Bahau although one had escaped. Baker and Abu bin Kassim took over the outlying area, including Bintulu, Tatau and Tubau. Because of some trouble among the Dyaks, Baker journeyed to the Tatau area and

day while the RAAF patrolled, the Japanese did not travel on the river.

Lieutenant Hume at Kapit headquarters continued to train the local levies. Kearny, who arrived at Kapit on 13 July from Belaga after a patrol further up the Rejang, was sent to reconnoitre the interior tracks from Kapit-Kanowit down to Song. The Japanese were masters of working round the back of the river block to outflank a position such as that at Kanowit. The Dyaks were equally masters at ambushing the Japanese using their own methods such as "cutting trees on the river banks practically through, tying them with rattan to steady them, and then cutting the rattan as a prahu load of Japanese was passing underneath"; and on the jungle paths, "by the use of their deadly blowpipes, the natives definitely kept the Japanese to known and well cleared paths."[21]

Oldham and his patrol investigated the area around Song but the village was well fortified. The Japanese had increased their attacks on the Ibans. Sgt. Embah (ex Sarawak Rangers) sent an agent to Song who offered to lead the Japanese against the Australians and their Allies. Embah's patrol ambushed and killed the 20 Japanese who set out. The Japanese garrison in Song was about 200 strong and killing all natives encountered. Sochon was now able to call on RAAF air strikes for occasional raids on entrenched Japanese positions; he soon called on the RAAF to carry out a bombing raid on Song. Small guerrilla bands were not equipped nor trained for frontal assaults; nor could they attack any large numbers of the enemy.

After Sochon had gone to Labuan on 21 July to discuss the overall situation and the timing for *Hippo*, Kearny and his patrol returned from the Rejang-Pelagus-Merit area. Now they set out from Sabatu to reconnoitre the back track Kapit-Kanowit west of Song at Poi. They reached Sungei Sapuloh where, on 24 July, Kearny ambushed a launch of Japanese reinforcements travelling from Kanowit to Song, killing 57 out of the 60 Japanese and sinking the launch.

Sochon returned the following day bringing Capt. (later Major) John C.D. Fisher, civil affairs officer, who now acted as 2 i/c to Sochon, and Cpl. Boon Tek Hin, a civilian Chinese operator. Fisher took over administrative control and civil affairs and effectively dampened the zeal of the Ibans. By this time Sochon had many recruits, both Chinese and Ibans.

While he was in Labuan, where Sochon reported on progress of the *Semut III*

operation at SRD headquarters, it was decided that Sibu must be taken before *Hippo* could be launched, delaying rescue of the prisoners at Kuching. Meanwhile, Captain Cheng and his *Hippo* party remained at Morotai continuing their Malay language lessons for another week before setting out for Labuan.

The Japanese were now headquartered in Song, a village on the Rejang about halfway between Kapit and Kanowit, with a fort commanding the juncture of a tributary with Batang Rejang. The RAAF destroyed selected targets in the village in a raid on the 27th. The Japanese survivors at Song were then driven out by Sochon and his native levies using every conceivable weapon from blowpipes to parangs, home-made spears, and shotguns.

Kearny and his patrol moved into Song as the escaping Japanese made for Kanowit. The fort and almost every building had been burned to the ground and the site was a wilderness until Fisher of civil affairs arrived. Temporary government buildings and local atap shops were soon built.

With Song secured, the next objective was Kanowit, a large village three hours' journey up river from Sibu. Here, Fort Emma commanded the Kanowit River where it flows into the Rejang.

The Oldham party blocked the river at Poi and when this was complete, Sochon sent Oldham to take over at Belaga. Oldham was then to patrol to Long Nawang in Dutch Borneo on the Batang Kayan to obtain rice before a Japanese party from Samarinda arrived. Oldham was also to obtain definite information about the Long Nawang massacre of 1942.

Although it was unusual for so many operatives to work together, Kearny, Walpole, and Bradbury, while reconnoitering Kidd's Estate about one and a half miles east of Kanowit, captured a Japanese whom they sent back with Walpole for interrogation. The captive preferred to drown and dived overboard. Since Walpole had had no sleep for two nights, he was not alert enough to stop him.

The Japanese by now were withdrawing outlying troops into Sibu for a last stand. Kearny and his party ambushed a boat at Kidd's Estate, killed two Japanese and four Chinese collaborators, and seriously wounded eight other Japanese.

By 1 August about 20,000 square miles had been liberated by the *Semut III* party, with 120 Japanese and four collaborators killed. It is doubtful whether the 19 Chinese killed by mistake were included in this number; there was no item in the tally list headed 'mistakes.'

Barrie arrived at Kapit from Belaga on 1 August, accompanied by Sgt. Frank Pippen of *Semut II* Signals. Barrie then began preparations for his own party to leave for Meluan.

An ambush by Kearny and his patrol at Kanowit caused ten Japanese casualties but Kearny himself by this time was ill and returned to Kapit. Meanwhile, Barrie went on to Manga Dap near Kanowit to replace him. Lack of proper food and rest could often lower the resistance of the operatives so that any cut or infection could become serious very quickly. The jungle may have been 'neutral' but it was also unhealthy. Even the Dyaks suffered serious health problems and needed outside medical attention. Kearny was soon back with his patrol after a few days' attention at headquarters. Maj. J.R. Wooler,[22] and WO2 R.C. Perry arrived from Labuan by Catalina on 2 August.

The Walpole and Bradbury patrol moved down river close to Kidd's Estate and crossed country to the Ulu Bawan to arrive at Kanowit from the downriver side. Unreliable Dyaks were cleared from the Bawan mouth by 5 August. Native troops were posted along the river across from Kanowit and they reported, on the following day, that the launch was being loaded. Positions below Bawan were set up to ambush the launch but it did not appear during daylight hours. The launch left at midnight with the entire Japanese garrison.

A signal from Labuan indicated that the Catalina carrying the *Hippo* party had been delayed, but a Liberator drop to Kapit of nine storepedoes and two packages on 7 August was made using *Eureka/Rebecca* and the *S.Phones*. The plane strafed Kanowit on its return to base; this brought a signal from the patrol that the Japanese had evacuated the town. Sochon signalled Morotai for additional mortars and ammunition to be dropped within the next 48 hours.

Sochon's patrols were already in Kanowit when Wooler set out to establish forward headquarters there 9 August. All other patrols were moved forward, forming river blocks in the Durin area. Kearny was now extracted by Catalina to Labuan. Baker reported that there were no Japanese at Tatau or Pendan but there were about 30 at Sebauh and 300 at Bintulu. John Douglas and Boon Teck Hin advised that there were 40 Japanese at Tanjong Kuluk, 40 miles up river from Mukah, who were barricaded in the church. Sochon called for aircraft to deal with them.

A signal was received from Labuan that the RAAF would strafe Kanowit and Sibu on 9 August. Sochon returned signal to stop the strafing of Kanowit since his patrols were already there. There appeared to be laxity at Labuan SRD "A" Headquarters in not cancelling with the RAAF after headquarters had been informed that Kanowit had been neutralized on the 7th.

Major Fisher left for Song, Poi, and Kanowit. He soon settled disputes between the Chinese and Ibans and was able to dampen some of the native guerrilla enthusiasm. He moved into Kanowit to settle any further local troubles.

Two Japanese planes machine gunned and strafed two villages in the Kuala Baleh area at Sungei Melekun, a tributary of the Baleh about ten miles east of Kapit, but there were no casualties. Sochon received word that another two Japanese had been ambushed at Kidd's Estate and a wireless message that Kanowit would not be strafed.

A C-47 stores drop 10 August at Kapit brought food, several tins of which were smashed because it was a free drop, that is without parachutes. Invariably some of the precious stores were destroyed when they were despatched in a free drop, yet it was a method that continued to be used, probably because the appropriate parachutes were not available.

Capt. Roger Cheng's group flew from Morotai, an island off the northwest tip of New Guinea, to Labuan where the group was briefed for Operation *Hippo*. The operation required them to land on the Rejang and proceed overland from Kapit to the Simanggang area, and on to Simujan. From Simujan, they were to again travel cross country to Kuching to assist in freeing and caring for the POWs and Internees. As Roy Chan expressed it: "We were supposed to recruit the natives and train them as guerrillas. We had to recruit 500 or 600 men or more. That was our briefing. All you have to do is arm one wrong guy, and you're dead!"

Undoubtedly the unfolding tragedy of Sandakan/Ranau would have been in the minds of SRD at Labuan and at Morotai when they sent in the *Hippo* party. Most of the officers from Sandakan survived because they had been moved to Kuching. The atomic bombs brought such an abrupt end to hostilities that many local Japanese commanders were bewildered and uncertain as to what action they should take.

On 10 August, while making preparations to move his headquarters from Kapit to Kanowit, Sochon received Captain Cheng, and Lieut. A.J.H. McCallum, the vanguard of *Hippo* with their wireless stores. "We went in by flying boat in the Rejang River some miles north of Sibu - about twenty or thirty miles

– courtesy Bob Long

Parang on right, scabbard far left

north of Sibu at a settlement there."[23] As part of the *Hippo* nucleus were the Canadians, WO James Shiu, and Sgts. Louey King, Roy Chan, and Norman Low, along with Sgts. G.H. Philpott and D.L. Foster, Cpl. Eusop bin Lansi, and Pte. C.E. Heron.[24]

Cheng's group received additional training from the Ibans. The natives taught them how to travel on jungle trails noise-lessly, and how to wield the parang, a short, 30-inch, broad knife, weighted slightly at its tip.

Malaria-carrying mosquitoes and leeches were almost as lethal as the Japanese in the dense jungle. Mosquito netting protected beds and hammocks at night from this disease carrier with hammocks swung as high as possible from the ground. The hammocks had a rubberized roof. Leeches dropped from trees and crawled up from the ground; if they were picked off, the head was left to fester and dangerous sores resulted. Any cut or skin puncture could rapidly lead to tropical ulcers. Dysentery, both amoebic and bacillary, tick fever, scrub typhus, and dengue were constant threats.

Operation *Hippo* was to have received a follow-up party consisting of twelve of Kendall's second group of Chinese Canadians.[25] *Hippo II* was not proceeded with when the Japanese surrendered, yet the POWs and Internees at Kuching were not relieved until 11 September, almost a month after the official surrender.

The day following Cheng's arrival, Sochon left Kapit and established headquarters at Kanowit at the district officer's house. Under Captain Fisher's civil administration, Kanowit was gradually being rehabilitated; Fisher installed himself in the Kubu. Wooler had already left to establish forward headquarters at Durin.

Also on the 11th, Barrie continued towards Meluan. On discovering there were no Japanese at Julau, he set out for Binatang and Sarikei to cut off the Japanese escape route in this area. When he arrived at the Ulu Assan, the natives informed him there were 50 Japanese at the mouth of the Assan being helped by locals. Barrie investigated and found no Japanese in the area. Some Japanese sympathizers were captured and escorted back to Kanowit but on the way "some of these offered resistance and were killed by local soldiers."[26]

The following day the advance patrol of Croton and Outhwaite was again moved ahead from Durin to Palau Kladi. This patrol, as with other patrols, was supported by a platoon of native troops.

Meanwhile Cheng set about getting his reconnaissance party away. The *Hippo* party had intended to establish a forward base in the Simanggang area on the Batang Lupar over-land from Kapit. The reconnaissance party reached Simanggang by 14 August. Simanggang is the capital of the Second Division, a trading centre where large numbers of Chinese and Malays reside, with the Ibans scattered in kampongs outside the main community. They halted here until clarification was received from headquarters since it was known that the war was almost over. It was now decided by headquarters at Labuan that the *Hippo* party would remain with Sochon's *Semut III* group since the distance overland to Kuching through dense jungle would still take many days.

On 15 August, while recruits were flocking in, a Catalina arrived with Col. G.B. Courtney, officer commanding the SRD Advance Headquarters at Labuan, and Capt. W.R. (Tiny) Fell, RN. They discussed the general position and the possibility of taking a naval vessel up the Rejang to Sibu to "pound the defences from the river while *Semut* attacked from the land, following the RAAF strike."

Courtney also brought an outline of the new Kuching operation. As part of a funeral procession, Chinese mourners were to be infiltrated into Kuching, the navy then to send a frigate up the river and evacuate the prisoners. While Australian paratroopers contained the Japanese garrison three miles away, the *Hippo* party under Sochon would then march into the capital. Sochon was to transfer to this new operation since there was "an immediate need to relieve the suffering of the men and women in the compounds."[27]

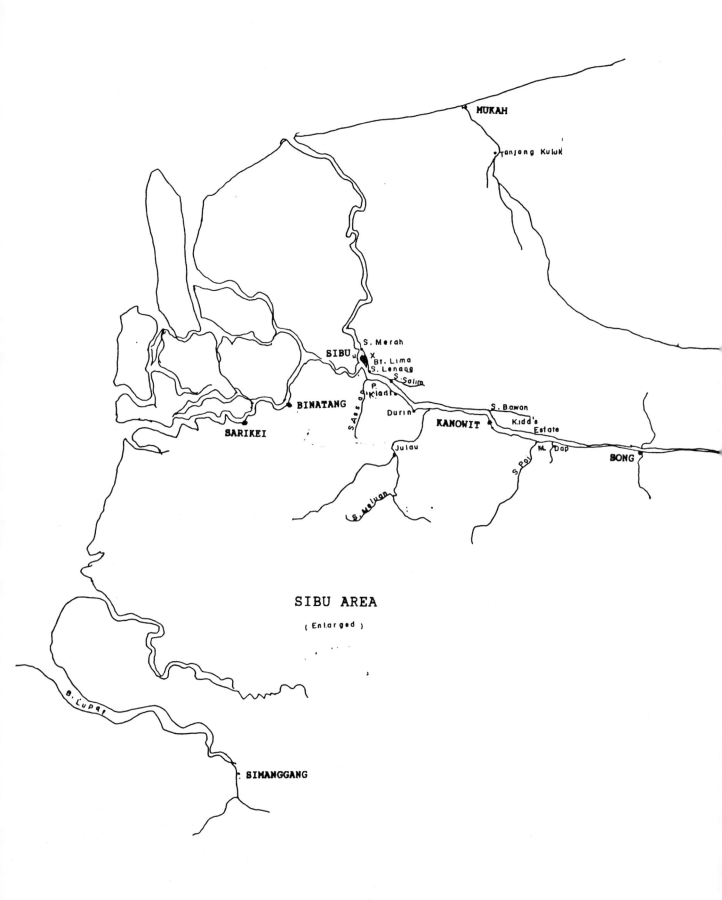

SIBU AREA

(Enlarged)

SARAWAK 207

The operation could not be undertaken, however, until Sibu had fallen. Courtney flew back to Labuan.

News of Emperor Hirohito's capitulation was also received 15 August; on this date "SRD was directed by HQs 9 Australia Division to suspend all offensive action against the enemy."[28] It had come as a surprise to the Australian Army to discover that about 100 'Z' Special Unit operatives with their local levies had cleared the enemy from the interior of Sarawak. This successful action had been possible only because they were able to nibble away at small parties. There was still a large group of the enemy in the north but they too were to be rounded up and delivered to the Australian Army by 'Z' Special Unit operatives.

Meanwhile, there was no news from Sibu. Sibu, the capital of the Third Division and the second largest town in Sarawak, was the Japanese military headquarters. Pamphlets were dropped from Catalinas over Sibu, with an escort of Kitty fighters. Sochon sent a final ultimatum to the Japanese commander at Sibu giving him 48 hours to surrender by midnight 16 August.

Croton, Outhwaite, and Fowler were sent to the western side of Sibu to guard the airstrip, about two-and-one half miles from Sibu. With five other patrols in the Sibu area, and at Salim a few miles downstream from Durin, and Barrie at Sarikei and covering Binatang, Sochon was in a position to prevent the Japanese from breaking out, either to the sea or up river. The Japanese commanding officer and the Kempei Tai refused to consider surrender.

Wooler returned to Labuan on the 19th; it was "considered that, as the surrender had taken place, the Hippo project was no longer required, and there was no necessity for Wooler to stay in the field."[29]

The Japanese made no response to Sochon's ultimatum, but instructions were received from Labuan to take no offensive action against them. Sochon's patrols were still active, however, and were now within the *Bukit* (hill) Lima area and Sungei Assan.

At this time, 17 August, Sochon was asked to consider a transfer to British Borneo Civil Administration Unit, a position which he accepted. He then asked HQs Labuan if patrols were to be withdrawn but there was no response to this request. Sochon next sent a letter to the head of the civilian Japanese to see if he could obtain a response from the garrison.

Baker was at Tatau, Abu at Tubau, Oldham at Long Nawang, Boon Teck Hin at Anup, and Barrie at Meluan. Foster and Norman Low were with the group at Sungei Lanang, a few minutes upriver from Sibu, when they heard on the radio of the Japanese surrender.

A report was received that 38 Japanese had been killed at Sebauh. By 18 August, 192 Japanese and four Chinese collaborators had been killed; as before, neither the 19 Chinese nor other casuals appear to be included in this number.

When he rejoined Sochon's group after the surrender, Sgt. Louey King patrolled down to the China Sea, working for a time with Sergeant Barrie in the Binatang area on the Lower Rejang. They travelled by motorized prahu with a skeleton crew of natives.

At one village Barrie and King went ashore to meet the people, many of whom were Chinese, leaving the prahu, Bren gun and ammunition in care of the Ibans. As they approached the villagers "there was a sudden outburst of what sounded like small arms fire." Just as they were about to flee back to the boat and their firearms, they suddenly realized the noise was made by Chinese firecrackers set off in celebration of their arrival. This incident reinforced the danger of over-confidence and they remained more alert to the possibility of attack. They travelled back to Binatang, however, somewhat chastened but more relaxed than they had been before the Japanese surrender.[30]

With Iban guerrillas, Sgt. Roy Chan patrolled east along the river as far as Kapit. For a time, Chan had been looked on suspiciously by the Ibans; they thought he looked like a Japanese and wanted to kill him.[31] Roy Chan's head very nearly graced an Iban longhouse.

Roy Chan with Ibans patrolling the Rejang

Sgts. Norman Low and Jimmy Shiu, in various positions around Sibu, maintained regular wireless contact with the 9th Divisional Headquarters at Labuan. Wireless security was still vital since the Japanese in Borneo had not surrendered.

The Catalina brought in Sgt. J.D.F. Hartley on 19 August and Wooler, who had been recalled, was extracted to Labuan. Bill

Jinkins came in to discuss the Belaga position and Abu bin Kassim at Tubau. Baker at Tatau needed supplies and Sochon arranged to have them sent by patrol launch.

Outhwaite and Croton returned from patrol and although there was to be no aggressive action against the Japanese, native security still had be to given first consideration. Labuan headquarters ordered the withdrawal of all formal patrols. Sochon refused to do this on the grounds that the natives required this security measure.[32] With the Japanese collected in Sibu and unwilling to surrender, there was every possibility that they were still ready to fight.

Bradbury and Walpole brought in two Japanese and one Chinese prisoner on the 22nd. One of the captured Japanese helped by describing the dispositions at Sibu. Barrie also arrived in Kanowit "to hand over local prisoners from the Assan, and to receive fresh supplies and instructions."[33]

Semut IV under Lieut. W.A. Chaffey with ten others, was inserted 22 August on the Similajan River area to link up with the *Semut III* base at Belaga. They were to operate along the coastal section near Bintulu to implement the surrender policy and to assist prisoners of war.

Major Fisher and Pip Hume left in the afternoon for Kapit. Sochon travelled to the forward headquarters at Durin to meet with Captain Cheng and Lieutenant McCallum. He outlined the need for patrols on both sides of the river and around the Japanese to prevent reprisals and to contain the former enemy.

Sochon was expecting the arrival of a Catalina on the 24th after an insertion at Sungei Pila for Belaga. Because of low water, the Catalina was unable to land at Pila and it landed at Kapit with Lt.-Col. David Leslie Leach,[34] liaison officer between SRD and 9th AIF; it also brought another small BBCAU party who were to proceed from Kapit to Belaga.

Les Leach and Bill Jinkins discussed with Sochon the future policy; *Semut IV* would take over Belaga and the other kampongs in that area, Tatau, Tubau, Sebauh and so on. Leach and Jinkins left for Labuan the following day taking with them Tom Crocker who was ill. Fisher and Pip Hume returned from Kapit.

Another insertion on the 25th brought Capt. (Dr) J.L. Stokes and Cpl. N.R.R. Mellet (medical orderly), the first attachment of medical assistance to the party. Sochon set about making fresh dispositions of his own patrols.

By the 26th, parties had been re-formed with main headquarters still at Kanowit consisting of Sochon, Fisher, Hume, Heron (who had returned ill from Durin but was acting as quartermaster), Doc. Stokes, Mellet, Campbell, Sgt/Signallers Pippin, Spurling, and James Shiu. The five Canadian *Hippo* members served in widely scattered areas after the capitulation.

Forward headquarters was at Durin under Captain Cheng and Lieutenant McCallum where Doc. Stokes and Mellet made an inspection 27 August. In the Bukit Lima patrol were Philpott, Croton, and Outhwaite at Sungei Merah; Hartley headed the North Bank Patrol at Assan; and for the South Bank Patrol, north bank at Assan, Louey King and Foster led the group. Perry and Roy Chan were in the Durin River Block at Palau Kladi.

With Keith Barrie at Sarikei; Astill and the new arrivals at Belaga; Baker at Tatau; Abu bin Kassim at Sembauh; Boon Teck Hin at Anup; Oldham at Long Nawang; and Fowler, Walpole and Bradbury at Meluan and the Lobak Antu, the Japanese could not move out of Sibu. Sochon's new arrangements for containment of the Japanese in his territory were again complete.

Oldham led a small patrol to Long Nawang 27 August to investigate reports of the massacre. "My records show a total of some 60 men, women & children were butchered between August & September 1942. I located the main mass grave in the jungle & opened it. They were there. . . . 21 British, 4 American missionaries, and thirty-five Dutch, Army and Airforce (give or take a head or two)."[35]

Also on 27 August a C-47 brought BBCAU stores and Sochon left on the Catalina for Labuan with a stop at Mukah where he met Les Leach. At Labuan, Sochon learned that nothing definite was decided concerning his attachment to BBCAU. Two days later he returned to Kanowit and the next day sent pay to Barrie's party. Sochon then made recommendations for decorations. Barrie received the Military Medal, and Kearny the Military Cross. Perry, who had been on two other operations before *Semut III*, also received the Military Medal.

When the Catalina arrived 2 September, it brought three additional BBCAU members and Astill from Belaga was sent out to Labuan. Church service was re-established in Sarawak, which Sochon and Fisher attended.

When a white flag was reported at Sibu 3 September, and the patrol at Rice Mill, Bukit Lima, was fired upon, Sochon proceeded down river with Doc. Stokes, Pippen and Hume to investigate these contradictory reports. The reports proved to be without foundation. Sochon and Hume returned to Kanowit.

After receiving another Catalina insertion 4 September at Kanowit, bringing Leach and three members for BBCAU, Sochon transferred his headquarters to Salim. Roy Chan and McCallum were already on their way there. Sochon set up his headquarters in a saw mill at Salim together with Doc. Stokes' medical clinic. Training of local levies continued at this new headquarters. The next day Hume arrived with the wireless party and 23 guerrillas to establish a depot. Sochon visited all patrol locations, in particular the forward one at Pulau Sunga.

Another Catalina arrived on the 8th at Salim and Lieut. F. Lambert joined *Semut III;* the Catalina also brought a Dr. Chee who was returning from Labuan to his local area.

At this time, Sochon had six patrols surrounding Sibu, each with a platoon strength of trained levies, with reinforcements at the Tai Koon School, about six miles from Sibu, consisting of Perry and some personnel of Captain Cheng's party. Barrie was at Binatang, with Kearny (who had returned to the Rejang by Catalina) and his party in the

SURRENDER OF JAPANESE FORCES

Address Delivered by

COMMANDER - in - CHIEF, AUSTRALIAN MILITARY FORCES
GENERAL SIR THOMAS BLAMEY

to

Lt - General Teshima, Commander Second Japanese Army
On the occasion of the signing of their Surrender

MOROTAI, 9th SEPTEMBER, 1945

LIEUT.-GENERAL TESHIMA, COMMANDER, SECOND JAPANESE ARMY :

"The Japanese Navy has been destroyed. The Japanese Merchant Fleet has been reduced to a mere fraction. The Japanese Air Force has been driven from the sky. The Japanese armies have been defeated everywhere and all that remained for them was to await their inevitable total destruction. Japanese cities lie in waste and Japanese industry has been destroyed. Never before in history has so numerous a nation been so completely defeated.

"To escape the complete destruction of the nation, the Emperor of Japan has yielded to the Allied Forces and an instrument of total surrender has been signed in his name. He has charged you to obey the orders which I shall give you.

"In carrying out these orders, the Japanese Army and Navy organisation will be retained for convenience. Instructions will be issued by the designated Australian Commanders to the Commanders of the respective Japanese Forces, placing upon you and your subordinate Commanders the responsibility for carrying out your Emperor's direction to obey all orders given to you by me.

"You will ensure that all Allied personnel, prisoners of war or internees in Japanese hands are safeguarded and nourished and delivered over to the Allied Commanders.

"You will collect, lay down and safeguard all arms, ammunition and instruments of war until such time as they are taken over by the designated Commanders. You will be given adequate time to carry this out. An official date will be named and any Japanese found in possession after that date of any arms, ammunition or instrument of war of any kind will be dealt with summarily by the Australian Commander on the spot.

"Orders will be given for these and other matters as I consider necessary and you will ensure the obedience to all such orders without delay.

"In receiving your surrender I do not recognise you as an honourable and gallant foe, but you will be treated with due but severe courtesy in all matters.

"I recall the treacherous attack upon our ally, China, in 1938. I recall the treacherous attack made upon the British Empire and upon the United States of America in December, 1941, at a time when your authorities were making the pretence of ensuring peace.

"I recall the atrocities inflicted upon the persons of our nationals as prisoners of war and internees, designed to reduce them by punishment and starvation to slavery.

"In the light of these evils, I will enforce most rigorously all orders issued to you, so let there be no delay or hesitation in their fulfilment at your peril."

Instrument of Surrender

In accordance with General Order Number One issued by the Japanese Imperial General Headquarters by direction of the Supreme Commander of the Allied Powers we hereby:–

A. **Proclaim** the Unconditional Surrender to the Commander in Chief, Australian Military Forces of all Japanese Armed Forces and all Armed Forces under Japanese control in the Netherlands East Indies, East of and exclusive of Lombok, and in Borneo.

B. **Command** all Commanders and members of the Japanese Armed Forces and Controlled Forces within the Territories, Islands and Areas aforesaid to cease hostilities immediately, lay down their arms, remain in their present localities and do all such acts and things as may be required of them by the Commander in Chief, Australian Military Forces or his authorised Representative or Representatives.

C. **Command** all Civil, Military and Navy officials and all members of the Japanese Armed Forces to obey and enforce all Proclamations, Orders and Directions issued by the Commander in Chief, Australian Military Forces or his authorised Representative or Representatives.

Signed at Morotai on the Ninth day of September 1945.

Commander Second Japanese Army.

By command and on behalf of

Japanese Imperial General Headquarters.

Accepted at Morotai on the Ninth day of September 1945.

T.A. Blamey General

Commander in Chief

Australian Military Forces

Simanggang area. Local levies were covering Julau and Meluan.

Conflicting instructions from SRD headquarters and the army only clouded the situation. Sochon thought he should have been kept informed since "to date have received no information or orders re surrender terms or instructions."[36]

The Japanese in Borneo finally surrendered formally on 9 September 1945, when Lt.-Gen. Fusataro Teshima and Gen. Sir Thomas Blamey, commander in chief, Australian Military Forces, signed the surrender document at Morotai.

In his address to the Japanese, General Blamey stated that the Emperor had placed them under his orders, that they were to assist in caring for POWs and Internees, that they were to be disarmed, and, finally, that he did not recognize them "as an honourable and gallant foe." However, they would be treated fairly.

On 10 September Lt.-Gen. Baba Masuo, the general officer commanding the 37th Imperial Japanese Army, the occupying force in Borneo, surrendered to Maj.-Gen. George F. Wootten, commander of the 9th Division.

These official surrenders had no effect on conditions at Sibu or with the group of Japanese in the north. Sochon sent a further ultimatum to the officer commanding in Sibu and "a favourable reply was received."[37]

Negotiations for the Japanese surrender at Sibu continued; the commanding officer indicated his willingness to cooperate but was unable to surrender without orders from Kuching. SRD advised by signal from Labuan that SRD "A" group were now under orders of the 9th Australian Division for the next six weeks. If the Japanese commander offered to surrender, Sochon was to advise Labuan and wait for instructions.

On 10 September, two warships sailed for Kuching and General Yamamura, commander of the Kuching area, surrendered. The Kuching Internee and Prisoner of War camps were entered on the 11th. There was one lone Canadian prisoner at Kuching.[38]

Sochon began discharging troops on the 12th and two days later received word from Labuan that it would be in order to contact the Japanese commander at Sibu. Accompanied by Hume and Doc. Stokes, Sochon met the Japanese commander and two of his officers at Bukit Lima on 16 September. Lambert and McCallum were in charge of two patrols accompanying them with Captain Cheng and Sergeants Chan and King in other patrols stationed in the area for security and to prevent looting. Norman Low and Jimmy Shiu, with other wireless operators, continued to maintain the wireless links with headquarters.

Formal surrender of the Japanese commander at Sibu was made to Sochon with Fisher present at 9 am on 17 September. The commander and his troops were to leave for Kuching the following day surrendering 90 percent of their arms. The Australian Army commander at Kuching would see to their repatriation once they arrived at the capital. The local population at Sibu gave their deliverers a "wonderful welcome."[39]

Personnel of BBCAU had been entering the country since the Emperor's capitulation and the area was gradually being handed over to them. On 18 September, arms were checked and there was a general programme of clearing up. The total composition of the trained guerrilla force at this time was two companies of Chinese and one company of Ibans, with a total strength of 450. The force had "a standard army organization of companies, platoons and sections."[40] The natives were armed with .303 rifles and the NCOs with SMGs and carbines. No arms were issued to anyone outside this trained force. Uniform clothing was issued as far as possible consisting of Australian jungle green shirts and trousers. The levies were paid at pre-war constabulary rates. Lieutenant Hume undertook most of the training and the degree of success was directly related to the amount of training the troops had received.

The *Semut III* party encountered and worked with Kayans, Kenyahs, Punans, Ibans, Malays and Chinese to name a few. Pre-war rangers and police formed the NCO basis. Shortage of shotguns prevented the arming of large numbers of natives. These weapons could have been issued one shotgun to every five doors of the native longhouses and the party would then have been much more aggressive than it was able to be. The natives were effective, however, with their blowpipes and parangs.

The badge worn by all members of the various *Semut* parties was "a representation of the Sarawak coat of arms" bearing "the motto 'Dum Spiro Spero' which translates freely as 'While I Breathe (live) I hope.'"[41] The Sarawak flag, although not used during the operation, was a red and purple cross on a yellow ground. Rajah Brooke was in the process of turning his country over to Great Britain and this symbol had been replaced by the Union Jack.

Harrisson parachuted into the Rejang area in late September or early October in an attempt to command all three *Semut* parties by organizing a pincer movement on the party of several hundred Japanese troops aiming to make a last stand in North Borneo. Sochon was not in favour of this request.

Sochon again journeyed to Labuan 19 September to clarify his position; he returned to Sibu on the 29th. On its return to Labuan the Catalina took Louey King, Roy Chan, Norman Low, James Shiu, and seven others. Before they left Sibu, the natives erected an arch saying "Good-Bye Canadians," and gave each member a posie for remembrance.

Roger Cheng and about 20 others remained with Sochon to help collect weapons and dismiss the levies. Sochon prepared a cash statement and met with the remainder of his party. Australian Military Forces Headquarters had ordered that all SRD personnel must be concentrated on Labuan by 15 October. The whole of the Rejang River area was turned over to BBCAU on that date.

The *Semut III* party had moved down the Batang Rejang, inflicting "heavy casualties on the enemy, capturing in turn Belaga, Kapit, Song, Kanowit and finally reaching Sibu," where the Japanese commander surrendered. They killed 227 Japanese

and four auxiliary troops and took no prisoners and lost none of their own. The reader should not place too much reliance on the numbers just quoted; another official figure is 265 Japanese killed.[42]

Although they had not been able to complete their original mission because of the unexpected rapidity with which the war ended, Cheng's group had been instrumental in helping to contain the Japanese in and around Sibu, and by patrolling the Rejang. The Prisoners of War and Internees at Kuching had been liberated without further loss of life.

On 15 October, Roger Cheng flew with other members of the *Semut III* party from Sibu to Labuan. Captain Fisher and Lieutenant Oldham were extracted a few days later. Roger Cheng was hospitalized at the 2/9th Australian General Hospital at Morotai for a week before his onward trip to Australia. Roy Chan, Norman Low, Jimmy Shiu, and Louey King had already joined the rest of Kendall's group at Tabragalba. At this time too, WO Shiu reverted to sergeant.

When these five returned to Australia, all 27 Canadians were now attached to the "No. 1 Special Wireless Group, R.C.Sigs. CA(A)," after being struck-off-strength SRD (British Military Establishment No. 100) having terminated duty with BSC on 31 October 1945.[43]

It was not until 28 October that Tom Harrisson of *Semut I* with two Japanese envoys and an Australian signals officer took the final surrender of about 358 out of the original 578 Japanese troops in North Borneo at Ba Kelalan, not far from Belawit. The Japanese had left Murudi 1 July. They had travelled incredible distances through what even the natives considered to be impassable jungles, over the mountains, harassed by the 'Z' Unit operatives and their native levies, with many dropping by the track, struck down by wounds, disease and hunger. Two other Japanese groups in the north had surrendered long before. Sgts. Ray Bennett and Bill Nibbs, both of 'Z' Special Unit, set out from Pa Bawang 6 November 1945 to escort the Japanese to Lawas where Maj. Rex

Blow handed them over to the Australian Army on the 15th.

Of the total number of operatives and RAAF men involved in SRD operations in the Southwest Pacific, 32 airmen and 14 SRD operatives died; most of them were killed in the Portuguese Timor and New Guinea operations.

The four Canadian sergeants were awarded the Military Medal after their return to Canada, and after National Defence undertook an investigation in April 1946, originally through BSC, New York (which had ceased operations in January) and then with the Australian Army, to substantiate Capt. Roger Cheng's recommendations. Their citations read as if the four men were dropped by parachute; they were inserted by flying boat. Also, Louey King was not trained as a wireless operator although all twelve had received some wireless instruction from Major Legg in the Okanagan.[44]

The awards were announced in 1946, but there was a delay in receipt of the medal, at least by Roy Chan, whose investiture did not occur until 1952 at Currie Barracks in Calgary. Ottawa apparently did not look on SOE activities as 'military' operations and all those who were employed by this civilian organization encountered a similar problem of recognition.

NOTES

Conversations with Louey King, Roger Cheng, and Roy Chan have been helpful in writing this chapter. Keith Barrie, Bob Long, Des Foster, Frank Oldham, and Col. Courtney (Retd) have also contributed essential material.

1. J. Keith Barrie, "Some Recollections of the Semut Operations, Borneo 1945" (unpublished copy in author's possession), p. 1, subsequently referred to as 'Barrie, Notes.'
2. Sgt. J. Keith Barrie, enlisted in the AIF in 1941 and served in the Middle East and New Guinea before joining SRD at Cairns, the 'Z' Experimental Station.
3. Edmeades was a captain in the 1st Australian Parachute Battalion; he is listed as lieutenant in the *Semut I* records; it is possible that Capt. Harrisson insisted on this lower rank initially.
4. Sgt. K.W. Hallam in Bob Long, *'Z' Special Unit's Secret War* (Maryborough: 1989), p. 105.
5. Barrie, Notes, p. 4.
6. Maj. William Lomas Phillipe Sochon, born 25 Dec. 1904 in London, England, was serving as major in the Home Guard. He had spent nine years in the Sarawak Rangers (disbanded 1932) and offered to return. Sochon was taken into SOE on 20 June 1944, trained and sent to Australia; he was signed on to 'Z' Special Unit 30 Sept. 1944 in the rank of captain.
7. Barrie, Notes, p.6.
8. Australian War Memorial, 3 DRL 6201, Brig. Sir Kenneth Wills, AIB 2 AIF, 1939-45.
9. AWM, 3DRL 6201, Wills, AIB 2 AIF, 1939-45.
10. Australian Archives, CRS A3270, Item 08, Vol.2, part 3, p.4.

11. AA, CRS A3270, Item 08, Vol. 2, Part 3, p. 49.
12. W.L.P. Sochon, "Transcription of Bill Sochon's Semut Diary Entries 1945," referred to as 'Sochon Diary' in the Notes (unpublished copy in author's possession).
13. Barrie, Notes, p. 7.
14. AA, CRS A3270, Item 08, Vol. 2, Part 3, p. 50.
15. Sochon Diary, p. 2.
16. Barrie, Notes, p. 11.
17. Barrie, Notes, p. 12.
18. Barrie, Notes, p. 13.
19. Barrie, Notes, pp. 13-14.
20. AA, CRS A3270, Item 08, Vol. 2, Part 3, p. 53.
21. AA, CRS A3270, Item 08, Vol. 2, Part 3, p. 55.
22. John Raymond Wooler, also a Canadian, was an ex-Sarawak civil servant. He served in England and the Mediterranean before posting to Australia in early 1945 and was parachute instructor and despatcher before volunteering for service with *Semut III*.
23. Cheng/Roy Transcript and interview with Roger Cheng 1989.
24. AWM, 3DLR 6201, Wills, AIB 2 AIF, 1939-45, gives the date 10 August by Catalina into the *Semut III* area for all five Chinese Canadians. AA, CRS A3270, Item 08, vol. 2, p. 49. gives August 11 as does Sochon's Diary. The international date line confounds the matter of dates in the Pacific theatre; it is not always known whether the correct local

time is being used (which would agree roughly with Tokyo time) or whether time east of the international date line is being cited (Hawaii time). The No. 1 Special Wireless Part II Orders and Elliot's *Scarlet to Green,* p. 398, give 13 July which is the date the *Hippo* party was ready for insertion but was being held at Morotai.

25. Cpl. Charlie J. Fong (Quong in document); Spr. K.F. (Henry) Cheng; Spr. Harden Lee; Spr. James Ming Wong; Pte. Ernest H.B. Wong; Spr. Dick W. Fong; Tpr. Jan Yuen; Tpr. Dick Lam; Pte. Georges E. Fong; Tpr. Doug Mar; Pte. Ming T. Hong; Pte. Yik Eng, and WO 2 R.P. Pritchard made up this party as given in Willis AIB 2 AIF, 1939-45, p. 21.

26. AA, CRS A3270, Item 08, Vol. 2, Part 3, p. 57. These men are also not listed in the final tally.

27. Col. G.B. Courtney, Notes, p.170, 176 (unpublished copy in author's possession).

28. WO C.W. McPherson in Long, 242; F/Lt. P. Bartram in Long, 487.

29. AA, CRS A3270, Item 08, Vol. 2, Part 3, p. 58. This is the first indication that Wooler is linked to the *Hippo* operation; he is shown only as a member of *Semut III* in other records.

30. Barrie letter to author 25 May, 1990, and interview with Louey King in Edmonton, 1989.

31. D.L. Foster letter to author 21 June 1990.

32. There is a pronounced feeling of concern for the Dyaks shown by the *Semut* operatives; more than 45 years after the events related in this chapter, Barrie can comment with sadness on the destruction of the habitat in which the nomadic Punans live as the forests are commercially exploited and the lumber shipped to Japan.

33. AA, CRS A3270, Item 08, Vol. 2, Part 3, p. 58.

34. Leach used the name 'David' rather than 'Leslie,' but Sochon called him 'Les' personally and in his diary entries.

35. Letter to author from Frank Oldham 15 July 1991 based on his records made at the time. The name of the village is now sometimes shown as 'Long Nawan.'

36. Sochon Diary, p. 10.

37. AA, CRS A3270, Item 08, Vol. 2, Part 3, p. 59.

38. NAC, RG 24, Vol.59, File 650-92-54, telegram to Col. R.S. Malone. The Canadian probably was the husband of Agnes Newton Keith.

39. Sochon Diary, p. 11.

40. AA, CRS A3270, Item 08, Vol. 2, Part 3, p. 60.

41. WO1 C.W. McPherson in Long, p. 235.

42. AWM, 3 DRL 6201, Willis, AIB 2 AIF, 1939-45. There is a discrepancy between the archival material and the account given above; there is no mention of the two Japanese and a Chinese prisoner taken 22 August; nor the 19 Chinese killed by mistake at Pasir Nai, and other casuals. The 265 figure is from AA CRS 3270 Item 08 Vol. 2, p. 60.

43. Daily Orders Part II by Lt.-Col. H.D.W. Wethey, p.1.

44. D.Hist. 112.21009, (D176). See also *Vancouver Sun* 9 September 1946.

Chapter XIII

Conclusion

Approximately 400 Chinese Canadian service men from British Columbia, were granted the franchise in March 1945. There were also some 50 Chinese Canadians still living who had served in the Great War in British Columbia, who were enfranchised. Then, in 1947, British Columbia enfranchised all Chinese citizens in the province. The federal government's new Dominion Elections Act of 1948 did not require that the voter also be on the provincial lists.

In spite of the fact that Chinese Canadians in British Columbia did not obtain the franchise for their military service in the Great War, the franchise and military service were irrevocably linked in political minds. Prime Minister W.L. Mackenzie King and Premier T.D. Pattullo of British Columbia saw military service in this light. Norman Robertson, Undersecretary of State for External Affairs, supported Pattullo's definition of compulsory military service and voluntary military service, saying "voluntary enlistment did not give as compelling a claim to enfranchisement as did compulsory enlistment."

When Chinese Canadians were called up under NRMA in British Columbia in 1944 the implication was that the franchise would follow. All those Chinese Canadians in British Columbia who were called up after July 1944 (whether they turned active, as most of them did), would seem to be the group to whom credit is due for obtaining the franchise for all Chinese Canadians in the services in that province, both First and Second World Wars, not those who enlisted voluntarily as would normally be supposed.

But more than their war service was involved in lessening hostility to the Chinese in Canada. The civilian Chinese Canadian war effort was exemplary; the Chinese communities over subscribed their quotas in each Victory Loan Drive, with the Vancouver community contributing more per capita than any other Canadian community. They were also active in the Red Cross and in war industries.

In Toronto, a Chinese Canadian group raised money to purchase an airplane for the Chinese Air Force but "it was only a little plane," said one of the members of the group. These efforts received favourable publicity.

China became an ally after 7 December 1941, when Canada declared war on Japan; this fact reflected favourably on the Canadian Chinese communities. Great publicity had been given to the fact that China had been fighting Japan in Manchuria since 1931 and in the rest of the country since 1937. The government and the Canadian Army, however, were reluctant to accord that country full Allied status.

The United Nations Charter, preceded as it had been by the Atlantic Charter, was another factor in lessening discriminatory practices in Canada. At times the discrepancy between what was professed and what was being done caused acute embarrassment on both the federal and provincial levels.

Then, too, some of the politicians had changed; many of the old guard were being phased out and by 1945 Premier John Hart headed the government in British Columbia. The Chinese Canadian Association in Vancouver had begun actively campaigning for enfranchisement from at least 1942 when speakers addressed church groups and service clubs. In February 1945, the Association presented a petition to the legislature along with 700 signatures in its support. The legislature, during the 1945 session, enfranchised Chinese, Japanese, East Indians, and native Indian veterans who were currently serving, and Chinese, East Indians, and native Indians who had served in the Great War. Japanese Canadian veterans of the Great War had received the franchise in 1931.

With the 1945 enfranchisement, Chinese Canadians aged 21 and over from British Columbia and Saskatchewan in the group of 117 in India on loan to the British War Office, were able to cast their ballots in the June election for the first time. Those in Australia from Ontario, Manitoba, and Alberta, who had always been able to vote, do not remember doing so. Saskatchewan, the only other province to deny the franchise to its Chinese Canadian citizens from 1908, had restored this civil right in 1944. The Saskatchewan restriction had been based on an oath that had prevented Chinese Canadians from casting their ballot.

Other than British Columbia and Saskatchewan, Chinese Canadians could vote municipally, provincially, and federally and were not legally barred from practice in the professions, in all other Canadian provinces. When the Cabinet War Committee placed a ban on compulsory military service for Chinese Canadians all across Canada, it was done on racial grounds not because of the franchise. War service and the franchise were linked, but only partly, and Chinese Canadian veterans were the first to be enfranchised in British Columbia. If it had been war service alone, then Chinese Canadian veterans of the Great War would have received the franchise at the same time as Japanese Canadian veterans in 1931. Trade and a vigorous home government, which seem to have extended protection to the Japanese, were also potent factors.

Although they could vote in other provinces, there had been restrictions, especially on the municipal level, such as in Hamilton, Ont, which passed a by-law to restrict the hours of operation for laundries, striking at the extended hours Chinese Canadians were willing to work in order to

make any living at all. British Columbia had passed a similar law in 1922. Ontario in 1923 had also passed the law forbidding white women to work in Chinese businesses following that of Saskatchewan in 1912 and Manitoba in 1914. British Columbia passed a similar act in 1924. The act in Ontario never seems to have been enforced. There had been similar petty restrictions in other municipalities and provinces as well, with the exception of Quebec, especially Montreal, which many Chinese Canadians from that part of the country consider to have been the least discriminatory of any Canadian province.

The Head Tax, or as it was delicately phrased, the Chinese Entry Tax, began at $50 in 1885 when the railway had been completed; the tax was raised to $100 in 1900 and finally reached $500 in 1904. Since payment of an entry tax had not been successful in preventing the Chinese from entering Canada, the Exclusion Act was passed in 1923.

The current agitation for repayment of this Head Tax and the Re-Entry Certificate Fees, together totalling a little over $23 million, is not from the individuals who paid the tax, nor their children, but rather from the new immigrants who have entered the country since 1967. With only two exceptions out of all those interviewed, Chinese Canadian veterans are hostile to the notion that this money should be repaid and more than one has said: "We were not forced to pay it; there is no similarity to the payment made to Japanese Canadians who lost everything in their forced removal from the BC coast." Like Mackenzie King himself, the majority of the veterans feel that it is 'a privilege not a right' to become a Canadian.

Chinese Canadians joined all three services, once the air force and navy restrictions had been removed, and they served without comment as to their racial origin. The Canadian Army, however, remained consistent throughout the war period; Chinese Canadians were 'Allied Aliens' to the end.

If there were any racial incidents, they were not recorded in the memories of the survivors nor in the regimental histories. The possibility of unpleasant racial incidents was always the fear of National Defence. The only Chinese Canadian identified as such in a regimental history is in Strome Galloway's *A Regiment at War: the Story of the Royal Canadian Regiment 1939-1945,* p.168.

On the other hand, although the Chinese Canadians in Australia and India operated separately from the main Canadian Army stream, they were Canadian soldiers receiving Canadian rates of pay throughout their service with the British. When they returned to Canada, they received the same benefits as any other Canadian soldier.

Those servicemen who had not completed their education before joining the services availed themselves of the opportunity for educational advancement after the war using their war service gratuities. Speaking for them all, Louey King in Edmonton said in 1988: "We didn't want to spend the rest of our lives in laundries and restaurants." Many were thus increasingly able to find employment outside the traditional restaurant, laundry, and ethnic businesses, partly because other Canadians had become used to working beside them, and partly because they had served together in the military. These Chinese Canadian veterans were pioneers in the white collar field and thus made it easier for new immigrants to be more readily accepted.

The change from British subject to Canadian citizen did not occur until the passage of *The Canadian Citizenship Act* in 1946, effective 1 January 1947.[1] Yet the terms "Canadian Nationality" and "Nationality at Birth: Canadian" were used in Europe on Army Form B. 2606, the Military Identity Card, as early as 9 April 1943 if not before.[2]

Also, as already noted, "Canadian citizenship" was used freely in the Exclusion Act of 1923 where Chinese Canadians were described as being without legal status in Canada. Federal legislation seems to have followed what was already the practice in British Columbia, as it had done with respect to the franchise. The new Citizenship Act also defined the franchise as a part of citizenship status; this change may have prodded the BC legislature into granting the franchise to all Chinese in that province in 1947.

The Canadian Citizenship Act of 1947 did not discriminate on the grounds of national origin nor of race and the "Certificate of Canadian Citizenship" issued to Chinese Canadians at the time, under the "Subject/Citizen of" category, states only "Canadian Citizen." It did weaken when it came to the "Colour" category for here "yellow" is used to describe a Chinese Canadian citizen. The Citizenship Act was another equalizing step, however, and in February of 1947, over 400 Chinese Canadian veterans in British Columbia, both men and women, celebrated their Canadian citizenship status.[3]

Many of the minority groups, such as Blacks, East Indians, and Chinese from Hong Kong, were British subjects even before they entered Canada, just as were all Canadians. It had been difficult, however, for Chinese nationals in Canada to become naturalized British subjects. Along with the reluctance of judges in British Columbia to grant naturalization, Canadian rules had changed in 1931 so that from that year, a Chinese wishing to become naturalized had to receive prior approval from China. At that time, the Chinese government was located in the north, and nearly all the Chinese in Canada came from the south, an area over which the north had little control. China had internally been in a state of turmoil from 1911 and from 1931 was attempting to keep the Japanese at bay. The Nationalist Chinese Government was not usually in a position to grant approval.

The Municipal Elections Act in British Columbia was amended in 1949 thus opening the way for Chinese Canadian participation in municipal affairs. The exclusion from practising law, pharmacy, and other professional occupations had been removed with the 1945 and 1947 enfranchisements, since membership in these organizations was based on the voters' lists.

From late 1945 social restrictions were also being lifted, such as use of the Crystal Pool in Vancouver, which was opened to all on 8 November 1945 at 1:00 pm. This restriction rankled in the minds of many of the veterans of both sexes. At least one theatre had imposed segregated seating and this practice too came to an end.

In the matter of immigration, it was not until 1967, 22 years after the war ended, that the Chinese were placed on an equal basis with other nationalities. The Exclusion Act of 1923 had been repealed and from 1947 immigration restrictions for the Chinese had been changing, at first allowing wives and unmarried children only to enter Canada as immigrants.

In 1951 there were 32,528 Chinese in Canada; by 1981 this figure had become 285,800, still only 1 percent of the total population. Sixty percent of the 1981 figure, however, were newcomers. There is often a sharp difference between the two groups in personality, expectations, and conduct.

During the period 1939 to 1945, Chinese Canadians from British Columbia especially were not fighting for the same freedoms as other Canadians; nor did they enlist in the same spirit of adventure as many others had done. Many considered it their duty to fight for the country in which they had been born, and that service in the military was something they owed in return. They hoped they would acquire the 'rights' of citizenship since they were fulfilling their 'obligations,' and in British Columbia, many of those who volunteered felt that enfranchisement must be only a matter of time.[4]

It would be naive to suppose that service in the Canadian Armed Forces was the only reason for the post-war change in British Columbia and Dominion policies; as indicated above there were many other reasons. And, in addition to the United Nations Charter, there was a change in political attitudes and in politicians, both federally and provincially. But the military service of Chinese Canadians from 1939 to 1945, and to a lesser extent from 1914 to 1918, was the first area in which equality was partly practised. Canada itself had matured during the war years, acquiring an assurance brought about by its own acceptance in the international arena and by its quite incredible war record. With this new assurance, it was easier for the federal government to be more generous in its treatment of this particular minority.

Equality for Chinese Canadians is rapidly proceeding to the point described by Maj.-Gen. Victor W. Odlum, Canadian ambassador to China during World War II, who forecast "a day when Chinese-Canadians would 'not be distinguished from other Canadians.'"[5] Some of the veterans interviewed insist, and rightly so, that they are "plain Canadians" without qualification.

This conclusion appears to be born out by a poll conducted in January 1992 for the Immigration Department, which states that those surveyed felt that it was important to "keep out people who are different from most Canadians." It was also found that the definition of a "good" immigrant was one who was "hard-working, self-supporting, flexible and adapting well to our culture," and that they "tend to be white or perhaps yellow."[6] The Chinese immigrant has always been "hard-working and self-supporting"; and he has also proved that he is "flexible and adapting well to our culture."

NOTES

1. *Statutes of Canada,* 10 George VI, Chap. 15, An Act respecting Citizenship, Nationality, Naturalization, and Status of Aliens, short title *The Canadian Citizenship Act.*
2. Col. C. Sydney Frost, CD, QC, LLD, *Once a Patricia* (St. Catharines, Ont., 1988), see picture No. 18, following p. 218.
3. *Vancouver Sun,* February 20, 1947, p. 3, where the seven representing the 400 veterans are listed: Louie [Louey] King, M.M.; Thomas Koo Chung, RCAF, radar air crew mechanic; Wilfred Bing Tong Seto; Donald Sung, Army Intelligence Corps; Lila Wong, CWAC; Jean Suey Zee Lee, RCAF (WD); Marion [name is Mary on birth certificate] Laura Mah, CWAC. See also Lee, "Enfranchisement," p. 64, where the figure of 200 BC Chinese Canadian war veterans attending the citizenship ceremony is given.
4. Cheng/Roy Transcript.

5. Quoted in Lee, p. 64.
6. "Immigration: Hostility growing toward foreigners moving to Canada" by Kirk LaPointe, *Canadian Press* reprinted in *The London Free Press,* 14 September 1992.

Abbreviations and Glossary

AA	Australian Archives
AA	Anti-Aircraft
ABC	Airborne Cigar
AC	Aircraftman
ACSEA	Allied Command South East Asia
A/CM	Air Chief Marshal
Admin	Administrative/Administration
Afr/Eur	Africa/Europe
AFTU	Advanced Flying Training Unit
AFU	Advanced Flying Unit
AG	Air Gunner
AG	Adjutant General
agas	sandfly
AIB	Allied Intelligence Bureau
AIF	Australian Imperial Force
AJUF	Anti-Japanese Union and Forces
Alta	Alberta
AM	Air Marshal
ANS	Air Navigation School
AOS	Air Observer School
APC	armoured personnel carrier
APIS	Air Photographic Interpretation Section
ASR	Air Sea Rescue
AT	anti-tank
ATA	Air Transport Auxiliary
atap	thatched
ATIS	Allied Translator and Interpreter Section
ATC	Air Transport Command
ATFERO	Atlantic Ferry Organization, name briefly used for Ferry Command
ATR4	transmitter receiver
Aus/Man	Australia/Manila
Aus/Sara	Australia/Sarawak
Aust	Australia
AVG	American Volunteer Group
A/VM	Air Vice Marshal
AW1	Airwoman, Class 1
AWM	Australian War Memorial
BAAG	British Army Aid Group
Battalion	3 or 4 infantry rifle companies with mortar, machine gun, anti-tank, pioneer, supply and administrative companies; 700 to 950 men
battery	unit of artillery of four to eight guns
B&GS	Bombing & Gunnery School
batang	river

BBCAU	British Borneo Civil Administration Unit
BC	British Columbia
BCATP	British Commonwealth Air Training Plan; same as Empire Air Training Scheme
BCD	British Columbia Dragoons
BCR	British Columbia Regiment
Bde	see Brigade
BEF	British Expeditionary Force
BEM	British Empire Medal
Berks	Berkshire
blind drop	parachute drop without a reception committee
"blockbuster"	4,000 lb. bomb
blowpipe	poison dart blown through hollow wood rod
BMAP	British Ministry of Aircraft Production
Bmdr	Bombardier (artillery)
BNB	British North Borneo
BOAC	British Overseas Airways Corporation
Bofors	Swedish light anti-aircraft gun (40 mm calibre)
BPF	British Pacific Fleet
BR	bomber reconnaissance
Bren	light-weight, quick-firing machine gun
Brigade	unit of three regiments or battalions with support arms and services
Brig	Brigadier
Brig-Gen	Brigadier General
BSC	British Security Coordination
BWM	British War Medal
B-17	Boeing Flying Fortress
Btn	see Battalion
B-24	Consolidated Liberator
B-25	Mitchell medium bomber
bukit	hill
BWM	British War Medal
CA(A)	Canadian Army (Active)
CAC	Canadian Armoured Corps
CAE	Canadian Aviation Electronics
Camp X	STS 103, Whitby/Oshawa, Ont
Canton AF	Canton Air Force
capital ship	term used from 1909 to describe largest fighting ship in fleet
Capt	Captain
carrier	escort carrier 20-35 aircraft; light carrier 40-50 aircraft; fleet carrier 50 and over
CAS	Chief of Air Staff
CATC	Central Air Transport Company (CNAC from 1945-1949)
CATF	China Air Task Force
C&Y	Carleton & York Regiment
CBI	China-Burma-India theatre
CBRG	Canadian Base Reinforcement Group
CBRD	Canadian Base Reinforcement Depot

CCOS	Combined Chiefs of Staff (US)
Cda/Eng	Canada/England
Cda/Nfd	Canada/Newfoundland
Cda/Nfd/Eng	Canada/Newfoundland/England
Cda/USA	Canada/United States
Cda/USA/SEAC/ SWP/HK	Canada/United States/Southeast Asia/Southwest Pacific/Hong Kong
Cda/US/Sing/HK	Canada/USA/Singapore/Hong Kong
CDC	Canadian Dental Corps
CdnDef	Canadian Defence
CdnMerNav	Canadian Merchant Navy
CdnParaBtn	1st Canadian Parachute Battalion
CdnScots	Canadian Scottish Regiment
CEF	Canadian Expeditionary Force
Central GovAF	Central Government Air Force (China)
C-46	Curtis Commando transport
C-47	Douglas Dakota transport
CFB	Canadian Forces Base
Cfn	Craftsman
CFS	Central Flying School
CGG	Canadian Grenadier Guards
CGS	Chief of General Staff
CGRU	Canadian Group Reinforcement Unit
Chindits	Long Range Penetration Groups, Burma
Chin/Ind	China-India
CIA	Central Intelligence Agency
CIC	Canadian Infantry Corps
ciphers	numbers
CLC	Chinese Labour Corps
Cmdr	Commander
CMHQ	Canadian Military Headquarters, London
CMI	Canadian Military Intelligence
CNAC	China National Avaiation Corporation
CNS	Central Navigation School
CO	Commanding Officer
codes	words
Col	Colonel
company	in rifle company, 100 to 150 men; called squadron in armoured units
conscription	compulsory military service
"Cookie"	4,000 lb. bomb
COPP	Combined Operations Pilotage Parties
Corps	command of variable number of divisions and attached formations or Corps troops such as artillery, engineers, and supply; two or more Corps makes up an Army
COS	Chiefs of Staff
COTC	Canadian Officers Training Corps (universities)
CPC	Canadian Pay Corps
Cpl	Corporal
CPR	Canadian Pacific Railway
CSDIC	Combined Services Detailed Intelligence Corps

CSM	Company Sergeant Major (WO Class II)
CWAC	Canadian Women's Army Corps
CWGC	Commonwealth War Graves Committee
CWC	Cabinet War Committee
DC-3	Douglas Dakota transport
DC-4	Douglas Dakota Skymaster transport
DCO	Duke of Connaught's Own
D-Day	6 June 1944
D Division	Deception (SEAC)
despatcher	in clandestine operations, person who accompanied operatives to infiltration or dropping point
DFC	Distinguished Flying Cross
D.Hist.	Directorate of History, Department of National Defence
Div	Division, combines every unit of army consisting of two or more infantry or tank brigades and artillery, engineer, supply, medical and administrative units; about 15,000 to 20,000 men
DM	Defence Medal
DMI	Director of Military Intelligence
DOT	Department of Transport
D/F	direction finding
drogue	target for gunnery practice, pulled behind aircraft
DSM	Distinguished Service Medal
Dyaks	generic term for all Borneo tribes
DZ	dropping zone
E Group	SEAC name for MI 9, Escape & Evasion
EastCmd	Eastern Command
EFTS	Elementary Flying Training School
88	German dual-purpose 88 mm anti-aircraft, anti-tank gun; also used on the 56-ton Tiger tank
Eng/China	England/China
escaper	POW who has escaped
evader	service man still able to move about in enemy territory
EWS(1)	Eastern Warfare School (1)
FAA	Fleet Air Arm
FC	Ferry Command
FE	Flight Engineer
Flail	tank with rotating drum, chains attached, to beat the ground ahead to explode land mines
flak	anti-aircraft fire, also called ack-ack
Flight	in 2 TAF, about 6 aircraft operating together
F/Lt	Flight Lieutenant
F/O	Flying Officer
F/Sgt	Flight Sergeant
Folboat	collapsible 16 ft. canoe of about 70 lbs. made of rubberized fabric on bamboo frame; could carry 800 lbs.
Force 136	SEAC name for SOE
FTS	Flying Training School

G-2	American Intelligence
gardening	mine laying by aircraft
Gdsm	Guardsman
Gee	radio aid for navigation and target identification
Gen	General
GenLst	General List
Generalissimo	Chiang Kai-Shek
George	automatic pilot
GGFG	Governor General's Foot Guards
GGHG	Governor General's Horse Guards
GIS	Ground Instruction School
GLO	Group Liaison Officer
GLT	Group Liaison Team
Glos	Gloucestershire
Gnr	Gunner
GOC	General Officer Commanding
GOCinC	General Officer Commanding-in-Chief
Grand Slam	22,000 lb. bomb
Group	15 Squadrons in RCAF No. 6 Group, Bomber Command; 8 Groups in Command with 100 Group (Bomber Support)
GRS	General Reconnaissance School
GS	General Service
GSO1	General Staff Officer, Grade 1; GSOs in various grades and ranks in planning, operations, intelligence, and at all levels
HAA	Heavy anti-aircraft; sometimes written AA (H)
Hants	Hampshire
HCU	Heavy Conversion Unit
HE	High Explosive
HF/DF	high frequency/direction finding (Huff-Duff)
HK	Hong Kong
HKVDC	Hong Kong Volunteer Defence Corps
HMCS	His Majesty's Canadian Ship
HMS	His Majesty's Ship
HMSO	His/Her Majesty's Stationery Office
HMT	His Majesty's Transport/Troopship
HQ	Headquarters
H2S	airborne radar navigation and target identification aid
Huff-Duff	high frequency radio direction finding equipment
Hump, The	The Himalayas
Hydra	radio station at Oshawa, Ontario
Ibans	one of the Borneo tribes
IFF	identification friend/foe
IIC	Industrial Intelligence Centre
Ijsselmeer	same as IJsselmeer (new name for Zuider Zee)
INA	India National Army
Ind/Burma	India-Burma
Ind/Eng	India/England
Ind/Mal	India/Malaya

IRC	Irish Regiment of Canada
ISLD	Inter-Services Liaison Department (SEAC name for Secret Intelligence Service or MI 9)
It/Eur	Italy/Europe
ITS	Initial Training School
Jedburgh	operatives in uniform who worked behind enemy lines
Joint COS	Joint Chiefs of Staff (US and British combined)
Ju88	German fighter-bomber aircraft built by Junkers
jumpmaster	person in aircraft charged with safe and timely exit of parachutists
junk	Chinese boat, larger than sampan
kampong	village
kangaroo	armoured personnel carrier
kanji	written Japanese
Kayan	Borneo tribe
KCB	Knight Commander (of the Order) of the Bath
Kelabit	Borneo tribe
Kempei Tai	Japanese Military Police
Kenyah	Borneo tribe
KIA	killed in action
kicker	person in aircraft charged to kick out packages and bundles
kuala	estuary
kubu	fort
Kuomintang	Chinese Nationalist
L capsule	cyanide pill
LAA	light anti-aircraft
LAC	Leading Aircraftman
Lanarks	The Lanark and Renfrew Scottish Regiment
lb	pound
LCI	landing craft infantry
L/Cpl.	Lance Corporal
LCT	landing craft tank
leave behind	group to operate behind enemy lines when main body withdraws
Leics	Leicestershire
LFS	Lancaster Finishing School
Lieut	Lieutenant
limpet	magnetic mine for attaching to metal hulls and bridges packed with plastic explosive and effective under water; fired by a time-delay fuse
Lincs	Lincolnshire
LMG	light machine gun
longhouse	extended building housing about 30 families
Loyal Eddies	Loyal Edmonton Regiment
Lt-Col	Lieutenant-Colonel
Lt-Cmdr	Lieutenant-Commander
Lt-Gen	Lieutenant-General
Luftwaffe	German air force
Maj	Major

Maj-Gen	Major General
Malays	inhabitants of the Malay peninsula and parts of Borneo
Man	Manitoba
Master Bomber	pilot in control of bomber raid
MC	Military Cross
MCR	minature communications receiver
MCS	Malaya Country Section
MD	Military District
ME	Military Establishment (alternative name for STS)
MEW	Ministry of Economic Warfare
MI	Military Intelligence
MI 5	Internal and overseas security service
MI 6	Secret Intelligence Service (SIS)
MI 9	Escape & Evasion
MI(R)	Military Intelligence (Research)
MiD	Mention in Despatches
MIT	Massachusetts Institute of Technology
MM	Military Medal
mortar	varying sized, easily handled, infantry weapon, throwing shells at high angles with wide zones of shell dispersal
MPAJA	Malayan Peoples' Anti-Japanese Army
MSM	Meritorious Service Medal
MU	Maintenance Unit
NAC	National Archives of Canada
NATO	North Atlantic Treaty Organization
NB	New Brunswick
NCO	Non-Commissioned Officer
NDHQ	National Defence Headquarters, Ottawa
NEI	Netherlands East Indies
Nfd	Newfoundland
nickel	propaganda leaflet dropped from aircraft
Nisei	second generation Japanese Canadian
Notts	Nottinghamshire
NPAM	Non-Permanent Active Militia
NRMA	National Resources Mobilization Act
NSHQ	Naval Service Headquarters
NSS	National Selective Service
NS	Nova Scotia
NWS	National War Services
OBE	Officer/Order of the British Empire
Oboe	blind bombing and target marking system controlled from ground radar stations
OC	Officer Commanding
Ont	Ontario
Ops	Operations
ORs	Other Ranks
ORA	Ontario Rifle Association
OSS	Office of Strategic Services

OTU	Operational Training Unit
P Division	coordinator of the 12 clandestine organizations in SEAC
PLieut (Temp)	Pay Lieutenant (Temporary)
PacCmd	Pacific Command
PacForce	Pacific Force
PACMIRS	Pacific Military Intelligence Research Section
PanAm	Pan American Airlines
padi	rice field
PBY	Consolidated PBY Catalina
PC	Privy Council (Order in Council when numbered)
PCO	Passport Control Office
PEI	Prince Edward Island
penghulu	chief
Perths	Perth Regiment
PFF	Pathfinder Force
P-40	Curtis Warhawk fighter; called Tomahawk and Kittyhawk in British service
PI	Philippine Islands
PIAT	Projector, Infantry, Anti-Tank weapon; throws anti-tank grenade about 100 yards
platoon	infantry sub-unit of 30 to 40 men in 3 sections
PLT	Patrol Liaison Team
POL	petrol, oil, lubricant
P/O	Pilot Officer
POW	Prisoner of War
PPCLI	Princess Patricia's Canadian Light Infantry
PR	photo reconnaissance
prahu	native boat (pronounced prow)
Pte	Private
PULHEMS	Physique, Upper and Lower extremities, Hearing, Eyes, Mental capacity, and Stability
Punans	Borneo tribe (nomads)
PWE	Political Warfare Executive
QM	Quartermaster
QOR	Queen's Own Rifles of Canada
Que	Quebec
RA	Royal Artillery
RAAF	Royal Australian Air Force
R/Adm	Rear Admiral
Radio Art	Radio Artificer
RAF	Royal Air Force
RAMC	Royal Army Medical Corps
RAN	Royal Australian Navy
RAPWI	Relief/Repatriation of Allied Prisoners of War and Internees
RCA	Royal Canadian Artillery
RCAC	Royal Canadian Armoured Corps
RCAF	Royal Canadian Air Force
RCAF(WD)	Royal Canadian Air Force (Women's Division)

RCAMC	Royal Canadian Army Medical Corps
RCAPC	Royal Canadian Army Pay Corps
RCASC	Royal Canadian Army Service Corps
RCCS	Royal Canadian Corps of Signals
RCE	Royal Canadian Engineers
RCEME	Royal Canadian Electrical & Mechanical Engineers
RCR	Royal Canadian Regiment
RCMP	Royal Canadian Mounted Police
RCN	Royal Canadian Navy
RCN(R)	Royal Canadian Navy (Reserve)
RCN(VR)	Royal Canadian Navy (Volunteer Reserve)
RCOC	Royal Canadian Ordnance Corps
RDF	radar/radio direction finding
Rear/Adm	Rear Admiral
Rebecca/Eureka	responder and interrogator between ground and aircraft
Recce	reconnaissance
reception party	group to receive parachutists
Reg	1. Infantry Regiment about 700 to 950 men; regiment may raise more than one battalion;
	2. Armoured Regiment 500 to 600 men: three tank squadrons, reconnaissance troop, and administrative
	3. Artillery Regiment about 800 to 1000 men: 3 batteries (18-24 guns)
rentis	path cut through jungle
Res and (Res)	Reserve
Rfn	Rifleman
RFS	Return Ferry Service
RHLI	Royal Hamilton Light Infantry
RMR	Rocky Mountain Rangers
RN	Royal Navy
RNAS	Royal Navy Air Service
RNI	Royal Navy Intelligence
RSM	Regimental Sergeant Major
R22e	Royal 22e Régiment
SAC	Strategic Air Command
SACSEA	Supreme Allied Command/er South East Asia
sampan	small Chinese boat
SAS	Special Air Service
Sask	Saskatchewan
SB	Special Branch (RCN)
SBC	small bomb container
SBS	Special Boat Sections/Squadrons
SD	Special Duty
SEAC	South East Asia Command
SEATIC	South East Asia Translators and Interpreters Corps
2 i/c	second-in-command
2nd TAF	2nd Tactical Air Force
Section B	Malaya Country Section SEAC
Section D	Z organization and Passport Control Office, SIS
semut	ant

Sgm	Signalman
Sgt	Sergeant
Skapan	sub-tribe of Kayan clan in Borneo
SFTS	Service Flying Training School
S/Maj	Sergeant Major
SHAEF	Supreme Headquarters Allied Expeditionary Force
Sic/It	Sicily/Italy
Sing/HK	Singapore/Hong Kong
SIS	Secret Intelligence Service
16 Cdn.Scots	16th Canadian Scottish (Reserve)
S/Ldr	Squadron Leader
SMG	Sub-machine gun
SOE	Special Operations Executive
SOS	struck off strength
SP	Self-propelled
S.Phone	radiotelephone
Spr	Sapper (Field Engineer)
Sqn	1. Armoured Squadron, 3 or 4 tank troops, about 110 to 125 men and 15 to 19 tanks;
	2. Air Force Squadron, about 20 aircraft;
	3. Navy Squadron, small unit such as 4 Cruisers
SRD	Services Reconnaissance Department
S/Sgt	Staff Sergeant
SS	Steamship
SSR	South Saskatchewan Regiment
S-20	S-20 Japanese Language School
stick	the number of bombs or men (about 6) dropped in rapid succession from aircraft
storepedoes	containers for dropping supplies
STS	Special Training School
Suluk	Borneo tribe
sungei	river
SWP	Southwest Pacific
TAF	Tactical Air Force
Tallboy	12,000 lb. bomb
telok	bay
Temp	temporary
Tiger Force	Canadian volunteers for Pacific War
TOS	taken on strength
Tpr	Trooper
Troop	4 tanks of about 16 men; or 4 guns in artillery
TTS	Technical Training School
tua rumah	head of household
25-pounder	standard field gun howitzer, with travelling field platform
2 i/c	second-in-command
UBC	University of British Columbia
UK	United Kingdom
UN	United Nations

US or USA	United States
USAAF	United States Army Air Force
USN	United States Navy
USS	United States Ship
UST	United States Transport/Troopship
ulu	interior
UWO	University of Western Ontario
V-1	flying bomb
V-2	artillery rocket
V/Adm	Vice Admiral
VE-Day	Victory in Europe, 8 May 1945
VGC	Veterans Guard of Canada
VIP	Very Important Person
VJ-Day	Victory in Japan 14 (15) August 1945
VM	Victory Medal (issued with BWM)
WAG	Wireless Airgunner
Warks	Warwickshire
WD	Women's Division (RCAF)
West Novas	West Nova Scotia Regiment
Window	metallic strips dropped from aircraft to confuse enemy radar
Wing	Air Force: three or more squadrons. Fighter Command and 2nd TAF operated in Wings, Squadrons, and Flights
WNSR	West Nova Scotia Regiment
Worcs	Worcester
WO	Warrant Officer, Class 1 or 2, senior non-commissioned officer, usually a sergeant-major
W/T	Wireless Transmitter
Y service	monitoring wireless signals (telegraphy and speech)
Yorks	Yorkshire
Z Force	name for Section D of SIS in Hong Kong
Z Organization	same as Z Force
'Z' Special Unit	SOE in Australia
Zombie	term for NRMA soldiers (non-volunteers)

Appendix

Chinese Canadian Veterans

The names of Chinese Canadians who served with Canadian and Allied Forces during World War II are listed below; the list is not complete. The Vancouver plaques were used as a basis, with additions and corrections made to that basic list. Every effort has been made to ensure accuracy, but this present list is in support of statements in the narrative and should not be considered in any way a legal document. It was not possible to contact each person. As listed here, the names are in the order used in the services as far as they are known.

The Lees, Chans, and Wongs are the most numerous Chinese surnames in Canada. Some of the confusion arises from the different spellings for the same surname and sometimes the same spellings for different surnames such as Chan, Chang, Chin, Chinn, and even Chun depending on a slightly different pronunciation of the same surname in the different dialects of the places of origin of their forbears, even if only a few miles apart. At the same time Chang and Chun could be the spellings of totally different surnames.

BAN QUAN, Pte Edward Mark (Bud)	K.7884	CIC	India
[surname Quan]			
BAW, Norman (Calgary)		Army	CdnDef
BING SUEY, Cpl Allan	R.267351	RCAF	CdnDef
[surname Bing Suey Lee]			
BING, WO2 Fred	R.242504	RCAF	Europe
BONG, Sgt John Ko	K.50956	RCA/CIC	Aus/Man
[surname Ko]			
BONG, Spr Peter Ko	K.7646	RCE	India
BUNN, Enoch		CNAC	Chin/Ind
[proper surname is really Ng]			
BUNN, Luke		CNAC	Chin/Ind
CHAN, Alan (Victoria)		CIC	CdnDef
[also spelt Chin, Chinn, Chun, Chang]			
CHAN, L/Cpl Allen Yee Poy	K.7429	CIC	India
CHAN, Pte Chuey Neill	K.7824	CIC	India
CHAN, Sgt Daniel Poy	B.140191	RCOC/RCEME	
CHAN, A/Cpl Dick		Army	CdnDef
CHAN, F/O E.C.F. (Sask)	J.46079	RCAF	
CHAN, George H. (Montreal)	D.	Army	
CHAN, RSM Harold	L or H	Army	
CHAN, LAC Herbert (Herby)	R.166288	RCAF	CdnDef
CHAN, Pte Herbert	K.12442	CIC	
CHAN, Pte Hong Gow	K.5573	CIC	

CHAN, Howard M.			
CHAN, Pte Jack	K.5616	CIC	Ind/Eng
CHAN, Pte Johnnie F.		Army	
CHAN, Kon Wat			
CHAN, Lloyd (Victoria)	K.	16th CdnScots(Res)	
CHAN, Spr Paul	K.7520	RCE	India
CHAN, Quai Sing		Army	
CHAN, Spr Raymond (Buster)	K.7647	RCE	India
CHAN, AC2 Richard Sir	K.10968	CIC	
	R.294654	RCAF	
CHAN, Sgt Roy Sin Twe	K.69908	RCA/RCASC	Aust/Sara
CHAN, Spr Toy (Ira)	K.7521	RCE	India
CHAN, Pte/Gnr Wallace	SK.14656	CIC/RCA	
- permanent force			
CHAN-KENT, Spr Robert	K.7558	RCE	India
CHANG, F/O Gan Yat	J.40080	RCAF	England
CHANG, Sgt Gwong	R.175640	RCAF	
CHANG, Robert		Army	
CHANG, Cpl Suey Hing (Albert)	K.7335	RCE	India
CHANG, Pte Teddy	B.165116	CIC	
CHANG, Theodore		COTC	
CHANG, Wallace			
CHANG, LAC Yat Chee	R.172216	RCAF	
CHENG, Spr Kam Fong (Henry)	K.7522	RCE	Aust
[Mandarin spelling]			
CHENG, Spr Kam Poy (Percy)	K.7530	RCE	
CHENG, Capt Roger Kee (Lillooet)		RCCS	Aust/Sara
CHEW, Sgm Bew	K.7600	RCCS	Aust
[also spelt Chiu, Joe]			
CHEW, Pte Jack LeRoy	B.139753	CIC/RHLI	Europe
CHEW, Pte James Delbert Harold	L.32372	VGC	
- also served World War I			
CHEW, Pte (L/Cpl) James Edward	M.37076	RCA/CIC	
CHEW, Norman (Montreal)	D.		
CHEW, Stanley (brother of Bew)			
CHEW, Pte Wing	K.7700	CIC	
CHIANG, F/Sgt Thomas Deong		RCAF	Europe
CHIN, Frank (Lucknow)	A	CIC	PacForce
[also spelt Chan, Chiang, Chinn, and Chun]			
CHIN, F/O/Capt Frank	J.224557	RCAF/CNAC	Eng/China
CHIN, Toy (George)		CdnMerNav	
CHIN, LAC Harry (Lucknow)	R.269181	RCAF	England
CHIN, Cfn Henry (Harry)	K.7418	RCEME	Ind/Eng
CHIN, Gnr Hon Ming (Teddy)	K.18402	RCA	
CHIN, Jack R. (bro. Teddy)	H.	Army	
CHIN, Pte James (Lucknow)	B.135924	RCASC	Europe
CHIN, Pte John Ying	K.13575	CIC	CdnDef
CHIN, Sgt Sir Jan (Danny)	K.7956	CIC/MI	Sing/HK
CHINN, Sgt Bing Lee (George)	K.5161	CIC	Ind/Mal
CHINN, Capt Harold		Canton AF/CNAC	Chin/Ind

CHINN, SSgt John Rose	SK.53628	RCASC	Sic/It
- served 1940-1964 permanent force			
CHIU, Sgt Matthew (Jack)	K.7511	CIC	India
[also spelt Chew]			
CHO, Pte Melvin	E.88330	Army	
[also spelt Tso]			
CHONG, Pte Daniel		Army	
[also spelt Cheong, Cheung, Jong]			
CHONG, Spr Stanley	M.3815	RCA	England
CHONG, William (Bill)		RCA	CdnDef
CHONG, William (Bill)	Agent No. 50	BAAG	China
CHONG, Pte Willie	K.7722	CIC	India
CHOO, Pte (L/Cpl) Juck Sun	K.7561	RCASC	India
[could be Chu or Gee ?]			
CHOW, Gnr Albert	K.18479	RCA	
[also spelt Joe or Jow]			
CHOW, Pte Bill Wing	K.5241	CIC	India
CHOW, C. Quan			
CHOW, Pte Delbert Yen	K.7786	GenLst	India
CHOW, Ed (Victoria)	K.	Army	
CHOW, Sgt Edward	B.91866	RCAMC	Aust
CHOW, Pte Fook Kwong (Harry)	K.7668	CIC	India
CHOW, Fred		Interp	China
CHOW, Gnr George	K.25810	RCA	Europe
CHOW, Bmdr George L. (Moose Jaw)	No.4136	HKVDC	Hong Kong
CHOW, Grant (Victoria)	K.	Army	PacForce
CHOW, Harry		China Air Force	
CHOW, LAC Henry	R.204895	RCAF	CdnDef
CHOW, Herbert - this is Herbert QUON, q.v.			
CHOW, Howard			
CHOW, Jack (Saskatoon)	L.	RCCS	
CHOW, F/Sgt Jackie (Jake)	R.293722	RCAF	Europe
CHOW, James			
CHOW, L/Cpl Jim Kwong	K.7840	CIC	India
CHOW, John (Victoria)	Army	CdnDef	
CHOW, Kee			
CHOW, Pte(L/Cpl) Lewis Roosey	K.7974	CIC	India
CHOW, Sgt Lloyd B.	K.7924	RCE	
CHOW, Marshall (Edmonton)	M.3667	RCCS	Europe
CHOW, Cpl Men Woo (Lloyd)	K.7536	RCE/CIC	India
CHOW, Pte Park Wing	K.5987	GenLst	CdnDef
CHOW, Percy		RCAF	
CHOW, Pte Percy	K.	Army	
CHOW, Pte Peter S.	L.109819	CIC	India
CHOW, Pte Quan Lai	K.7560	GenLst	India
CHOW, Wilbert			
CHOW, Sgt William S. (Bill)	L.51129	RCCS	India
CHOW KEM, Bill (Calgary)		Army	Overseas
CHOW [-LEONG], P/O Charles	J.35171	RCAF	Ind/Burma
CHU, Albert		Army	Overseas

CHU, Pte Clarence		Army	CdnDef
CHU, Ronald L.			
CHUN, Fred	K.	Army	
- enlisted twice; real surname was LOW Chun, q.v.			
CHUNG, Sgt Charley	K.5487	CIC	Ind/Mal
[also spelt Jone]			
CHUNG, Henry J.		US Inter	China
CHUNG, WO2 Thomas Kuo	R.197678	RCAF	
CON, Sgt Harry Gen Ping	K.7534	CIC	India
DAN, Manuel (1941-1946)	K.76963	RCASC	Europe
[also spelt Tang, Teng, Dong, or Dang]			
DARLING, [Dar Leung] Gdsm. Ted (1939-1946)	K.89870	CGG	Europe
DER, Jimmy [also spelt Dear or Tse]			
DER, Joe			
DER, Pte Sui Kenneth	E.5612	CIC	
DER, Walter (Victoria)	K.	Army	CdnDef
DER WOON, — (Calgary)			
DOFOO, Paul (Calgary)		Broadcasting	Chungking
DONG, David			
[also spelt Dan, Dang, Tang, Teng]			
DONG, J.K. (Jack)		CNAC	Chin/Ind
DONG, Pte Wing Herbert	K.7792	CIC	India
ENG, George [also spelt Ng or Ing]			
ENG, Jack			
ENG, Pte Keyea	K.	Army	
ENG, Pte Peter (Victoria)	K.609234	RCOC/CIC	CdnDef
ENG, Peter (Calgary)			
ENG, Pte Robert (Bob)		Army	
ENG, Spr Wing Fung (Frank)	K.7510	RCE	India
ENG, Spr Wing Wong (Jerry)	K.7643	RCE	India
ENG, Pte Yick (Harry)	K.7915	CIC	Aust
FEE, Pte Joe		CIC	
FEE, Pte Thomas (Junction)	K.7810	CIC	India
FONG, Berkley			
[Mandarin Feng; Fong could also be used to represent Kwong]			
FONG, Cpl Charles Joseph	B.118836	RCAMC	Aust
FONG, Pte Dick (P.Rupert)	K.7432	CIC	Nfd
FONG, Pte Dick Wing (Edward)	K.7546	CIC	Aust
FONG, Cpl Eddie (Lethbridge)		RCAF	
FONG, L/Cpl Georges E.	C.49137	RCAMC/RCAPC	Aust
FONG, LAC Harry (New Brunswick)		RCAF	CdnDef
FONG, Pte Jim Lee (Mont Joli)	E.601397	R22e	Europe
FONG, Johay			
FONG, John (Edward) (Victoria)	K.		
FONG, Pte John (Prince Rupert)	K.5603	CIC	Ind/Eng
FONG, Johnny (Calgary)			
FONG, Pte Jong Leung (James)	K.7547	CIC	Ind/Eng

FONG, Pte Rupert	K.7979	CIC	Aust
FONG, Samaul [*sic*] (New Brunswick)		BCATP/FC/ATA	Cda/Eng
FONG, Stanley			
FONG, Stanley (Vancouver)		CNAC	Chin/Ind
FONG, Pte Tuck Quon (Harry)	K.5885	CIC	India
- Dominion Marksman, First Class			
FONG, Pte Willie (Mont Joli)	E.	R22e	It/Europe
- killed in Korea 1952			
FUNG, C.T. (Vancouver)		CNAC	Chin/Ind
FUNG, Pte Hinn Wing (Henry)	K.5224	CIC	Ind/Mal
GAY, Jack W.			
GEE, Pte Margaret		CWAC	
[sometimes spelt Chee or Chu]			
GIN, Gan Sang (Alfred) - this is Alfred Quinn LEE, q.v.			
GINN, Alfred [this may be Alfred Gin above]			
GONG, Albert			
GONG, Sgt Harry (Clinton BC)	R.	RCAF/RAF	Ind/Burma
GONG/GWONG, Tony		Army	
[could be Fong or Gung]			
GOON. Sgm Lawrence (Vancouver)	K.7949	RCCS/CIC	India
[usually spelt Yuen]			
HANG, CSM Harry (Toronto)		RCASC	It/Eur
HAY, Pte YOUNG Wing	K.57403	CdnScots	Europe
HEM, Pte Percy F. (New Brunswick)	? 19872		CdnDef
[also spelt Hum, Thom, and Tom]; (letter for NB is G)			
HING, Pte Dan	K.5362	CIC	India
HING, Pte Johnnie Fook (Joe)	K.5357	CIC	
HO, Sgt Fat Chung (Harry)	K.7593	CIC	Ind/Mal
HO, Pte Fred (died of wounds)	B.37564	IRC	Italy
HO, G. (from SW Ontario) KIA		RCAMC	Italy
HO, Lin Fat (Fred)　KIA			Italy
HO, Pte Joe		Army	
HO, Pte Kwok Chung (Charlie)	K.7543	CIC	India
HO LEM, Lieut Frank (Calgary)		CIC	PacCmd
HO LEM, George (Calgary)		Army	CdnDef
HO, Pte Samuel (Vancouver)	K.	Army	
HO, Pte Willy		Army	
HOAN, Tommy I. (Hamilton)	R.256205	RCAF	Eng/Eur
[father's surname NG Hoan]			
HOE, Pte Helen	W.100858	CWAC	CdnDef
HONG, Pte Billie (Pat)	C.49383	RCASC	India
HONG, Fred (Windsor)	A.		Europe
HONG, Pte George (Windsor) KIA	A.117703	WNSR	Italy
HONG, F/O Joseph (Windsor) KIA	J.37185	RCAF	Europe
HONG, King Lewis CHOW (SS Marie)	B.80078	RCAC	It/Eur
[surname is CHOW]			
HONG, Pte Ming T. (SS Marie)	B.166370	Army	Aust

HONG, Pte Wing Shu (Chatham)	A.606615	Army	
- Chinese National - Services no longer required			
HOWE, Tpr Jolly (Streetsville)	B.26617	RCE/CAC	
HOY, Pte Charlie (Vancouver)	K.5749	CIC	India
[should probably be spelt Hui]			
HUM, Sgt Art Ten (Henry)	E.100068	R22e	CdnDef
[also spelt Hem, Thom, Tom, or Tam]			
HUM, Georges E.	R.268705	RCAF	England
HUM, Victor (Montreal)		RCN(VR)	
ING, Henry (Kingston)	C.	Army	
[also spelt Eng, and Ng]			
ING, Pon Chong		Army	
JANG, Albert (Victoria)	K.	Army	
[popular spelling of Cheng; also spelt Chang]			
JANG, Pte Alvin (Toronto)	B.106813	CIC	PacForce
JANG, Charlie - army name WING, Jang Yok, q.v.			
JANG, Pte (L/Cpl) Clarence Walter	K.7316	RCE/CIC	India
- name now changed to Bevan Jangze			
JANG, Harry			
JANG, Harry K.			
JANG, Pte Maurice Eugene	K.7390	CIC	India
JANG, Pte Raymond (Toronto)	B.145543	RCR	Italy
JANG, Pte Thomas		Army	
JANG, Cpl Timothy Gim (Duncan)	K.7419	CIC	India
JOE, LAC Andrew	R.294680	RCAF	CdnDef
[also spelled Chow or Jow]			
JOE, Spr Chong Gan (Victoria)	K.7512	RCE	India
JOE, John (Victoria)		Army	CdnDef
JOE, Thomas			
JOE, Sgt Walter D. (Vernon)	R.197926	RCAF	CdnDef
JOH, Spr E.K. (Saanich)		RCE	Europe
[probably a corruption of Joe]			
JOH, Pte Ke Cheong (Lyon)	K.7599	CIC	India
JONE, Pte Hin Wing	K.7769	CIC	India
[also spelt Jung]			
JONG, F.C. (Alfred)	C.130969	RCASC	CdnDef
[also spelt Chang, Cheung, and Jang; this is probably Albert Jang from Victoria, above]			
JOW, Pte Herbert		CIC	England
[also spelt Chow and Joe]			
JUNG, F/L Arthur Ernest	J.35156	RCAF	England
[also spelt Jone or Chung or Tsang]			
JUNG, Pte Chew Chuck	K.7554	RCASC	Cda/USA
JUNG, Sgt Douglas	K.50902	CMI/S-20	Aust
JUNG, Harry			
JUNG, Pte Herb		Army	
JUNG, F/Sgt Irwin	R.270236	RCAF	England
JUNG, Kenneth			
JUNG, Capt Ross		RCAMC	Europe

JUNG, Pte Thomas Kampbell	K.5156	CIC	India
KANG, Spr(L/Cpl) Mar George	K.7592	CIC	India
[surname probably Mar]			
KEE, Jimmy (Toronto)		RCA	PacForce
KEEN, Pte Chew Lung Bew (Bill)	K.7614	CIC	India
[surname probably Chew]			
KHEONG, Harry Leuy (Calgary)		US Liaison Officer.	China
[surname should be Louey or Louie]			
KHEONG, Sgt Jack Leuy (Calgary)		US Army	China
KHEONG, Joe Leuy (Calgary)		US ATC	China
KHEONG, Ken Leuy (Calgary) Interpreter		US QM Corps	China
KIANG, Hugh			
KING, Sgt Louey, (Alberta)	K.50207	RCAC	Aus/Sara
[surname originally Yee]			
KIWAY [DER], Tpr (L/Cpl) Hayward	K.7598	CIC	India
KO BONG, L/Cpl Andrew	K.440472	2nd (Res) BCR(DCOR)	CdnDef
KO BONG, Pte Mary (Victoria)	W.115036	CWAC	CdnDef
KO, Cpl Donald Wing Kan (Toronto)	B.164741	CIC	CdnDef
KWONG, Pte George Yet (Revelstoke)	K.1813	RCASC/CIC	Europe
[sometimes pronounced Fong]			
KWONG, Pte Harry	M.2871	RCEME	
KWONG, W/O Henry (pilot) (Calgary)		RCAF	Europe
KWONG, James Kuo (Revelstoke)	B.106092	RCOC	CdnDef
KWONG, Pte Joe	K.5816	CIC	India
KWONG, Pte Larry (Vernon)	K.	Army	
LAM, Sgt Cecil (Victoria)	K.	Army	CdnDef
[same as Lem, Lim, Lum, or Lin]			
LAM, Pte Dick (Victoria)	K.7574	CIC	Aust
LANG, Harry			
[same as Leung, Long, Liang, or Leong]			
LANG, Howard G.		CIC	Europe
LANG, Johnny (Montreal)	D.	CIC	
LANG, F/Lt Norman (Three Rivers)	J.	RCAF	
LAW, Pte Gee Man	K.7920	CIC	India
[same as Lore, Lor, or Lo Mandarin spelling]			
LAW, Harry [radar 1ST HAA Bty]		RCA	England
LAW, Pte Lum Man	K.7584	CIC	Ind/Eng
LEE, Pte Alfred Gett	K.7712	CIC	India
LEE, Pte Alfred Quinn (Winnipeg)	H.28434	CIC	CdnDef
LEE, B.O.(Silent)			
LEE, Pte Bak Foong (Fred)	L.8993	CIC	
LEE, Pte Benny (Windsor)	A.117827	Perths	It/Eur
LEE, Sgt Billy Kong	K.7597	RCE	Ind/Mal
LEE, Sgt Bing Chu (Vancouver)	K.7405	RCE	Ind/Mal
LEE, Spr Chew Quon (Charlie)	K.6934	RCE	India
LEE, Cpl Daniel	R.170973	RCAF	Cda/Eng
LEE, David (Montreal)		RCN	
LEE, Pte Ed (Vancouver)	K.	QOR	CdnDef
LEE, Eddie (Montreal)	D.		Overseas

LEE, Pte Eddie A.		Army	Overseas
LEE, LAC Edward (Windsor)	R.187538	RCAF	England
LEE, LAC Edward (London)	R.259998	RCAF	CdnDef
LEE, Pte Edward Feey (Vancouver)	K.7837	CIC	India
LEE, Bmdr Ernest (High River, Alta)	M.	RCA	CdnDef
LEE, F/O Ernie Thomas (Nav)	J.	RCAF	England
LEE, Pte Fay		CWAC	CdnDef
LEE, Pte Frank	A.109047	CIC	
LEE, Lieut Frank (Montreal)		RCEME	PacForce
LEE, Pte Frank (Toronto)	B.	CIC	PacForce
LEE, Pte Frank (Baldur)	H.27868	Army	India
LEE, Fred (Montreal)	D.	Army	
LEE, Pte Fred (Chan Toy) (P.Alberni)	K.7883	CIC	
LEE, Gar Chong			
LEE, George (Calgary)			
LEE, George (Kenora)	R.215888	RCAF	Cda/Nfd
LEE, George	K.18145	Army	CdnDef
LEE, LAC George (Big George)	R.168494	RCAF	Europe
LEE, George A. (Vancouver)			
LEE, George G.K. (Montreal)		RCAF	
LEE, George S.C. (Edmonton)		Interp	China
LEE, Pte Gordon (Winnipeg)	H.27855	CIC	India
LEE, Grant (Calgary)		Army	CdnDef
LEE, Pte Harden (Victoria)	K.7557	RCE	Aust
LEE, Harvey (Prairies)	L.	Army	
LEE, F/Lt Harvey A. (Harold)		RCAF	England
LEE, Sgt WAG Henry		RCAF	England
LEE, L/Cpl Herbert Qui Shiu (Vic)	K.5619	CIC	India
LEE, Sgt Horace Bing Dang (Vic)	K.7313	CIC	Ind/Eng
LEE, Pte Howard (Victoria)	K.7834	RCASC	India
LEE, Pte Hubert (Victoria)	K.7917	RCEME/CIC	India
LEE, Pte Ivan G. (Montreal) KIA	D.143578	SSR	Europe
LEE, LAC Jack (Brantford)	R.272738	RCAF	CdnDef
LEE, Pte Jack(man) (Vancouver)	K.	Army	CdnDef
LEE, Pte James (Brantford)	B.548346	RCEME	CdnDef
LEE, AW1 Jean Suey Zee (Kimberley)		RCAF/WD	EastCmd
LEE, Jerail			
LEE, Cpl Jim (Wingham)	A.66726	RCASC	Europe
LEE, F/O Jim Gen (Winnipeg) KIA	J.42216	RCAF	Europe
LEE, Pte Jimmy (Brandon)	K.7756	CIC	India
LEE, John (Hamilton)		RCAF	England
LEE, Kam		RCAF	
LEE, Pte Kee Tun	K.13502	CIC	
LEE, LAC Kenneth Kwong (Baldur)	R.163591	RCAF	CdnDef
LEE, Kim Dong (P.Rupert)		COTC(Air)	
LEE, Sgt Kim Yuen (P.Rupert)	R.221953	RCAF	CdnDef
LEE, Pte Leonard Richard	K.7916	CIC	India
LEE, Pte Louis Joseph	K.5665	CIC	
LEE, LAC Monying (Monty)	R.275784	RCAF	
LEE, Nelson (Montreal)	D.	Army	

LEE, Pte Oscar (Baldur, Man.)	L.109769	CIC	India
LEE, Sgt Peter (Windsor)	A.61469	RCA	England
LEE, Quan E.			
LEE, Pte Quon Kee (Charlie)	K.13483	CIC	
LEE, Maj Raymond Harry (Vancouver)		BAAG	China
LEE, Rfn (Bandsman) Robert	B.168081	QOR/CIC	CdnDef
LEE, Lieut Robert (Montreal)		COTC	
LEE, Cpl Robert W.J.	K.7836	Army	India
LEE, L/Cpl Ronald (P.Rupert)	K.7426	RCE	India
LEE, Pte S.A. (Si) (P.Rupert)	K.	Army	
LEE, Maj S. Fraser (Regina)		SSR	Europe
LEE, Pte Samuel (Montreal)	D.189647	CIC	
LEE, Stanley (Montreal)	D.	Army	
LEE, Victor (Montreal)	D.	Army	
LEE, Vincent	K.		
LEE, Wa Jil (special duty ?)		Army	
LEE, Wally Wahying (Vancouver)		Chinese Army	
LEE, Pte Walter (Victoria)	K.	Army	CdnDef
LEE, Walter (Montreal)	D.	Army	CdnDef.
LEE, Walter Pong (Vanc/Mont)	K.	RCA	
LEE, Spr Watts Duck	K.7319	RCE	India
LEE, Pte William D. (Bill)	H.27694	CIC	India
LEE, William K.			
LEE, Lieut William Youk Sin (Montreal)		COTC	
LEE, Capt Wilson (Montreal)		RCAMC	Cda/Nfd/Eng
LEE, P/O Wilson John (Kimberley)	J.50015	RCAF	CdnDef
LEE, L/Cpl Yuk	K.7617	RCE	India
LEM, George (Oshawa, Ont.)		CdnMerNav	
[same as Lam, Lim, Lum and Lin]			
LEM, LAC William Frederick	R.251549	RCAF	England
LEONG, Daniel T.Y.			
[same as Lang, Long and Leung]			
LEONG, Lt Dennis T.S.		Army	CdnDef
LEONG, WO Jackie (pilot) (Calgary)		RCAF	CdnDef
LEONG, Jack (Y.C.) (Victoria)	K.424163	RCA	
LEONG, Pte Richard Charles	K.7732	RCEME	
LEONG, Roy		Army	Overseas
LEONG, Sgt Stanley T.S.	R.189416	RCAF	CdnDef
LEUNG, Pte Paul (Victoria)	K.7492	Army	CdnDef
[same as Leong, Lang, Long or Liang]			
LEUNG, Capt So Won (Edm/Vanc)		RCAMC	CdnDef
LEW, Pte Henry	K.5176	CIC	India
[sometimes also spelt Liu]			
LEW, Sgt Robert Won (Vancouver)	K.5677	CIC	Ind/Mal
LEW, Pte Y. Kong (George)	K.10207	Army	
LIM, P/O Allen (Carleton, Ont.)		RCAF	Europe
[same as Lam, Lem, Lin (Mandarin spelling), Ling and Lum]			
LIM, Don (bro. On LIM)		COTC	
LIM, Pte Harry Bing Mon	K.16400	RCASC	Italy
LIM, Pte Harvey (Victoria)	K.	Army	CdnDef

LIM, Spr Herbert T.A.	K.7487	RCE	India
LIM, Pte John (Victoria)	K.5271	CIC	India
LIM, Pte Lillian M. (Althamer, BC)		CWAC	
LIM, Nurse Nellie (New Westminster)		BAAG	China
LIM, Tpr On Wah	K.10766	RCAC	CdnDef
LIM, Tpr Po On (Victoria)		BCD	It/Eur
LIM, Quan E.			
LIM, Sgt Shu Kwong (Victoria)	K.	Army	CdnDef
LING, Tom			
LING, William			
LOCK, Sgt George Thomas (Toronto)	B.113018	CDC/CIC	Aust
LOCKE, Pte Leong Chew	K.7334	CIC	India
LONG, Pte Chu Hoy (Charles)	K.5621	CIC	India
[see Lang, Leong, Leung]			
LONG, Gilbert			
LONG, LAC Joe (Edm/Lethb)		RCAF	
LONG, L/Cpl P.K.		Army	Overseas
LONG, Richard H.			
LORE, Capt Henry (Toronto)		RCAMC(Res)	CdnDef
LORE, Tommy (Toronto)		FC	
LORE, Lieut William K.L.	O-42700 RCN(VR) (SB)		Cda/US/SEAC/SWP/HK
- served from 1939 to 1943 with DOT; 1943 to 1969 with RCN			
LOUIE, Pte Alexander Shu Kee	K.5411	CIC	India
[also spelled Luey or Lui]			
LOUIE, Gayle			
LOUIE, Pte Henry (Vancouver)	K.1788	Army	CdnDef
LOUIE, Sgt Kim Wing (Ernie)	K.5163	CIC	Ind/Mal
LOUIE, F/O Quan Jil KIA	J.38242	RCAF	England
LOUIE, Sgt Victor Joy Ying	K.7785	CIC	Ind/Mal
LOW, Fred (same as Fred CHUN, enlisted 2x)		CIC	
LOW, Sgt Norman Mon	K.49785	CIC	Ind/Aus/Sar
LOWE, Pte Choa Sing (Harry)	K.7573	CIC	Ind/Eng
LOWE, Pte Chor (Charlie)	K.7872	CIC	CdnDef
LOWE, Pte Dave	K.11379	Army	
LOWE, Pte Edna Silaine	W.11703	CWAC	CdnDef
LOWE, Pte Frank (Victoria)	K.	Army	CDnDef
LOWE, Pte Gaye (Victoria)	K.	Army	CdnDef
LOWE, George (Victoria)	K.		
LOWE, Spr Harvey	K.5176	RCE	
LOWE, Pte (L/Cpl) Harry	K.6926	CIC	India
LOWE, Harvey (reserves Shanghai Volunteers	(US Section)		China
LOWE, Huene (reserves Shanghai Volunteers	(US Section)		China
LOWE, James (Nav)		RCAF	Afr/Eur
LOWE, John		RCAF	England
LOWE, Capt Kwong Chee (Charlie)	1046585	Army	Cda/US/Sing/HK
- served from 1939 to 1947			
LOWE, Matthew (Mike)		RCAF/USAAF	
LOWE, R. (Tagish, Y.T.)		Army	Overseas
LOWE, Sgt Raymond Young	H.71083	CIC	Ind/Aus/Man
LOWE, Pte Richard	K.	Army	

LOWE, Stanley H. (Victoria)		14th USAAF	China
LOWE, Pte Victor (Victoria	K.	Army	CdnDef
LOWE, Pte William Hong Yuen (Bill)	K.16401	RCASC	Italy
LUM, Bert	K.	RCAC(Res)	CdnDef
[also spelt Lam, Lem, Lim, and Lin]			
LUM, Pte Charles	K.7838	CIC	India
LUM, Don			
LUM, Cpl Francis Ming (Ashcroft)	K.50418	CIC	Europe
LUM, Francis Y. (Vancouver)	K.10931	Army	
LUM, Sgt Robert (Ashcroft)	R.204964	RCAF	
LUM, Thomas			
LUNG, Alex (Calgary)	M.4868	CIC	CdnDef
LUNG, Gnr Frank M. (Calgary)	M.4328	RCA	CdnDef
MA, Daniel (Toronto)	R.	RCAF/FC	
[Ma, Mah, Mar, and Marr are the same name]			
MA, Cfn James Hyma (Toronto)	B.165553	RCEME	India
MA, LAC John (Toronto)	R.256279	RCAF	Europe
MA, Joseph (Toronto)		COTC	
MAH, Capt Albert (P.Rupert)		BCATP/CNAC	Cda/China
MAH, Capt Cedric (P.Rupert)		BCATP/CNAC	Cda/China
MAH, Spr Dodson (Nanaimo)	K.7652	RCE	India
MAH, Donald Luk			
MAH, Sgm Edward	M.46082	RCCS	
MAH, Pte Eleanor		CWAC	
MAH, Pte Frank (Calgary)		Army	
MAH, Pte George (Vancouver)	K.	Army	CdnDef
MAH, Gordon (Vancouver)	K.		
MAH, Pte James F.S.	K.	Army	
MAH, Capt Kuo Lim KIA	Canton AF/Central GovAF/CNAC		China/Ind
MAH, Pte Mary Laura	W.111243	CWAC	CdnDef
MAH, Robert			
MAH, Sgt Roy Quock Quon (Vic)	K.5358	CIC	India
MAH, Pte Wally (Victoria)	K.	Army	CdnDef
MAR, Alfred			
MAR, Pte Bing Lung (Jack)	K.5503	CIC	
MAR, Pte Douglas (P.Alberni)	K.7513	RCAC	Aust
MAR, Douglas (P.Rupert) instructor		BCATP	
MAR, George		CAC	
MAR, James			
MAR, Spr Quan Dan (Wilfred)	K.5562	RCE	
MAR, Cpl Richard (Victoria)		1st Cdn Para Btn	Europe
MAR, Lieut William (Bill) (Vic.)		RCN(VR)	PacForce
MAR, L/Cpl York Soon (Gilbert)	K.7641	RCASC/CIC	India
MARHULL, Arthur	K.10581	CIC	CdnDef
MARHULL, Robert	K.7559	RCEME	CdnDef
MARR, Pte Alfred Edwin	K.	Army	
MARR, Cecil [P.Rupert]	K.	Army	
MARR, Pte George Phillip	K.7859	CIC	India
MARR [MAH], Tpr William (Bill)	K.4035	Army	CdnDef

MEE, S/Sgt Lai Sham (Sammy)	K.74279	RCAC/RCASC	England
- served from 1939 to 1946 [surname may be Lai]			
MING, Pte Ching Foo	K.7839	CIC	India
[Surname could be Foo]			
PONLAND, Frank (Calgary)	M.	Army	Overseas
[surname probably Pon]			
QUAN, Sgm Chong Loy (John)	K.7718	RCCS	India
[Quan or Quon - Sometimes spelt Kwan]			
QUAN, Bandsman Jack W.	H.		
QUAN, Pte Juy Kong (Gordie)	K.7657	CIC	India
- Master WO in reserve 1952 - 1982			
QUAN, Pte Robert Allen (Vic)	K.7861	CIC	India
QUON, Albert		OSS	China
QUON, L/Cpl.Diamond (Calgary) KIA	M.9074	RCCS	It/Eur
QUON, Herbert		OSS	China
QUON, Lyman		HKVDC/CdnMerNav	
SAM, Pte Fong Wing (Tom)	K.7454	CIC	India
[sometimes spelt Shum]			
SAM, P/O Kam Len Douglas	J.86388	RCAF	England
- served from 1942 to 1967			
SAM, Samuel (Vancouver)	K.10563	CIC	CdnDef
SETO, AC2 Robert	R.223885	RCAF	
[double character surname]			
SETO, Capt Wilfred Bing Tong	Army		CdnDef
SHEIN, Paul Kam (SIN Kam)		CdnMerNav	
SHIU, Pte Do Gay (Daniel)	K.7690	Army	India
SHIU, Sgt James	K.69286	RCE	Ind/Aus/Sara
SHIU, Sgt Joseph T.W.		RCAF	
SHUEN, George [also spelt Soon or Sun]			
SHUEN, Johnnie P.			
SHUM, Pte Randy		Army	
[see Sam above]			
SING [Chan], Charles	H.	Army	
[correct surname is CHAN Sing]			
SING [Chan], Edward	H.	Army	
SING [Chan], Pte Ernest Ornne	K.7650	RCEME/RCOC	India
SING, Tpr George Chan	K.12375	RCAC	CdnDef
SING, Jack (Calgary)			
SING [Chan], Jim L.			
SING [Chan], Wally A.	H.	Army	
SOO, Robert (Bob) (Oshawa)	B.		
SOO, Tpr William (Bill) (Oshawa)	B.135498	GGHG	It/Eur
SOON, Pte Ben		Army	
[Soon and Soone same as Shuen]			
SOON, Pte Charlie F.		Army	
SOON, Frank			
SOON, Pte Frederick Leong	K.7519	CIC	

SOONE, Cpl Harry Gaye	K.7455	RCE	
SOONG, Henry		US Navy	
[Soong same as Sung]			
SOONG, Pte Howard (Ottawa)	C.9708	CIC	
SOONG, Pte Sammy (Victoria)	K.7651	CIC	CdnDef
SUEYORK, Spr Kenneth	K.7989	RCE	CdnDef
[correct surname was Eng or Ng]			
SUNG, WO2 Donald	M.36555	MI	India
SUNG, Pte Oliver Lloyd	K.5136	Army	India
TENG, John (P.Rupert)	K.	Army	
[same as Dan, Dang, and Deng]			
THOM, Gnr Jack Edward (Nanaimo)	B.631325	RCA	
[same as Hem and Hum]			
THOM, Pte Jack Melvyn	M.600647	RCASC/CIC	CdnDef
TOM, Choy Wah (Toronto)	B.	Army	
TOY, F/L Simon (Montreal)	J.	RCAF	
[sometimes spelt Choi or Tsai]			
TSO, F/O Hong Yuen (Victoria)	J.44216	RCAF	Ind/Burma
[sometimes spelt Cho]			
WING, AC2 Frank	R.278179	RCAF	
WING (Saunders) Cpl Harry	B.133518	RCAC	
WING, AC2 James	R.172446	RCAF	
WING, Sgm JANG Yok	K.18659	RCCS	CdnDef
WON, Gnr (L/Bdr) Kin Quon	K.7664	RCA	
WON, Pte Quinton (Victoria)	K.	Army	CdnDef
WONE, Pte Allen		Army	
WONE, William (Billy) (Vancouver)	K.	Army	
WONE, L/Cpl William (Burnaby)	L.109734	CIC	India
[name sometimes Won or Wong]			
WONG, Pte Alfred (Victoria)	K.7431	RCE	India
WONG, Allen			
WONG, Andrew (Andy) (Victoria)		US MerNav	
WONG, Armand (Montreal)	D.	RCAMC	Europe
WONG, Pte Bing Chew	K.5323	CIC	PacForce
WONG, P/O Charlie (Thunder Bay)	J.95019	RCAF	Overseas
WONG, Pte Cheong Gok (Tommy)	K.4888	CIC	India
WONG, AC1 Chue Gim	R.289079	RCAF	
WONG, David (New Brunswick)		Army	
WONG, Don (Montreal)		RCAF	
WONG, Lieut Doug (Brantford)		RCN(VR)	
WONG, Nurse Elsie (New Westminster)		Hong Kong/CNAC	
WONG, Pte Ernest Bark Hong	K.7709	CIC	Aust
WONG, Pte Fong Bing (Frank)	K.45536	RCOC/RCEME	Europe
WONG, Foon			
WONG, Cpl G.T.		Army	
WONG, Pte Gein Bark	K.10566	CIC	Cda/USA
WONG, Spr George	K.7633	CIC	India
WONG, Lieut George D. (Montreal)		RCN(VR)	CdnDef

WONG, L/Cpl George Edward	A.104597	RCASC	Europe
WONG, P/O Gim Foon	J.52601	RCAF	CdnDef
WONG, L/Cpl Glen C.	K.289079	Army	
WONG, Pte Gordon	K.18461	CIC	
WONG, Gordon		RCAF	
WONG, Cpl Gordon Patrick	K.7685	CIC	India
WONG, Harry Kuo			
WONG, Pte Hastings Hong	C.78955	CIC	PacForce
WONG, Henry (Montreal)		RCAF	
WONG, Henry (Calgary)			
WONG, Sgt Henry Albert	A.50317	CIC	Aust
WONG, Howard (Gus) (Montreal)		FC	
WONG, Radio Art J.R. Marcel	V.64736	RCN(VR)	High Seas
WONG, James (P.Rupert)		Army	
WONG, Cpl James (Vancouver)	K.	Army	Overseas
WONG, Tpr James Ming (Victoria)	B.167696	RCAC	Aust
WONG, Jimmy (Montreal)		RCAF	Europe
WONG, John (Montreal)	D.		
WONG, Jonathan			
WONG, Pte Kee Mow	K.7297	CIC	India
WONG, Pte Kuo Wei (Alfred)	K.440526	BCR (Res)	
WONG, Pte Kug Him (Daniel)	K.5554	CIC	
WONG, Pte Kye Don (Winnipeg)	H.27556	RCA/RCAPC	India
WONG, Pte Larry George (Sask)	K.7986	CIC	Cda/Nfd
WONG, Pte Larry Yuen (Vanc)	K.8905	CIC	India
WONG, Lee (Calgary)			
WONG, Pte Lila	W.111494	CWAC	
WONG, S/Sgt Norman Donald	A.61714	CIC	Kiska/Aust
WONG, Pte Norman Gun (Victoria)	K.	RCE	CdnDef
WONG, Sgt On (Ted) (Vanc)	K.7425	CIC	Ind/Mal
WONG, Peter		RCAF	
WONG, Peter B.			
WONG, Pte Peter Glen	K.3311	CIC	
WONG, Peter S. (Montreal)		FC	
WONG, Pte Poon Lock (Vanc)	K.7721	CIC	India
WONG, Gnr Richard (Victoria)	K.	RCA	Overseas
WONG, Pte Robert Quoying	K.7673	RCAMC/CIC	Aust
WONG, P/O Robert Shun (instructor)		RCAF/BCATP	
WONG, Pte Seak Lou (George)	K.7719	CIC	India
WONG, Cpl Soot Yee (Sidney)	K.7682	CIC	India
WONG, Ted (Victoria)			USA
WONG, Pte Theodore	K.491704	BCR(Res)	
WONG, Thomas		RCAF	
WONG, Cpl Thomas K.	K.7680	CIC	India
WONG, Sgt Thomas Kwok Hung	R.172154	RCAF	CdnDef
WONG, Capt Tommy (Seu Kwong)		BCATP/CNAC	Cda/China
WONG, Sgt Tommy Shun (Victoria)	R.204010	RCAF	CdnDef
WONG, Pte Tom (Vic/Tor)	B.131675	WNS/C&Y	Italy
WONG, Tony		RCA	
WONG, Gnr Victor Eric (Vic)	K.7726	RCA	India

WONG, Wilbur Bruce (Montreal)		FC	
WONG, Willy (Victoria)			
WONG, Capt William Andrew		RCAMC	Cdn.Def.
WONG, William E.			
WONG, Sgt Wing Lee (Regina)	L.100443	RCCS	Aus/Man
WONG, Pte Woey (Willy)	K.5675	CIC	India
WONG, Cpl Young Ming (Vanc)	K.7767	RCASC	India
WOO, Harry S. (Montreal)	D.	RCEME	Europe
[sometimes spelt Wu]			
WOO, Ma Fay (Sask)			
WOO, Pte Marie	W.111515	CWAC	CdnDef
WOO, Pte William (Bill)	K.10443	CIC	Europe
WOO, William (Vancouver)	K.	CIC	
YEASTING, Pte Robert Willis	K.7787	CIC	India
[surname possibly was Yee]			
YEE, Pte Jack	K.18644	CIC	
YEE, Wah	K.71471		
YEE, Pte William (Willie)	B.	RCA	Europe
YEP, LAC Charles Herbert	R.187265	RCAF	
[Yep and Yip sometimes spelt Ip]			
YIP, Pte Dake Wing (Dick)	K.7853	RCA/CIC	India
YIP, Pte(L/Cpl) Dan Wing (Danny)	K.7701	CIC	
YIP, Pte Doo Tong (Dick)	K.5614	CIC	India
YIP, Tpr Kwock Fann (Danny)	L.109727	CAC	India
YIP, Pte Peter Wing	K.5292	CIC	India
YIP, Gnr Poy Wing (Steve)	K.10637	RCA	PacForce
YIP, Pte Wing See (Cecil)	K.18793	CIC	PacForce
YIP, Pte Wing Soone (Fred)	K.5290	CIC	India
YOUNG, David			
[sometimes spelt Yeung or Yang]			
YOUNG, Jack	US 39448800		
YOUNG, Pte Louie (Y.)	K.5310	CIC	India
YOUNG, Pte Wa (Victoria)	K.7963	CIC	Ind/Eng
YOUNG, Pte Wong (Phil) (Vic)	K.7964	CIC	India
YUEN, Henry (Montreal)	D.		
[one family in Vancouver spelt this name Goon]			
YUEN, A/C Hong F.		RCAF	
YUEN, Pte James Wing	K.7493	CIC	
YUEN, Pte Jan (Victoria)	K.7727	CIC	Aust.
YUEN, Gnr Robert (Montreal)	D.147175	RCA	Europe
YUEN, Simon (Montreal)	D.	RCA (Res)	Cda/US
YUEN, Willie (Montreal)		RCN	
YUN, Tee [S.E. (Sam) Yee]	L.	SSR (Res)	CdnDef
[also spelt Yin or Yan]			

Bibliography

Primary Sources
Australian Archives ACT.
   A 3269/1 Item 09 SOA Vol. 1. "History of SOA. Chapter 1. Directorate of training. Chapter XI. Personnel."
   ACT CRS A 3270 Item Vol. 1, selected pages from 38 to 66.
      CRS A 3270 Item 08 Vol. 2, *Semut III,* pp. 48 to 69.
                     Oblivion Operations (2 pages).

Australian War Memorial.
   SDRL 6201. Papers of Brig. Sir K. Willis, AIB 2 AIF, 1939-45. Item 33 Folder No. 6. Part 1, Completed Operations.
   Handwritten notes prepared by Allan Fraser, Researcher, giving nominal rolls of Special Reconnaissance Detachment (Z Special Force) AWM PR 64/119 File 419/118/30 (Archives); and File CRS A 3269 W9 (card index); and AWM PR 85/325 Items 11/1, 11/2, "Extract from 'SRD Operations'"; and "Summary of Field Operations SRD."

Canada. National Archives.
   MG 26J W.L. Mackenzie King Papers
   RG 2 Privy Council Office
   RG 24 Department of National Defence
   RG 25 Department of External Affairs
   RG 26 Department of Citizenship & Immigration
   RG 27 Department of Labour

Canada. Department of National Defence. Directorate of History.
   A.C.S.E.A. - Sundry Material.
   H.M.C.S. *Prince Robert.*
   H.M.C.S. *Crescent* (Reports of Proceedings 1949-1957) 8000
   77/267. No. 435 Squadron India/Burma.
   R S7. No. 436 Squadron India/Burma.
   Special Committee on Orientals in B.C.
   And other files cited in the notes.

United Kingdom. Foreign and Commonwealth Office.
   SOE Adviser. Selected summaries and reports.

Other Unpublished Primary Sources
Barrie, Sgt. Keith. "Some Personal & Training Background and Recollections of the Semut Operation, Borneo, 1945," 24 April 1991.
Courtney, Colonel G.B. "Five pages of Major Sochon's memoirs."
"Daily Orders Part II by Lt-Col. H.D.W. Wethey, Commanding No. 1 Special Wireless Group R.C. Sigs., CA (A), Order No. 73, 26 Nov. 45."

"Master File (Diary) of Canadian Radar Detachment on Loan to Australian Military Forces."
Penticton (R.N. Atkinson) Museum.

     Major Hugh John Legg. Interview by Major Victor Wilson, M.C., 1975.

Sochon, Major W.L.P. "Transcription of Bill Sochon's Semut Diary Entries 1945."

University of British Columbia. Special Collections. G.R. Pearkes Collection, Archives Box 16.

     F.W. Kendall. Interview by Reginald H. Roy, 16 July 1968.

     Major Roger Cheng. Interview by Reginald H. Roy, 22 Feb. 1971.

Published Works: Official

Canada. Official History of the Canadian Army in the Second World War.

   Vol. 1. Col. C.P. Stacey. *Six Years of War: the Army in Canada, Britain and the Pacific.*
Ottawa: Queen's Printer, 1955.

   Vol. 2. Lt.-Col. G.W.L. Nicholson. *The Canadians in Italy 1943-1945.* Ottawa: Queen's Printer, 1966.

   Vol. 3. Col. C.P. Stacey. *The Victory Campaign.* Ottawa: Queen's Printer, 1966.

Canada. *Statutes of Canada.* An Act Respecting Chinese Immigration, 1923, 13-14 George V, Chap. 38, pp. 301-15.

    _____. _____. An Act to Amend the Immigration Act 1947, 10 George VI, Chap. 19, pp. 283-285.

    _____. _____. An Act respecting Citizenship, Nationality, Naturalization and Status of Aliens, 1946, 10 George VI, Chap. 15, pp. 67-82.

Douglas, W.A.B. *The Creation of a National Air Force: The Official History of the Royal Canadian Air Force.* Vol. 2. Toronto: University of Toronto Press, 1986.

Feasby, Lt-Col. W.R. *Official History of the Canadian Medical Services 1939-1945.* Ottawa: Queen's Printer, 1956.

Melnyk, T.W. *Canadian Flying Operations in S.E. Asia 1941-45.* Ottawa: Minister of Supply and Services, 1976.

Schull, Joseph. *The Far Distant Ships: An Official Account of Canadian Naval Operations in the Second World War.* Ottawa: King's Printer, 1950.

Stacey, Col. C.P. *Arms, Men and Governments: The War Policies of Canada 1939-1945.* Ottawa: Queen's Printer, 1970.

    _____. *The Canadian Army 1939-1945: An Official Historical Summary.* Ottawa: King's Printer, 1948.

Tucker, Gilbert Norman. *The Naval Service of Canada: Its Official History.* 2 vols. Ottawa: King's Printer, 1952.

Books and Articles

Adachi, Ken. *The Enemy that Never Was: an Account of the Deplorable Treatment Inflicted on Japanese Canadians during World War Two.* Toronto: McClelland and Stewart, 1979.

Allen, Louis. *Burma: The Longest War 1941-45.* London: J.M. Dent & Sons Ltd., 1984.

Andrew, Christopher. *Her Majesty's Secret Service: The Making of the British Intelligence Community.* New York: Viking, 1986.

Baker, A.D. *Merrill's Marauders.* New York: Ballentine Books, 1972.

Barber, Noel. *Sinister Twilight: The Fall of Singapore.* London: Arrow, 1988.

    _____. *War of the Running Dogs.* London: Arrow, 1989.

Barker, A. J. *Yamashita.* New York: Ballantine Books Inc., 1973.

Beesly, Patrick. *Very Special Intelligence: The Story of the Admiralty's Operational Intelligence Centre 1939-45.* London: Hamish Hamilton, 1977.

Bosanquet, David. *Escape through China: Survival after the Fall of Hong Kong.* London: Robert Hale, 1983.

Bowyer, Michael J.F. *2 Group R.A.F.: A Complete History, 1936-1945*. London: Faber & Faber, 1974.

Bowman, Phyllis. *We Skirted the War*. pp, 1975.

Brickhill, Paul. *The Dam Busters*. London: Pan Books Ltd., 1969.

Broadfoot, Barry. *Six War Years 1939-1945: Memories of Canadians at Home and Abroad*. Toronto: PaperJacks Ltd., 1976.

Browning, Christopher R. *Ordinary Men: Reserve Police Battalion 101 and the Final Solution in Poland*. New York: Harper Perennial, 1993.

Bruce, Phillip. *Second to None: the Story of the Hong Kong Volunteers*. Hong Kong: Oxford University Press, 1991.

Bryden, John. *Best-kept Secret: Canadian Secret Intelligence in the Second World War*. Toronto: Lester Publishing, 1993.

_____. *Deadly Allies: Canada's Secret War 1937-1947*. Toronto: McClelland & Stewart, 1989.

Calvert, Michael. *Prisoners of Hope*. London: Jonathan Cape, 1971.

_____. *Slim*. New York: Ballantine Books Inc., 1973.

Calvocoressi, Peter, and Guy Wint. *Total War: Causes and Courses of the Second World War*. 2 ed. New York: Pantheon, 1989.

Cambon, Kenneth, M.D. *Guest of Hirohito*. Vancouver: PW Press, 1990.

Canada. Veterans Affairs. *Uncommon Courage: Canadian Secret Agents in the Second World War*. Ottawa: Veterans Affairs Canada, 1985.

Canucks Unlimited: the Record in Story and Picture of the History, Life and Experiences of the Men of 436 R.C.A.F. Squadron, India, Burma 1944-1945. Toronto: pp, nd.

Cederberg, Fred. *The Long Road Home: The Autobiography of a Canadian Soldier in Italy in World War II*. Toronto: General Paperbacks, 1989.

Churchill, Winston S. *The Second World War*. 6 vols. Cambridge, Mass.: Houghton Mifflin, 1948-1953.

Commonwealth Air Training Plan Museum. *They Shall Grow not Old: a Book of Remembrance*. Brandon, Man.: 1992.

Con, Harry, Ronald J. Con, Graham Johnson, Edgar Wickberg. *From China to Canada: a History of the Chinese Communities in Canada*. ed. by Edgar Wickberg. Toronto: McClelland & Stewart, 1982.

Conrod, Hugh. *Athene (Goddess of War) The Canadian Women's Army Corps (Their Story)*. Dartmouth, NS: Writing & Editorial Services, 1983.

Copp, Terry and Robert Vogel. Maple Leaf Route. *Caen*. Alma, Ont.: MLR, 1983.

_____. _____. *Falaise*. Alma, Ont.: MLR, 1983.

_____. _____. *Antwerp*. Alma, Ont.: MLR, 1984.

_____. _____. *Scheldt*. Alma, Ont.: MLR, 1985.

_____. _____. *Victory*. Alma, Ont.: MLR, 1988.

Cruickshank, Charles. *SOE in the Far East*. Oxford: Oxford University Press, 1986.

Curtis, Lettice. *The Forgotten Pilots: A Story of the Air Transport Auxiliary 1939-45*. 2nd ed. Olney, Bucks.: Nelson & Saunders Ltd., 1985.

Dancocks, Daniel G. *The D-Day Dodgers: The Canadians in Italy, 1943-1945*. Toronto: McClelland and Stewart, 1991.

_____. *In Enemy Hands: Canadian Prisoners of War 1939-45*. Toronto: M&S Paperback, 1990

_____. *Welcome to Flanders Fields: The First Canadian Battle of the Great War: Ypres, 1915*. Toronto: McClelland and Stewart, 1988.

Davidson, Basil. *Special Operations Europe: Scenes from the Anti-Nazi War*. London: Grafton Books, 1987.

Dawson, R. MacGregor. *The Conscription Crisis of 1944*. Toronto: University of Toronto Press, 1961.

Deacon, Richard. *A History of British Secret Service*. London: Grafton Books, 1980.

D'Este, Carlo. *Decision in Normandy*. New York: Harper Perennial, 1991.

Douglas, W.A.B., and Brereton Greenhaus. *Out of the Shadows: Canada in the Second World War*. Toronto: Oxford University Press, 1977.

Dunlap, Air Marshal C.R. "Memories of 139 Wing." *High Flight*. Vol. 2, No. 5, Sept/Oct. 82: 189-200.

_____. "Noballs." *Airforce*. Vol. 14, No. 2, Jul/Aug/Sept. 1990: 8-10.

Edwards, Jack. *Banzai you Bastards*. Hong Kong: Corporate Communications, 1990.

Elliot, S.R. *Scarlet to Green: A History of Intelligence in the Canadian Army 1903-1963*. Toronto: Canadian Intelligence and Security Association, 1981.

Ellis, John. *Brute Force: Allied Strategy and Tactics in the Second World War*. New York: Viking, 1990.

Embry, Sir Basil. *Mission Completed*. London: White Lion Publishing, 1976.

Falconer, D. Wilf. *Battery Flashes of World War II: A Thumb-nail sketch of Canadian Artillery Batteries during the 1939-1945 Conflict*. np, 1984.

Faraguna, Debra. "Commando Bay." *Okanagan Historical Society Forty-first Report*. November 1, 1977: 85-89.

Fergusson, Bernard. *Beyond the Chindwin*. London: Fontana, 1955.

_____. *The Watery Maze: The Story of Combined Operations*. London: Collins, 1961.

Foot, M.R.D. *SOE in France: An Account of the Work of the British Special Operations Executive in France 1940-1944*. London: HMS Office, 1966.

_____. *SOE: An Outline History of the Special Operations Executive 1940-46*. London: British Broadcasting Corporation, 1984.

Foot, M.R.D. and J.M. Langley. *MI9: The British Secret Service that Fostered Escape and Evasion 1939-1945 and its American Counterpart*. London: Bodley Head, 1979.

Frost, C. Sydney. *Once a Patricia (Memoirs of a Junior Infantry Officer in World War II)*. St. Catharines, Ont.: Vanwell Publishing Limited, 1988.

Galloway, Strome. *Bravely into Battle: the Autobiography of a Canadian Soldier in World War Two [The General who Never Was]*. Toronto: Stoddart, 1986.

Garfield, Brian. *The Thousand-Mile War: World War II in Alaska and the Aleutians*. New York: Nelson Doubleday, Inc., 1983.

German, Commander Tony. *The Sea is at Our Gates: the History of the Canadian Navy*. Toronto: McClelland & Stewart, 1991.

Gilbert, Martin. *Road to Victory: Winston S. Churchill 1941-1945*. Toronto: Stoddart, 1986.

Granatstein, J.L. *The Generals: The Canadian Army's Senior Commanders in the Second World War*. Toronto: Stoddart, 1993.

_____. *Nation Forged in Fire: Canadians and the Second World War 1939-1945*. Toronto: Lester & Orpen Dennys, 1989.

Griffiths-Marsh, Roland. *The Sixpenny Soldier*. North Ryde: Angus & Robertson, 1990.

Gwynne-Timothy, John R.W. *Burma Liberators: RCAF in SEAC*. 2 vols. Toronto: Next Level Press, 1991.

Harris, Marshal of the R.A.F. Sir Arthur. *Bomber Offensive*. Toronto: Stoddart, 1990.

Hastings, Max. *Bomber Command*. New York: The Dial Press/James Wade, 1979.

Horton, D.C. *Ring of Fire: Australian Guerrilla Operations against the Japanese in World War II*. London: Secker & Warburg, 1983.

Howarth, David. *The Shetland Bus*. London: Thomas Nelson and Sons Ltd., 1951.

Hyatt, A.M.J. *General Sir Arthur Currie: a Military Biography*. Toronto: University of Toronto Press, 1987.

Hyde, H. Montgomery. *The Quiet Canadian: The Secret Service Story of Sir William Stephenson*. London: Hamish Hamilton, 1962.
  Also published under the title, *Room 3603*. New York: Dell, 1964.
  _____. *Secret Intelligence Agent: British Espionage in America and the Creation of the OSS*. New York: St. Martins, 1983.

Ind, Colonel Allison. *Allied Intelligence Bureau*. New York: David McKay Company, Inc., 1958.

Infield, Glenn B. *Disaster at Bari*. New York: Macmillan Company, 1971.

Irving, David. *Churchill's War*. New York: Avon Books, 1991.
  _____. *Hitler's War*. New York: Avon Books, 1990.

Ito, Roy. *We Went to War: The Story of the Japanese Canadians who Served during the First and Second World Wars*. Stittsville: Canada's Wings, 1984

Jack, Ronald. "C.L.C. Headdress and Cap Badge with Notes for Collectors." *Military Collectors' Club of Canada*. Spring 1988: 16-18.
  _____. "Awards to the Chinese Labour Corps, B.E.F." *Military Collectors' Club of Canada*. Winter 1987: 143-145.

Keenleyside, Hugh L. *Memoirs of Hugh L. Keenleyside*.
  Vol. I. *Hammer the Golden Day*. Toronto: McClelland and Stewart, 1981.
  Vol. 2. *On the Bridge of Time*. Toronto: McClelland and Stewart, 1982.

Keith, Agnes Newton. *Three Came Home*. Boston: Little, Brown, and Company, 1947.

Kinvig, Clifford. *Death Railway*. New York: Ballantine Books Inc., 1973.

Kirby, S. Woodburn. *Singapore: The Chain of Disaster*. London: Cassell, 1971.

Kostenuk, Samuel and John Griffin. *RCAF: Squadron Histories and Aircraft 1924-1968*. Toronto: Samuel Stevens Hakkert & Company, 1977.

Ladd, James and Keith Melton. *Clandestine Warfare: Weapons and Equipment of the SOE and OSS*. London: Blandford Press, 1988.

Lai, David Chuenyan. *Chinatowns: Towns within Cities in Canada*. Vancouver: University of British Columbia Press, 1988.

Lamb, Richard. *Montgomery in Europe: Success or Failure?* London: Buchan & Enright, 1984.

Lane, Tony. *The Merchant Seamen's War*. Manchester University Press, 1990.

Langer, William L., comp. and ed. *An Encyclopedia of World History*. rev. ed. Cambridge, Mass.: Houghton, Mifflin Company, 1952.

Laqueur, Walter. *The Terrible Secret: an Investigation into the Suppression of Information about Hitler's Final Solution*. London: Weidenfeld and Nicolson, 1980.

Leary, William M., Jr. *The Dragon's Wings: The China National Aviation Corporation and the Development of Commercial Aviation in China*. Athens, GA: University of Georgia Press, 1970.

Leasor, James. "The Man who Kept Hong Kong British." The *Telegraph: Sunday Magazine*. 12 August 1984.

Lee, Carol F. "The Road to Enfranchisement: Chinese and Japanese in British Columbia." *BC Studies* No. 30, Summer 1976: 44-76.

Li, Peter S. *The Chinese in Canada*. Toronto: Oxford University Press, 1988.

Liddell Hart, B.H. *History of the First World War*. London: Papermac, 1992.
  _____. *History of the Second World War*. London: Papermac, 1992.

Lindsay, Oliver. *At the Going Down of the Sun: Hong Kong and South-East Asia 1941-45*. London: Hamish Hamilton, 1981.
  _____. *The Lasting Honour: the Fall of Hong Kong, 1941*. London: Hamish Hamilton, 1978.

Long, Bob. *'Z' Special Unit's Secret War: Operation Semut I. Soldiering with the head-hunters of Borneo*. Maryborough: pp, 1989.

Long, Gavin. *The Six Years War: A Concise History of Australia in the 1939-45 War.* Canberra: Australian War Memorial, 1973.

Lorain, Pierre. *Clandestine Operations: The Arms and Techniques of the Resistance 1941-1944.* Adapted by David Kahn. New York: Macmillan Publishing Company, 1983.

Lynch, Capt. J.A.M. *Orion: Mighty Warrier.* Toronto: Lugus Publications, 1993.

Lynch, Capt. J.A.M., ed. *Salty Dips.* Vols. 1-4. Naval Officers Association of Canada, 1983-85-88-93.

MacDonald, Malcolm. *Borneo People.* Singapore: Oxford University Press, 1985.

MacLaren, Roy. *Canadians Behind Enemy Lines, 1939-1945.* Vancouver: University of British Columbia Press, 1981.

Malone, Colonel R.S. *Missing from the Record.* Toronto: Collins, 1946.

Manchester, William. *American Caesar: Douglas MacArthur 1880-1964.* Boston: Little, Brown and Company, 1978.

_____. *The Arms of Krupp: 1587-1968.* np: Bantam, 1973.

Maule, Henry. *Caen: The Brutal Battle and Breakout from Normandy.* Newton Abbot, Devon: David & Charles, 1988.

McKee, Fraser M. "Princes Three: Canada's Use of Armed Merchant Cruisers during World War II." *RCN in Retrospect 1910-1968.* James A. Boutilier, ed., pp. 117-137. Vancouver: University of British Columbia Press, 1982.

McKee, Ronald. *The Heroes.* Sydney: Angus and Robertson, 1960.

McVicar, Don. *A Change of Wings.* Shrewsbury, England: Airlife Publishing Ltd., 1984.

_____. *Ferry Command.* Shrewsbury, England: Airlife Publishing Ltd., 1981.

_____. *North Atlantic Cat.* Shrewsbury, England: Airlife Publishing Ltd., 1983.

Merrick, K.A. *Flights of the Forgotten: Special Duties Operations in World War Two.* London: Army and Armour, 1989.

Messenger, Charles. *'Bomber' Harris and the Strategic Bombing Offensive, 1939-1945.* London: Arms and Armour Press, 1984.

Middlebrook, Martin. *Berlin Raids: RAF Bomber Command Winter, 1943-44.* London: Penguin, 1990.

_____. *Nuremberg Raid 30-31 March 1944.* Harmondsworth, Middlesex: Penguin, 1986.

_____. *The Peenemunde Raid: The Night of 17/18 August 1943.* London: Penguin, 1988.

Middlebrook, Martin and Chris Everitt. *The Bomber Command War Diaries: An Operational Reference Book: 1939-1945.* London: Penguin, 1990.

Moffitt, Athol. *Project Kingfisher.* North Ryde, NSW: Angus & Robertson, 1989.

Moir, John S., ed. *History of the Royal Canadian Corps of Signals 1903-1961.* Ottawa: RCCS, 1962.

Morton, Desmond. *A Military History of Canada.* Edmonton: Hurtig Publishers, 1990.

Morton, James W. *In the Sea of Sterile Mountains: The Chinese in British Columbia.* Vancouver: J.J. Douglas Ltd., 1977.

Mowat, Farley. *And No Birds Sang.* Toronto: McClelland and Stewart, 1979.

Neave, Airey. *Nuremberg: A personal record of the trial of the major Nazi war criminals in 1945-46.* London: Grafton Books, 1989.

_____. *Saturday at M.I.9.* London: Grafton Books, 1969.

Nicholson, G.W.L. *Gunners of Canada: the History of the Royal Regiment of Canadian Artillery.* Vol. 2. Toronto: McClelland & Stewart, 1972.

_____. *Seventy Years of Service: a History of the Royal Canadian Army Medical Corps.* Ottawa: Borealis Press, 1977.

Nolan, Brian. *King's War: Mackenzie King and the Politics of War 1939-1945.* Toronto: Random House, 1989.

O'Brien, Terence. *The Moonlight War: The Story of Clandestine Operations in South-East Asia, 1944-5.* London: Collins, 1987.

Oranje, Vincent. *Coningham: a Biography of Air Marshal Sir Arthur Coningham, KCB, KBE, DSO, MC, DFC, AFC*. London: Methuen, 1990.

Overy, R.J. *The Air War 1939-1945*. New York; Stein & Day, 1981.

Palmer, Howard. *Patterns of Prejudice: A History of Nativism in Alberta*. Toronto: McClelland & Stewart, 1985.

Peden, Murray. *A Thousand Shall Fall*. Toronto: Stoddart, 1988.

Percival, Lieut-Gen. A.E. *The War in Malaya*. London: Eyre & Spottiswoode, 1949.

Powell, Alan. *The Shadow's Edge: Australia's Northern War*. Melbourne University Press, 1988.

Powell, Griffith. *Ferryman*. Shrewsbury, England: Airlife Publishing Ltd., 1982.

Purcell, Victor. *The Chinese in Malaya*. London: Oxford University Press, 1945.

The RCAF Overseas: The First Four Years. With an Introduction by C.G. Power. Toronto: Oxford University Press, 1944.

Richards, Denis. *Portal of Hungerford: the Life of Marshal of the Royal Air Force, Viscount Portal of Hungerford KG, GCB, DAT, DSO, MC*. London: Heinemann, 1978.

Ride, Edwin. *BAAG: Hong Kong Resistance 1942-1945*. Oxford University Press, 1981.

Robertson, John. *Australia at War 1939-1945*. Melbourne: Heinemann, 1981.

Robertson, Terence. *The Shame and the Glory: Dieppe*. Toronto: McClelland and Stewart, 1962.

Roosevelt, Kermit. *War Report of the OSS (Office of Strategic Services)*. New York: Walker and Company, 1976.

Roy, Patricia E.. "The Soldiers Canada Didn't Want: Her Chinese and Japanese Citizens." *Canadian Historical Review*. LIX, 3, 1978: 342-358.

Roy, Patricia, J.L. Granatstein, Masako Iino, Kiroko Takamura. *Mutual Hostages: Canadians and Japanese during the Second World War*. Toronto: University of Toronto Press, 1990.

Roy, Reginald H.. *For Most Conspicuous Bravery: A Biography of Major-General George R. Pearkes, V.C., through Two World Wars*. Vancouver: University of British Columbia Press, 1977.

Royal Canadian Corps of Signals. *Souvenir Booklet 1944-1945*. No. 1 Canadian Special Wireless Group, nd.

Ruck, Calvin W. *The Black Battalion: 1916-1920: Canada's best kept Military Secret*. Halifax: Nimbus Publishing Limited, 1987.

Runciman, Steven. *The White Rajahs: A History of Sarawak from 1841 to 1946*. Cambridge at the University Press, 1960.

Russell, Edward F. L. (Lord of Liverpool). *The Knights of Bushido: A Short History of Japanese War Crimes*. London: Cassell & Company Ltd., 1958.

_____. *The Scourge of the Swastika*. London: Corgi Books, 1966.

Ryan, Cornelius. *A Bridge Too Far*. New York: Simon and Schuster, 1974.

_____. *The Last Battle*. New York: Simon and Schuster, 1966.

_____. *The Longest Day June 6, 1944*. New York: Pocket Books, 1967.

[Saunders, Hilary St. George]. *Combined Operations: The Official story of the Commandos*. New York: The Macmillan Company, 1943.

Schaller, Michael. *Douglas MacArthur: the Far Eastern General*. New York: Oxford University Press, 1990.

Shirer, William. *The Rise and Fall of the Third Reich*. New York: Simon and Schuster, 1960.

Schultz, Duane. *Maverick War: Chennault and the Flying Tigers*. New York: St. Martin's Press, 1990.

Slim, Field Marshall the Viscount. *Defeat into Victory*. New York: David McKay Company, 1961.

Smith, E.D. *Battle for Casino.* Newton Abbot, Devon: David & Charles, 1989.

Smith, Peter C. *Task Force 57: The British Pacific Fleet 1944-1945.* London: William Kimber, 1969.

Smith, R. Harris. *OSS: The Secret History of America's First Central Intelligence Agency.* Berkeley: University of California Press, 1972.

Somerville, Donald. *World War II Day by Day.* London: Bison, 1989.

Speer, Albert. *Inside the Third Reich: Memoirs.* New York: Collier Books, 1981.

Spencer Chapman, Frederick. *The Jungle is Neutral.* London: Chatto & Windus, 1963.

Stafford, David. *Camp X: Canada's School for Secret Agents, 1941-45.* Toronto: Lester & Orpen Dennys, 1986.
    Also published by General Paperbacks, 1987 (contains interview with Jack Clayton).

Stanley, George F.G. *Canada's Soldiers: The Military History of an Unmilitary People.* Rev. Ed. Toronto: The MacMillan Company, 1960.

Stevenson, William. *A Man called Intrepid: The Secret War.* New York: Harcourt Brace Jovanovich, 1976.

Sweet-Escott, Bickham. *Baker Street Irregular.* London: Methuen & Co. Ltd., 1965.

Tan, Jin and Patricia E. Roy. *The Chinese in Canada.* Ottawa: Canadian Historical Association, 1985. Booklet No. 9 in Canada's Ethnic Groups.

Tancock, Elizabeth. "Secret Trains Across Canada 1917-1918." *Military Collectors Club of Canada.* Summer 1992: 66-71.

Taylor, Telford. *The Anatomy of the Nuremberg Trials.* New York: Alfred A. Knopf, 1992.

Trenowden, Ian. *Operations Most Secret: SOE: The Malayan Theatre.* London: William Kimber, 1978.

Tuchman, Barbara. *Stilwell and the American Experience in China 1911-45.* Toronto: Bantam Books, 1989.

Tunner, William H. *Over the Hump.* New York: Duell, Sloan & Pearce, 1964.

van der Vat, Dan. *The Atlantic Campaign: World War II's Great Struggle at Sea.* New York: Harper & Row, 1988.

Villa, Brian Loring. *Unauthorized Action: Mountbatten and the Dieppe Riad.* Toronto: Oxford University Press, 1989.

Walker, James W. St.G. "Race and Recruitment in World War I: Enlistment of Visible Minorities in the Canadian Expeditionary Force." *Canadian Historical Review.* LXX, No. 1, March 1989: 1-26.

Wall, Don. *Sandakan under Nippon: the Last March.* rev. ed. pp, 1989.

Wang, Gungwu, ed. *Malaysia: A Survey.* New York: Frederick A. Praeger, 1964.

Ward, G. Kingsley. *Courage Remembered . . . Military Cemeteries and Memorials of the Wars of 1914-1918 and 1939-1945.* Toronto: McClelland & Stewart, 1989.

Warren, Arnold. *Wait for the Wagon: The Story of the Royal Canadian Army Service Corps.* Toronto: McClelland and Stewart, 1961.

Waterman, Angeline. "Commando Bay Reunion." *The Fifty-Third Report of the Okanagan Historical Society.* 1989: 19-24.

Watt, Commander Frederick B. *In All Respects Ready: The Merchant Navy and the Battle of the Atlantic, 1940-1945.* Toronto: Totem, 1987.

Wedemeyer, Albert A. *Wedemeyer Reports.* New York: Henry Holt & Company, 1958.

Whitaker, W. Denis and Shelagh Whitaker. *Rhineland: the Battle to End the War.* Toronto: Stoddart, 1989.

_____. *Tug of War: the Canadian Victory that Opened Antwerp.* Toronto: Stoddart, 1987.

Wills, Archie. "Chinese coolies built CPR and defences for Canadians." *The Islander.* [Vancouver Island] nd, p. 8.

Winterbotham, F.W. *The Ultra Secret.* New York: Harper & Row, 1974.

Ziegler, Philip. *Mountbatten: a Biography*. New York: Alfred A. Knopf, 1985.
_____, ed. *Personal Diary of Admiral, the Lord Louis Mountbatten, Supreme Allied
    Commander South East Asia, 1943-1946*. London: Collins, 1988.

Regimental Histories

Baylay, George Taylor, ed. *The Regimental History of the Governor General's Foot Guards*.
    Ottawa: pp, 1948.
Barnard, Lt-Col. W.T. *Queen's Own Rifles of Canada 1869-1960*. Don Mills: Ontario
    Publishing Co., 1960
Barrett, Lt. W.W. *The History of the 13 Canadian Field Regiment, Royal Canadian Artillery,
    1940-1945*. np, nd.
Beattie, Kim. *Dileas: History of the 48th Highlanders of Canada 1929-1956*. Toronto: The 48th
    Highlanders of Canada, 1957.
Bird, Will. *No Retreating Footsteps: the Story of the North Nova Scotia Highlanders*. Kentville,
    NS: Kentville Pub., 1954.
_____. *North Shore (New Brunswick) Regiment*. Fredericton, NB: Brunswick Press, 1963.
Boissonnault, Charles-Marie. *Histoire de Royal 22e Regiment*. Quebec, PQ: Editions du peli-
    can, 1964.
Brown, Kingsley, Sr. and Jr. and Brereton Greenhaus. *Semper Paratus: the History of the Royal
    Hamilton Light Infantry*. Hamilton, Ont: RHLI Hist. Assn., 1977.
Buchanan, Lt-Col. G.B., M.B.E. *The March of the Prairie Men; A Story of the South
    Saskatchewan Regiment*. Weyburn, Sask., pp, [1957].
Burhans, R.D. *The First Special Service Force: A War History of the North Americans, 1942-
    1944*. Washington: Infantry Journal Press, 1947.
Cassidy, Major George L. *Warpath: The Story of the Algonquin Regiment 1939-1945*. Toronto:
    Ryerson Press, 1948.
Castonguay, Jacques. *Les Bataillons et le Dépôt du Royal 22e Régiment: Vingt ans d'histoire
    1945-1965*. Quebec: Réie du Royal 22e Régiment, 1974.
Chambers, Ernest John. *Governor General's Horse Guards: The Governor General's Body
    Guard*. Toronto: Canadian Military Journal [1953].
Churchin, Leonard A. and Brian D. Sim. *The Elgins: the Story of the Elgin Regiment (RCAC)
    and its Predecessors*. St. Thomas, Ont.: np, 1977.
Conron, A. Brandon, ed. *A History of the First Hussars Regiment, 1856-1980*. London, Ont.:
    pp, 1981.
Corfield, William E. *Citizen Soldiers (Canadian Fusiliers, City of London Regiment, Oxford
    Rifles 1798-1953, Perth Regiment 1866-1964, 4th Battalion RCR (London & Oxford
    Fusiliers)*. London: RCE, 1983.
Duguid, Col. Archer Fortescue. *History of the Canadian Grenadier Guards, 1760-1964*.
    Montreal: Gazette Printing Co., 1965.
Farran, Major Roy, M.C. *The History of the Calgary Highlanders 1921-54*. np: Bryant Press
    Ltd., nd.
Fetherstonhaugh, R.C. *The Royal Montreal Regiment 1925-1945*. Westmount, Que.: pp, 1979.
Galloway, Strome. *A Regiment at War: The Story of the Royal Canadian Regiment 1939-1945*.
    (First published in 1946 under the title, "55 AXIS"). np, nd.
Greenhaus, Brereton. *Dragoon: the Centennial History of the Royal Canadian Dragoons, 1883-
    1983*. Ottawa: Guild of the RCD, 1983.
Harker, Douglas E. *The Story of the British Columbia Regiment 1939-1945*. Vancouver: pp,
    1950.
_____. *The Dukes: The Story of the Men who have Served in Peace and War with the
    British Columbia Regiment (D.C.O.) 1883-1973*. [Vancouver]: The British Columbia
    Regiment (D.C.O.), 1974.

Hayes, Geoffrey William. *The Friction of War: a Study of the Lincoln and Welland Regiment 1940-1945*. Master's thesis, Wilfred Laurier University, 1985.

Hutchison, Colonel Paul F., ed. *Canada's Black Watch: The First 100 Years (1862-1962)*. Don Mills: Black Watch (RHR) of Canada, 1962.

Jackson, H.M., ed. *Argyll and Sutherland Highlanders of Canada (Princess Louise's) 1928-1953*. Montreal: pp, 1953.

_____. *The Princess Louise Dragoon Guards: A History*. np: [1951].

Johnston, Stanford. *The Fighting Perths . . .* Stratford, Ont.: pp, 1964.

Lamontagne, Leopold. *Les Archives Regimentaires de Fusiliers du St. Laurent*. pp, nd.

McAvity, J.M. *Lord Strathcona's Horse (Royal Canadians): A Record of Achievement*. Toronto: pp, 1947.

[Meanwell, R.W.] *1 Battalion The Essex Scottish Regiment 1939-1945*. Aldershot, England: Wellington Press, 1946.

Mowat, Farley. *The Regiment*. Toronto: M&S Paperback, 1989.

Paterson, Major R.A. *A History of the 10th Canadian Infantry Brigade*. np: 1945.

Quigley, John Gordon. *A Century of Rifles, 1860-1960: The Halifax Rifles (RCAC) (M) . . .* Halifax: pp, 1960.

Raddall, Thomas H. *The West Novas; A History. . .* Liverpool, NS: pp, 1947.

Rogers, Major R.L. *History of the Lincoln and Welland Regiment*. St. Catharines, Ont.: The Regiment, 1954.

Ross, Major Armand, DSO and Major Michel Gauvin, DSO. *Le Geste du regiment du la Chaudiere*. Levis, Que: The Regiment, 1968.

Ross, Lt-Col. W., CD. *The Stormont, Dundas and Glengarry Highlanders (1783-1951)*. Ottawa: Runge Press, 1952.

Ross, Lieut-Col. Richard M. *The History of the 1st Battalion Cameron Highlanders of Ottawa (M.G.)*. Ottawa: The Regiment, 1946.

Roy, Reginald H. *Seaforth Highlanders of Canada 1919-1965*. Vancouver: pp, 1969.

_____. *Sinews of Steel: History of the British Columbia Dragoons*. Brampton, Ont.: pp, 1965.

_____. *Ready for the Fray: History of the Canadian Scottish Regiment (Princess Mary's) 1920-1955*. Vancouver: Evergreen, 1958.

Ruffee, G.E.M. and J.B. Dickie. *History of the 14th Field Regiment RCA 1940-1945*. Amsterdam: Wereldbibliotheck N.V., 1945.

Smith, Kenneth B. *Duffy's Regiment: A History of the Hastings and Prince Edward Regiment*. Toronto: Dundurn Press, 1987.

Stanley, George. *In the Face of Danger: The History of the Lake Superior Regiment*. Port Arthur, Ont: The Regiment, 1960.

Stevens, G.R. *A City Goes to War*. np: 1964.

Tascona, Bruce, and Eric Wellslo. *Little Black Devils: A History of the Royal Winnipeg Rifles*. Winnipeg: Frye Pub., 1983.

Tooley, Robert. *Invicta: The Carleton and York Regiment in the Second World War*. Fredericton, NB: New Ireland Press, 1989.

Willes, John A. *Out of the Clouds: The History of the 1st Canadian Parachute Battalion*. Kingston, Ont.: pp, 1981.

Williams, Jeffery. *Princess Patricia's Canadian Light Infantry*. London: Leo Cooper, 1972.

Wood, Gordon. *Story of the Irish Regiment of Canada 1939-1945*. Heirenveen, Neth.: pp, 1945.

Worthington, Larry. *The Spur and the Sprocket: The Story of the Royal Canadian Dragoons*. Kitchener, Ont.: Reeve Press, 1968.

INDEX

Bold page numbers indicate a photograph or document.

Abu bin Kassim, Sgt, 192, **194,** 196, 198, 199, 200, 201, 207, 208, 209
Acknowledgment, **135,** 137, 147
Advanced Operations School, Trincomalee, 154
Air Transport Auxiliary, ATA, 54-8
    Ferry Pilots Pools, 57-8
    Maintenance Units, 54, 57-8
Airborne Cigar (ABC), 32
AIRCRAFT;
    Anson, 49. 50, 51, 53; Austers, 191; US B-17s, 36; Beaufighters, 40-1; Blenheims, 40, 41; Boston, 42, 44, 55, 58, 191; Catalina, 41, 55, 58, 115, 162, 199, 200, 203, 205, 207-9, 213-4; Consolidated Canso, 50; Consolidated Catalina, 50; Cornell, 50; Dakota, 27, 53, 55, 115-6, 156; Dakota C-46 Commando Transports, 20; Douglas Dakotas, DC-3, 20, 27; C-47, 55; Flying Fortresses, 41, 53, 55, 84; Halifax, 40; Halifax III, 38; Halifax III A, 39; Halifax VI, 55; Hampdens, 55; Harvard, 49; Hudsons, 41, 55, 115; Hurricanes, 31; Junkers Ju88 fighter bomber, 83; Lancasters, 32-6, 55; Liberator AL504, 57; Liberator squadrons, 179; Liberators, 29, 41, 53, 55, 57, *passim;* Lockheed Hudsons, 54; Lockheed L-1011, 88; Lysander, 115; Marauders, 55; B-25 Mitchell, 41-3, **44,** 47, 55, 58; Mosquitoes, 34-7, 40, 42, 47, 55, 205; Mustangs, 36, 40; PBY Catalina, 58; P-40 Kittyhawk, 21; Kitty, 207; P-40 Tomahawk, 21; P-40 Warhawk, 21; Short Sunderland, 58; Spitfire, 31, 40, 41, 42, 84, 200; Stirling, 34, 115; Sunderlands, 41; Supermarine Stranraer, 50; Typhoons, 41; Ventura, 42, 55; Vickers Wellingtons, 37; Waco glider, 55; Wellingtons, 34, 37, 41; Whitley, 115
Akyab Island, Burma, 27, 29, 30
Alacrity Achorage, 66
Alam Bazaar, India, 139, 154
Albert Canal, Bel, 84
Alberta Provincial Rifle Association, 101
Aldershot, Eng, 82, 86, 92, 97, 101, 148
Aldershot, NS, 97
Alençon, Fr, 33
Aleutians, 78, 128
Alexander, Lt.-Col. D.R., 164
Algonquin Regiment, 92
Alien and Aliens, 9, 19, 60, 68, 71, 73, 74, 75, 76, 77, 78, 80, 106, 107, 114, 146, 219; Allied alien, 9, 19, 74, 77, 78, 79, 80, 146, 217; Enemy alien, 71, 74; Neutral alien, 74; Registered Aliens, 77
Allied Intelligence Bureau (AIB), 114, 115, 118, 144

Allan, Col. Hugh, 123
Alliford Bay, BC, 50
Alor Star, Kedah, 174
American Volunteer Group, AVG, 21, 22
Amnesty, 66
Ampang Gombak, Selangor, 166
Ancona War Cemetery, Italy, 91
Angers, Fr, 37
Ansalam, Sara, 192
Anticosti Island, 60
Anti-Comintern Pact, 89
Anti-Japanese Union and Forces, 161
Antwerp, Bel, 47, 96
Antwerp-Turnhout Canal, 91
Anup, Sara, 207, 209
Arakan, Burma, 27
Ardennes offensive, 35, 87, 89
Armstrong, Brigadier, 150
Army, Navy, and Air Force Veterans in Canada, 2, 91
Army Examiner's Report, 9
Arnhem, Neth, 47, 87, 90, 94
Aro, Vic, 39
Assan, Sara, 205, 207, 208, 209; Ulu Assan, 205
Astill, Capt. R.A., 200, 201, 209
Atlantic Charter, 216
Atlantic Ferry Organization, ATFERO, 54; see Ferry Command
Atomic bombs, 62, 164, 183, 184, 204
ATR4 wireless set, 192, 196, 199, 200
Attestation, 9, 76
Au Fevre, Fr, 38
Augsburg, Ger, 37
Australian 21st Minesweeper Squadron, 64
Australian Imperial Force, 144, 185, 188, 190, 208, 214, 215; HQs, 213; HQs, Melbourne, 138
    Australian Parachute Battalion, 180
    8th Division, 180
    9th Division, 196, 212; HQs 207, 208
    First Australia Corps
    7th and 9th Divisions, 190
    2/9th Australian General Hospital, 213
Austria, 3, 6
Avellino, Italy, 93, 97
Aviation College (California Flyers), 20
Ayrs, Leslie, 49

Ba Kelalan, Dutch Borneo, 213
Baba Masuo, Lt.-Gen, 212
Bachelor society, 133

Bad Zwischenahn, Ger, 96

Badges, 7, 31, 42, 44, 49, 55, 108, 151, 213, 145 n.17

Bahau River, Dutch Borneo, 190, 193

Baker, Lieut. R.J., 200, 201, 203, 207, 208, 209

Balau, Johore, 173

Balikpapan, Dutch Borneo, 190

Baling, Tua Rumah, 198

Bangkok, Siam, 29, 163

Baram River, Sara, 192, 193, 195, 196, 199; Ulu
    Baram, 196

Bareo, Sara, 191, 192, 194, 196

Barneveld, Neth, 94

Barrie, Sgt. J. Keith, **191**, 192, **194**, 196, 199, 200,
    201, 203, 205, 207, 208, 209

Barriefield (Kingston), 86, 87, 88, 130, 148, 149, 150,
    183

Balui Batang, Sara, 198

Belaga Batang, Sara, 198

Batavia, NEI, 64

Batu Gaja, Perak, 180

Batu Pahat, Johore, 173

Batu Talam, Pahang, 163

Bawan, 203; Ulu Bawan, 203

Bawang River, 192

Beaverbrook, Lord (Max Aitken), 57

Beaulieu, Eng, 115, 139

Beckhausen, Ger, 96

Belaga, Sara, 195-6, 198-9, 200, 201-3, 208-9, 213;
    Ulu Belaga, 198

Belawit, Dutch Borneo, 191-2, 213

Bennett, Sgt. Ray, 213

Benoit, Maj. Joe H.A., 172-3, 184

Berhala Island, BNB, 190

Berlin, Battle of, 35, 37

Berlin 1939-1945 War Cemetery, Charlottenberg, Ger,
    40

Bernhard Line, Italy, 93

Bernière-sur-Mer, Normandy, 83

Bhamo, Burma, 29

Biak Island, NG, 62, 137, 143

Biggin Hill, Eng, 53

Binatang, Sara, 205, 207, 209

Bing, Cpl. Allan, 39, 48

Bing, WO2 Fred, 42, **43**, 44, 47, 48

Bintulu, Sara, 198, 200, 201, 203, 208;
    Bintulu-Paku rentis, 199

Bisley, Aldershot, 74, 101

Blacks, 60, 218

Blamey, Gen. Sir Thomas, 212

Blind drop, 162, 163, 165, 191

"blockbusters," 35, 91

Blow, Maj. Rex, 190, 213-4

Blowpipes, 198, 201, 202, 213

Bofors (AA gun), 83, 84

Boisenburg, Ger, 89

Bombay, India, 121, 151, 180

Bong, Sgt. John Ko, **75**, 106, **126**, 127, **131**, **139**,
    143-4

Bong, Peter Ko, 106, **149**

Boon Teck Hin, Cpl, 202, 203, 207, 209

Bordeaux, Fr, 35, 175, 184

Borneo, 62, 114, 122, 165, 175-214
        British Borneo, BNB, 159, 185, 188, 190,
    213; Brunei, 185, 190, 191; Dutch Borneo, 185,
    190, 192, 195, 196, 202; Sarawak, 185-214

Boulogne, Fr, 38, 47

Bourg-Leopold, Bel, 38

Bournemouth, Eng, 85

Bower, S/Sgt. Doug, 191

Bowes, Major, 127

Bradbury, Cpl. R.W., 200, 202, 203, 208, 209

Bramshot, Eng, 5

Brand, Capt. Eric, 67

Bremen, Ger, 32, 36

Bren gun, 84, 94, 201, 207

Breskens/Flushing, Neth, 47

Bretteville-sur-Laize Canadian War Cemetery, 33

Brisbane, Qd, 55, 62, 116, 140, 143

Bristol, Eng, 57

British Army, 167, 171, 173, 188
        21st Army Group, 35, 41; 2nd British Army, 89;
    8th British Corps, 2nd Army, 89; 8th British Army,
    55; British 49th Division, 94; 7th Armoured
    Division, 94; 30th Corps HQs and Troops, 94; 6th
    British Airborne Division, 89; 6th British Tank
    Brigade, 89; 4th Battalion Grenadier Guards, 89;
    Scots Greys, 89; British Army Hospital No. 2 Field
    Dressing Station, 92

British Army Aid Group, BAAG, 12-6, 113, 121, 140;
    see also E Group and MI 9

British Borneo Civil Administration Unit, BBCAU,
    207, 208, 209, 212, 213

British Chiefs of Staff, 112, 113

British Columbia Dragoons (9th Armoured Regiment),
    49, 95, 96, 98

British Columbia Legislature, 7, 80, 149, 151, 216,
    217, 218

British Commonwealth Air Training Plan (BCATP),
    19, 20, 24, 29, 54, 60, 61
        No. 1 ANS, Rivers, Man, 47; Rivers, Man, 49;
    No. 2 AOS, Edmonton, 20, 48; No. 5 AOS,
    Winnipeg, 20, 31, 51; No. 7 AOS, Portage la
    Prairie, 39, 47; No. 8 AOS, Ancienne Laurette,
    Quebec City, 20; No. 10 AOS, Chatham, NB, 24, 57
        No. 7 B&GS, Paulson, 48; No. 8 B&GS,
    Lethbridge, 36, 42; No. 9 B&GS, Mont Joli, 36, 50
        No. 5 EFTS, High River, Alta, 33; No. 19
    EFTS, Virden, Man, 27
        No. 1 General Reconnaissance School,
    Summerside, 51; No. 31 General Reconnaissance
    School, Charlottetown, 54
        No. 2 ITS, Regina College, 27; No. 3 ITS
    Victoriaville, Que, 50; No. 4 ITS, Edmonton, 50;
    No. 7 ITS, Saskatoon, 48
        No. 1 Manning Depot, Toronto, 51; No. 2
    Manning Depot, Brandon, Man, 31; No. 3 Manning
    Depot, Edmonton, 27, 30, 48, 49, 50; No. 5
    Manning Depot, Lachine, 53
        No. 9 Pre-Aircrew Educational Detachment at
    McGill, 36

No. 5 OTU, Boundary Bay, 36; No. 6 OTU, Comox, 27; No. 31 OTU, Debert, NS, 30, 54; No. 34 OTU, Pennfield, 42; No. 36 OTU, Greenwood, NS, 51

No. 4 SFTS, Saskatoon, 48; No. 7 SFTS, MacLeod, 30, 33; No. 15 SFTS, Claresholm, Alta, 53; No. 17 SFTS, Souris, 27; No. 18 SFTS, Gimli, Man, 53; No. 19 SFTS, Vulcan, Alta, 49

No. 2 Training Command, MacDonald, 49; No. 3 Training Centre, Edmonton, 49; No. 4 Training Command, 49

No. 1 Air Gunner Ground Training School, Quebec, 36

Central Navigation School, 47; No. 1 Central Navigation School, 49; Central Flying School, Trenton, 36

No. 1 Wireless School, Montreal, 49, 50; No. 2 Wireless School, Calgary, 42; No. 3 Wireless School, Winnipeg, 48; No. 4 Wireless School, Guelph, 31

No. 1 Flight Engineer School, Aylmer, Ont, 49
No. 1 TTS, St. Thomas, Ont, 20, 33, 49, 51, 53
No. 2 Release Depot, Jericho Beach, Vancouver, 49; No. 9 Release Centre, Boundary Bay, 36; Winnipeg Release Centre, 48

British Empire, 101, 121
British Empire Grand Aggregate, 101
British Empire Medal, 13
British Empire War Office, 6
British Expeditionary Force, 112
British Guiana, 3, 78
British Indian Fleet, 180
British Intelligence, 13
British Military Administration, 180
British Military Government, 163, 176
British Ministry of Aircraft Production, BMAP, 54
British Overseas Airways Corporation, BOAC, 54, 55, 58
British Security Coordination, BSC, 8, 78, 111, 113, 116-8, 123-4, 131-2, 137, 146-7, 149, 150-1, 155, 213-4; British Security Coordinator, 116
British War Medal, 4, 5, 6
British War Office, 1, 12, 79, 80, 112, 117, 121, 123, 132, 133, 146, 148, 155, 179, 217
Broadhurst, Lt.-Col. D.K., 165-6, 170-1
Brockville officers' training, 82, 126
Brooke, Rajah James, 115, 175, 185, 199, 213
Brooks, F/O W.H., 32
Broome, Capt. R.H. (Richard), 161, 162, 184
Bruges, Bel, 92
Brunei Bay, Borneo, 190, 192, 193, 196
Brussels, Bel, 30, 36
Bukit Lima, Sara, 207, 209, 212
Bulgaria, Italy, 93
Buna, NG, 137
Bunn, Enoch, 25, 26
Bunn, Luke, 25
Burma, 12, 13, 15, 21-3, 26-9, 41, 59, 61, 115, 118, 159, 175, 179-180, 184, 188
Burma Road, 22

Burma Star, 151
Burma-Siam railway, 159, 161, 163, 176, 180
Burr, Derek, 174

Cabinet War Committee, CWC, 69, 70, 70-5, 76, 79, 80, 107, 113, 117, 146, 147, 217
Caen, Normandy, 83, 84, 87, 90, 91, 96, 97, 100; Caen-Falaise, 83, 84
Calcutta, India, 11, 14, 20, 22, 23, 28, 55, 116, 139, 154, 156, 176, 179, 180
Calgary, Alta, 5, 8, 16, 31, 42, 49, 73, 86, 89, 90, 97, 99, 101, 110, 128, 149, 150; Currie Barracks, Calgary, 101, 104, 214
Calgary *Herald,* 101
Calgary Regiment, 5
Cambrai, Belg, 38
Camp Borden, Ont, 82, 92, 94, 95, 98, 100, 104, 127, 128, 148, 149, 150, 183
Camp Savage, Minn, 109, 110
Camp X, STS No. 103, 116
Campbell, R.H., 209
Campbell-Miles, Lt-Col A.C., 172
Camrose, Alta, 89, 92
Canada Manpower and Immigration, 39
Canadair, 16
Canadian Air Liaison Mission, 26
Canadian Army, 47, 180
1st Canadian Army, 41; 1st Canadian Corps, 90; HQs, 94; Canadian Corps, 97; Corps Troops, 94; Dental Corps, 128
Canadian Infantry Corps, 90; Canadian Infantry Training Centres, 82; 1st Infantry Division, 175; 2nd Infantry Division, 83, 84, 91, 97; 3rd Infantry Division, 83, 84, 90, 94; 1st Infantry Brigade, 95; 2nd Infantry Brigade, 91; 6th Infantry Brigade, 91; 7th Infantry Brigade, 90; 8th Infantry Brigade, 83; 11th Infantry Brigade, 90; 13th Infantry Brigade, 129; 14th Infantry Brigade, 128
Canadian Intelligence Corps, 78, 105, 143
Canadian Armoured Corps, 94; 4th Armoured Division, 5, 96, 99; 5th Armoured Division, 90, 94, 95; HQs, 94; 22nd Armoured Regiment, 96; 2nd Armoured Brigade HQs, 89; 4th Armoured Brigade, 96, 99; Tank Corps, Camp Borden, 127, 128
1st Canadian Parachute Battalion, 67, 89
Canadian Army Filter, 154
Canadian Aviation Electronics, 87, 88
Canadian Broadcasting Corporation, CBC, 31
Canadian Citizenship Act, 80, 218
Canadian Expeditionary Force, 5
47th Battalion, 5; 47th (Western Ontario) Battalion, 5; 52nd Battalion (The New Ontario Battalion), 3; 102nd RMR Regiment, 4; 10th Battalion, CEF, 3, 5; 50th Battalion, CEF, 3
Canadian Forces HQs, RCAF, 31
Canadian Fusiliers (City of London Regiment), 128, 129
Canadian Grenadier Guards, 96, 97
Canadian Group Reinforcement Unit, CGRU, 151
No. 1 Base Reinforcement Depot, 97

Canadian Military Headquarters, CMHQ, London, 3, 137

Canadian Military Intelligence, CMI, 121, 123
    Military Intelligence, MI, 18, 76, 79, 109, 112, 113, 114, 116, 117, 126, 128, 184; No. 1 Discrimination Unit, 109, 110, 118; No. 6 Canadian Field Security Section, 105

Canadian Officers Training Corps, COTC, 74, 82, 87, 91, 102; see also University by name

Canadian Pacific Airlines, 20

Canadian Pacific Steamship Lines, 16, 68

Canadian Repatriation of Prisoners of War group, 65, 143

Canadian Scottish Regiment (Princess Mary's), 90

Canadian Women's Army Corps, 106, 148, 219

Canton, China, 9, 11, 12, 13, 14, 24, 25, 26, 68, 101, 119, 120, 133

Canton Air Force, 25

Carleton & York Regiment, 93

Carmen, Man, 31

Carpiquet, Normandy, 83, 84, 100

Carter, Maj. G.S. (Toby), 190-4, 198-9

Casablanca, 20, 55

Casalavecchio, Italy, 95

Caserta, Italy, 95

Castel Di Sangro, Italy, 93

Caza, Capt. Roger M., 173, 184

Celle, Ger, 89

Census, 8, 71, 73

Central Air Transport Company, 25, 26, 29, 31

Central Government Air Force, 25

Central Intelligence Agency, CIA, 16, 82

Ceprano, Italy, 95

Cervia, Italy, 94, 95

Chaffey, Lieut. W.A., 208

Chai Wan Military Cemetery, HK, 66

Chaklala, India, 115

Chan Chak, Admiral, 120

Chan, L/Cpl. A.Y.P., 149

Chan, LAC Herbert (Herby), 14, **48**, 59, 127

Chan, Ira (Toy), 9, 48, 68, 127

Chan, Lloyd, **75, 149**

Chan, Paul, 9, 48, 68, 127, **153**

Chan, Sgt. Roy S.T, 48, **75**, 127, **138, 139**, 144, 148, 185, **189**, 204, 205, 207, **208**, 209, 213, 214

Chan, Raymond, **149**

Chan Kent, Robert, **149**

Chang, Albert, **149**

Chang, Robert, 82

Chang, Dr. Theodore, 82

Chassé, Maj. Pierre E., 174-5

Chee, Dr, 209

Chemnitz, Ger, 35

Cheng, K.F. (Henry), **141**

Cheng, Capt Roger Kee, 62, 126-7, 132-4, **139**, 144; Sarawak: 185, **189**, 193-4, 202, 204-5, 208-9, 212-4

Chennault, Maj. Gen. Claire, 14, 21, 22

Chester, Maj. F.G.L., 188

Chew, Pte. James Delbert Harold, 3

Chiang Kai-Shek, Generalissimo, 12, 13, 21, 22, 25, 26, 120, 156

Chilliwack, BC, 148, 149, 183

Chin, George, 68

Chin, Pte. James, 99

Chin, S.J. (Danny), 110

Chow, Pte. Quan Lai, 150

China Air Task Force, 14, 21, 22

China National Aviation Corporation, CNAC, 11, 14, 20, 20, 22, 23, 24, 25, 26, 29

China Unit, 15

Chinatowns, 155

China-Burma Theatre, 22, 121

China-Burma-India Theatre, 121

Chindits, see Long Range Penetration Groups

Chindwin River, Burma, 23

Chinese Adjustment Statement Programme, 66

Chinese Air Force, 21, 216

Chinese Air Force/aircraft factory, 16

Chinese Battalion, 73, 79, 91, 101

Chinese Canadian Association, 79, 148, 149, 216

Chinese Communists, 114, 116, 159, 176, 183

Chinese Dialects, 175; Cantonese, 134, 168; Hakka, 18, 134; Mandarin, 12, 134, 168, 173, 179

Chinese Entry Tax, 217

Chinese Immigration Act 1923, 76

Chinese Labour Battalions, 2, **5**

Chinese Labour Corps, 6

Chinese Nationalist, **168, 183**

Chinese Nationalist Army, 16

Chinese Nationalist Government (Kuomintang), KMT, 26, 163

Chinese Secret Service, 120

Chinese Signal Unit, 73

Chinese wives, 133

Chinn, Sgt. Bing Lee, 165, **168**

Chinn, Capt. Harold, **25**

Chinn, S/Sgt. John Rose, 97

Chittagong, India, 29, 30

Chiu, L/Cpl. M. (Jackie), 149, **157**

Chong, Stanley, **84, 85, 86**

Chong, Willie, 86

Chong, William Gun, 13

Chow, P/O Charlie, **30**, 31

Chow, Sgt. Edward, 127, 128, **131, 139**

Chow, Gunner George, 83-4

Chow, Bombardier George L., 11, 68

Chow, M.W. (Lloyd), **153**

Chow, Marshall, 89,

Chow, Pte. Quan Lai, 150

Chung, Sgt. Charley, **174**, 175

Chungking, China, 13, 14, 16, 18, 23, 25, 116, 120, 121

Churchill, Sir Winston, 35, 57

Cipher, 78, 106, 115, 118, 133

Citizens and Citizenship, 1, 7, 25, 70, 73, 76, 77, 78, 84, 102, 132, 216, 217, 218, 219

Civil Service Commission, 65

Civilian Chinese operator, 202

Clayton, Sgt. Jack K., 124, **125**, 126, 131
Clayton Knight Committee, 20, 54, 58
Cleve, Ger, 84
Clough, Major, 179
Coders, 154, 157, 164, 165
Colchester, Eng, 83; Convalescent Hospital, 99
Cologne, Ger, 38
Colombo, Ceylon, 62, 162, 173, 174, 179, 180
Colonial Airlines, 60
Comacchio, Bay of, Italy, 95
Combat Cargo Task Force (India), 27
Combined Operations, 57
Combined Operations Pilotage Parties, COPP, 113
Combined Services Detailed Intelligence Corps, 61
Combined Services Radio Intelligence Unit, 61
Combe, Maj. R.G.P.N., 188
Commando, 37, 43, 57, 83, 113, 124, 128, 131, 132,
    133, 184, 190; see also Independent Companies
Commando Bay, BC, 124, 127, 138
Commando Order, 113
Commonwealth War Graves Commission, 93
Communist Party, 176
Communists, 12-4, 23, 25, 66, 89, 114, 121, 140, 159,
    161, 184
Con, Sgt. Harry, 148, 149
Conca River, Italy, 94
Coningham, A/VM Sir Arthur, 41
Conscription, 3, 70, 146, 161; see also NRMA
Contact man, 180, 192
Convoys, 41, 42, 50, 67, 68, 91, 97, 118, 125, 171
Coolangatta (near Brisbane), 143
Coriano Ridge, Italy, 94
Cosgrave, Col. L. Moore, 137, 143, 146
Cossor (Canada) Limited, 87
Côté, Sergeant, 126, 130
Courtney, Col. G.B., 205, 207
Creery, Capt. Wallace B., 63
Crocker, Tom, 200, 209
Croix de Guerre avec Etoile d'Argent, 38
Cross, John, 174
Croton, Cpl. R.J., 200, 205, 207, 208, 209
Crystal Pool, Vancouver, 218
Cumberland Force, Italy, 94, 95
Currie Barracks, Calgary, 101, 104, 214
Curtis-Reid Flying School, Montreal, 56
Cusack, WO Rod, 191
Custodian of Enemy Alien Property, 72
Czechoslovakia, 97

Dams Raid, 36
Dan, Manuel, 97
Dapoi, Sara, 197; Ulu Dapoi, 196, 197
Darling, Gdm Ted **96,** 97
Dartmouth, NS, 33
Darwin, NT, 118, 190, 191
Davis, Col. John H.L., 161, 162, 164, 171, 174, 184
D-Day, 31, 38, 41, 42, 57, 61, 82, 83, 86, 89, 90, 100,
    175
Debert, NS, 83, 85, 90, 92

Deer Lodge Hospital, Winnipeg, 47
Defence Medal 1939-1945, 11
Delfzijl, 94; Delfzijl Pocket, 95
Delhi, India, 14, 20, 21, 55, 110
Denmark, 22, 89, 112
Department of External Affairs, 117
Department of Justice (RCMP), 66
Department of Transport, DOT, 53, 54, 60, 65
Deputy Supreme Allied Commander, 41
Der, Billy, **88**
Der, Ken, 104
d'Erlanger, Commodore Gerard, 58
Despatcher, 156, 214
Distinguished Flying Cross, DFC, 20
Didam-Doetinchem, Ger, 94
Diest, Belg, 40
Dinjan, Assam, India, 22, 23, 24, 25
Director of Military Intelligence, DMI, 12, 79
Director of Naval Intelligence, 67
Disposal Order, 132; No. 100, 147; (PC 3464), 133
Distinguished Service Medal, 6
Dobree, Capt. P.G.J., 162, 163
Dominion Elections Act, 7, 216
Dong, Jack K., 25
Dong, Pte. Wing Herbert, 150
Donovan, Gen. William, 117
Dortmund-Ems Canal, Ger, 34, 89
Dorval, Que, 53, 54, 55, 56, 60
Douglas, John, 203
Drake, Col. Ed, 61
Dresden, Ger, 35, 36
Drew-Brook, T.G., 117, 121, 123, 124, 132, 133, 146,
    147, 148, 149, 151
Dropping Zone, DZ, 162, 166, 173, 192
Duclair, Fr, 47
Dulit Range, Sara, 196, 198
Dum Dum airport Calcutta, 22
Dunkirk, Fr, 112, 113
Dunsfold, Surrey, 41, 44
Durban, SA, 125
Duren, Ger, 35
Durin, Sara, 203, 205, 207, 208, 209; Durin River, 209
Dyaks, 114, 185, 200, 201, 202, 203

E Group, 12, 113, 156, 166, 179, 180; see also MI 9
    and BAAG
Eagle Squadron, 22
East Indians, 74, 217, 218
Eastern Air Command, Rockcliffe, 51, 54
Eastern Warfare School, 153
Edmeades, Lieut. Eric, 191, 192
Edmonton Fusiliers, 104
8th Reconnaissance Regiment (14th Canadian
    Hussars), 84
Eindhoven, Neth, 40
Elbe River, Ger, 89
Electra House, 112, 113
Elephant Point, Burma, 29
Embah, Sergeant, 202

Emden, Ger, 34
Emmerich, Ger, 94, 95
Ems Canal, Ger, 34
Emut, Jok, 198
Enfranchisement, 7, 10, 74, 108, 216, 217, 218
Eng, Harry, **141**
Eng, Frank W., **149**
Eng, Jerry W. Wong, **149**
Ermelo, Neth, 95
Eschede, Ger, 89
Esquimalt, BC, 6, 63, 66, 106, 132
Eurasians, 11, 161
Eureka, 162, 203
Eusop bin Lansi, Cpl, 205
Eastern Warfare School, EWS, 154
Exclusion Act, 9, 69, 71, 76, 77, 144, 217, 218, 219;
    "An Act Respecting Chinese Immigration," 77;
    Certificate, **77**; US Exclusion Act of 1881, 56
Exmouth Gulf, WA, 173

Falaise, Normandy, 96
Falardeau, Lieut. R., 93
Far East Liaison Group, SEAC, 143
Far Eastern Office of the Ministry of Economic
    Warfare, Singapore, 116
Farge, Ger, 36
Federation of Malaya Police, 38
Fell, Capt. W.R. (Tiny), 205
Fenner, Maj. Claude, 172
Ferry Command, 22, 24, 30, 53-7, 58, 60
    Return Ferry Service, 54. 55; No. 112 Wing at
    Dorval, 55; No. 113 Wing at Nassau, 55; No. 280
    Wing, the Pacific, 55; No. 301 Composite Unit at
    Dorval, 53; RAF at Dorval Airport (Ferry
    Command), 51
Fifth Column, 120, 133-4
Fifth Replacement Depot, Manila, 143
15th Canadian Light Horse, 101
Filipinos, 62
Filter Board, 153-5
Finland, 118
1st Calgary Tank Regiment, 101
1st Gurkha Regiment, 164, 166
1st Hussars, 83
First Special Service Force (the North Americans), 89,
    129
Fisher, Maj. John C.D., 198, 202, 203, 205, 208, 209,
    212-3
Fiumicino River, Italy, 95
Fleet Air Arm, 67
Flushing, Neth, 47
Flying Tigers, see American Volunteer Group
Folkestone, Eng, 92
Fong, Cpl. Charlie J., 140
Fong, Ed, **141, 142**
Fong, George, **149**
Fong, Georges, **142**
Fong, Pte. Jim Lee, 93
Fong, Rupert, 143

Fong, Samaul, **57,** 58
Fong, Stanley, 25
Fong, Pte. William, 93
Force 136, SOE in India, 12, 28, 29, 105, 113, 114,
    116, 133, 147, 148, 156, 157, 159, 161, 165, 173,
    176, 179, 183; Force 136, Calcutta and Colombo
    HQs, 180
Force "J," 85
Forestry Draft, 4
Forme d'Aquino, Italy, 95
Formosa, 26, 64, 159
Fort Benning, Ga, 89
Fort Emma, Sara, 202
Fort Garry Horse (10th Armoured), 96
Fort Sylvia, Sara, 200, 201
Fort Vyner, Sara, 199
Fosso Vecchio, Italy, 95
Foster, Sgt. D.L., 205, 207, 209
4th Princess Louise Dragoon Guards (4th Recce Reg),
    95
XIVth Army, Burma, 27
14th Canadian Hussars (8th Recce Reg), 84
Fowler, Cpl. H.N., 200, 207, 209
Franchise, 1, 6, 7, 70, 71, 72, 74, 75, 79, 80, 121, 133,
    149, 151, 216, 217, 218
Frankfurt, Ger, 37
Fraser, Admiral Sir Bruce, 64
Fraser, Capt. Hugh, 170
Fraser Island, Qd, 139, 140
Free French, 38, 44
French Indo-China, 180
French National Anthem, 44
French Resistance, 35, 38; Maquis, 176
Fung, C.T. (Fatty), 25
Fung, Sgt. Hinn Wing (Henry), 165, 166, **167,** 168,
    183

G-2 (American Intelligence) Allied Command Hqs, 62
Galloway, Strome *A Regiment at War,* 218
Gander, NFd, 54, 55, 60, 127, 133; No. 19 Sub-Repair
    Depot, 51
Gandy, Lt.-Cmdr. G.H., 120
Gaspe/Yarmouth, NS, 50
Gdynia on the Baltic, 36
Gemas, Johore, 163
General Electric, Schenectady, NY, 87
General Headquarters, Delhi, 12
Generalissimo, see Chiang Kai-Shek
Geneva Convention, 73
Gerard, F/O Bill, 38
Ghent, Bel, 38, 87
Gibraltar, 53, 62
Gimson, Colonial Secretary Sir F.C., 16, 64
Gironde River, Fr, 35
Gona, NG, 137
Gong, Sgt. Harry, 31
Gong Gajah, Kedah, 163
Goodwin, F/O D.W., 33
Goodyer, Sergeant, 171

Goose Bay, Labrador, 53, 54
Gordon Head, BC, 83, 87, 91, 101, 110
Gothic Line, Italy, 94, 95
Governor General's Foot Guards GGFG (21st
    Armoured), 96
Governor General's Horse Guards GGHG (3rd
    Armoured Recce), 94, 95
Grand Slam, 36
Grant, Janet, 92, 93, 144
Grant, Richard William, 93
Grasett, Gen. A.E., 119, 120
Gravenhorst, Ger, 34
Great Britain, 53, 55, 213
Great Depression, 8, 11
Greater East Asia Co-prosperity Sphere, 159, 185
Grebbe Line, Neth, 94
Greenock, Scot, 37, 86, 151
Grentheville, Normandy, 96
Grik Valley, Perak, 162, 163
Grimsdale, Brig. G.E., 12
Groningen, Neth, 94
Groos, Lt.-Cmdr. D.W., 66
Group A Schools, Arisaig at Inverness, 115
Group B Schools, 115
Group Laison Team GLT, 164, 166
Group Liaison Officer GLO, 164
Guam, Marianas, 65, 143
Guerrilla Training Unit, 153
Gujrat, India, 26
Gurkhas, 162, 164, 166, 170, 171, 175, 180

Haifa, Palestine, STS No. 102, 115
Hainan, China, 119
Halifax, 4, 31, 37, 39, 68, 69, 82, 87, 88, 92,   115,
    127, 128, 144, 151, 157, 180
Halifax Rifles, 96
Hallam, Sgt. K.W, 191, 192, **194**
Halpenny Force, Normandy, 96
Hang, CSM (WO2) Harry, 97, **98**
Hanna, Capt. John E., 173
Hannah, Maj. J.F., 163, 164
Harcourt, R/Adm. Cecil, 62, 64-5
Harding, Lieut. John J., 151, **157**
Hardwicke Island, BC, 83
Harris, AM Sir Arthur, 35
Harrison, Maj. Harry, 164
Harrisson, Maj. T.H., 190-4, 196, 213
Harrod's No. 1 Camp, Pisa/Leghorn, 95
Hart, Capt. F.G., RCN, 63
Hart, Premier John, 216
Hart, Maj. John V., 173, 174
Hartley, Sgt. J.D.F., 208, 209
Hasler, Maj. G.A., 163
Hay, Young Wing, 1, 90, 106
Head Tax, 3, 24, 81, 144, 217
Headly, Maj. Derek, 163
Heelis, Maj. John E., 164, 166
Heidrich's 1st Parachute Division, 93
Heine, Capt. K. Robert, 169-171
Heinsburg, Ger, 35

Hem, Pte. Percy F., **100, 101**
Hengyang, China, 14
Henney, Sgt. Tom R., 166
Heron, Pte. C.E., 205, 209
Himalayas, 20, 23; see also The Hump
Hirohito, Emperor, 62, 140, 189, 207
Hiroshima, Japan, 62
Hitler, Adolph, 113
Ho, Sgt. Fat Chung (Harry), **174,** 175, **183**
Ho, Pte. Fred, 93
Ho, Lin Fat, 93
Ho Lem, Frank, 73-4, 101, 101, **102,** 106, 110,
Hoan, Tommy I., 40
Hoe, Alfred, 11
Hoe, Pte. Helen, 106, 148
Hoffmeister, Maj.-Gen. B.M., 94
Hollandia, NG, 62
Holman, Capt. John, 171
Holmes, D. Ronald, 12, 13, 14, 15, 16, 112, 119, 132,
    134, 140, 151
Holt's Wharf, Tsimshatsui, HK, 64
Home Defence, 31, 48, 100
Hong, Pte. George, 33, 91
Hong, F/O Joseph, **33,** 91
Hong, King Lewis Chow, 94,
Hong Kong, 2, 8, 9, 29, 72
            Hong Kong Field Ambulance, 12; Hong
    Kong Volunteer Company, 15; Hong Kong
    Volunteer Defence Corps, HKVDC, 11, 12, 16, 68
            Hong Kong University, 14
Honolulu, Hawaii, 55, 65
Horana, Ceylon, 156, 172, 183
Hordouseaux, Normandy, 96
Horsham, Eng, 85
Horsnell, WO Don L., 192, **194,** 196
Houffallize, Belg, 35
Hsuchow, China, 26
Hoy, Sgt. Charles, **157**
Hudson's Bay Company, 120
Hukawng Valley, Burma, 23
Hum, Sgt. Art Ten (Henry), **88, 104**
Hum, Victor, 67
Hume, Lieut. P.W. (Pip), 200, 201, 208-9, 212
Hump, The, 20, 23, 25, 26, 59
Hunter, Maj. A.J., 166
Hydra, 109, 116, 118
Hywood, Sgt. A.W.C., 189

Iban tribe, Sara, 115, 185, 193-200, **201, 208,** 212
Ibrahim bin Ismail, Capt, 162
Igoville, Fr, 47
IJsselmeer (Zuider Zee), Neth, 90, 94, 95
Immigration Branch, Department of Mines and
    Resources, 55
Immigration Department, 66, 219
Imphal, India, 27, 29
Independent Companies, 113
India National Army, INA, 159
Indian Army, 159, 167
            Indian Division, 180; Indian ORs, 155

India-Burma Theatre, 22, 30, 121
Industrial Imperial School, 98
Industrial Intelligence Centre, 113
Innes, Controller, 128
Innisfail, Alta, 101; Innisfail, NQ, 144
Inter-Services Liaison Department (ISLD), 165, 166, 173, 174, 184; see also MI 6
Invitational Travel Orders, **136,** 137, 140
Ipoh, Perak, 164, 198
Irish Regiment of Canada, 93, 95
Irrawaddy River, Burma, 23
Itagaki Seishiro, Lt.-Gen, 171, 179
Italian Partisans, 95

Jacobi, F/Sgt, 40
Jambogen Island, BNB, 188
Jane's Fighting Ships, 62, 64
Jang, Clarence, **149, 153**
Jang, Raymond, 93
Japanese Army HQs in Saigon, 179
Japanese Canadian linguists, 113
Japanese Canadians, 73, 80, 110, 117, 217
Japanese fire balloon, 50
Japanese linguists, 151
Japanese surrender documents, **210, 211**
Japanese work parties, **169, 170**
Jacques, WO J.G., 33
Jason Bay, Johore, 174
Javanese labour, 198
Jedburgh teams, 114, 147, 175, 176
Jensen, Sgt. T.A., 101
Jesselton, BNB, 188
Jessore, India, 115, 156, 165
Jews, 32
Jinkins, Maj. W.L., 208
Joe, Cpl. Walter D., 49
Johnstone Strait, BC, 83, 131
Johore, Malaya, 161, 163, 172, 173, 174, 179
Johore Bahru, 174, 179
Joint Chiefs of Staff, 118
Joint Intelligence Unit, 65, 110
Jong, F.C. (Alfred), 97
Julau, Sara, 205, 212
Julich, Ger, 35
Jumpmasters, 27, 29
Jung, F/Lt Arthur Ernest, 33, **34,** 36, 105
Jung, Sgt. Douglas, 105 110, 128, **139,** 140
Jung, Capt. Ross, **81,** 82, 105
Junks, 133
Juno Beach, Normandy, 90, 96
Juvincourt, Fr, 36
Kachau, Saelangor, 165, 170, 171; Kachau-Broga, 171
Kajang, Selangor, 165, 167
Kampar, Perak, 164
Kangar, Kedah, 175
Kangla, Imphal (Manipur), 27
Kanowit, Sara, 193, 194, 202, 203, 204, 205, 208, 209, 213
Kanowit River, 202
Kapit, Sara, 195, 198, 199, 200, 201, 202, 203, 204,

205, 207, 208, 209, 213; Kapit-Kanowit, 201, 202
Karachi, India, 20, 27, 29, 54, 55, 151
Karens, Burma, 184
Kattegat near Kiel, 41
Kayan River, Sara, 202
Kayan tribe, 115, 192, 193, 195, 196, 197, 199, 212
Kearny, Capt. D.J., 200-203, 209
Kedah, Malaya, 159, 163, 174, 175
Keenleyside, Dr. Hugh L., 70
Kelabit tribe, Sara, 190, 191, 192
Kelantan, Malaya, 159, 163
Kempei Tai, 138, 161, 207
Kendall, Francis Woodley (Mike), 15, 78-9, 100, 105, 112, 118, **119,** 120-1, 123-4, 126-7, 130-4, **138,** 140, 143-6, 153, 184, 185, 205, 213
Kent Regiment, 94, 128
Kenyah tribe, Sara, 115, 192, 193, 196, 212
Kerangan, Sara, 198
Kerling, Selangor, 165, 168
Kharakvasla, Poona, India, 153
Kheong, Harry, Joe, Jack, Ken, 16
Kiangyin, China, 66
Kiang-Chang, China, 66
Kickers, 27
Kidd's Estate, Sara, 202, 203
Kiel, Ger, 40
King, Sgt. Louey, 16, 100, **101, 127,** 128, 131, **139,** 144, 185, **189,** 207, 209, 212, 213, 214, 218
King, Prime Minister W.L. Mackenzie, 5, 14, **52,** 63, 70, 72, 87, 146, 216, 217
Kiway, Hayward, **149**
King's Regulations and Orders, 19, 164
Kingston, Ont, 81, 87, 89, 90, 104, 148, 150
Kiska, Aleutians, 78, 80, 128, 129
Kluang, Johore, 173
Knight Commander (of the Order) of the Bath, KCB, 120
Ko Bong, Andrew, 106
Ko Bong, Mary, 106
Korea, 31, 82, 93, 184
Kota Bahru, Kelantan, 163
Kowloon, HK, 64
Krupps Works, Essen, 37
Kuala Bahau, Sara, 201
Kuala Baleh, Sara, 200, 201, 203
Kuala Krai, Kelantan, 163
Kuala Kubu Bahru, Selangor, 168
Kuala Lipis, Pahang, 163, 170
Kuala Lumpur, Selangor, 159, 165, 167, 169, 170, 171, 179, 180
Kuala Maa, Sara, 198
Kuala Papan, Johore, 174
Kuala Pila, Negri Sembilan, 172
Kuala Sungei Pila, Sara, 199
Kuala Sungei Pawan, Sara, 197
Kubaan, Sara, 192
Kubu Lio Matu, Sara, 196
Kuching, Sara, 180, 185, 188, 194, 202, 204, 205, 212
Kukong, China, 13
Kunming, China, 14, 16, 22, 23, 25, 120, 184

Kusten Canal, Ger, 96
Kutenhausen, Ger, 89
Kwangtung Province, China, 2, 11, 12, 13, 14, 82, 121
Kweilin, China, 11, 13, 22
Kweiyang, China, 25
Kwong, Pte. George Yet, **88, 92**
Kyaukpyu, Ramree Island, 29

L capsules, 164
Labuan, Borneo, 93, 161, 185, 190-1, 196, 199, 200, 201-5, 207-8, 209, 212, 213
Lachine, Que, 27, 50
Lahad Datu, BND, 190
Lake, Maj. B., 90
Lake Superior Regiment (Motor), 3, 96
Lam, Cecil, **75**
Lam, Dick, **141, 142**
Lambert, Lieut. F., 209, 212
Lanark and Renfrew Scottish, 95
Landes, Roger, 175
Landing Craft Infantry, LCI, 143
Landing Craft Tanks, LCTs, 83, 85, 86
Land's End, Eng, 40
Lashio, Burma, 29
Lastuk, F/O Bill, 38
Lawai Bisarai, Penghulu, 191
Lawas, Sara, 213
Leach, Lt.-Col. David Leslie, 208, 209
Leaflet, 16, **17**, 33, 36, 37, 44, **45-6**, 179
'Leave behind' parties, 116, 120, 159
Leavens Flying School, Barker Airport, Toronto, 57
Ledo Road, Burma, 23, 29
Lee, Alfred Quinn, 104, **105**
Lee, Arthur, 16, 104
Lee, Ben (Perth Reg), 83, 90
Lee, Sgt. Billy Kong, **149, 153, 179, 183**
Lee, Sgt. Bing Chu, **153, 165,** 171, **183**
Lee, Charlie Q., **149, 153**
Lee, Cpl. Daniel, **53**
Lee, David, 67
Lee, Edward, **88**
Lee, Cpl. Edward (No. 404), 40, 83, 90
Lee, Ernie Thomas, 31, 51
Lee, Lieut. Frank, **88**
Lee, Pte. Frederick, **5**
Lee, George, 51
Lee, Hanson, **4**
Lee, Harden, **141, 142**
Lee, F/Lt. Harvey A. (Hal), 31, 32
Lee, Horace, **157**
Lee, Pte. Ivan G., 91
Lee, LAC Jack, 50
Lee, Sgt. James, 88
Lee, AW1 Jean Suey Zee, 51, **52**
Lee, Cpl. Jim, 100
Lee, F/O Jim Gen, **32**
Lee, Mr. K.C., 84
Lee, LAC Kenneth Kwong, 50
Lee, Sgt. Kim Yuen, 24, 50, **51**
Lee, 'Mech,' **88**

Lee, Peter, 83, 90
Lee, Maj. (Dr.) Raymond Harry S., 14
Lee, Rifleman/Bandsman Robert, 4, **105**
Lee, Robert (Montreal), 102
Lee, Cpl. Robert, **157**
Lee, Ronald, **149, 153**
Lee, S. Fraser, **91**
Lee, Pte Samuel, 102, **103,** 104
Lee, Watts, **149**
Lee, William, 102, **103,** 104
Lee, Capt. Wilson, 82
Lee, P/O Wilson John, **51**
Lee, Y.C., 4, 105
Legg, Maj. Hugh John, 105, 113, 117, 124, **125,** 128, 130, 131, 133, 137, 144, 147-8, 150-1, 154, 183
Leigh-Mallory, A/CM Sir Trafford, 41
Leipzig, Ger, 34, 35
Leir, Hugh, 126
Le Mans, Fr, 38
Lem, George, 68
Lem, William, 33, 68
Lengaleh, Sara, 194
Leonard, Maj. G.R., 163
Leong, Sgt. Stanley T.S., 49, 50
Leong, Yee Chong, 4
Leopold Canal, Belg, 96
Lethbridge, Alta, 30, 48
Leung, Capt. So Won, 82
Levy, Capt. M.G., 158, 166, 179, 180, **183,** 184
Lew, Sgt. R.W. (Bob), 165, **170,** 171
Leyburn, Qd, 116, 140, 190
Leyte, PI, 62, 143
Lim Bo Seng, 161, 180
Lim, RSM Harry Bing Mon, **75,** 91, 97, **98**
Lim, Nurse Nellie, 14
Lim, Pte. On Wah, 104
Lim, Pu On, **88,** 94, 95
Lim On, Joan, 143
Limpet, 120, 125, 130, 132, 184
Lin, Dr. David, 18
Lingling, China, 22
Liri Valley, Italy, 94, 95
Little, F/O Pilot R.R., 32
Liverpool, Eng, 4, 39, 61, 62, 98, 157, 184
Lobak Antu, Sara, 209
Lobang River, Sara, 198
Lochtenboerg, Belg, 91
Lock, Sgt. George Thomas, **126,** 128, **139,** 143
Lockheed Aircraft Corporation, 88
Lolang, Sara, 180
Lombardo, Guy, 98
Long Akah, Sara, 193, 194, 195, 196, 199; Kubu, **196**
Long Branch Ranges, Toronto, 101
Long Labid, Sara, 192
Long Lama, Sara, 193
Long Lelang, Sara, 192, 194
Long Nawang, Dutch Borneo, 199, 200, 201, 202, 207, 209
Long Pawan, Sara, 197; Ulu Pawan, 197
Long Range Penetration Groups, 15, 27

Long San, Sara, 195
Long Seniai, Sara, 194
Lord Strathcona's Horse (Royal Canadians), 95
Lore, Capt. Henry, 82
Lore, Molly, 65, 144
Lore, William King Lowd, 60, **61,** 66-7, 82
Louie, Pte. Henry, 104
Louie, Sgt. K.W. (Ernie), 40, **172,** 173, **183,** 184
Louie, P/O Quan Jil, **39,** 40
Louie, Sgt. Victor Joy, **172**
Louie, Wee Hong, **4,** 5, 7, 49
Louie, Pte. William Thomas (Wee Tan), 4, **5,** 7, 49
Louvain, Bel, 38
Low, Sgt. Norman Mon, 100, **101,** 128, 133, **139,** 140, 144, 185, **189,** 205, 207, **208, 213**
Lowe, Edna Silaine, 106
Lowe, Harry, **75, 149**
Lowe, Harvey, 16
Lowe, Huene, 16
Lowe, Sgt. K. Chee (Charlie), 16, 110
Lowe, Sgt. Raymond Young, 128, **133,** 143
Lowe, Stanley H., 14, **15,** 106
Lowe, Pte. William Hong Yuen, **15, 75,** 91, 97, **98,** 106
Loyal Edmonton Regiment, 91, 97
Lum, Charles, **157**
Lum, Francis, 104
Lung, Alex, **86**
Lung, Bombardier Frank, **86**
Lupar River, Sara, 205
Luthe, Ger, 89
Lutzkendorf, Ger, 34
Luzon, PI, 62
Lynch, F/Sgt, 40

Maas River, Neth, 96
Macao, China, 11, 13
MacArthur, General, 62, 118, 137, 171
MacDonald, Captain, 11
Macdonald, Maj. Ian A., 166-7
Mackenzie, Colin, 176; letter **177-8**
MacRitchie, Cmdr. Peter, 64, **65**
Madagascar, 125
Madgeburg, Ger, 40, 184
Mah, Capt. Albert, 16, 20, **21,** 13, 24, 51, 59
Mah, Bernice, 24
Mah, Capt. Cedric, 20, **21,** 23, 24, 26, 30, 59
Mah, George, 104
Mah, Capt. Kuo Lim, 25
Mah, Mary Laura, 106
Mah, Sgt. Roy Q.Q., **75,** 149
Mah, Wally, 104
Malacca, Malaya, 161, 172
Malaya Country Section, MCS, 154, 162, 164, 180; MCS, Group B, 180
Malayan Emergency, 38
Malayan Peoples' Anti-Japanese Army, MPAJA, 161-174, **175,** 176
   1st MPAJA Regiment, 165; 2nd MPAJA Regiment, 172; 3rd MPAJA Regiment, 172; 5th

MPAJA (Perak) Regiment, 163, 164, 172; 6th MPAJA Regiment, 163; 7th MPAJA Regiment, 174
Maltby, Maj.-Gen. C.M., 11, 120
Malton, Ont, 49, 55
Manchuria, 8, 161, 216
Manchus, 66
Mandalay, Burma, 27
Mandriole, Italy, 95
Manga Dap, Sara, 203
Manila, PI, 62, 63, 65, 143, 184; Manila Bay, 62
Manson, Honourable Mr. Justice A.M., 74-7, 79, 107
Manus Island, Admiralty Group, 62
Mao Tse-Tung, 26
Maple Creek, Alta, 148, 149, 150, 183
Mar, George, 104
Mar, Cpl. Richard, 67, **88,** 89
Mar, Lieut. (Temp.) William, 67
Mark, Ross, 16
Marr, Doug, **141**
Martin, Maj. W.P.S.B., 173, 174, 180
Maryborough, Qd, 140
Massachusetts Institute of Technology, 87
Master Bomber, 34
Matera, Italy, 95
Mauritius, 58
Mawnubyin, Akyab Island, 27
Maxwell, Maj. C.E., 168
May, Capt. Wilfred R. (Wop), 20
McCallum, Lieut A.J.H., 204, 208, 209, 212
McCallum, Capt. (Dr) Ian A.N., 192
McClure, Sgt. Andrew Wylie, **124,** 125, 126, 132, 137, **138**
McGill University, 67, 102, 126
McKenzie, Lt.-Col. Arthur P., 109, 110, 111
McLaren, Maj. Jock, 107, 122, 190
McNaughton, Gen. A.G.L., 146
MCR radio, 196
Mediterranean, 115, 125
Mee, S/Sgt Lai Sham (Sammy), 92, 93, 98, 99
Meerut, India, 128, 133, 154, 156, 173, 180, 183
Meiktila, Burma, 27; Meiktila-Toungoo-Pegu, 27
Melanaus tribe, Sara, 185
Melbourne, NSW, 62, 138, 139, 143, 148, 154, 188
Melfa River, Italy, 95
Mellet, Cpl. N.R.R., 209
Melsbroek, Bel, 47, 58
Meluan, Sara, 203, 205, 207, 209, 212
Memorandum (Secret No. 1), 71
Mentakab, Pahang, 163
Merapoh, Pahang, 163
Merchant Navy Reserve, 67, 125
Merchant seamen, 144; Manning pools, seamen, 68
Mereville, Fr, 38
Meritorious Service Medal, 6
Mesopotamia (Iraq), 6
Meteorologists, 23, 54
Metz, Fr, 38
Mezzano, Italy, 95
MI 5 British Security Service, 116
MI 6 (SIS), 12, 38, 112, 113, 116, 117, 119

MI 6 (Section D, Z Organization), 112, 119
MI 9 (Escape & Evasion), 9, 12, 23, 38, 113
Military Cross, 93, 124, 209
Military District No. 1 (London), 148
    MD No. 2, Toronto, 117, 123, 126 , 148
    MD No. 3 (Kingston), 148
    MD No. 4 Longueuil, Que, 82
    MD No. 5 Quebec City, 104
    MD No. 10 Winnipeg, 148
    MD No. 11 Vancouver, 123, 148
    MD No. 12 Calgary, 3
    MD No. 13 Saskatchewan, 148
Military Establishment 100, 115, 138, 213
Military Intelligence rolls, 12
Military Intelligence (Research), MI(R), 112
Military Medal, 123, 209, 214
Military Service Act, 3
Minden, Ger, 89
Minister of National Defence, 72, 75, 79, 117
Minister of National War Services, 70
Ministry of Economic Warfare, MEW, 113
Miri, Sara, 185, 193
Mirs and/or Bias Bays, China, 13, 120, 140, 156
Mittelland Canal, Ger, 34
Mobile, Ala, 43, 68
Mobile Salvage Unit, 51
Montone River, Italy, 95
Montreal General Hospital, 82
Montreal Military Hospital, Queen Mary Road, 82
Morib Beach, Selangor, 171, 180
Moro River Cemetery, Italy, 93
Morotai, 116, 143, 185, 189, 190, 191, 192, 194, 200,
    202, 203, 204, 212, 213
Mount Ced Mah, 24
Mountbatten, Lord Louis, 22, 57, 121, 161, 171, 179,
    180
Muar, Johore, 173
Mukah, Sara, 203, 209
Mullaly, Lt.-Col. B.R., 109
Municipal Elections Act, 218
Munro, Maj. Colin D., 175
Murudi, Sara, 193, 213
Musgrave, Col. R., 175
Myitche, Burma, 27
Myitkyina, Burma, 23, 29
'M' organization, 114

Naga Hills, Burma, 23
Nagasaki, Japan, 62
Nanaimo, BC, 7, 106, 128
Nanking, China, 12, 66
Naples, Italy, 95, 97
National Research Council, NRC, 50, 104
National Resources Mobilization Act, NRMA, 1, 8, 9,
    19, *passim*
National Selective Service, NSS, 24, 74, 76, 78, 79,
    106, 107, 121; NSS Mobilization Boards, 74; NSS
    Mobilization Regulations, 74
National War Service, NWS, 71, 72, 74, 106, 107,
    108; NWS Boards, 74; NWS Regulations, 74

Nationalist Chinese, 12, 13, 21, 42, 66, 168, 180
Nationalist Chinese Government, 11, 23, 161, 218
Naval Control Service, 67, 68
Naval Intelligence Unit, 65
Naval Radio Interception Centre, Gordon Head,   61
Naviglio Canale, Italy, 95
National Defence Headquarters, NDHQ, 9, 73, 78, 79,
    80, 151
Neder Rijn, Neth, 94
Nederweert War Cemetery, Neth, 90
Negri Sembilan, Malaya, 161, 172
Negroes, 19; see also Blacks
Nelles, V/Adm. Percy F., 61
Netherlands East Indies, NEI, 159, 163, 179
New Guinea, NG, 62, 116, 137, 138, 204, 214
New Territories, HK, 12, 64, 120, 133
New Zealanders, 20, 95
Nibbs, Sgt. Bill, 213
Nickel (propaganda leaflet), 33
Nieuport, Bel, 84
Nijmegen, Neth, 87, 90
Nimitz, Adm Chester, 62, 143
19th Hospital, HK, 18
Nisei, 109, 110, 122
Noad, Lt.-Cmdr. Algy, 61
Noemfoor, NG, 137
Non-Permanent Active Militia, NPAM, 49
Norris, S/Maj. A., 174
North Atlantic Treaty Organization, NATO, 24
North Bay, Ont, 54
North Sea, 34, 37
Northeast Airlines, 60
Norway, 36, 40, 89, 112
Nuremberg, Ger, 37

Officer (of the Order) of the British Empire, OBE, 20,
    118, 184
Occupation Force, 41
Odlum, Maj.-Gen. Victor W., 14, 18, 219
Office of Strategic Services, OSS, 12, 16, 117, 118,
    163, 165, 176, 184
Official Secrets Act, 124
O'Hoy, Myrtle, 143
Oisemont, Fr, 38
Okanagan Special Trainign Camp, 80, 101, 117, 118,
    124-32, 138, 144, 183, 214
Okanagan Mountain Provincial Park, 124
Okinawa, 63
Oldenburg, Ger, 96
Oldham, Lieut F.R., 200, 201, 202, 207, 209, 213
Olsen, Air Gunner, 43
Ontario Rifle Association ORA, 101
OPERATIONS - BORNEO:-
    Agas, 188, 190, 191; *Agas II,* 188; *Agas IV,* 190;
Agas V, 190; *Hippo,* 143-4, 189, 193-4, 202-5, 207,
209, 215; *Hippo II,* 205; *Kingfisher,* 180, 184, 188,
190; *Oboe,* 190, 200; *Semut,* 122, 190, 192, 195, 200,
205, 209, 213-5; *Semut I,* 190, 192, 213; *Semut II,*
192, 193, 200-1, 203; *Semut III,* 192-4, 200, 202-3,
208, 209, 212, 213; *Semut IV,* 208; *Stallion,* 200

BURMA:-
     Dracula, 29, 62
CHINA:-
     Oblivion, 117, 121, 124, 132, 133, 140, 144, 146, 154, 156, 185
EUROPE:-
     Cleanser, 94, 95; *Destroyer,* 94; *Dragoon,* 175; *Exodus,* 36; *Goldflake,* 90; *Goodwood,* 83; *Husky,* 93; *Market-Garden,* 41; *Overlord,* 41, 85; *Thunderclap,* 35; *Totalize,* 83, 84, 96, 97; *Tractable,* 96, 97
MALAYA:-
     Carpenter, 156, 173-4, 180; *Fighter,* 163; *Funnel,* 163; *Galvanic,* 165; *Galvanic Blue,* 166-7. 170; *Galvanic Brown,* 165-7, 170-1; *Galvanic Green,* 165, 168; *Galvanic Orange,* 165, 166, 170; *Galvanic Slate,* 165, 169; *Gustavus,* 161-22, 164, 174, 180; *Hebrides,* 162; *Humour,* 172; *Humour Orange,* 172; *Humour Slate,* 170-2; *Jaywick,* 157; *Mint,* 156, 173-4; *Multiple,* 154, 163; *Oatmeal,* 162; *Pontoon,* 163; *Rimau,* 157; *Sergeant,* 174; *Sergeant Brown,* 174-5; *Snooper,* 179; *Tideway,* 172; *Tideway Green,* 172-3; *Zipper,* 157, 164, 171, 173, 176, 180
SEAC:-
     Mastiff, 180
Order in council, 24, 68, 80, 81, 144, 146
     Order in Council PC 10924, 74
     Order in Council PC 1986, 60
     Order in Council PC 79/11160, 19
     Order in Council PC 83/8848, 147
     Secret order in council, 78
"Order of the Day," 180, **181-2**
Orkneys, Scot, 58
Oro Bay, NG, **137**
Orsogna, Italy, 93
Ortona, Italy, 93
Ostend, Bel, 87
Otterloo, Neth, 94, 95
Outhwaite, Cpl. R.M., 200, 205, 207, 208, 209

Pa Bawang, Sara, 213
Pa Tik, Sara, 192
Pacific Force, 109; see also Tiger Force
Pacific Military Intelligence Research Section (PACMIRS), 109, 110
Pacific Star, 151
Pacific Theatre, 156; Pacific War, 36, 63
Pahang, Malaya, 161, 163
Palau Kladi, Sara, 205, 209
Pan American Airways, 20, 25-6
Paradise Ranch, 124, 130
Pare, Sgt. C.W., 192, **194**
Particulars of Family under NRMA, 76
Partisan (guerrilla), 114, 176
Partridge, P/O W.J., 39, 40
Pasir Nai, Sara, 199
Passport Control Office, PCO, 112, 116
Pas-de-Calais, Fr, 38
Pathfinders, 31, 32, 35, 38
Patrol Liaison Officer, PLO, 166
Patrol Liaison Team, PLT, 164, 165, 168, 172

Pattullo, Premier T.D., 70, 71, 72, 106, 216
Pearkes, Maj.-Gen. George R., 7, 10, 79, 80, 107, 122-4, 133, 144
Pearl Harbor, Hawaii, 27, 49, 63. 72
Peking, China, 6
Pelagus Rapids, Sara, 198, 199
Penang, Malaya, 11, 64, 161, 180
Pendan, Sara, 203
Penticton, BC, 2, 124, 126, 131, 144
People's Republic of China, 26
Pepper, Captain, 172
Perak, Malaya, 161, 162, 163, 164, 171
Perlis, Malaya, 159, 175
Perry, WO2 R.C., 203
Personal History Form (Alien), 9, 78
Perth Regiment, 90, 95
Petawawa, Ont, 83
Peterborough, Ont, 148, 149, 183
Petition, 7, 70, 149, 151, 216
Philippeville, Algeria, 91, 93, 97
Philippines, 62, 63, 137, 159, 165, 190, 191
Philpott, Sgt. G.H., 205, 209
Pippen, Sgt. F.C., 203
Pittsburg, Cal, 140
Pockley, S/Lr Graeme, 191, 192
Pofi, Italy, 95
Poi, Sara, 202, 203
Poissant, Pilot Cy, 42
Poland, 41, 97
Polish Division, 96, 97
Political Warfare Executive, PWE, 113, 147; PWE School, 154
Politz, Ger, 34
Pontecorvo, Italy, 95
Poona, India, 121, 148, 153, 154, 155, 183
Port Dixon, Negri Sembilan, 180
Porter Force, Italy, 94, 95
Portuguese East Timor, 114, 165, 191, 214
Powell River, BC, 131
Power, C.G., Minister for Air, 146
Power, Admiral, 64
Prahu, 190, 195, 196, 199, 202, 207
Prestwick, Scot, 54, 57, 58
Prince George, BC, 3, 20, 50, 59, 63, 69, 105, 129
Princess Patricia's Canadian Light Infantry, PPCLI, 47, 91
Prisoners of War and Internees, POW&I, 12, 16, 40, 73, 109, 143, 159, 171, 176, 179, 180, *passim* Kuching, 194, 205, 212, 213; Sandakan, 188; Singapore, 179; Outram Gaols, 159; Changi, 176, 179; Malai POW camps, 179; Indian POWs, 159, 174; Sham Shui Po POW Camp, 11, 14, 65; Padu Gaol, Kuala Lumpur, 159 German POWs, 80, 128; POW camp, Seebee Alta, 104
Pu Yi, Emperor, 7
Pulau Sunga, Sara, 209
PULHEMS, 92, 130, 150
Punan tribe, 197, **198**, 212
Punjabis, 164, 173

Pure European descent, 19, 36, 72;
    pure white race, 72
Puso, Penghulu, 196, 198, 199

"Qualifications and Registration of Voters Act," 7
Quan, Pte. Chong Loy (John), 150
Queen Mary Hospital, HK, 11
Queen's Own Rifles of Canada, 4, 105
Queen's University, Kingston, 87
Querenstede, Ger, 96
Quon, Albert, 16
Quon, L/Cpl. Diamond, **90,** 108
Quon, Herbert, 16
Quon, Lyman, 16, 68

Rabaul, NG, 64
Radar Detachment, 137, 143
Radio Interception Centres, 61
Ralston, Col. J.L., 76, 106, 146
Ramree Island, Burma, 27, 29
Ranau, BNB, 179, 188, 189, 204
Rangoon, Burma, 29, 62, 121, 175, 176
Rasa, Selangor, 165
Rastede, Ger, 96
Raub, Pahang, 163
Ravenna, Italy, 95
Rawalpindi, India, 115
Rawang, Selangor, 166
RDF (radar direction finding), 78
Rebecca/Eureka, 162, 203
Reception committee, 162
Reconnaissance Unit (Z Force), 119, 120
Recovery/Repatriation of Allied Prisoners of War and
    Internees, RAPWI, 16, 36, 40, 138, 143 173, 179,
    212
Red Cross, 216; American, 14; Canadian, 14
Red Deer, Alta, 92, 127, 148, 149, 183
Reddish, Maj. D.G., 173
Reeves, J.F., 13
Regina, Sask, 50, 83, 91, 130, 150
Regina Rifle Regiment, 90
Reichswald, Ger, 84
Reinforcements, 89, 92, 95, 97, 129, 146, 151, 166,
    189, 202, 209
Rejang River, Sara, 115, 189, 192-209, 213; Rejang-
    Pelagus-Merit, 202
Rejection certificate, 78
Remi River, Italy, 93
"Report and Recommendations of the Special
    Committee . . ." 8, 71; "1940 Report," 8, 9
Reydt Ger, 47
Re-Entry Certificate Fees, 217
Rheims, Fr, 38, 110
Rhenania-Ossag oil refinery, Harburg, 34
Rhine River, 35, 41, 84, 87, 89, 94, 95
Rhineland, 91, 96
Rhine-Herne Canal, 34
Rhone Valley, Fr, 175, 184
Richardson, Sgt. David John, 163, 165-6, 180
Richardson, Maj. J.A., 163

Richmond, NSW, 116, 140, 143
Ricklingen, Ger, 89
Ride, Col. (Dr.) Lindsay T., 12, 13,14, 16, 18
Rideau Military Hospital, Ottawa, 150
Riestedt, Ger, 89
Rimini Line, Italy, 95
Ringway, Eng, 115
Ringwood Special Intelligence School, 115
Ripley, F/Lt. G.C., 188-9
Rising Sun, 64
Robertson, F/O J., 165
Robertson, Norman, 216
Rocky Mountain Rangers, RMR, 75, 96, 98
Rogers, Mid-upper Gunner T.A., 38
Romagna, Italy, 94, 95
Ronning, S/Ldr. Chester A., 61
Roosevelt, President F.D., 14, 21, 42
Rositz, Ger, 34
Ross, Captain, 179
Rotterdam, Neth, 31
Rouen, Fr, 47
Roulers, Bel, 95
Royal Air Force, RAF, 14, 19, 22, 26, 27, 29, 31, 32,
    40, 41, 42, 43, 51, 53, 85, 97, 180
        Personnel Reception Centre in Bournemouth,
    34, 37; RAF Bomber Command, 31; Coastal
    Command, 31, 54; RAF Transport Command, 55
        Training: No. 10 OTU, Abingdon, Berks, 33;
    No. 14 OTU, Market Harbourgh, Leics, 34; No. 22
    OTU, RAF, 37; No. 22 OTU, Wellesbourne, 38,
    39; No. 24 OTU, 33; No. 5 Lancaster Finishing
    School, Syerston, Nott, 34; No. 6 Advanced Flying
    Unit, Little Kissing, 33; No. 6 Battle School,
    Thirsk, 37; No. 7 AFTU, Bishops Court, County
    Down, 39; No. 7 EFTS, Desford, Leics, 33; No.
    1516 Battle Flight, Pershore, Worcs, 34; No. 1654
    Heavy Conversion Unit, Wigsley, Lincs, 34; RAF
    Regiment School (British Marines), 43
        Groups; No. 2 Group, 41, 42; Nos. 1, 5, 6, and 8
    Groups, 36; No. 1, 3, 6, and 8 Groups, 35; No. 6
    Group, 38, 40; No. 8 Group, 38, 40; No. 1 and 5
    Groups, 32; No. 4 Group, 31; No. 5 Group, 34, 35,
    36; Nos. 5 and 8 Groups, 35; No. 6 Bomber Group,
    37; No. 8 Group, 31, 40; No. 41 Group, 57; No. 38
    Transport Group, 41; No. 46 Transport Group, 41;
    No. 45 Group, RAF Transport Command, 55; No.
    45 (Atlantic Transport) Group, 55; No. 100 Group,
    40; No. 216 Group RAF, 54
        Squadrons: No. 50 Squadron, 34; RAF No. 101
    Squadron No. 1 Group, 32; RAF No. 117
    (Transport) Squadron, 30; No. 404 Coastal
    Command (Buffalo) Squadron, 40-1; No. 405
    (Vancouver) Pathfinder Squadron, 31; No. 426
    (Thunderbird) Squadron, 37, 38; No. 430 (Sudbury)
    Squadron, 40; No. 431 (Iroquois) Squadron, 33; No.
    434 (Bluenose) Squadron, 33; No. 435 (Chinthe),
    26, 27, 29, 41; No. 436 (Elephant), 26, 27, 29, 41;
    No. 437 in No. 120 (RCAF) Wing, 41; No. 617
    Squadron, the 'Dam Busters, 36; Nos. 400 and 414
    in No. 39 (RCAF) Wing, 40;

2nd Tactical Air Force, TAF, 29, 31, 41-7, 58; No.46 Group, 41; Nos. 83 and 84 Groups, 41; Fighter Bomber Wing, 41; Fighter Command, 41; Fighter Reconnaissance, 31, 40, 41; No. 137 Wing, 42; No. 139 Wing, 41, 47, 58; No. 85 (Base) Group, 41; No. 98 Squadron, 41, 43, 44, 47; OTU at RAF Finenere, 43

Royal Australian Air Force, RAAF, 190, 191, 201, 202, 203, 205, 214; RAAF ASR Squadron, 199; 113 Air Sea Rescue Flight Catalinas, 191; Special Duties Flight 200 RAAF, 115, 191

Royal Canadian Air Force, 1, 7, 19, 20, 22, 24, 26, 28, *passim*
    No. 5 (Bomber Recce) Squadron, 50; No. 6 (Bomber Recce) Squadron, 50; No. 1 Canadian Army, Air Photographic Interpretation Section APIS, 40
    Canadian Transport Squadrons, 29; No. 168 Heavy Transport Squadron, 53
    RCAF Headquarters in Bombay, 156
    RCAF No. 2 Recruiting Centre, Calgary, 19
    RCAF Recruiting Station, Montreal, 60
    RCAF Station Patricia Bay, 48, 50
    RCAF Station Whitehorse, Yukon, 48
    RCAF (Women's Division), 51
    Photographic School at Rockcliffe, Ont., 40

Royal Canadian Army Medical Corps, RCAMC, 81-2, 105, 127; No. 1 Advanced Dressing Station, 92 No. 1 Roman Way, Convalescent Hospital, Colchester, 92; No. 21 Canadian General Hospital, Oldham, 92, 97; No. 9 Canadian General Hospital, Horsham, 92

Royal Canadian Army Service Corps, RCASC, 92, 97-100, 126; Directorate of Supplies and Transport, 98; 69th Transport Unit, 97; Group 83, 92

Royal Canadian Artillery, RCA, 83, 85-6
    2nd Medium Regiment RCA (Reserve), C Battery, 84; 2nd Army Group RCA, 100; 2nd Anti-Tank Regiment, 84; 3rd and 4th LAA Regiments, 84; 3rd LAA Regiment, 83, 84; 4th LAA, 84; 4th Medium AA Regiment, 84; 5th AA Battery, 11; 6th LAA Regiment, 84; 13th Field Regiment, 84; 14th Field Regiment, RCA, 83, 100; 15th Battery, Winnipeg, 83; 16th AA Battery, 83; 16th Battery, 84; 17th LAA Battery, 83; 19th Army Field Regiment, 83, 100; 19th Field Regiment, 100; 22nd (Gleichen), 84; 24th LAA Battery, 83; 25th AA Regiment, 82; 43rd HAA Regiment, 84; 44th Field Battery, 84; 56th HAA Battery, 127; 78th (Red Deer), 85; 96th AT Battery, 96

Royal Canadian Corps of Signals, RCCS, 89, 90, 106, 118, 145, 148; RCCS (Reserve), 87; 1st AA Brigade Signals, 90; No. 1 Special Wireless Group, 79, 110, 137, 143, 144, 213

Royal Canadian Electrical and Mechanical Engineers, RCEME, 79, 86, 87, 88, 148
    1st Army Troops Workshop RCEME, 86

Royal Canadian Engineers, RCE, 125

Royal Canadian Legion, 2

Royal Canadian Mounted Police, RCMP, 9, 39, 60, 72, 76, 117, 121, 123

Royal Canadian Navy, RCN, 1, 41, 56, 58, 60, 61, 64, 65, 67, 68, 69, 70, 72, 81, 82, 87, 128; RCN(VR), 82; NSHQ, 61, 65, 67
    Operational Intelligence Centre, 61

Royal Canadian Ordnance Corps, RCOC, 42, 88, 128, 157; Advanced Workshop Detachment, 83

Royal Canadian Regiment, RCR, 93

Royal Rifles of Canada, **63**; 2nd Battalion, 104

Royal Marines, 174

Royal Navy, RN, 61, 62, 64, 65, 67, 179, 205
    Admiralty, 65, 66, 67
    11th Aircraft Carrier Squadron, 62; British Naval Task Force, 16, 29, 57, 63; British Pacific Fleet, 62, 63, 64

Royal 22e Régiment, 47, 93, 104

Royal Winnipeg Rifles, 48, 90

Royan, Fr, 35

Ruhr, Ger, 37

Ryan, Navigator/Bomb Aimer Peter (Doc), 42

S.Phone, 162, 172

Sabatu, Sara, 201, 202

Sage War Cemetery Oldenburg, Ger, 32

Sai Wan Hill, Lyemun, HK, 11

St. Ghislain, Belg, 38

St. Hubert Airport, Que, 53, 54, 60

St. Jean, Que, 104

St. John's, Nfd, 68

St. Louis, Col. A.R., 123, 126

St. Martins-l'Hortier, Fr, 38

St. Pol, Fr, 38

Salim, Sara, 207, 209

Salween River, Burma, 23

Sam, Kam Len Douglas, 36, **37,** 38-9, 110

Samarinda, Dutch Borneo, 202

Sampan, 24, 120

San Diego, California, 55

San Francisco, 14, 25, 65, 137, 140

San Jose Air Base, Mindoro I, 191, 192

Sandai, Penghulu, 199

Sandakan, BNB, 179, 180, 188, 190, 204

Sanderson, Sgt. C.F., 191, 192

Sangro, Italy, 93

Sant'Alberto, Italy, 94, 95

Sarawak: Fourth Division, 193
    Second Division, 205
    Third Division, 198, 207

Sarawak Constabulary, 197

Sarawak Rangers, 202

Sarcee Camp, Calgary, 101

Sarikei, Sara, 205, 207, 209

Saskatchewan Telecommunications, 91

Saskatoon, 92, 128

Scheldt, Battle of, 47, 84, 91, 96

School of Eastern Interpreters, 138

School of Oriental and African Studies, 109

Schoonselhof Cemetery, Antwerp, Bel, 91

Schü mine, 93
Schweinfurt, Ger, 37, 38
Seaforth Highlanders, 91, 93, 97, 184
Sebauh, Sara, 203, 207, 208
Secret Circular Memorandum No. 25, 74
Secret Memorandum No. 1, 74, 76, 79
Seine River, Fr, 47, 87, 96
Selangor, 161, 164, 165, 168, 170, 171
Sembauh, Sara, 209
Semporna, BNB, 190
Senio River, Italy, 95
Sepang (Lolang), Selangor, 180
Seremban, Negri Sembilan, 172
Serendah, Selangor, 165, 166, 170, 171
Seria, Brunei, 185
Servaes, R/Adm. R. M., 64
Services Reconnaissance Department, SRD, 114, 116,
    138, 185; see also Special Operations Australia
        SRD HQs, 202, 205, 212; SRD "A" group, 212;
        SRD "A" HQs, 200, 203;
            Z' Special Unit, 114, 116, 138, 144, 148, 164,
        185, 194, 213; Z' Special Unit operatives, 188, 189,
        190, 195, 207
Seto, Lieut. Wilfred B.T., 72, 73, 91, 106, 107, 110,
    111
7th Japanese Army, Singapore, 179
Sham Shui Po, 64
Shanghai, China, 25, 50, 64, 65, 66, 69, 82, 157, 184;
    Shanghai Volunteers, 16
Shangri-La, 42
Shaw, Allen, 172
Shein, Paul K., 68
Shetland Bus, 125
Shetland Islands, 40, 58
Shilo, Man, 84, 148, 149, 183
SHIPS;-
        HMS Adamant, 62; Andes, 39, 61, 95, 98; SS
    Athenia, 60; HMT Awatea, 63; HMS Belfast, 66;
    Carmania, 5; HMS Cleopatra, 64; HMS Cossack, 66;
    HMCS Crescent, 65, 66, 69; SS Cyclops, 68; US Don
    Jose, 63; HMS Duke of York, 64; Duntroon, 138;
    Empress of Australia, 65; Empress of Japan/Canada,
    50, 65, 68; English Prince, 144; UST Fred Ainsworth,
    140; UST General Meigs, 65; General Brewster, 143;
    General Gordon, 16; Ile de France, 89, 97, 180; HMS
    Indomitable, 62; HMCS Iroquois, 67; Kitsilano Park,
    144; SS Laetitia, 92; HMCS Louis Pasteur, 43;
    Lurline, 137; Mauritania, 157; SS Megantic, 4;
    Micmac, 67; Monarch of Bermuda, 157; SS Monterey,
    143; Moreton Bay, 180; HMS Nelson, 64; Nieuw
    Amsterdam, 38, 92, 151; Northland, 4; HMCS
    Ontario, 65; HMCS Prince Robert, 63-5; Queen
    Elizabeth, 87, 97; Queen Mary, 87; SS Scandinavian,
    5; HMCS Uganda, 63; HMS Venerable, 62
SHORE STATIONS:-
        HMCS Cornwallis, Deep Brook, NS, 61, 67;
    HMCS Donnacona, Montreal, 65, 69; HMS Golden
    Hind, Sydney, NSW, 62; HMS Lanka, Ceylon, 62;
    HMS Mayina, Ceylon, 62; HMS Mercury, England,
61; HMCS Montreal, 61; HMCS Naden, Victoria, BC,
67; HMCS Peregrine, Halifax, 61; HMCS Protector,
Sydney, NS., 67; HMS Tamar, Victoris, HK, 64
Shiu, Sgt. James, 126, 128, 133, **139**, 144, 185, **189,**
    200, 205, 209, 212, 213
Shwebo, Burma, 27
Sibu, Sara, 198, 202, 203, 204, 205, 207, 208, 209,
    212, 213
Sichel, S/Ldr. Herbert, 117, 124, 133
Sicily, 93, 97
Sikhs, 107
Silver Cross, 31
Simanggang, Sara, 204, 205, 212
Sime, Maj. D., 173, 174
Similajan River, Sara, 208
Simmonds, Lt.-Gen. G.G., 83
Simujan, Sara, 204
Singapore War Crimes Committee, 110
Singapore War Crimes Trials, 110
Singarh Fort, Poona, 121
16th Canadian Scottish (Reserve), 75, 97, 127
Skapan tribe, Sara, 195
Slim, Lt.-Gen. Sir William, 26
Slim River, Perak, 164
Sochon, Maj. W.L.P. (Bill), 192, **193, 194** 195-213
Soltau, Ger, 40
Somme, Fr, 96
Song, Sara, 127, 200, 201, 202, 203, 213
Soo, Tpr. William, 94
South Johore, 156, 173, 174
South Saskatchewan Regiment, 91, 92
Southeast Asia Command, SEAC, 22, 29, 31, 109,
    110, passim; D Division, SEAC, 162; P Division,
    114; South East Asia Translators and Interpreters
    Corps, SEATIC, 109, 110
Southwest Pacific Theatre, SWP, 112, 118, 146, 162,
    214
Spain, 112, 118
Special Branch (SB), 61, 64, 65
Special Duty, SD, 116, 180; SD Squadrons, 179
Special Air Services, 113
Special Boat Sections, 113
Special category, 73, 80
Special Committee on Orientals in British Columbia,
    71
Special Operations Australia, 116, 120, 146, passim;
    see also Services Reconnaissance Department
Special Operations Executive, SOE, 1, 8, 12, 18, 23,
    passim
Special Training School, STS, 115-8, 124, 184
Special Training School No. 101, 114, 116, 119, 159,
    162
Special Training School No. 103, 115-8, 123-4
Spencer Chapman, Frederick W., 161, 163, 184
Spurling, Sgt. E.R., 200, 209
Stalin, Joseph, 35
Stanley Camp, 16, 65
Stanley Cemetery, HK, 66
Stanley Park, BC, 83

Stephenson, Sir William, 113, 116, 117
Stewart, Lt.-Col. Arthur, 179, 184
Stilwell, Gen. Joseph W., 12, 14, 22
Sticpewich, WO Bill, 189
Stokes, Capt. (Dr) J.L., 209, 212
Stone Cutters Island, HK, 120
Stores, **167, 169, 197**
Straits Settlements, Malaya, 161
Subic Bay, PI, 62, 63
Sueyek, Ida Tang, 144
Suez Canal, Egypt, 6, 62, 68
Sultan, Lt. Gen. Daniel, 22
Suluk tribe, Borneo, 188
Sumatra, 118, 140, 179
Summerland, BC, 2, 131
Sun Yat-Sen, 7
Sun Yat-Sen Gardens, 9
Sung, WO2 Donald, 105, **157**
Sungei Lanang, Sara, 207
Sungei Melekun, Sara, 203
Sungei Merah, Sara, 209
Sungei Paku, Sara, 198
Sungei Patani, Kedah, 175
Sungei Pila, Sara, 199, 200, 208
Sungei Rusa, Selangor, 166
Sungei Sama, Sara, 200
Sungei Sapuloh, Sara, 202
Sungei Mo, Sara, 196
Sunnybrook Hospital, Toronto, 93
Supreme Allied Command South East Asia, SACSEA, 180
Supreme Allied Commander, General Eisenhower, 41
Supreme HQs Allied Expeditonery Force, SHAEF, 31, 35, 41
Sussex, Eng, 85, 90, 99
Sutcliffe, Lieut. F.M., 151
Swatow, China, 119
Sweden, 36, 112, 118
Switzerland, 112, 118
Sydney, NSW, 55, 62, 63, 68, 116, 140
S-20 Japanese Language School, 38, 91, 102, 105, 109-111, 128

Tabragalba, Qd, 143, 213
Tacloban, Leyte, 143
Tai Koon School, Sara, 209
Tai Li, General, 12
Taik Hing, Selangor, 166
Taiping, Perak, 164
Takashima, Pte. Joseph, **157**
Talan, Maj. Monia, 119, 120
Tallboy, 36
Tama Weng Ajang, Penghulu, **195,** 196
Tamabo Range, Sara, 192
Tamils, 180
Tampin, Negri Sembilan, 172
Tangja Tuloh, Johore, 174
Tanjong Kuluk, Sara, 203
Tapah, Perak, 163, 164

Tarakan I, Borneo, 190, 191, 192, 196
Tatau, Sara, 201, 203, 207, 208, 209
Tedder, AM Arthur W., 41
Teh Soen Hin, Sgt, 192, **194**
Tekok Rapids, Sara, 198
Telok Anson, Perak, 163
Tempsford, Eng, 115
Terlet, Neth, 95
Terrebonne, Que, 24, 51
Teshima, Lt.-Gen. Fusataro, 212
13th Canadian Machine Gun Corps, 101
37th Imperial Japanese Army, 212
Thomson, Lieut. Gordon, 133
Thompson-Walker, Maj. P.T., 165
Three Rivers Officers' Training, Que, 91
Thru, Sgt. J., 148
Tibet, 23
Tiger Force, 33, 38, 82, 84, 87, 92, 94, 104
Tinfoil (Window), 44
Tinjar track, Sara, 196, 198
Tokyo, Japan, 29, 42, 109, 171
Tonsberg, Norway, 36
Torbay, Nfd, 51
Toronto Daily Star, 101
Toronto Union Station, 128
Townsville, Qd, 138
Tracadie, NB, 85
Travers, Maj. W.I.L., 164
Tredrea, Sgt. Jack, 191
Trenggenu, Malaya, 159
Trevaldwyn, Capt. D.E., 174
Trianon Club at Luilen Hospital, 97
Trincomalee, Ceylon, 154, 156
Trondheim, Norway, 36
Truk, Caroline Islands, 63
Trun, Normandy, 96
Trythall, Commander, 62
Tso, F/O Hong Yuen, **26,** 28-9
Tubau, Sara, 200, 201, 207, 208
Tulihal, Imphal Valley, 27
Tutoh River, Sara, 192

U-boat, 36, 50, 68
U-boat pens, 36
Ulu Anak, Sara, 200
Ulu Merit, Sara, 200
Ulu Yam, Selangor, 165, 166
Ulu Yam Bahru, Selangor, 165
Unattached List ("Q" List) NDHQ, 133
Undersecretary of State for External Affairs, 117, 216
Union Jack, 28, 64, 195, 213
United Nations Charter, 216, 219; UN Peace Keeping Force, 47; United Nations Rehabilitation and Relief Association, 97
United States Army Air Force, 12, 21
    US Chiefs of Staff, 62
    USAAF, 14, 29, 31, 36, 37, 97; US Special Duty Squadrons, 115; US Tactical Air Force, 42; USAAF 317th and 319th Troop Carrier Squadrons,

29; Air Transport Command, 14, 20, 23, 53, 54; 14th USAAF, 14, 21; 10th USAAF, 14, 21, India-China Wing, 23; US Ferry Command, 25
US 17th Airborne Division, 89; US 18th Airborne Corps, 89; US 82nd Airborne, 87
US 13th Naval District, 61; US 3rd Fleet, 63; US 5th Fleet, 63; US 7th Fleet, 62; US Liberty ship, 68; US Merchant Marine, 68
US 3rd Army, 38; US Army Medical Corps, 82; US Army Quartermaster Corps, 16
US International Settlement, 16
Universal Trading Corporation (1933), 84
University of British Columbia, UBC, 39, 50, 91, 111
University of Chicago, 4
University of Toronto, 18, 81, 82
University of Western Ontario, 83

Valli di Commachi, Italy, 94
Vancouver Sun, 9
Varel, Neth, 96
Verle Bay, Norway, 36
Vermillion, Alta, 106
Vernon, BC, 4, 49, 86, 95, 97, 98, 127, 129, 130, 131
Verrières Ridge, Normandy, 83
Veterans Guard of Canada, 3
VE-Day, 33, 62, 82, 84, 87, 90, 96, 97, 100
Victoria Flying Club, 49
Victory Aircraft, Malton, 55
Victory Loan Drive, 216
Victory Medal, 4, 5
Villa Gnaldo, Italy, 93
VJ- Day, 47, 55, 82, 84, 183
Vladivostok, USSR, 42
Voorthuizen, Neth, 94, 95
V-1 flying bomb launching sites, 40, 42
V-2 rocket sites, 42

Waichow, China, 13, 14, 120
Wales, 83, 98, 138
Walker, Admiral, 64
Wallis, Barnes, 36
Walpole, Cpl. B.B., 200, 202, 203, 208, 209
Wan Osman, 198
War Amputations of Canada, 94
War Brides, 29, 65, 100, 143, 144; Australian War Brides, 143
War Crimes Trials, 110, 179
War Establishment, 12, 32, 120
Watson, F/Lt. K.W. (Bill), 39, 40
Watt, Lieut. E.F.H., 68
Wayne Coal Industries Match, 101
Wedemeyer, Maj.Gen. Albert C., 12, 14, 22, 121, 140
Wesel, Ger, 35
West Nova Scotia Regiment, 91, 93
Wetaskiwin, Alta, 104, 148, 149, 183
Whangpoo, China, 66
White, Capt. L.V.C., 172
White race, 58, 60
Whites, 155, 192

William Head, Vancouveer I, 6
Wilson, Maj. Victor, 124
Wilson, Mrs. Victor, 124, 130
Wingate, Maj.-Gen. Orde, 15
Winnipeg Grenadiers, 63, **69**
Winter Line, Italy, 93
Wismar, Ger, 89
Wittenberg, Ger, 89
Wolpinghausen, Ger, 89
Wong, Andrew, 68
Wong, Armand, 82
Wong, Bing Chew, 87
Wong, Charles, 11
Wong, Dr. David, 12
Wong, Pay Lieut. (Temp.) Doug G., 67
Wong, Elsie, 11
Wong, Cpl. Fong Bing (Frank), 86
Wong, Lieut. George D, 56, 67
Wong, L/Cpl. George Edward, **98**
Wong, P/O Gim Foon, **49**
Wong, Henry, 12
Wong, Cpl. Henry Albert (Hank), **77,** 128, **139,** 143, **150, 198**
Wong, Howard (Gus), 56, 67
Wong, J.L. (James), **157**
Wong, Radio Artificer Jean Raymond Marcel, 67, 82
Wong, Pte. Larry George, 104
Wong, Cpl. Lila, 106
Wong, Moi, 143
Wong, Sgt. Norman Donald, **127,** 128, 133, **138, 139**
Wong, Sgt. On (Ted), 82, 165, **166,** 171, **183**
Wong, Peter, 12
Wong, Peter, 56
Wong, Peter S., 56
Wong, Sid Y., **149, 153**
Wong, Sgt. Thomas Kwok Hung, 7, 49
Wong, Tom, **88,** 93
Wong, Capt. Tommy, **24,** 25
Wong, Wilbur Bruce, **55,** 56, 67
Wong, Capt. William Andrew, **82**
Wong, Sgt. Wing Lee, 130, **139,** 143
Woo, Harry S., 87
Wooler, Maj. J.R., 203, 205, 207, 208
Woosung, China, 66
Wooten, Maj.-Gen. George F., 212
Wright, S/Sgt. H.A., 143
Wunsdorf, Ger, 89
Wykoff, F/O C.B., 33
Wylie, Lt.-Col. Ian S., 172

Yalta Conference, 35
Yamashita Tomoyuki, Gen, 62
Yamamura H., General, 212
Yangtze River, China, 66, 120
Yarmouth, NS, 50
Yeasting, Robert, **157**
Yee, Lannie, 16
Yee, Maj.-Gen. S.K., 120,
Yee, Pte. William, 83-4

Yeiling, China, 64
Yep, LAC Herbert, 48
Yeung, Sgt. Vincent, 13, 14, 15, 19, 121, 132, 134, **139,** 140
Yorke Island, BC, 83, 131
Ypres, 3
Yuen, Tpr. Jan (John), 16, **141**
Yuen, Gnr Robert, 83
Yuen, Simon, 84
Yuen, Willie, 67

Yugoslavia, 121
Yukon, 71
Yunnan Province, China, 22, 23
YW Halifax, NS, 51

Z Force, Hong Kong, 12, 112, 119; see also Reconnaissance Unit
Zombie, 128
'Z' Special, see Services Reconnaissance Department